DATABASE

Step-by-Step

Other Wiley-Interscience Books by Mark L. Gillenson:

Strategic Planning, Systems Analysis, and Database Design
(with Robert Goldberg), 1984

DATABASE

Step-by-Step

Second Edition

Mark L. Gillenson
University of Miami

John Wiley & Sons
New York / Chichester / Brisbane / Toronto / Singapore

Library of Congress Cataloging in Publication Data:

Gillenson, Mark L.
    Database: step-by-step / Mark L. Gillenson. – 2nd ed.
        p.   cm.
    Includes bibliographical references.
    ISBN 0-471-61759-8
    1. Database management.
QA76.9.D3G523   1990
005.74–dc20
                                                                                90-38137
                                                                                CIP

Printed in the United States of America

10 9 8 7 6 5 4 3 2 1

To my Parents:

Sam and Sarah Margolis

Contents

CHAPTER 2:   SIMPLE FILES AND STORAGE MEDIA 27

CHAPTER 3:   FILE ORGANIZATIONS AND ACCESS METHODS 43

CHAPTER 4:   BENEFITS OF THE DATABASE APPROACH 70

Preface

In the four short years since the publication of the first edition, the field of database has continued its rapid expansion. The major changes to the field have been exciting and numerous. Relational database management systems (DBMSs) are constantly improving their performance characteristics and increasingly have been used for serious commercial applications. The SQL language has been adopted as both a U.S. and an international standard. DBMSs are now considered "standard equipment" on personal computers and several mainframe DBMSs have been adapted for the PC. Interest is beginning to be shown in converting some of the huge set of industrial hierarchical and network database applications to relational database. Increasing interest is being shown in distributed databases and data dictionaries. The new concept of object-oriented databases is being developed.

In order to keep up with this rapidly changing field, this edition includes extensive updating of many first-edition chapters. In addition, minor improvements have been made throughout; new topics have been added; the number of chapters has been increased from 15 to 17. The major changes are as follows.

The chapters on relational and pseudo-relational database have been moved before the chapters on hierarchical and network database, to reflect the present intense interest in relational database and the projected long-term importance of the relational concept. But, the hierarchical and network chapters have not been reduced in content or relegated to appendices because these topics continue to be of major importance in the commercial world and will be for some time to come.

The most major change to the book regards the topic of relational database, which was covered in one chapter in the first edition, but now has three chapters devoted to it (plus a separate chapter on pseudo-relational database). The introductory material on relational database has been rewritten and expanded. The material on the now standard SQL language has been expanded and given its own chapter. Joining Query-by-Example (QBE), in another new chapter devoted to other relational tools, are Query Management Facility (QMF) and the popular personal computer DBMS: dBASE III + and dBASE IV. The material on the IBM System/38 in the chapter on pseudo-relational database has been updated to include the follow-on IBM AS/400 system.

Other changes include the inclusion of the Date-Wilson method of database design in the database design chapter, additional material on relational-style catalogs in the chapter on data dictionaries, and the inclusion of material on object-oriented databases and expert databases in the chapter on evolving topics.

Always remember that no matter how fast or exotic computing hardware becomes, the fundamental issues in how to efficiently and effectively handle a company's data will remain.

I would like to thank Raymond Frost and Vicar Hernandez for their help in the preparation of the second edition. I would also like to thank my Wiley editor, Diane Cerra, for her encouragement and diligent support of this project.

Mark L. Gillenson

Coral Gables, Florida
October 1989

Preface To The First Edition

Database, the study of data storage and management, is a burgeoning discipline in the rapidly expanding fields of computer science and data processing. As in the evolution of any discipline, it began as the study of a relatively small body of knowledge, by a limited group of practitioners in industry, and, by faculty and graduate students in universities. Today, we find that both the number and depth of database subtopics have grown dramatically. A wide variety of data processing and non-data processing personnel, across the gamut of industrial and nonindustrial organizations, are exposed to the topic. As a university subject, it is increasingly migrating to the undergraduate computer science and business administration curriculums.

An unfortunate, if not surprising, characteristic of the database field, is that to have a thorough understanding of it, to eliminate the mysteries of how so significant an accomplishment can actually be made to work in the cold silicon and metals of the machines, a large amount of interconnected information must be assimilated. It is difficult to understand why a hierarchical data structure might be used without understanding the problems of data redundancy and multiple relationships. It is difficult to understand how to gain access to the records in a network structure without understanding the fundamentals of access methods. It is difficult to understand the need for a data administration function without understanding the principles behind the database approach. Such a list of interconnected concepts could go on indefinitely in this field.

The purpose of this book is to explain the PRINCIPLES behind the database and the broad range of database subtopics IN A MANNER WHICH LEAVES

NOTHING TO THE IMAGINATION. On the other hand, it does not attempt to exhaustively cover every detail of the field. It does not require a substantial data processing background as a prerequisite, but assumes only that the reader understands elementary computer principles and elementary concepts of computer programming. It approaches the subject in a methodical progressive manner, which will insure a *confident understanding* of the subject of database.

This book is intended to be used as the text for a first course in database, or as an introduction to the field for data processing professionals or others whose work exposes them to the database environment. Included is material on basic data definitions and structures, access methods, database management systems characteristics and approaches, database design, management aspects of the environment, and other assorted topics in the field.

I would like to leave the following thought with my fellow computer scientists, lest I offend their collective sense of precision. In its attempt to cut through the maze of database detail and yet hit hard at the basic concepts while surveying the entire field, this book may generalize or oversimplify a few points. I simply suggest that the tradeoff is well worth it. The readers of this book who need only a basic understanding of database will benefit from the tradeoff, while those who expect to go on in database will, after building a solid foundation here, have plenty of opportunity to go into more detail and be more precise in further courses, work experiences, and books. This book is intended to be a "user-friendly" introduction to the (entire) field of database–period.

A number of my database colleagues reviewed chapters of this book, making invaluable comments and suggestions in the process. Chief among them were Charley Bontempo and Judy King, both of whom read large sections of the book and were always available to discuss ideas about its construction. Additionally, I would like to acknowledge Art Amman, Jake Ever, Chuck Haspel, Alice Jones, Jack Lebow, Mike McGuire, Fred Page, Dick Schlough, John Sears, and Moshe Zloof. My thanks also to those students of the IBM Systems Research Institute and of Pace University in New York City who read and commented on the manuscript and tested the exercises at the ends of the chapters.

I would also like to thank the management of the IBM Systems Research Institute, specifically Allen L. Morton, Jr., Program Director, Alfred M. Pietrasanta, Director, and Robert W. DeSio, Director of The Corporate Technical Institutes, for providing a stimulating and supportive atmosphere for the writing of this book.

To Jim Gaughan and the crew at John Wiley & Sons, my thanks for their support of this project and their professionalism in publishing.

Lastly, I am grateful to Irene Gillenson, Edith and Marty Sherr, and Marion and Jack Zack, for a very special kind of help given to me while I was writing this book.

The views expressed in this book are those of the author and do not necessarily reflect those of the IBM Corporation.

Mark L. Gillenson

New York, New York
July 1985

1

Introduction

Introduction

This book is about data. Facts. Pieces of information that we need to manage our businesses, governments, banks, universities, and every other kind of human endeavor. It's about ways of managing the data itself, so that the exact data we need will be there when we need it. It's about computers and the way that a computing environment known as "database" can solve the problems caused by the huge amounts of data we increasingly are storing in them. It's about a key part—maybe the most important part—of today's data processing technology, about which everyone associated with data processing must have a fundamental understanding.

Let's begin by tracing man's concern with data from its beginnings to the present.

Data and Computers

The Origins of Record Keeping

Mankind has been interested in data for at least the past 12,000 years. While today we often associate the concept of data with the computer, historically, there have been many more primitive methods of data handling. In fact, some of them are still in use today.

In present-day Iraq, one can find shepherds who keep track of their flocks with pebbles, as shown in Figure 1.1. As each sheep leaves its pen to graze, the shepherd places one pebble in a small sack. When the sheep

Figure 1.1.   Shepherd using pebbles to keep track of sheep.

return, the shepherd discards one pebble for each animal and thus has a way of knowing whether he has lost any of his flock. In fact, this method of record keeping is a variation of the most ancient method known.

Excavations in the Zagros region of Iran, dated to 8500 B.C., have unearthed clay "tokens" or "counters" that, it is theorized, were used for record keeping in primitive forms of accounting. Such tokens have been found in sites from present-day Turkey to Pakistan to the east and Khartoum to the south. They date from as long ago as 7000 B.C.

By 3000 B.C., at the present-day city of Susa in Iran, the use of such tokens had reached a greater level of sophistication. Tokens with special markings on them (see Figure 1.2) were sealed in hollow clay vessels, which apparently served as bills of lading, accompanying commercial goods in transit. The tokens represented the quantity of goods being shipped and, obviously, could not be tampered with without the clay vessel being broken open. Inscriptions on the outside of the vessels and the seals of the parties involved provided a further record. The external inscriptions included words or concepts such as "deposited," "transferred," and "removed."

Figure 1.2.   Ancient clay tokens used to record merchandise in transit.

At about the same time that the Susa culture existed, people in the city-state of Uruk in Sumeria kept records in clay texts. With pictographs, numerals, and ideographs, they described land sales and business transactions involving bread, beer, sheep, cattle, and clothing.

Other neolithic means of record keeping included storing tallies as cuts and notches in wooden sticks and as knots in rope. The former continued in use in England as late as the medieval period, the latter was used by South American Indians.

Data through the Ages

In retrospect, the primary origins of the interest in data can be traced to the rise of cities. Simple subsistence hunting, gathering, and, later, agrarian cultures, had little use for the concept of data. But as we have seen with Susa and Uruk, cities and the attendant culture that began with the Bronze Age forever changed the way people live. The beginnings of mass production, the specialization of labor, the use of money, and the bartering of services and products for the necessities of life all required the keeping of data in records.

As time went on, more and different kinds of data and records were kept. These included calendars, census data, surveys, land ownership records, marriage records, data on temple contributions, and family trees (see Figure 1.3). Merchants had to keep track of inventories, shipments, and wage payments in addition to production. As farming went beyond the subsistence level and progressed to the feudal manor stage, there was a need to keep data on the amount of produce to consume, to barter with, and to keep as seed for the following year.

The Crusades took place from the late eleventh to the late thirteenth centuries. One side effect of the Crusades was a broader view of the world from the perspective of the Europeans, with an accompanying increase in interest in trade. A common method of trade in that era was the establish-

Figure 1.3. Increasing number of kinds of data with the advance of civilization.

ment of partnerships among merchants, ships' captains, and owners to facilitate commercial voyages. That increased level of commercial sophistication brought with it another round of increasingly complex record keeping, specifically, double-entry bookkeeping.

Double-entry bookkeeping originated in the trading centers of fourteenth-century Italy. The earliest known example is from a merchant in Genoa and dates to the year 1340. Its use gradually spread, but it was not until 1494, in Venice (about 25 years after the first movable type printing press in Venice came into use), that a Franciscan monk named Luca Pacioli published his *Summa de Arithmetica, Geometrica, Proportioni et Proportionalita*. That work had an important effect in spreading the use of double-entry bookkeeping. Of course, the increasing use of paper and the printing press also furthered the advance of record keeping.

As the dominance of the Italian merchants declined, other countries became more active in trade and, concomitantly, with data and record keeping. Furthermore, as the use of temporary trading partnerships declined, and more stable, long-term mercantile organizations were established, other types of data became necessary. For example, annual as opposed to venture-by-venture statements of profit and loss were needed. In 1673 the "Code of Commerce" in France required that a balance sheet be drawn up every two years by every businessperson.

Early Calculating Devices

It was also in the seventeenth century that people began to take an interest in devices that could *automatically process* their data, if only in a rudimentary way. One of the earliest and best known was produced in France in the 1640s by Blaise Pascal, reportedly to help his father perform his job as a tax commissioner (see Figure 1.4). It was a small box that contained interlocking gears and was capable of doing addition and subtraction. In fact, it was the forerunner of today's automobile odometers.

In about 1694, Gottfried Wilhelm von Leibniz built a more sophisticated device, consisting of cylinders and wheels with interlocking teeth, shown in Figure 1.5. It was capable of multiplying and dividing, with one multidigit number entered initially and the other represented by turning a gear that number of times. In practice, Leibniz's device suffered (as did Pascal's) from the poor machining skills of the day, but its principles were later to be used in fairly contemporary mechanical calculating devices.

In 1805, Joseph Marie Jacquard of France invented a device that automatically created patterns during the textile weaving process. The heart of the device was a series of cards with holes punched in them; the holes allowed strands of material to be interwoven in a sequence that produced the desired pattern (see Figure 1.6). While Jacquard's loom wasn't a calculating device as such, his method of storing fabric patterns as holes in

Figure 1.4. Pascal and his adding machine. (Courtesy IBM Archives.)

Figure 1.5.   Liebniz and his mechanical multiplier. (Courtesy IBM Archives.)

Figure 1.6. The Jacquard loom. (Courtesy IBM Archives).

punched cards was a very clever means of *data storage*, which would have great importance for computing devices to follow.

The last of the early computing geniuses was truly a man ahead of his time. Charles Babbage was a nineteenth century English mathematician. During the 1820s and 1830s he developed and built a machine that he called the "Difference Engine," shown in Figure 1.7. Sophisticated for its time, it was capable of tabulating series of numbers derived from complicated polynomials. Such tables were needed in navigation and astronomy. Beginning in 1833, Babbage began to think about another invention, which he called the "Analytical Engine." He never completed it (again, the state of the art of machinery lagged the creativity of the mind), but included in its design were many of the principles of modern computers. The Analytical Engine was to consist of a "store" for holding data items and a "mill" for operating on them. Babbage was very impressed by Jacquard's work with punched cards. In fact, the Analytical Engine was to be able to store calculation instructions in punched cards, which would be fed into the machine together with punched cards containing data, to operate on that data and produce the desired result.

Practical Large-Scale Calculating

The development of practical computing and tabulating devices required two things: (1) a large-scale data storage and processing demand and (2) a certain base level of manufacturing skills and mechanical and electrical devices. By the late nineteenth century, machining skills had reached a sufficiently advanced level, and a need involving a massive amount of data occurred as well: the U.S. census.

The 1880 U.S. census took about seven years to compile by hand. It was estimated that using the same manual techniques, the compilation of the 1890 census would not be completed until after the 1900 census data had begun to be collected. The solution to processing the census data was provided by a government engineer named Herman Hollerith. Basing his work on Jacquard's punched card concept (as had Babbage), he arranged to have the census data stored in punched cards. He built devices to punch the holes into cards and devices to sort the cards. Hollerith and some of his machines are pictured in Figure 1.8. Wire brushes touching the cards completed circuits when they came across the holes and advanced electromechanical counters. Using Hollerith's equipment, the total population count of the 1890 census was completed one month after all of the data was in. The complete set of tabulations, including data on questions that had never before been practical to ask, took two years. In 1896, Hollerith formed the Tabulating Machine Company to produce and commercially market his devices. That company, combined with several others, eventually formed what is today the International Business Machines Corporation (IBM).

ure **1.10.** Electro-mechanical, punched card-based data processing equipment, circa
). (Courtesy IBM Archives.)

data was stored in punched cards, while the processing instructions
e implemented as collections of wires plugged into specially designed
rds, which in turn were inserted into slots in the electromechanical
ice

orld War II approached, the pace of development quickened.
rR. Stibitz at Bell Laboratories, and Howard H. Aiken at Harvard
d sophisticated electromechanical digital computers. Aiken's Mark
ted in 1944, had 72 numerical counters, or storage positions, and
seconds to do a multiplication operation.

st large, viable, fully electronic computer was also hastened by
tics needs of the military during the war. Called the Electronic
l Integrator and Calculator (ENIAC) it was begun in 1943 at
e School by John W. Mauchly and J. Presper Eckert, and was
l in 1946 (see Figure 1.11). It had 18,000 vacuum tubes and could
000 additions per second. It was about 1000 times faster than the

e advance into fully electronic computers was made other devel-
llowed rapidly. In 1945 John von Neumann, working from his
ideas, proposed a stored program computer. The first such
alled the Electronic Delay Storage Automatic Computer (ED-
completed in 1949 at Cambridge University by Maurice Wilkes.
MIT Whirlwind I, on which work had begun in the late 1940s,
t to incorporate core memory.

Figure 1.7. Babbage and his "Difference Engine." (Courtesy IBM Archives.)

9

Figure 1.8. Hollerith and some of his early punched card equipment. (Courtesy IBM Archives.)

The census bureau, while using Hollerith's equip[ment] experimenting on its own. One of its engineers, James [P. Powers,] devices to automatically feed cards into the equipment [and automat-]ically print results. In 1911 he formed the Powers Tab[ulating] Company, which eventually formed the basis for the UN[IVAC division of] the Sperry (now UNISYS) Corporation.

It was also around this time that another major advanc[e in] data tracking was made. The cash register, invented in 18[?? and inten-]sively marketed by the National Cash Register Compan[y, progres-]sively gained acceptance in retail businesses of every descr[iption. An early] NCR cash register is shown in Figure 1.9.

As society increased in sophistication, so did the volu[me of data] and the complexity of the ways in which the data had to [be handled.] Inventors made further advances in response. During the 19[??s,] Vannevar Bush at the Massachusetts Institute of Technolo[gy, and] others at such institutions as the Moore School of Engineeri[ng, Uni-]versity of Pennsylvania developed important "analog" comp[uters based] on continuous measuring devices as opposed to discrete item[s (such as] holes in cards), primarily for military ballistics calculations.

During that same period, and continuing into the early [1950s, com-]mercial data processing was performed on a variety of el[ectromechan-]ical punched card–based devices. They included calcul[ators,] sorters, collators, and printers, some of which are show[n ...]

Figure 1.9. An early NCR cash register[.]

Figure 1.11. The ENIAC. (Courtesy Unisys Corporation.)

Commercial Computers

After World War II, scientific advances and increasing business needs brought on by new societal expectations caused still further increases in the kinds and volumes of data to be processed. This brought renewed pressure on data processing capabilities. In 1947, Eckert and Mauchly formed the Eckert-Mauchly Computer Corporation and in 1951 delivered the UNIVAC I (Universal Automatic Computer), shown in Figure 1.12, to the census bureau. That company was eventually absorbed by Remington Rand (later Sperry Corporation), which continued to produce computers with the UNIVAC name. In 1953 IBM, which had a very strong presence with electromechanical calculating equipment and some early vacuum tube-based devices, produced its first electronic computer. The IBM 701 was a scientifically-oriented machine with a vacuum tube memory. It was followed by the business-oriented 702 and then in 1955 by the 705, which had a core memory, (see Figure 1.13). Those machines and others of their ilk came to be known as "first generation" computers.

The late 1950s and early 1960s saw the advent of computers based on transistors, rather than on vacuum tubes, (see Figure 1.14). These machines—the "second generation" computers—were much more reliable, smaller, and faster than those of the first generation. In addition to being incorporated into large computers, this new technology, combined with

Figure 1.12.   The UNIVAC I. (Courtesy Unisys Corporation.)

Figure 1.13.   The IBM 705. (Courtesy IBM Archives.)

Figure 1.14. A second generation computer: The NCR 304. (Courtesy NCR Corporation.)

improvements in core memory technology, created the first viable smaller scale computers, which became highly successful and proliferated rapidly. Such machines were the first computers for many thousands of corporations. The mid- and late 1960s saw the rise of the "third generation" of computers. Based on integrated circuits, third generation computers were another major step forward. Figure 1.15 shows a third generation mainframe computer.

Figure 1.15. A third generation computer: The UNIVAC 1108. (Courtesy Unisys Corporation.)

Modern Data Storage Media

Paralleling the growth of equipment to process data was the development of new media on which to store the data. The earliest form of modern data storage was punched holes in some appropriate paper medium. In the 1870s and 1880s punched paper tape was introduced in conjunction with early teletype equipment. Of course, we've already mentioned that Hollerith in the 1890s and Powers in the early 1900s used punched cards as a storage medium. In fact, punched cards were the only data storage medium used in the increasingly sophisticated automated accounting machines of the 1920s, 1930s, and 1940s. They were used extensively in the early computers of the 1950s and 1960s and could still be found well into the 1970s, in smaller data processing installations and in a progressively reduced capacity.

By 1936, both Eastman Kodak and Bush, with his "Rapid Selector," were recording digital data photographically. While the data could be read back with photoelectric cell technology, this was a nonerasable medium. Nonerasability in a data storage medium can be an advantage for some data processing applications, but it is too limiting for most, and thus photographic storage has always had only limited use.

The middle to late 1930s saw the beginning of the era of magnetic storage media, with Bell Laboratories experimenting with magnetic tape for sound storage. In 1937 there was early work in Germany on oxides for use in magnetic storage. In 1937 and 1938 Bush expressed some early ideas on magnetic storage on plate-like objects. In 1939 at MIT, magnetic strips on the backs of accounting cards were wound around a drum for reading. With the advent of World War II, these efforts slowed or stopped.

In 1942 at MIT, Perry Crawford wrote a thesis describing the idea of magnetic drum storage. Beginning in 1943, and continuing into the early 1950s, Engineering Research Associates (ERA) conducted experiments with and developed such devices, such as the one shown in Figure 1.16.

In the late 1940s there was early work on the use of magnetic tape for recording data and further thought on flat plate magnetic storage. In 1947 Eckert and Mauchly developed a magnetic tape unit; in 1948 and 1949 IBM furthered magnetic tape development. Also in 1947, ideas on flat plates and flat donut-shaped plates for large-scale random access data storage were expressed at the Aberdeen Proving Grounds and at the National Bureau of Standards, respectively. In 1948 and 1949, Potter Instrument experimented with strips of magnetic tape stretched on a flat frame.

By 1950, others, including RCA and Raytheon, were developing the magnetic tape concept, too. Also in the early 1950s, Aiken developed tape units with vacuum columns. In 1952, both UNIVAC and Raytheon offered commercially available magnetic tape units. In 1953 IBM offered the tape units pictured in Figure 1.17. From the mid-1950s to the mid-1960s, magnetic tape gradually became the dominant data storage medium

Figure 1.16. An early ERA magnetic drum unit, circa 1948. (Courtesy Imprimis Technology Incorporated.)

Figure 1.17. An early IBM magnetic tape drive. (Courtesy IBM Archives.)

Figure 1.18.   A later magnetic tape drive. (Courtesy IBM Corporation.)

in computers. Magnetic tape technology has been continually improved since then, and is still in broad use today, particularly for archived data. Figure 1.18 shows a more recent tape drive.

In 1952 and 1953, first ERA and then UNIVAC offered the first commercially available magnetic drums, such as the one in Figure 1.19. In 1953 and 1954 IBM offered drums in some of its early computers. They were joined in 1955 by Control Data. Also in 1955, UNIVAC "File Computers" contained the first large capacity drum storage.

In 1956 and 1957, IBM developed magnetic cards as a memory device for typewriters.

In 1953, IBM began work on its 305 RAMAC (Random Access Memory Accounting Machine) fixed disk storage device. By 1954 there was a multiplatter version, which became commercially available in 1956 (see Figure 1.20). In 1957 the first shipment of devices with movable-head disk drives was made. At about that time, experiments began with removable disk packs which were introduced commercially in 1963. One of these is pictured in Figure 1.21. During the mid-1960s a massive conversion from tape to disk as the preeminent secondary storage medium began to take place. At first, the disk storage environment was geared towards the removable pack philosophy, with a dozen or more packs commonly being juggled on and off a single drive. As data recording densities increased, the pack-to-drive ratio decreased to the point that in 1976 IBM marketed a disk drive with a nonremovable pack. Continual improvements in disk technology

Figure 1.19. A later ERA magnetic drum unit, circa 1950. (Courtesy Imprimis Technology Incorporated.)

have led it to become the standard data storage medium in use today. Figure 1.22 shows a modern disk drive unit.

Among the newest data storage media are "mass storage" devices and the diskette. In 1974 IBM introduced the "Mass Storage System." It consisted of a "honeycomb" of small cylinders with magnetic tape wrapped around them and is shown in Figure 1.23. On command, the device would select a cylinder, wrap its tape around a reading device, and transfer the data. While slow compared to disk storage, this technique is capable of storing huge amounts of data. At the other end of the spectrum, the diskette is a small, flexible, inexpensive, coated plastic disk, which was introduced in different forms in 1971 and 1973. The latest version is enclosed in a hard, plastic case, (see Figure 1.24). Diskette drives are the principal secondary storage devices used in today's microcomputers.

Today's Data Processing Environment

Eventually, the boundaries between computer generations became indistinct. We speak of today's fourth generation of computers as being based on "very large scale integrated" (VLSI) circuits. This technology and countless other improvements have continued the simultaneous trend of decreasing price and increasing performance.

Figure 1.20. The IBM RAMAC disk device. (Courtesy IBM Archives.)

Computers now range from desktop microcomputers like the one in Figure 1.25, to incredibly powerful large machines such as that shown in Figure 1.26. Storage facilities have become faster, more reliable, and capable of packing data in an increasingly dense fashion. Networks of far-flung computers, tied together by a variety of communications media, have flourished.

Software, the various kinds of instructions that make the machines run, has also continuously advanced. Highly sophisticated operating systems allow many people to use the machines simultaneously. Database management systems permit nonredundant data storage and complex data access. Special development systems permit certain application programs to be created quickly, bypassing the slow traditional programming process.

In short, the computer has become a part of virtually every business process. This is a trend that is sure to continue.

Figure 1.21. A disk drive unit of the mid-1960s. (Courtesy Imprimis Technology Incorporated.)

Figure 1.22. A modern, sealed, disk drive unit. (Courtesy IBM Corporation.)

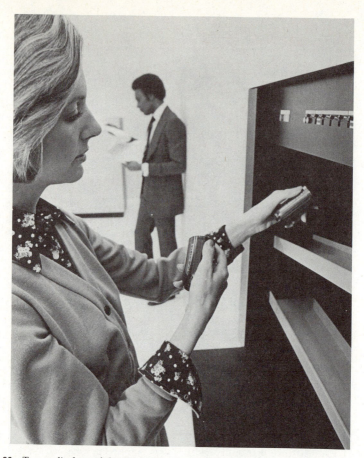

Figure 1.23 Tape cylinders of the IBM Mass Storage System. (Courtesy IBM Corporation.)

Figure 1.24. Diskettes. (Courtesy IBM Corporation.)

Figure 1.25. A microcomputer: The IBM Personal System/2. (Courtesy IBM Corporation.)

Figure 1.26. A modern, large-scale computer: The IBM 3090. (Courtesy IBM Corporation.)

The Information Age

Which brings us back to the starting point for all of that activity: data. It took thousands of years for people to cultivate an interest in the simplest kinds of data. It took a few hundred years to develop basic calculating methods and devices to the point that an interest in more sophisticated uses of data became practical. And it has taken only about the last 30 years for data processing to reach a point at which people are speaking of the decline of the "industrial age" and the birth of the "information age."

One crucial aspect of the information age, and one that we have already had to begin dealing with, is managing the huge volumes of data involved. Walk into a large company's data processing installation today and you're likely to find shelves of tape reels and stacks of disk packs, together with rows of devices to read from them and write onto them. Of course, new developments in hardware are continually producing devices that can cram more data in the same amount of space, but in a way that only adds to the problem, because it encourages people to capture and store more and more data without having sufficient means to manage it properly.

The amount of data that large and even not-so-large firms have today is almost unbelievable. We're talking about more than trillions of individual pieces of data, and more often than not, the way that they are managed—or, more accurately, mismanaged—is horrendous, if somewhat understandable. It's not as if we're talking about managing a company's employees. Even the largest companies have only a few hundred thousand of them, and they don't change that frequently. Nor does the money that a company has match this complexity: sure, there is a lot of it, but it's all the same in the sense that a dollar that goes to payroll is the same kind of dollar that goes to paying a supplier for raw materials.

In data, we have a commodity of tremendous volume, each piece of which is different from the next. Much of it is in a state of change at any one time, and nowadays it seems that everyone in the company wants access (usually instant access) to it for one purpose or another. Furthermore, with so much data processing development taking place, it's difficult to keep track of what data already exists. For these and other reasons, the same data tends to be stored several (or many) times over for different applications.

Is there no hope? Are we to be buried forever in a seemingly endless mass of unmanageable data?

Fortunately, there is a class of methodologies—really more of an environment—for storing, accessing, and in general, managing data, which can form the foundation for survival in a world that is going to become ever more data-oriented as time goes on. That class of methodologies or environment has come to be known as **database**.

This Book

Database emerged as a recognizable subject and discipline in the mid-1960s, but for some time concern about it was limited to a relatively small portion of the data processing population. Through the 1970s it grew to be a major focus of data processing activity for many organizations; but with more and more data processing people exposed to it and expected to understand and use it, it became clear that there was a tremendous lack of understanding of the fundamental concepts of the subject. The advent of the 1980s made that situation even more acute.

Database is a very powerful concept. It forms an ingenious solution to some vexing problems. As a result, it unfortunately tends to be a multifaceted and complex subject, which appears difficult when one attempts to swallow it in one gulp. But database is approachable and understandable if one proceeds carefully, cautiously, and progressively, step by step.

This book is a straightforward introduction to database. It takes a step-by-step approach that leaves no gaps in its explanation. Each chapter progressively adds more to an understanding of the fundamentals of database. It is an understanding that no one in data processing can any longer afford to be without.

References

Crawford, P., conversation on February 3, 1984.

Gleiser, M., "Men and Machines Before Babbage," *DATAMATION* **24** (10) (October, 1978): 125–130.

Goldstine, H. H., *The Computer from Pascal to von Neumann*, Princeton University Press, Princeton, NJ; 1972.

Gordon, M. J., and Shillinglaw, G., *Accounting: A Management Approach*, 4th ed., Richard D. Irwin, Homewood, IL; 1969.

Hendriksen, E. S., *Accounting Theory*, revised ed., Richard D. Irwin, Homewood, IL; 1970.

Littleton, A. C., and Yamey, B. S., *Studies in the History of Accounting*, Richard D. Irwin, Homewood, IL; 1956.

Rosen, S., "Electronic Computers: A Historical Survey," *Computing Surveys* **1** (1), (March, 1969): 7–36.

Schmandt-Besserat, D., "The Earliest Precursor of Writing," *Scientific American* **238** (6), (June, 1978): 50–59.

Shurkin, J., *Engines of the Mind*, W. W. Norton, New York; 1984.

Stevens, L. D., "The Evolution of Magnetic Storage," *IBM Journal of Research and Development* **25** (5), (September, 1981): 663–675.

Tropp, H., "The Effervescent Years: A Retrospective," *IEEE Spectrum* **11** (2), (February, 1974): 70–79.

Questions and Exercises

1.1. Draw a time line for the last 200 years comparing the development of data processing devices to the development of data storage media.

1.2. Do you think that the comparative development of data processing devices and data storage media was uneven? Did the rate of growth of one inhibit the growth of the other?

2

Simple Files and Storage Media

What is Data?

Records and Entities

Let's begin by thinking about a single piece of data. A single piece of data represents a single fact about something in which we are interested. In our company, it may be the fact that John Smith's employee number is 31719; it may be the fact that our largest supplier of bolts is located in Chicago; or it may be the fact that the telephone number for one of our customers, the Acme Company, is 555-8003. A *piece of data* is a single *fact* about something that we care about in our surroundings.

Usually we have many facts to describe something of interest to us. For example, let's consider the facts that we might be interested in about that employee of ours, John Smith. We want to remember that his employee number is 31719, his salary rate is $5.50 per hour, his home city is Detroit, his home state is Michigan, and so forth. We need to know these things in order to process Smith's payroll check every week, to notify his family in case he will be home late, to send him a company greeting card at New Year's, and so forth. It certainly seems reasonable to collect all of the facts about Smith that we need for those purposes and to hold all of them together. Figure 2.1 shows all of the facts about John Smith that concern payroll and related applications.

Since we have to generate a paycheck each week for every employee in our company, not just for Smith, we are obviously going to need a collection of facts like those in Figure 2.1 for all of our employees. Figure 2.2 shows a portion of that collection.

Employee Number	Employee Last Name	Employee First Name	Salary Rate	Home city	Home state	Home Telephone
31719	Smith	John	5.50	Detroit	MI	313-555-5186

Figure 2.1.   John Smith's payroll facts.

It will simplify matters later if at this point we can relate some of the items that we have already come across to some of the many terms that are a part of file and database terminology. The collection of facts about a particular employee (one line or row of the table in Figure 2.2) is called a **record**. Each kind of fact (e.g., employee number or home city) is called a **field**. The collection of payroll facts for all of the employees, that is, the entire table in Figure 2.2, is called a **file**.

The file in Figure 2.2, which is about the most basic kind of file imaginable, is often called a **simple**, or **linear**, **file** (linear since it is a collection of records listed one after the other in a long "line"). We will speak of the layout of each record of a file (the column headings in Figure 2.2) as the **record type**, and each individual record (each row in Figure 2.2) as an **occurrence** of that record (or of that record type).

Put in a slightly different, but closely related way, each thing that we are interested in keeping track of (the real physical object or event, not the facts about it) is called an **entity**. John Smith—the real, living, breathing person who you can go over to and touch—is an entity. A collection of entities of the same type (e.g., all of the company's employees) is called an **entity set**. An **attribute** is a property or characteristic of an entity. Smith's telephone number, employee number, home city, and so forth, all are his attributes. Relating these terms back to files, we can see that a record *describes* a particular entity (at least in terms of one or several applications).

Employee Number	Employee Last Name	Employee First Name	Salary Rate	Home city	Home state	Home Telephone
06337	Jones	Fred	4.30	New York	NY	212-555-9207
09155	Smith	Susan	5.90	Atlanta	GA	404-555-2287
16840	Adams	John	10.00	Atlanta	GA	404-555-4301
31719	Smith	John	5.50	Detroit	MI	313-555-5186
38102	Baker	George	7.00	Atlanta	GA	404-555-7739
. . .						

Figure 2.2.   Payroll file.

A file describes an entire entity set. A given attribute is represented as a field value.

Another handy feature of the file in Figure 2.2 has to do with the employee numbers field: Its values are unique. Since each employee has a unique employee number, we can use that field to distinguish between the different employee records. Such a field (or combination of fields) is called a **key** field of the file.

Relationships

So far we've been concerned with maintaining facts about a particular entity. Another very important kind of information is the collection of ways that different entities *relate to each other*. Such interactions are described as **associations** and **relationships**.

Suppose that in addition to the information about the employee previously mentioned, there is a need to store data about each employee's identification badge (or card), his or her manager, and the rooms in which the employee is authorized to be. There is exactly one identification badge and one manager associated with each employee, facts that are called **unary associations**. In addition, looking at it the other way, for a given identification badge there is exactly one employee associated with it. In this case there is a unary association in each direction; this is called a *one-to-one relationship*, (see Figure 2.3a).

Returning once again to employees and managers, while for a given employee there is only one manager, for a given manager there may be many subordinates. Thus there is a unary association in one direction and a **multiple association** in the other direction, and the combination is called a **one-to-many relationship**, (see Figure 2.3b). (Note that the single arrowhead denotes the unary association, while the double arrowhead denotes the multiple association.)

Finally, consider the situation of employees and secure rooms. An employee may be authorized to be in several rooms, while a room will have several employees authorized to be in it. That's a **many-to-many relationship**, (see Figure 2.3c).

Figure 2.3. Relationships: (*a*) one-to one, (*b*) one-to-many, and (*c*) many-to-many.

Simple Files

Let's review what we've established thus far. It may all seem rather simple, but it forms a solid foundation for what lies ahead.

The basic notion of data is establishing a collection of needed facts about things (entities) that we care about in our environment. In concept at least, we can envision each such collection to form a row of a table (record of a file) that brings together the data of each occurrence of that type of entity. Again, the table or file in Figure 2.2 contains a row's worth of data about each of our employees.

This brings us to the first of several times in this book that we shall face the following question:

> That last paragraph sounds perfectly logical to me, as a human being, but how can a "nuts and bolts" (or more accurately, a "circuits and chips" computer be made to make sense out of it?

At each such juncture, this book will answer such questions at a level appropriate for a practitioner or student of data processing or a user or manager of it. It will not get into the electrical or mechanical engineering details.

In order to approach this question, it will be necessary to take a look at the appropriate kinds of data representations and data storage devices available, information that will actually be quite useful throughout the book. The characteristics of those devices will be important considerations both in the ways that we can access data and in the performance that we can expect to achieve in doing so.

Data Storage Concepts

Data Representations

You're probably familiar with the concepts of bits and bytes and the basic ways of forming data with them, but in the spirit of completeness let's begin with a review of that material.

A **bit** or binary digit is simply a two-way switch, which at any moment is set either one way or the other way. Over the years, this idea has been physically embodied in little metal rings (or "cores") being magnetized in one direction or the other, spots on punched cards either being left alone or being punched out, spots on metal oxide–coated plastic, aluminum being magnetized in one direction or the other, and so on.

Since there is not much in the way of data that can be recorded in a single bit, groups of bits are combined together to form a medium for data storage. In many of today's computers, eight bits are grouped together to form a **byte**. Groups of bytes, or in some computers other groups of bits, are combined to form **words**. The two main kinds of data that we are interested in storing are numeric data and alphabetic data.

There are three common ways of storing numeric data, usually called binary, decimal, and floating point. A "binary number" is simply a number represented in the binary, or base two, number system, in a string of bits, each of which has the value zero or the value one, as the binary system requires. For example, the string of bits

0111001

represents the number 57.

A "decimal number" is formed by assigning a particular bit sequence in a byte to have the value 0, another sequence the value 1, and so on through 9. For example, if 11110101 represents the decimal digit 5 (note that the last four bits form the number 5 in binary), and if 11110111 represents the decimal number 7, then

11110101 11110111

represents 57 in this system. Since only four bits are needed to represent the 10 different decimal digits, this representation can be compressed so that two decimal digits appear in a single byte

01010111

in this example. This system is known as "packed decimal" and is quite straightforward, except that an additional byte may be required to represent the sign of the number. The decimal system was devised for business applications with high data input and output requirements, which it meets through its relative ease in transferring data to and from input and output devices.

Floating point numbers are intended for scientific applications, which often require very large or very small numbers. While there are some variations on the theme, a floating point number consists of three parts: the sign, the characteristic, and the fraction. In general, the characteristic is an exponent that raises the base of the number system to some power. The result is then multiplied by the fraction to obtain the result. For example,

5E243

might be a notation for 10 (the base of the number system) raised to the power 5, times 0.243, or 24,300. If the amount of storage allotted to the fraction is small, and the range of the exponent allows very large or very small numbers, some precision may be lost, but with the numbers and applications being dealt with that usually doesn't matter.

Characters are represented as assigned bit sequences in a particular "code" with which the computer operates. Two of the most common such codes are the Extended Binary Coded Decimal Interchange Code (EBCDIC), which represents each character as an eight bit sequence (one character per byte), and the American Standard Code for Information Interchange (ASCII) which is a seven bit code. For example, in EBCDIC the bit sequence 11000001 represents the character A, 11000010 represents the character B, and so on. To form the word SMITH in a computer's memory would require five bytes of storage, the first containing the bit pattern for S, the second the pattern for M, and so on.

So storing a record in a computer's memory is a matter of a program causing the correct bit patterns for the alphabetic fields of the record and the correct representations for the numeric fields of the record to be stored in consecutive storage positions. The record in Figure 2.1 would be stored as several bytes to represent the employee number 31719 in, say, packed decimal format, followed by a byte with the bit pattern for a character S, followed by a byte with the bit pattern for a character M, and so on. For an entire file, the records might simply follow each other in memory. This brings us to the different kinds of memory and some of the various types of storage devices that are available today.

Basically, there are two levels of storage or memory in a computer system: primary memory and secondary memory.

Primary Memory

Primary memory is the place where data being processed, application programs in the process of executing, and portions of the system control programs (the operating system, database management system, and network control program) must be placed. At the byte or word level, each storage location can be singled out and directly reached by the computer's central processing unit. Because it is so critical to the overall operation of the system, primary memory must be extremely fast in terms of the storage and retrieval of its contents. In theory, it might be nice if primary memory was unlimited in size and all of the programs and data files associated with a system could be stored in it. But because of the speed and other requirements placed upon it, primary memory requires comparatively expensive technologies. That, and the fact that primary memory is limited in size by the system's addressing schemes used to access its contents, allows it to be only large enough to store a very small fraction of a system's programs and data files at any one moment.

Primary memory used to be made of little doughnut shaped pieces of iron called "cores" (the term "core memory" used to be synonymous with the term "primary memory"), which were strung together with wires running through them. Each core represented a single bit, and the wires running through them could both set the two directions of magnetism on the cores, which represented the zero and the one values, and could sense them to determine their current values at any later time. Today, primary memories are made with newer integrated circuit technologies. The concept of the bit remains the same, but the speeds involved have increased tremendously.

In any case, primary memory can be thought of as a vast array of bits, arranged into bytes and/or words. Each byte or word has an address and can be accessed by the central processing unit, to store new data or retrieve existing data, very rapidly.

Secondary Memory

The Need for Secondary Memory. Because of the scarcity of primary memory, the vast volumes of data and the programs that process them are held on secondary memory devices. Individual records or groups of records of a file are loaded from secondary memory into primary memory when required for processing (as are programs when they are to be executed). A loose analogy can be drawn between primary and secondary memory in a computer system and a person's brain and a library (see Figure 2.4). The brain cannot possibly hold all of the information that a person might need, but, let's say, a large library can. So when a person needs some particular information that's not in his or her brain at the moment, he or she finds a book in the library that has the information and, by reading it, transfers the information from the book into his or her brain.

Sequential and Direct Access. While data processing applications come in a countless number of variations, there are fundamentally only two kinds of access to stored data that any of them requires. In this book we shall refer to these two kinds of access as **sequential access** and **direct access**.

The term sequential access means that the application must retrieve and process all or a portion of the records of a file one after another until all of the required records have been processed. The records in the file may

Figure 2.4. Primary and secondary memory are like a brain and a library.

be ordered by the values of some key field, they may be in chronological order, with the most recently inserted record placed at the end of the file, or they may be in no particular order at all. A common example of sequential processing is producing a company's payroll checks every week. Since all of the company's employees must be paid, it might as well plow through all of the employee payroll records, which will probably be ordered by the employee number field, one after another until a paycheck has been generated for each employee. Ordering the file by employee number will facilitate control and update of the file and will probably simplify distribution of the paychecks.

The other mode of access will be referred to in this book as direct access. This mode meets the need to find one specific record in a file and retrieve it with the usual, but not strict, assumption that it must be retrieved very quickly. The record is retrieved either to simply present it to someone for perusal, to process or modify it in some way, or both. An example of this type of data access requirement is an airline's reservation system. When a customer telephones an airline to make a reservation or simply to get information about a flight on a certain date, the reservations clerk, usually sitting in front of a video display terminal, must be able quickly to retrieve the data on the requested flight. We might also pursue the employee payroll file example a bit further in this direction by suggesting that there will be times when an employee payroll record must be retrieved directly. For example, if one specific employee gets a salary raise and we want to record that new data, then we want to find and process just his or her employee payroll record and no other.

The two predominant forms of secondary memory in use today are magnetic tape and magnetic disk. Magnetic tape is a sequential storage medium and thus supports sequential access. Data is stored one character after another down the length of the tape, and there is no direct access to it. Most database applications today require direct access, and so tape is not much of a factor in the realm of database.

Disk Storage Devices.   Databases require storage devices that are very large in storage capacity, are very fast in terms of storage and access times (although not as fast as primary memory), provide a direct access capability to the data, and are less expensive than primary memory units of comparable capacity. By far the most common such device in use today is the **magnetic disk** unit.

A single magnetic disk is a hard, round, aluminum platter with an iron oxide coating on its two surfaces. Usually several disks are stacked together, mounted on a central rod, with some space between them, into a **disk pack**, shown in Figure 2.5. The disk pack arrangement is a permanent one; the disks are not interchangeable or removeable. The disk pack is placed in a device known as a **disk drive**, which has read/write heads capable of storing data on and retrieving data from the disks' surfaces;

Figure 2.5. A disk pack.

Figure 2.6 shows such an arrangement. The disk pack spins on the disk drive at a high velocity (e.g., 2400 rpm), causing any given piece of data to be potentially accessible many times each second.

It is important to understand how data is arranged on the disks and the related performance factors in retrieval operations. Data is stored, serially by bit, on concentric circles on the disk known as **tracks**, illustrated in Figure 2.7. There may be fewer than one hundred or several hundred tracks on each disk surface, depending on the particular device. Let's number the outermost track 0, the next track 1, and so on. You might assume that the way a file is loaded onto a disk pack would be by filling up all of the tracks of one disk surface, then all of tracks on the next surface, and so on. In fact, that is not the way that it is done.

Track 0 on surface 0, track 0 on surface 1, and each of the other "track 0s" on the pack, (one per surface) are logically combined into **cylinder**

Figure 2.6. A mounted disk pack showing the access arm mechanism with its read/write heads.

Disk surface

Tracks

Figure 2.7.   Tracks on the surface of a disk.

0. The same logical cylinder arrangement is made for every such set of tracks with the same index number on their respective surfaces. It's as if you looked at the disk pack from the top and could select a set of the concentric circular tracks, one per surface and each right over the other, forming a cylinder. Thus the total number of cylinders in a disk pack is equal to the number of tracks on any one disk surface.

The reason for the emphasis on the cylinder concept has to do with the read/write hardware in the disk drive. It would be too expensive and cumbersome to have a read/write head for every track of every surface, so the read/write heads are designed to move from track to track as required. The arrangement shown in Figure 2.6 is one of the earliest and simplest of that sort. There is a movable access mechanism that consists of a set of arms with read/write heads. Each arm has two read/write heads on its far end and fits into the space in between two of the disks. In that design, one of the read/write heads on an arm is capable of accessing the disk surface above the arm, and the other head is capable of accessing the surface below the arm. Thus, as can be seen in Figure 2.6, there is one read/write head per surface. Furthermore, this entire comb-like access arm assembly is designed to move as one solid object. You can't have the head for surface 0 positioned at track 10 of that surface and at the same time have the head for surface 3 positioned at track 35 of that surface. If one head is at track 10 of its surface, then they are all at track 10 of their respective surfaces. This arrangement has two consequences. One is that it holds down the cost and the complexity of the disk drives. The other is that it creates the concept of the logical cylinder for the following performance-oriented reasons.

There are four major steps or timing considerations in the transfer of data from the disk pack to primary memory:

1. *Seek Time:* Moving the access arm assembly to the correct cylinder from whatever cylinder at which it's currently positioned.
2. *Head Switching:* Selecting the read/write head that accesses the particular track (surface) of that cylinder on which the data resides.
3. *Rotational Delay:* Waiting for the desired data to arrive under the read/write head as the disk pack is spinning on the drive.
4. *Transfer Time:* The time to actually move the data from the disk to primary memory once steps 1–3 have been completed.

Head switching takes virtually no time, since it is simply a matter of throwing an electrical switch. On the average, rotational delay takes half the time of one full rotation of the disk, and of course is unavoidable anyway. Transfer times are rather fast, and, again, are necessary in any case. The slowest part of the process is the seek time: the movement of the access arm assembly. But there is a way to turn this situation to advantage, and that's where the concept of the cylinder comes in.

If the records of a simple file are in order by some (key) field, it is a good assumption that for at least some of the applications that use the file, the records will be accessed, one after the other, in the same key order. Furthermore, for reasons which we will delve into later in this book, there are many database situations in which closely related pieces of data stored in different record formats will be accessed together. In both of these cases, if we store the data initially by filling all of the tracks on one cylinder, then all of that data can be retrieved *without having to move the access arm assembly.* We position the assembly to the correct cylinder, start reading from the first required track of that cylinder, and then just flip an electronic switch to activate a different read/write head and read another track of that same cylinder. The alternative, filling all of the tracks of one disk surface and then moving on to the tracks of another surface, would always require access arm assembly movement to go from the data on one track to related data on a nearby track (on the same disk surface).

Over the years there have been tremendous improvements and a wide range of variations in disk technology. These include:

- A range of from 1 to as many as 16 disks in a disk pack. This amounts to from 2 to 30 tracks or surfaces per cylinder, since in multidisk disk packs the top surface of the top disk and the bottom surface of the bottom disk are normally not used.)
- Some disk drives are designed so that disk packs can be removed and replaced with other packs as frequently as desired. Others have permanently mounted, nonremovable disk packs. An advantage of nonremovable packs is that engineering tolerances can be finer, allowing for a higher data recording density.
- In some cases the access arm assembly with its read/write heads is part of the disk drive unit, in others it is actually part of the disk pack and connects to the drive when the pack is mounted in it.

- As opposed to the original design of one access arm assembly reaching all of the data on the disk pack, there are more recent designs with more than one such assembly. In some cases different assemblies access different disk surfaces, in others they access different cylinders of the same set of surfaces. Obviously, these variations open the way for multiple, parallel accesses of a given disk pack.
- Recently, particularly in the field of microcomputers, there has been the advent of the diskette. This is a variation that has a single disk (two surfaces), is only a few inches in diameter, and is made of a thin, pliable, iron oxide–coated plastic base. When spun in a disk drive it flattens and can be used as a disk normally would be.
- A related kind of device is called a **magnetic drum**. It is a cylindrical unit with circular tracks wrapped around it. A drum is permanently mounted in a device that spins it and that provides one read/write head *per track*. The consequences of that arrangement are that access to data is extremely fast, but because of limited storage capacity and high cost drums are normally used to hold systems programs and associated data, as opposed to application data files.

Data and Disk Formats.   There are two other issues, both concerning aspects of the ways that data can be arranged, that we will take up now. The first involves variations in the way that records can be structured. The second involves issues of data placement on the disk.

Record Formats.   The records in the file in Figure 2.2 are called **fixed length** records. Every record in the file is of the same length, with the same field types in the same order as every other record in the file. Alternatively, there are files that consist of **variable length** records, each of which may consist of different fields and vary in length within a specified range.

Each record in the file in Figure 2.2 is called a **logical record**. Since the rate of processing data in the central processing unit is much faster than the rate at which data can be brought in from secondary memory, it is advisable to transfer several consecutively stored records at a time. Again, as mentioned previously, this has implications both for simple sequential files and for database structures. Once a **physical record** or **block** of several logical records has been brought into primary memory from secondary memory, each logical record can be examined and processed as necessary by the executing program.

Track Formats.   Finally there is the question of how to place the data records on the disk tracks, so that they can be found once the system has determined that they are on a particular track.

Typical of track formats are the "count-data" format and the "count-key-data" format used in the IBM 3330, 2305 (with some modifications), 3340, 3344, 3350, 3375, and 3380 disk devices. Figure 2.8*a* illustrates the count-data format. The beginning of the track is denoted by a marker known as

Figure 2.8a. IBM disk track formats: Count-data format.

the "index point." Following that is a small gap. Gaps of varying lengths separate all of the different items on the track and give the disk drives time to perform certain functions. Next is the "home address," which includes such information as the cylinder number, track number, and a flag indicating whether the track is defective. Next is a special record called the "track descriptor record," which contains such information as the number of bytes left on the track after the last data record and if this track has a defect in it, and the address of the alternate track that contains the data that should have been on this one. Finally we reach the data records, which consist of three parts: an "address marker," a "count area," and a "data area." The address marker is a special indicator that will allow the drive to determine where the beginning of the record is on subsequent retrievals. The count area repeats the cylinder and track numbers and the indication of whether or not the track is defective, and contains such additional information as the record number (of the records on that track), the length of the data area to follow, and the fact that this file is in count-data, as opposed to count-key-data format. The data area contains all of the actual data of a physical record or block.

The count-key-data format, Figure 2.8b, is the same as the count-data format, except that there is a "key" area between the count and data areas of each data record and an indication in the count area of the length of the

Figure 2.8b. IBM disktrack formats: Count-key-data format.

key. The key area usually contains the value of the highest key among the key values of the logical records in that block. Because of these key areas, the count-key-data format can be used by the system to more quickly locate records on the basis of key value.

A more recent development is the "fixed-block architecture" (FBA) used in the IBM 3310 and 3370 disk devices. While in the other devices previously discussed the user sets the length of a block (the "blocking factor" is the number of logical records in a physical record) for a particular data file, the FBA devices have fixed, 512-byte blocks for all data files. Special hardware and software features juggle the data in ways unique to the FBA based devices.

Storing Simple Files

Now, let's return to our earlier question of how to take the concept of the simple file and convert it into a form suitable for computer storage and use.

As we've seen in this chapter, both numeric and alphabetic data can be represented as series of bits. A given record is simply a composite string of all of the bits needed to represent each of its fields, and a file is a composite string of all of the bits needed to represent each of its records.

A decision is made as to how many logical records should go into making up one physical record. Then using say, the count-key-data format, the file is loaded, one physical record at a time, onto a disk pack. The data is loaded, serially by bit, on one track of a cylinder, then the next track of the cylinder, and so on until the cylinder is full. Then the process continues with the next cylinder, and the next, until the entire file has been loaded.

References

Bohl, M., *Information Processing*, 4th ed., Science Research Associates, Chicago, IL, 1984.

Bohl, M., *Introduction to IBM Direct Access Storage Devices*, Science Research Associates, Chicago, IL, 1981.

Grauer, R. T., and Sugrue, P. K., *Microcomputer Applications*, 2nd ed., McGraw-Hill, New York, 1989.

Tom, P. L., *Computer Information Systems*, Scott, Foresman, Glenview, IL, 1989.

Questions and Exercises

2.1. What is data? Do you think the word "data" should be treated as a singular or plural word? Why?

2.2. Name some entities and attributes in a university environment.

2.3. Name some entities and attributes with which an insurance company would be concerned.

2.4. Name some entities and attributes with which a furniture store would be concerned.

2.5. What is the difference between a record type and an occurrence of that record. Give some examples.

2.6. This file is used in the data processing system of an automobile manufacturer.

Vehicle Number	Vehicle Model	Color	Date of Manufacture
. . .			
527360	Sedan	Blue	9-12-89
527482	Coupe	Red	9-23-89
630975	Sedan	Red	9-27-89
644182	Sedan	Brown	9-27-89
. . .			

a. Name one of the entities described in the file. How would you describe the entity set?

b. What are the attributes of the entities? Choose one of the entities and describe it.

c. Choose one of the attributes and discuss the nature of the set of values that it can take.

2.7. Consider the entities you found in question 2.2, 2.3, or 2.4 and describe some relationships among them.

2.8. Why are relationships between entities important?

2.9. Write the number 84 in the binary, decimal, and floating point representations.

2.10. Discuss the reasons for having both primary and secondary memories in a computer system.

2.11. Describe an application that would require sequential access and an application that would require direct access to the automobile file in question 2.6.

2.12. What is a cylinder in a disk pack? Why is it important to data processing applications?

2.13. In your own words, describe how data moves from a disk pack to main memory.

2.14. Why is it necessary to have special formats for data on disks? Describe one such arrangement.

3

File Organizations and Access Methods

Accessing Data

In the last chapter we established the concept of the simple file, using a payroll file as an example. Now let's talk about the ways we can use it in the payroll and other related applications.

There are four actions that we can take with a file:

1. Simply look at a record without changing it.
2. Modify a record (e.g., an employee's salary rate changes).
3. Insert a new record (e.g., a new employee is hired by the company).
4. Delete an existing record (e.g., an employee leaves the company).

Depending on the nature of a particular application, a given program might perform all or only some of those four functions on a file that it accesses. But in addition, there is the question of *which* record or records we want to operate on at a given time.

It's easy enough to visualize the data in a payroll file and to understand the concepts of sequential and direct retrieval, and we've talked about the general principles behind actually putting data on a disk, but arranging data on a disk so that it will be available in an efficient manner for sequential retrieval, direct retrieval, or both is another level of detail that we must pursue before we can go any farther. It is a somewhat complex matter, but certainly understandable if we take it gradually, step by step.

We refer to the way that we store the data for subsequent retrieval as the **file organization.** The way that we retrieve the data, based on it being stored in a particular file organization, is called the **access method**. (Note that the terms "file organization" and "access method" are often used synonymously, but this is technically incorrect.)

File Organizations and Access Methods

Introduction

Let's pursue the question of file organizations and access methods with the same example data that we've been using. Remember that, as Figure 3.1 demonstrates, each record consists of the same set of fields as every other record in the collection. For every employee we want to maintain the person's employee number, last name, first name, salary rate, and so forth. Again, we will refer to the general outline or structure of the record as the "record type" and the data for a specific employee (31719, Smith, John, 5.50, . . .) as an "occurrence" of that record, or simply a "record." We will take a look at the major file organization and access method possibilities that exist for such simple collections of records, all of the same type.

Simple Linear Files

Sequential Files. The simplest way to store a collection of records is in one long list. If the records are in sequence, in terms of one or more of the fields, then we call the arrangement a **sequential** (or **key-sequential**) file. Thus, the payroll file in Figure 3.1 is really a sequential file. The field(s) that the file is sequenced on is called the **sequence field**. A field with unique values that identify the records of the file is called a **key field**. In the payroll file the records are sequenced by a key field (employee number), as is often, but not always, the case.

In a simple sequential file, the only way to retrieve the data is to start at the beginning of the file and read one record after another, in sequence,

Employee Number	Employee Last Name	Employee First Name	Salary Rate	Home City	Home State	Home Telephone
06337	Jones	Fred	4.30	New York	NY	212-555-9207
09155	Smith	Susan	5.90	Atlanta	GA	404-555-2287
16840	Adams	John	10.00	Atlanta	GA	404-555-4301
31719	Smith	John	5.50	Detroit	MI	313-555-5186
38102	Baker	George	7.00	Atlanta	GA	404-555-7739
. . .						

Figure 3.1. Payroll file.

until you reach the record you want. That sounds terrible if you are only looking for one specific record—and it is. Sequential files, without additional devices that we will discuss shortly, were never meant for direct access applications. But they do have the beauty of simplicity, and there are many applications for which they are very well suited. Back to payroll: Every Friday we want to write a payroll check for every employee in the company. In order to do so, we need each employee's record in the payroll file. We might as well read them, one after another, from the payroll file shown in Figure 3.1. If we are interested in writing the checks in an order other than employee number order, then perhaps that file should be stored in that other order.

Sequential files have been around for a long time, and the peculiar ways that they have to be processed are classic parts of computer lore. In addition to the problem of simple access discussed previously, there are the problems of insertion and deletion of records. After all, you can't insert a new record between two records that are physically nudged up against each other on the storage device, and you can't delete a record unless you can find it first, which brings us right back to the direct access problem again. The way to update a sequential file (called the "master file") on a tape is illustrated in Figure 3.2. A "transaction file" is set

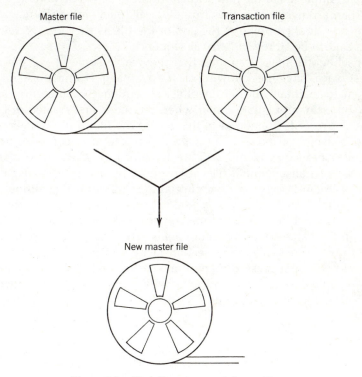

Figure 3.2. Updating a sequential tape file.

up on another tape. It includes the new records to be inserted, the key field values of the records to be deleted (with an appropriate delete code appended), and the key field values of the records to be updated, plus the new data that constitutes the update. All of these are sorted together in the same key field sequence that the master file is in. A program starts reading through the two tapes in tandem, looking for matches of the key fields for the delete and update operations and for the proper spot to place the new records for the insert operations. While it's reading through the master and transaction tapes, it's also creating a new tape, called the "new master," which will contain all of the data from the master tape, subject to the changes dictated by the transaction tape. Unaffected records are simply copied onto the new master tape; records to be deleted are simply not copied onto the new tape. Records to be inserted are placed onto the new tape, merged into the correct location to maintain the key sequence. Updates are performed and the updated records are copied over to the new tape in sequence. At the end of the entire operation, the new master tape and file become the master tape and file. The original tape is often kept around as backup in case something goes wrong with the new tape.

Nonsequential Files.   There are circumstances in which it makes sense to have a simple linear file that is not sequenced by any field. One example of such an arrangement is the chronological "pile," in which new data or records are plunked down at the end of the file as they are received. The data is said to be stored in "arrival sequence."

Nonsequential files, assuming that they serve some useful purpose in the first place, have the following clear advantage. No time or effort must be spent to maintain the file in physical sequence by merging, sorting, or any other manipulation, either when the file is first created or later on when new records are added to the end of the file. But what about their serving a useful purpose? And if they're not in any sequence, how can you find a particular record you are looking for? Clearly, to make any sense out of nonsequential files there must be a way to find particular records in them directly. Another intriguing thought is that although such files are not maintained in any *physical* sequence, it might be useful to be able to, at some times and for some applications, read the file in sequence based on the values of one or more fields. That may sound contradictory, but it's not, as we shall soon see. In fact, such files are quite common today and will be discussed many times in this book. The mechanism for providing direct access to, and externally maintaining the sequence of, such files is described in the next section.

Indexed Files

As we have said, there are legitimate reasons for wanting to store records in simple linear files that are not in physical sequence by any field while at the same time:

1. Expecting to be able to access those records directly, and
2. Expecting to be able to retrieve those records in sequence by some field, whether or not the file is stored in physical sequence by that or any other field.

All of this sounds *so good* that we are at once tempted to expand on it and say that it might also be desirable to have *sequential files* whose records can be accessed directly and whose data can be retrieved in sequence based on a field *other than* the key field by which the file is physically sequenced. While all of this may sound like it's counter to what we've already said about linear files, there is a device that can be added to the picture to accomplish just these goals. That device is called an **index.**

The interesting thing about an index is that, while we will explain it here in terms of computers, the principle involved is exactly the same as for the index in the back of a book. After all, a book is a storage medium for information about some subject. Think of the page numbers as addresses of "chunks" of information, namely, whatever words are on those particular pages. The table of contents in the front of the book merely summarizes what is in the book by major topics and is written in the same order as the material in the book. But what do you do if you want to find some specific piece of material, too minor to be mentioned in the table of contents, without having to laboriously read through the whole book? What you do is turn to the very end of the book and look up the item in the index. The index is arranged alphabetically by item, without regard to where a given item appears in the book. Humans have the ability to efficiently do a quick alphabetic search through an index to find the topic of interest. Then what? Next to the item in the index appears a page number: in fact, it is a "direct pointer" to the page in the book where the material appears. You go directly to that page and find the material there, (see Figure 3.3).

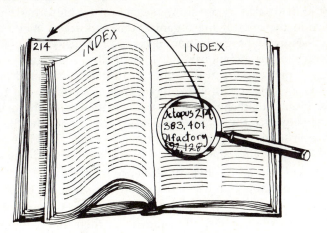

Figure 3.3. The index in a book.

The simplest kind of index for a data file, the **simple linear index**, will be discussed and illustrated in this section. Of course, this term should sound familiar, since we have been talking about simple linear files, and in fact such an index is merely a usage variation of that kind of file.

Based on the foregoing discussion, there are four distinct cases to discuss in the use of an index (simple linear or otherwise) with a simple linear file. The four cases are distinguished by whether or not the file is stored in sequence by some field and whether the desired operation involves the direct retrieval of a single record or the retrieval of all of the records of the file in order by some set of field values. The following chart and text explain the four cases.

	The file is in physical sequence by some field.	The file is not in physical sequence by any field.
The concern is direct retreival of a single record.	Case 1	Case 3
The concern is retrieval of all of the records in order based on the values in some field.	Case 2	Case 4

1.   The file is stored in physical sequence by some field and, in addition, direct access is needed via one of the fields (which may or may not be the sequence field).

When the **search field**—a specific value of which will be used to identify the record sought in a direct access—is the *same* field as the sequence field (the field used to physically sequence the file), then this case is a classic in the area of file organizations and access methods, called **indexed-sequential organization**. Because of its historic importance and interesting implementations, it will be treated separately in the next section of this chapter. In the other case, the file is stored in physical sequence by some field, and direct access is required, but the search field is *different* than the sequence field. In that case, the fact that the file is in sequence (by that other field) is irrelevant. The file might as well not be stored in any physical sequence at all. Thus in essence, the situation is really the same as that of case 3 and will be discussed there.

2.   The file is stored in physical sequence by some field and there is a requirement to be able to retrieve the records in sequence by some field.

Obviously, if the field on which the retrieval is to be based is the field on which the file is physically sequenced, then this requirement just amounts to reading the records in their physical sequence. The other, somewhat more interesting case is when the requirement is to retrieve the records in sequence based on the values in a field *other* than the one on which the file is physically sequenced. The right-hand side of Figure 3.4 shows the EMPLOYEE NUMBER, EMPLOYEE LAST NAME, and EMPLOYEE FIRST NAME fields of the Payroll file of Figure 3.1 (the rest of the fields are assumed to be there, too). Notice also that the records of the file are numbered, 1,2,.... These numbers, known as "relative record numbers," are clearly a form of addressing individual records. Given a relative record number, the systems software is capable of making some address calculations and directly finding the record associated with it. Remember that the Payroll file is in sequence by EMPLOYEE NUMBER. The left-hand side of Figure 3.4 shows a simple linear index, designed to provide sequential access to the Payroll file by EMPLOYEE LAST NAME. The left-hand column of this index is identical to the EMPLOYEE LAST NAME column of the Payroll file, except that it has been sorted so that the values are in alphabetic order. The right-hand entry of each row of the index is intended to provide the address of the record in the Payroll file that contains the value of the LAST NAME field in that index row. The address can take the form of an absolute or actual, disk address or of a relative record number, which is the case in Figure 3.4. Thus, if we wish to retrieve the records of the file alphabetically by EMPLOYEE LAST NAME, we simply read the index, line by line, and pick up record number 3 (the one for Adams) in the Payroll file, followed by record number 5 (the one for Baker), and so forth. Notice that there are two employees whose last names are Smith. That's why there are two lines in the index for the name Smith (in no particular order), each pointing to a different "Smith record" in the Payroll file.

3. The file is not stored in any physical sequence, but direct access is needed via one of the fields.

Figure 3.5 shows the sample payroll records of Figure 3.1, physically stored so that they are not in sequence by any field. It also shows an index into that new file based on the EMPLOYEE LAST NAME field.

Employee Last Name	Record Address		Rec. No.	Employee Number	Employee Last Name	Employee First Name	•••
Adams	3		1	06337	Jones	Fred	•••
Baker	5		2	09155	Smith	Susan	•••
Jones	1		3	16840	Adams	John	•••
Smith	2		4	31719	Smith	John	•••
Smith	4		5	38102	Baker	George	•••

Index   Payroll File
(Sequenced on Employee Number)

Figure 3.4. Sequential file indexed on a different field.

Employee Last Name	Record Address		Rec. No.	Employee Number	Employee Last Name	Employee First Name	...
Adams	5		1	31719	Smith	John	...
Baker	4		2	06337	Jones	Fred	...
Jones	2		3	09155	Smith	Susan	...
Smith	1		4	38102	Baker	George	...
Smith	3		5	16840	Adams	John	...

Index   Payroll File
                              (In No Particular Sequence)

Figure 3.5. Nonsequential indexed file.

This index is and must be in sequence by EMPLOYEE LAST NAME. Suppose that there is a need to directly find the payroll record for Jones. First, a program known as a "search" program or routine would find Jones in the third line of the index. We won't stop here to discuss search routines, but in concept they work in much the same way as that a person searching for an item in the index at the back of a book, quickly "homing in" on the desired item. Once Jones is found in the index, the associated index entry indicates that the record in the main file with an EMPLOYEE LAST NAME field value of Jones is relative record number 2. The system can then go directly to record number 2 in the main file and pick up the record for Jones.

4.   The file is not stored in any physical sequence, but there is a requirement to be able to retrieve the records in sequence by one of the fields.

Let's revisit the unordered file in Figure 3.5. In case 3, we showed how to use the index in that figure to find a record in the file directly. But that same index can also be used to retrieve the records of the file in the sequence of the field on which the index is based (EMPLOYEE LAST NAME in this case), even though the file is not stored in physical sequence based on any field. As in case 2, this is accomplished by starting with the first line of the index (which is in order by that field) and reading down it line by line, each time retrieving the record in the main file indicated by the address in the index line. In this case, we would retrieve record number 5 first (the one for Adams), followed by record number 4 (the one for Baker), and so on.

Let's review a few of the points about indexes and notice a few others. By the way, these characteristics are conceptual in nature at this point and may vary in actual implementations.

- An index can be built based on any field of a file, whether or not the file is in physical sequence based on that or any other field.
- An index can be built based on a combination of fields. For example, in the Payroll file example, we might want to be able to directly find

a record based on EMPLOYEE LAST NAME *and* EMPLOYEE FIRST NAME. The index in that case would include both an EMPLOYEE LAST NAME column and an EMPLOYEE FIRST NAME column, as well as the required column with the corresponding address into the main file.

• Any index can be used both for direct access based on the indexed field and for sequential retrieval of the records according to the sequence of that field.

• Many separate indexes into a file can exist simultaneously, each based on a different field or combination of fields of that file. The indexes are quite independent of each other.

• When certain changes are made to the file, the indexes must be updated. For example, if the value of one of the fields in one of the records in the file changes, and if there is an index built for that file based on that field, then that index must be updated. For example, in Figure 3.5, if Susan Smith marries and adopts her husband's last name (Eller), then not only does record number 3 in the Payroll file have to be updated, but the fifth row of the index must be changed as well. Eller must replace Smith in that row of the index, and the entire index must be resorted into alphabetic order. Obviously, the field values in the index must at all times match the corresponding field values in the main file for the concept of the index to make any sense. This is also true if a new record is inserted into the file, or an existing one is deleted. The index must actually be resorted with the new data, either on the spot or at some later time. If it is to be done at a later time (which, as we shall see, is usually advantageous in terms of performance), then the updates must be kept in a list that can somehow be accessed, in case a retrieval must be done based on one of the new entries before the index is resorted.

Indexed-Sequential Files

Introduction. As we said in the last section, when a file is sequenced on a particular field, and an index for that file is built based on that *same* field, then the arrangement is known as an indexed-sequential file. The benefits of such a structure are clear for certain applications. For example, consider the Payroll File constructed in an indexed-sequential fashion, with the Employee Number field used both as the sequence field and as the field on which the index is based. Using that one file, we can generate payroll checks in sequential, employee number order every Friday, and using the index, we can directly find individual records for updates (e.g., if employee 31719's salary increases).

Indexed-sequential files have a long history in data processing, emerging as a natural extension of simple sequential files. Two aspects of indexed-sequential files have been studied in depth over the years, and a number of variations of them have emerged. These two aspects are the structure of the index and the way that new records are added to the file so that both the sequential and direct access nature are maintained. We will take a look at three ways of structuring indexed-sequential files, paying particular attention to the index structure and the insertion method for new records. The three variations are the simple index, the multilevel, hardware-dictated index, and the B-tree oriented index.

Simple Index. Figure 3.4 showed the Payroll File sequenced on the EMPLOYEE NUMBER field, together with an index based on a different field of the file. Figure 3.6 shows the same file still sequenced on the EMPLOYEE NUMBER field, but with a simple linear index based on the *same* field. Such an arrangement, using a simple linear index, is perhaps the simplest kind of indexed-sequential file. It should be clear at this point that the records in the file in Figure 3.6 can be accessed sequentially by employee number, since they are stored one after the other on the disk pack in that order. They can also be retrieved directly by employee number, using the index with an appropriate search routine.

You may well wonder what the point is of creating a separate index that repeats one of the fields of the original file in the same order. If you can apply a search routine to such an index to find a record on a direct basis, why not apply the same search routine to the main file and save all of the bother of having a separate index? The answer lies in the fact that whatever is being searched has to be dragged into main memory for the actual search work. The larger the file gets, the larger the index becomes, and the larger the index becomes, the bigger a job it becomes to bring it into main memory and search through it for a particular key value. If the index is too large for all of it to be in primary memory at one time, then a scheme has to be developed to shuffle parts of it into and out of primary memory from secondary memory during the search. This can quickly become an unacceptable bottleneck. And if the entire records, rather than just the search fields, have to be brought

Employee Number	Record Address	Rec. No.	Employee Number	Employee Last Name	Employee First Name	...
06337	1 ⟶	1	06337	Jones	Fred	...
09155	2 ⟶	2	09155	Smith	Susan	...
16840	3 ⟶	3	16840	Adams	John	...
31719	4 ⟶	4	31719	Smith	John	...
38102	5 ⟶	5	38102	Baker	George	...

Index

Payroll File
(Sequenced on Employee Number)

Figure 3.6. Sequential file indexed on the sequence field.

into primary memory for the search (as would be the case if the search routine were applied to the main file, rather than the index), then the problem is compounded to a much worse degree. (Of course, for a large file, so many index records would have to be brought into primary memory that it wouldn't matter how small they are, and this organization would be impractical.)

As for the question of how to insert new records into the file, the situation is the same as for the sequential files that we discussed earlier. The file has to be rewritten, with the new record(s) inserted in the correct sequence, or it has to be resorted in place. Entries for the new record(s) must, of course, also be placed in the correct sequence in the index, necessitating a sorting operation there, too.

Multilevel, Hardware-Dictated Index. To introduce another type of index, consider the following situation. Let's say that you go to a large, eight-story department store to buy a copy of a particular book, Figure 3.7. You could wander down every aisle of every floor until you find it, but even the most compulsive shopper would find that unacceptably tedious. More likely the first thing that you would do on entering the store is to look for the store directory. It alphabetically lists all of the different departments in the store and indicates on which floor each is to be found. You find the entry for "Books" and note that it is on the fourth floor, so you take the escalators up to the fourth floor. There are a number of different departments on that floor, and so, rather than wander around the floor looking for the books department, you ask a store employee where it is. He or she points you to it, and you walk over. You could look through every shelf in every bookcase in the books department until you find the one that you want, but the different bookcases have signs on them indicating topical categories (fiction, cookbooks, etc.), so you scan the signs and find the bookcase with the category of books into which the one you're looking for fits. The books in each bookcase are organized alphabetically by author, so you scan the shelves of that bookcase until you find the book that you want.

Figure 3.7. The levels of search in a department store.

Figure 3.8. IBM ISAM file: Index and data.

Think about that series of actions. You successively narrowed the search, based on physical characteristics of the environment (first floors, then departments on a floor, then display cases—bookcases in this example) until you had it down to a small enough number of pieces of merchandise to scan for the one that you wanted. It sure beats an exhaustive search of every item in the store from the ground floor up!

An example of an analogous search procedure for a record in a computer file is IBM's Indexed Sequential Access Method (ISAM). It too successively narrows the search for an item (record) based on physical characteristics of the environment (the disk packs).

Figure 3.8 shows a personnel file and its associated three-level index organized in the ISAM style. (The third index level is stored in the combination of the "track 0s" of all of the cylinders.) Each record consists of a number of fields: the five-digit employee number, which will serve as the key field, the employee's last name, and so on. Employees were assigned employee numbers on a random basis when they joined the company, so their names are in no particular sequence relative to the employee numbers. Let's assume that we are dealing with disk packs that have six recording surfaces, meaning that there are six tracks per cylinder (numbered 0–5). Initially, the records are stored sequentially, based on the key field, in the "prime area," which in Figure 3.8 is tracks 1–4 of each of the 12 cylinders. Figure 3.9 shows cylinder 6 in more detail. There are 16 records in our personnel file with key values from 38007 to 42159, and they happened to fall into the prime area of cylinder 6 when the file was loaded. Before going into the matter of the index, note and remember that whatever else can be said about the ISAM organization, the data is laid out sequentially in the prime area. By reading each prime area track of each cylinder in sequence, the file can easily be retrieved, record by record, in order by the employee number (key) field.

Now let's see how the multilevel (also called "nonlinear") index provides for direct retrieval of the records based on the employee number field. As Figure 3.8 illustrates, there are basically three levels of index, each of which contains a subset of the keys of the file. Each index level maintains its keys in sequence. The first level is called the "master index"

	Normal Entry for Track 1	Overflow Entry for Track 1		
Track Index	39118 T1 39118 XX	39772 T2 39772 XX	40755 T3 40755 XX	42159 T4 42159 XX
Prime Area	38007 Jones . . .	38642 Adams . . .	38750 Taylor . . .	39118 Hall . . .
	39206 Carter . . .	39353 Newton . . .	39541 Jones . . .	39772 Allen . . .
	39945 Smith . . .	40230 James . .	40617 Sloan . . .	40755 Potter . . .
	41699 Baker . . .	41837 Dodd . . .	41922 Logan . . .	42159 Smith . . .
Overflow Track				

Figure 3.9.   IBM ISAM file: Cylinder 6 in detail.

and can be assumed to be in primary memory. The pointers from the master index lead to groups of cylinder pointers in the "cylinder index." In Figure 3.8, the cylinder index has three such groups (each row is a group). Each pointer in the cylinder index points, uniquely, to a particular cylinder. The first track (track 0) of each cylinder is called a "track index" and leads to a given track on that cylinder, where the record with a particular key value will be found.

Let's take an example and see how that process works with the file shown in Figure 3.8. Suppose that the record sought is the one for employee 40230. The access method scans the master index from left to right looking for the first key value *greater than or equal to* 40230. That's 53097. It then follows the pointer associated with value 53097 to the second row, or group of key values, in the cylinder index. It repeats the process, scanning that group of keys from left to right, looking for the first value greater than or equal to 40230. That's 42159. Now it follows the pointer attached to that value to the beginning of cylinder 6, as shown in the figure. The first track of that cylinder (track 0) contains the track index for that track. Switching to Figure 3.9, we see that the track index consists of a "normal entry" and an "overflow entry" for each track in the prime area of that cylinder. A normal entry contains the highest key value on the track and the track number (or address). An overflow entry, initially, also contains the highest key value on the track and a dummy entry (shown as XX in Figure 3.9). The system scans the normal entry values, again looking for the first value greater than or equal to 40230. That's 40755. The pointer associated with 40755 indicates that the record with key value 40230 will be found on track 3 of that cylinder. The system then scans track 3 until it finds the record with key value 40230. As in the department store example, that may sound complicated at first, but it's vastly more efficient than conducting a sequential search for the same record.

As you look at Figure 3.9, a problem may occur to you. It looks like the data, as initially loaded, fills each of the prime area tracks, and it does. Where do new records go when they are added to the file, how does the file remain in sequence, and how is the direct access to all records preserved? Good questions!

The answer begins with the overflow tracks at the end of each cylinder (and other so-called "independent overflow areas") and includes the overflow entries in each track index. Suppose that we want to add a new record, with key value 38693, to the file. The system will proceed through the three index levels, as if it were trying to find the record with that key value. Following the same search reasoning described earlier, it would decide to place the record on track 1 of cylinder 6 (see Figure 3.9). But of course, it finds that track to be full. It then proceeds to insert the new record in its rightful place on the track, slides all of the other records down one position to the right, and bumps the last record on that track off to the overflow track, as shown in Figure 3.10. The track index values for track 1 are changed so that:

38750 T1 39118 T5 Rec 1	39772 T2 39772 XX	40755 T3 40755 XX	42159 T4 42159 XX
38007 Jones . . .	38642 Adams . . .	38693 Hughes . . .	38750 Taylor . . .
39206 Carter . . .	39353 Newton . . .	39541 Jones . . .	39772 Allen . . .
39945 Smith . . .	40230 James . . .	40617 Sloan . . .	40755 Potter . . .
41699 Baker . . .	41837 Dodd . . .	41922 Logan . . .	42159 Smith . . .
39118 Hall . . . T1			

Figure 3.10. IBM ISAM file: Cylinder 6 with record 38693 added.

1. The normal entry shows the new highest key value of all of the records on the track proper (which is now 38750).
2. The overflow entry shows:
   a. The *last* overflow record in key sequence, logically belonging to that track, by *key* value (which is 39118), and
   b. The *first* overflow record in key sequence, logically belonging to that track, by *address* (which is track 5, record 1).

(Note: It should now be evident that when the index search procedure reaches the track index, it must use the *overflow* key value in doing its "greater-than-or-equal test" because that value always indicates the highest key value *logically* associated with a given track, regardless of whether the record with that key value is on the prime data track or on the overflow track.)

Figure 3.11 continues the illustration with the addition of the record with key value 38444. It gets placed in that same track 1, and the record with key value 38750 gets bumped into the overflow track. Maintaining the sequence, the track index now shows 38693 as the highest key value on track 1 proper, 39118 as the key value of the last record of that track that was placed on the overflow track, and track 5, record 2 as the address of the first overflow record for that track. Notice also that all of the overflow records for a given track are "chained" together in a linked list. As shown

38693 T1 39118 T5 Rec 2	39772 T2 39772 XX	40755 T3 40755 XX	42159 T4 42159 XX
38007 Jones . . .	38444 Evans . . .	38642 Adams . . .	38693 Hughes . . .
39206 Carter . . .	39353 Newton . . .	39541 Jones . . .	39772 Allen . . .
39945 Smith . . .	40230 James . . .	40617 Sloan . . .	40755 Potter . . .
41699 Baker . . .	41837 Dodd . . .	41922 Logan . . .	42159 Smith . . .
39118 Hall . . . T1	38750 Taylor . . . T5 Rec 1		

Figure 3.11. IBM ISAM File: Cylinder 6 with record 38444 added.

in Figure 3.11, if a record that should be on track 1 of that cylinder isn't there (and has a value higher than 38693), the track index points first to the record with key value 38750. Then, if that's not the desired record, it has a pointer associated with it that points to the next record, in sequence, that would have been on track 1 had there been enough room there, and so on. The logic of the overflow entries in the track index sounds more complicated than it is. In effect it tells you *where* (by physical address) the first overflow record for the track is and *what* (by key value) the last overflow record for the track is.

The system must obviously use the overflow arrangement both in conducting subsequent sequential retrievals and direct searches. As more records are added to the file, more prime area tracks will have one or more of their records bumped to overflow. First the overflow track on the same cylinder will be used, then, when that fills up, independent overflow tracks on other cylinders will be used. Retrieval and search operations will get progressively slower, because two tracks have to be read in the case where the regular overflow track is used, and the disk access arm mechanism has to jump around among the different cylinders in the case where the independent overflow tracks must be used. To help fix that problem, the file occasionally must be reorganized. In that operation the entire file, overflowed records and all, is read in key sequence and written onto the *prime areas* of another set of cylinders, while the system builds a new set of appropriate indexes.

B-Tree Oriented Index.   While the ISAM multilevel index concept was an important step forward in the history of data processing, it does have its shortcomings. For one thing, its inherent dependence on the physical attributes of the storage devices limits its flexibility. The way that overflow records are handled makes retrieval cumbersome as the number of overflow records builds up. And in the same vein, it requires comparatively frequent reorganizations to move the overflow records back on to the prime areas.

A newer kind of multilevel indexed-sequential file has been developed that is hardware independent and is capable of absorbing new records in a much less traumatic way than in ISAM. It is based on a structure known as a "B-Tree." An example of this newer organization is the Key Sequenced Data Set (KSDS) of IBM's Virtual Storage Access Method (VSAM). The term Virtual Storage Access Method (singular) is really something of a misnomer, as VSAM is actually a collection of three different access methods, one of which is KSDS. The other two are Entry Sequenced Data Set (ESDS), which is designed for sequential files, and Relative Record Data Set (RRDS), which is used for hashed (see the next section) files.

Figure 3.12 illustrates the KSDS arrangement. The storage space in KSDS is divided into **control intervals** and **control areas**. A control interval is the unit of data transferred between primary and secondary memory.

Figure 3.12. IBM KSDS file: Index and data.

It may be, but need not be, a disk track. A control area is made up of a number of control intervals. It may be, but need not be, a disk cylinder. A multilevel index, like that of ISAM, is hierarchical in nature and may increase in depth as the file grows. There is one index record at the topmost level, and the index fans out downwards from there. The number of levels in the index is dependent on the size of the file and the size of the index records. All of the index records of the lowest level of the index are collectively known as the **sequence set**. There is a single sequence set record for each control area of the data file, and there is the option for each sequence set record to be stored with the control area that it indexes. This is for performance reasons and is illustrated in Figure 3.12.

The entries in the index are constructed in much the same way as they were in ISAM. An index entry at a given level of the index represents the highest index entry of one of the index records at the next lower level of the index and points to that index record. For example, in Figure 3.12, entry 30465 in the top level index record points to the index record in the next level down which ends with (its own copy of) entry 30465. Each entry of a sequence set record points to a single control interval of the data file control area that it indexes, and, consistent with the indexing scheme, contains the highest key value of the data records in that control interval. This is illustrated, for control area 6, in Figure 3.13.

It will turn out, as we shall soon see, that while the data in a given control interval will always be in sequence, the control intervals may, as time goes on, get out of sequence because of insertions. The question then becomes: How can the file be retrieved in key sequence? The answer is that the sequence set records always keep track of the correct sequence, and the sequence set records are all linked together by a set of "horizontal pointers," as shown in Figure 3.12. By following the chain of sequence set records, and ignoring the higher levels of the index, the file can be retrieved in key sequence.

Again as in ISAM, to find a record on a direct basis, the system starts at the left of the single index record at the top of the index hierarchy and scans to the right looking for the first value greater than or equal to the key value of the record being sought. It then follows that pointer down to an index record at the next level of the index and continues this process until it reaches the correct data file control interval, which it scans for the target data record.

The real beauty of KSDS lies in the way that new records are inserted into the file. In ISAM, insertions caused increasingly long access paths to

	Entry for Track 1			
Sequence Set	39118 T1 39772 T2 40755 T3 42159 T4 free T5				
	38007 Jones . . .	38642 Adams	38750 Taylor	39118 Hall	free space
	39206 Carter	39353 Newton	39541 Jones	39772 Allen	free space
	39945 Smith	40230 James	40617 Sloan	40755 Potter	free space
	41699 Baker	41837 Dodd	41922 Logan	42159 Smith	free space
	free control interval				

Figure 3.13.   IBM KSDS file: Control area 6 in detail.

some records as the overflow chains grew. In KSDS, all records have the same access path length regardless of how many new records have been inserted. The frequent reorganizations needed in volatile ISAM files are reduced. One of the things that makes this possible is the way that free space is deliberately left in the file as it is loaded. Figure 3.13 shows free space left in each control interval containing data records and one control interval left entirely free. Additional free control areas are also provided. This free space, used as described in the following, forms the basis for the KSDS insertion technique.

Figure 3.14 shows control area 6 with the addition of the record with key value 38693. Based on key sequence, this record should be placed in control interval 1, and, in fact, it can be, because there is sufficient free space in that control interval to accommodate it. The new record is inserted in between the records with key values 38642 and 38750; the records with key values 38750 and 39118 are shifted to the right so that the insertion does not disturb the file sequence.

Figure 3.15 shows control area 6 with the addition of the record with key value 38444. As in the last case, that record should go into control interval 1. But this time there is no room for it, all of the free space in the control interval having been used up already. So the system goes through an exercise known as "splitting." It begins by looking for a completely free control interval in the control area. If it finds one it divides all of the data on the full control interval plus the new record being inserted, leaving about half the data on the original control interval and putting the other half on what was the completely free control interval. Thus, in Figure 3.15, the records with keys 38007, 38444 (the new record), and 38642 remain on control interval 1, while 38693, 38750, and 39118 are all moved to control interval 5. The sequence set is changed, as shown in that figure, so that the keys in it, representing the highest key on each control interval, remain in sequence, even though the control intervals no longer are.

What would happen if this process continued to the point that a new record had to be inserted into a full control interval and there were no more free control intervals left in its control area with which to perform a control interval split? Then a new, completely free control area would be

39118 T1	39772 T2	40755 T3	42159 T4	free T5
38007 Jones . . .	38642 Adams	38693 Hughes	38750 Taylor	39118 Hall . . .
39206 Carter	39353 Newton	39541 Jones	39772 Allen	free space
39945 Smith	40230 James	40617 Sloan	40755 Potter	free space
41699 Baker	41837 Dodd	41922 Logan	42159 Smith	free space
free control interval				

Figure 3.14. IBM KSDS file: Control area 6 with record 38693 added.

38642 T1	39118 T5	39772 T2	40755 T3	42159 T4	
38007 Jones	38444 Evans	38642 Adams	free space		
39206 Carter	39353 Newton	39541 Jones	39772 Allen . . .	free space	
39945 Smith	40230 James	40617 Sloan	40755 Potter . . .	free space	
41699 Baker	41837 Dodd	41922 Logan	42159 Smith . . .	free space	
38693 Hughes	38750 Taylor	39118 Hall	free space		

Figure 3.15.   IBM KSDS file: Control area 6 with record 38444 added.

obtained and the entire control area would split. About half of the control area's data would remain on it, and the other half would be moved to the new control area. But, as you will remember from Figure 3.12, every control area must be pointed to from the next to the lowest level of the index (the level just above the sequence set). So the addition of a new control area to the file means that a new entry must be added to that level of the index. That's fine, as long as there is room in the appropriate index record. If not, then it splits, causing another entry to be added to the index level above it. The highest index level may only consist of one index record. So if this process ever backs all the way up to the top index level and finds the index record there to be full, the system must split that index record and add another index record at a new higher level (which will be the new top level) of the index.

Hashed Files

There are many applications in which all file accesses are to be done on a direct basis and speed is of the essence. For such situations, the best approach is the **hashed file**. Let's assume, just to be consistent, that we're still working with our payroll records, but that now we are only concerned with fast direct access. Let's also assume, just for the sake of argument, that each of the records is 100 bytes or characters long.

So we have some unspecified number of records, each 100 bytes long, each with a 5-digit, unique numeric key field. If there were no restrictions at all on how to store the file on a disk pack, how might we go about storing the records for the fastest possible access? Figure 3.16 shows a view of one way to store the data. Suppose that we choose an arbitrary starting point, or address, on the disk, and place the record (if it exists) with key field value (EMPLOYEE NUMBER) 00000 there. Then we place the record with key value 00001 at the point 100 bytes beyond the arbitrary starting point. The record with key value 00002 starts 200 bytes beyond that point, and so on for every record (or, really, the ones that exist) through the record with key value 99999.

If we want to find the record with key value 00500, then after multiplying that number by the record length 100, we look at the position on

Address	Employee Number	Employee Last Name	• • •
0	00000	Dobbs	• • •
100	00001	Taylor	• • •
200	00002	Miller	• • •
. . .	. . .	. . .	
50,000	00500	Garner	• • •
. . .	. . .	. . .	
9,999,900	99999	Monroe	• • •

←————— 100 bytes —————→

Figure 3.16. Full-size file.

the disk 50,000 bytes forward from the arbitrary starting point of the file, and there we find the record we're looking for. What could be simpler? Or faster?

But as so often is the case when something seems so simple, there is a fly in the ointment (or, since we're dealing with computers, maybe we should say a bug in the ointment). Although we can accommodate 100,000 different records with a 5-digit decimal key, we probably don't have 100,000 records to store. Perhaps there are only 200 employees in the company. The point is that, in order to use the simple method of storage and retrieval previously suggested, we would have to reserve 10 million bytes on the disk, enough for the full potential of 100,000 records, even though we know that we only have 200 records to store, which only require 20,000 bytes of storage. The difference between 10,000,000 bytes and 20,000 bytes represents a huge and unacceptable amount of wasted space on the disk. That's the catch. But still, being able to *associate* a key value with a storage location is a very tempting thought.

What about the following variation? Can we work on the premise of having only a limited amount of storage space set aside for the file and converting the key field value into one of those available storage addresses? For example, can we take a 5-digit key field with value 52866 and convert it to relative storage location 116 (out of, say, 250)?

Figure 3.17 shows a schematic of a disk storage area, in which we can store 250 records (numbered 0 to 249), each 100 bytes long. Perhaps we have 200 records to store and want to leave room for further expansion.

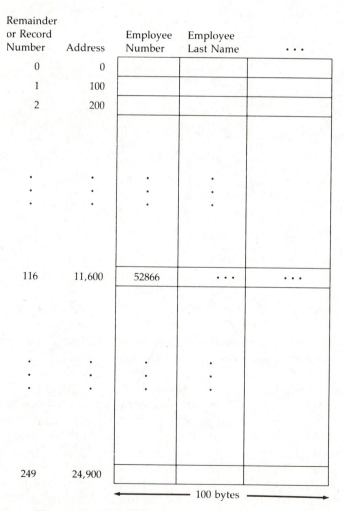

Figure 3.17. Hashed file, division-remainder method.

Try the following method as a straightforward way of converting from the key value to a storage location. Divide the key value (52866) by the number of storage locations (250). The result is 211.464. But remember back to grammar school and "long division"; another way of expressing that result is a quotient of 211, and a remainder of 116. The remainder, in that division, will *always* be an integer from 0 to the divisor (250) minus 1, or 249 in this case. But that is the same number of storage slots (each 100 bytes long) that we allocated in the area shown in Figure 3.17. What if we simply store the record with a particular key value at the storage location indicated by the remainder of the division of the key value by the number of storage locations, as demonstrated above? In order to retrieve the same record at a later time, we would go through the same procedure and look for the record at the location indicated by the division operation. The technique we have been talking about is called the **division-remainder method**, and is one of many so-called **hashing methods** that can be used for key conversion in hashed file storage.

There is one problem that may have occurred to you. Surely, continuing with the previous example, there may be many 5-digit numbers that, when divided by 250, have 116 as the remainder. But only one of them (the first one that came along) can be stored at that location. This problem is known as the **collision** problem, and the two (or more) key values that "hash" to the same storage location are called **synonyms**. But all is not lost; there are several ways to deal with that situation. Figure 3.18 shows the same diagram as in Figure 3.17, but with some extra storage space added beyond the original 250 slots and a new pointer or address field added to each record. As an example, assume that we stored three records, with key values 52866, 37616, and 25116. These three key values happened to hash to the same storage location, 116. One is stored at location 116, another is at 250, and the third at 251. Notice how the new pointer field forms a *chain* connecting the three together. If you try to find the record with key value 25116 at location 116, you find the record with key value 52866 there instead. Then you follow the pointer at the end of that record to location 250 (27,500 bytes into the file), and there you find the record with key value 37616. This record in turn points to location 251 where you finally find the record you were looking for, the one with key value 25116.

There are several other things to point out about hashed access methods.

- There is no physical sequence of the stored data. The nature of the hashing methods is to scatter the records in the allocated storage area in a way that makes direct access as efficient as possible, without regard to anything else, including sequence.
- Over the years, many different hashing methods have been developed, the division-remainder method being but one.

Remainder or Record Number	Address	Employee Number	Employee Last Name	...		Pointer For Synonyms
0	0					
1	110					
2	220					
.	.	.	.			
.	.	.	.			
.	.	.	.			
116	12,760	52866	...	...		27,500
.	.	.	.			
.	.	.	.			
.	.	.	.			
249	27,390					
250	27,500	37616				27,610
251	27,610	25116				-1
252	27,720					
253	27,830					

←——————————— 100 bytes ———————————→ ←— 10 bytes —→

Figure 3.18. Hashed file, division-remainder method (with chained synonyms).

- The most important measure of the goodness of a hashing method is how well it minimizes the number of collisions. The only way to find that out is to actually try to store a given set of records with a given hashing method. Sometimes changes can be made in the parameters of a method. For example, in the division-remainder method, it's known that, in general, if the number of storage locations, and thus the divisor, is a prime number, or is odd and can't be evenly divided by any number less than 20, then there is a better chance of having fewer collisions. So in the example that we were looking at, instead of allocating 250 storage locations, we would allocate a number equal to the next prime number above 250.

Conclusion

It's still early in the book, but we've already made tremendous progress in developing data storage concepts. In Chapter 2 we saw how bits and bytes can be arranged to represent data and how that data can be organized into simple files. We also discussed the manner in which these bits and bytes representing the data can be placed on disk media.

In this chapter, we developed another critical data storage idea: There are some applications that require records of a file to be available in sequence by some field value and some applications that require records of a file to be available on a direct basis. Based on the types of applications that access them, some files must be set up for sequential retrieval, some for direct retrieval, and some for both. We proceeded to discuss different schemes for organizing data records for those three categories of retrieval requirements.

But while we've built a strong base to work from, the simplicity of (independent) simple files unfortunately leaves much to be desired in efficiency in some common data storage situations. We will take a look at these problems in Chapter 4.

References

Bohl, M., *Introduction to IBM Direct Access Storage Devices*, Science Research Associates, Chicago, IL, 1981.

Folk, M. J. , and Zoellick, B., *File Structures*, Addison-Wesley, Reading, MA, 1987.

Kroenke, D. M. , and Dolan, K. A. , *Database Processing*, 3rd ed., Science Research Associates, Chicago, IL, 1988.

Lewis, T. G. , and Smith, M. Z. , *Applying Data Structures*, 2nd ed., Houghton Mifflin, Boston, MA, 1982.

Salzberg, B., *File Structures: An Analytic Approach*, Prentice-Hall, Englewood Cliffs, NJ, 1988.

Tremblay, J. P. , and Sorenson, P. G. , *An Introduction to Data Structures with Applications*, 2nd ed., McGraw-Hill, New York, 1983.

Questions and Exercises

3.1. What is a file organization? What is an access method? What do they accomplish?

3.2. What is a sequential file? What are some advantages and disadvantages of their use?

3.3. Describe the procedure for adding records to a sequential file.

3.4. Do you think that records in a sequential file can be updated without generating a new master file? Why or why not?

3.5. In your own words, describe what an index is.

3.6. Since using an index to find a record in a file entails some work, that is, executing the index search algorithm, why is such a retrieval considered to be "direct"?

3.7. Describe the use of a simple linear index for direct retrieval of a single record. Does it matter whether or not the file is in physical sequence by the field that is indexed?

3.8. Describe the use of a simple linear index for sequential retrieval of all of the records in a file. Does it matter whether or not the file is in physical sequence by the field that is indexed?

3.9. Create a simple linear index for the file in Figure 3.1 based on the SALARY RATE field.

3.10. What are the implications for index-based direct retrieval and for index-based sequential retrieval if the indexed field is not unique?

3.11. What is an indexed-sequential file organization? Describe a set of applications that requires a file to be organized that way.

3.12. What is the advantage of a multilevel index over a simple linear index?

3.13. Consider the IBM ISAM index in Figure 3.8. Assume that a personnel record with employee number 77000 is the third of four records on track 3 of cylinder 11. Describe a direct search through the index for that record.

3.14. Consider the portion of the IBM ISAM file shown in Figure 3.9. Add the following records in the order shown, in each case taking into account the previous insertions. What would happen if the overflow track were full?

    a. 42000 Barber
    b. 39200 Madison
    c. 41800 Morgan

3.15. Describe the splitting mechanism in the VSAM KSDS structure.

3.16. Compare the IBM ISAM and VSAM KSDS file organizations in terms of:

    a. direct retrieval capability.
    b. sequential retrieval capability.
    c. method of record insertion.
    d. retrieval performance after a substantial number of insertions have taken place.

3.17. Consider the portion of the VSAM KSDS file shown in Figure 3.13. Add the following records in the order shown, in each case taking into account the previous insertions. What would happen if the free track were full?

   a. 42000 Barber

   b. 39200 Madison

   c. 41800 Morgan

3.18. Describe how a direct search works in a hashed file.

3.19. What are the prospects for a sequential search in a hashed file?

3.20. What is a hashing method?

3.21. Describe how the division-remainder method of hashing can be used to effect the direct retrieval of a record in a file.

3.22. What are the advantages and disadvantages of a hashed file vs. an indexed file?

3.23. What is a collision in a hashed file? What are synonyms? Describe a collision resolution technique.

3.24. Insert records with the following employee numbers into the personnel file shown in Figure 3.18.

   a. 32869

   b. 00866

3.25. A hashed file has space for 70 records, each 30 bytes wide. Each record has an additional 10 byte slot for a collision chain pointer, and there are an additional 15 record spaces for storing synonym records.

   a. Draw a diagram illustrating this situation.

   b. Using the division-remainder method, store records with each of the following 4-digit keys, indicating the address at which each is stored.

      i. 4000

      ii. 5207

      iii. 0360

      iv. 1410

4

Benefits of the Database Approach

Introduction

Now that we've taken a good look at the ways in which simple linear files are built and accessed, it's time to pause and consider just how well these files handle the real world of data and data processing. But first, a point we have been taking for granted has to be noted and emphasized. In speaking about simple linear files, we have been assuming that these files exist totally independent of each other; as yet, there has been no reason to assume otherwise. It will turn out, as we shall eventually see, that manipulating combinations of such files, in certain ways, can lead to a more powerful data storage concept (in fact to a legitimate database form). So, to distinguish between the two cases, we will from here on refer to the case that we have been discussing thus far as "independent linear files."

To be sure, independent linear files are just right in certain situations. But, as we shall see in this chapter, they are lacking in several key respects for the more complex data processing applications and environments that exist today.

Let's take a look at five key areas of discussion in that regard. They are:

1. Certain characteristics of today's data processing environment
2. Problems associated with redundant data
3. The ability to store data involved in multiple relationships
4. Certain data management control topics
5. The concept of data independence

Data Processing Environment Characteristics

Data as a Manageable Resource

In the earlier days of data processing most of the time and emphasis in applications development was placed on the programs, as opposed to on the data and data structures. Hardware was expensive and limited in addressing scope. Programming was a new discipline and there was much to be learned about it in order to achieve the goal of efficient processing. Partial mechanization of the programming process, or even standardization of style, was unknown. In this environment, the treatment of the data was hardly the highest priority concern.

As data processing continued to grow, a number of the ground rules began to change. Hardware became cheaper, software development took on a more standardized, "structured" form, and large backlogs of new applications to be implemented built up, making the huge amount of time spent on maintaining existing programs more and more unacceptable. It became increasingly clear that the way in which we handled (or mishandled) data in the past was one of the major factors in the program maintenance mess in which we found ourselves. We found that:

- Data was stored in different formats in different files.
- Data was often not shareable among different programs that needed it, necessitating redundant files.
- Data was often not easily recoverable or secure.
- Programs were usually written in such a manner that if the way that the data was stored changed, the program had to be modified to continue working.

Data was all too often inaccurate, inconsistent, or not up to date. Changes in everything from access methods to tax tables required programming changes.

At the same time, as an increasing amount of the enterprise's operational and strategic work became dependent on automated data processing, an increasing awareness evolved that the data itself was an important **enterprise resource.**

Money, capital equipment, inventories, and so forth are all important property to an enterprise. We have applied numerous management techniques to them (many of which, of course, have involved computers). Many people are now coming to the conclusion that data is also a manageable resource. A firm's data about its products, manufacturing processes, customers, suppliers, employees, competitors, and so on can, with proper storage and use, provide a significant competitive advantage.

At the intersection of all of the above issues is the question: "How?" We want to manage data as an enterprise resource, while at the same time improving its treatment in terms of the technicalities of data processing. It becomes clear, even before we reach the discussion of the specifics later in this book, that some sort of a uniform system to manage data as an enterprise resource is needed. The database environment, with its supporting software and accompanying management techniques, will provide the framework for treating data as a standardized, manageable, shareable resource.

Standardization and Specialization

In a data processing environment driven by independent applications, it is often difficult to maintain standards in programming and data storage conventions. Programmers tend to go their separate ways, especially when other programs are not directly dependent on their work. Unfortunately, a lack of standardization makes it difficult for anyone, often even the original programmer, to understand a program well enough to make required maintenance changes to it later on.

The sharing of data files among different applications and the use of consistent data description and access statements in the programs in the database environment force a more careful and standardized look at the entire application development process. Now, whatever one programmer does may affect others too, for instance, in terms of data accuracy, update schedules, and performance. Standardization in programming techniques and storage schemes can only serve to make for a less error-prone environment.

In addition, the database environment leads to new levels of job specialization, which is really another form of standardization. Typically, a data administration function is formed to be responsible for the data. Within that function are people who specialize in database design, security, backup and recovery, performance, and so on. As the commitment to the new, data-oriented environment increases, the application programming and operations groups develop a dependency on the data administration function to assume an increasing amount of the data-oriented legwork of the applications development and execution processes. This can include data collection and verification, monitoring, database design, integrity monitoring, security, and backup and recovery; in effect, a thorough custodianship of the enterprise's data. It doesn't happen overnight, but rather takes place as a gradual transition. But again, this kind of standardization—functional standardization in this case—can only lead to a more efficient, error-free environment.

Redundant Data

Data stored in a data processing system is a reflection of the facts of the real world environment. In a data processing system, data is redundant *only* if a particular fact about the real world environment is stored more than once. Let's take a look at the problem of redundant data and its

SALESPERSON NUMBER		SALESPERSON NAME	
137		Baker	
186		Adams	
204		Dickens	
361		Carlyle	
.		.	
.		.	
.		.	

(a)

CUSTOMER NUMBER		SALESPERSON NUMBER	
0121		137	
0839		186	
0933		137	
1047		137	
1525		361	
1700		361	
1826		137	
2198		204	
2267		186	
.		.	
.		.	
.		.	

(b)

Figure 4.1. Separate files: (a) Salesperson, (b) Customer.

companion, the problem of data integrity. First we will consider it in the context of one file, then in the context of many files.

Redundancy within One File

Suppose that we are a sales organization and, of course, have to have a way of keeping track of our customers and our salespeople. Figure 4.1 shows two independent linear files, one for salespeople and one for customers. The Salesperson file is keyed on the (unique) SALESPERSON NUMBER field and includes, as one of its other fields, the SALESPERSON NAME field. The Customer file is keyed on the (also unique) CUSTOMER NUMBER and has, as one of its other fields, the SALESPERSON NUMBER, that is, the number of the salesperson who is assigned to that customer account. There is one record per salesperson in the Salesperson File. A particular record contains the data that we hold about a particular salesperson, such as salesperson number, name, home address, home telephone number, and so on. There is a like situation for the data on each customer in the Customer file. This kind of data storage is said to be **nonredundant**, because the detail data on each entity is stored only once. That is as it should be.

If someone comes along and wants to know the name of the salesperson who is identified by a particular salesperson number (e.g., 186), he or she merely looks up that salesperson's record in the Salesperson file, Figure 4.1a, using the SALESPERSON NUMBER as the key, and reads off the name (Adams). Similarly, if someone wants to know the number of the salesperson who is responsible for a particular customer account, he or she goes to the Customer file, Figure 4.1b, and looks up that customer's record, using the CUSTOMER NUMBER as the key. So far, so good.

Now, what if someone comes along and wants to know the *name* of the salesperson who services a particular customer account, identified by customer number. Can that information be obtained from only one of the files in Figure 4.1? Clearly it cannot, since the customer number information exists only in the Customer file, and the salesperson *name* information exists only in the Salesperson file. The only way to answer that question is to first look up that customer's record in the Customer file, find the number of the salesperson on that account, then use that number to find the person's record in the Salesperson file, and finally to find his or her name in the record. For example, in Figure 4.1, given customer number 1525, we would access the fifth record in the Customer file and find that the responsible salesperson is number 361. We would then access the record for salesperson number 361 in the Salesperson file and find Carlyle as the salesperson name. That kind of custom-made, multicommand, multifile access is error prone in terms of programming, expensive in terms of execution performance, and depending on the software involved, may have to be coded separately for each such access combination.

Ah, but if we knew that we were going to make such queries, why did we bother breaking the data up into two files in the first place? If it's all contained in one file, in a meaningful way, then there are no costly multicommand, multifile accesses. Figure 4.2 shows the same data represented in one file. Notice that we show the salesperson (by number) assigned to a particular customer, just as we did in the two files in Figure 4.1, but now the salesperson's name is also carried along. We can still answer the two original simple questions that we put to the files in Figure 4.1, but now, in addition, we can answer the tougher, previously multifile question, "What is the name of the salesperson on a particular account?" with just the one file in Figure 4.2 and one command. Fine! Or is it? In the file in Figure 4.1*a*, there is one record per salesperson, each containing the particulars for a given person once. Indicating which salesperson services a particular account is simply a matter of attaching the salesperson's number to the single record that describes that customer in the file in Figure 4.1*b*.

But in the combined file of Figure 4.2, where all of the fundamentally different kinds of information are intermingled, the particulars of a specific salesperson must be repeated for every account that he or she services. A given salesperson may appear in several records in that file, and it makes no sense from a logical or a retrieval standpoint to specify, for example, the salesperson name for one customer the salesperson services and not for another. To be complete, the data must be repeated in every appropriate slot. Thus, whereas in the two files of Figure 4.1 the name "Carlyle" is attached to the salesperson number "361" just once, in the combined file of Figure 4.2 the name "Carlyle" appears with salesperson number "361" in as many records as customers that Carlyle services.

This situation of data redundancy causes a number of problems. For one thing, the data takes up a lot more storage space. (Try adding a home

SALESPERSON NUMBER	CUSTOMER NUMBER	SALESPERSON NAME	• • •
137	0121	Baker	
137	0933	Baker	
137	1047	Baker	
137	1826	Baker	
186	0839	Adams	
186	2267	Adams	
204	2198	Dickens	
361	1525	Carlyle	
361	1700	Carlyle	
•	•	•	
•	•	•	
•	•	•	

Figure 4.2. Combined file.

address field of 40 bytes and see how you feel about storing it say, 50 times, as opposed to once.) For another thing, it causes extra work when it comes to updating. If Carlyle changes his or her name, the change must be recorded many times. The time consumed in doing that can be very costly, particularly if the records involved are scattered all over a disk. Also, there is the nagging doubt that all of the occurrences may not have been updated, due to anything from programming bugs to execution time system failures. When that happens, it's called a **data integrity** problem.

There appears to be a trade-off, but then trade-offs are hardly rare in the computer field. In the two files of Figure 4.1, we have no redundancy, but a query of the type that we've been looking at requires a multicommand, multifile access. In the combined file of Figure 4.2, we have eliminated the need for a multicommand, multifile access for that type of query, but we have introduced data redundancy. Neither of these situations is tolerable, for the reasons indicated previously.

Can we have our cake and eat it too? This question brings us to one of the key features of the database environment. An **integrated** data management system, that is a true *database system,* is one in which data can be held nonredundantly (in the sense of the files in Figure 4.1) while at the same time, a query that requires a mixture of different kinds of data (such as the query that we've been looking at) can be specified in a single command from the highest level programming interface (*as if* the access was being made to the file in Figure 4.2). Any system that does not have this property really should not be called a database system; "file management" system would be a more accurate term.

There are several approaches to designing a true database system, which revolve around several storage structures and different times and ways of "mixing" the various pieces of data together. We will explore them later on.

Another benefit of the integrated approach is the encouragement that it gives to finding new uses for the data in the database. The richness of having so many different portions of the organization's data interconnected leads to many more usage possibilities than when they were stored separately.

Redundancy among Many Files

There is another kind of redundancy that, while perhaps a bit more obvious than the one discussed previously, is not necessarily easier to combat, but it's difficult for different reasons.

Frequently, certain data is needed by different departments in an enterprise in the course of their normal, everyday work. For example, customer name and address may be needed by the sales department, the accounts receivable department, and the credit department. There will also generally be other pieces of information involving customers that are needed only by one or two departments. Typically the solution to this multiple need is redundancy. The sales department has its own stored file that, among other things, contains the customer name and address, as do the accounts receivable and credit departments.

While it's true that this keeps the departments from competing for the data, it opens up a can of worms reminiscent of the problems that we encountered in single file redundancy. First of all, storing a piece of data three times takes three times the amount of storage as storing it once. In addition, every time the data must be updated, it must be changed in each file in which it resides. This wastes processing time, causes control nightmares, and has the potential of leading to integrity problems if all of the data is not updated correctly and at the same time. Furthermore, the question arises as to whose responsibility it is to update the data in all of these different files, which are probably owned by widely separated departments.

Wouldn't it make more sense for such data to be stored just once, in a way that makes it accessible to all of the different groups that need it? This way there would be one group in charge of updating it, little wasted space, few integrity problems, and so on.

The database approach includes the concept of a common shared database with controlled management and update responsibility.

Multiple Relationships

In Chapter 2, we discussed the different ways that entities can relate to each other in terms of unary and multiple associations, and one-to-one, one-to-many, and many-to-many relationships, which are diagramed

Employee   ⟷   Identification Card

(*a*)

Employee   ⟸⟶   Manager

(*b*)

Employee   ⟸⟹   Secure room

(*c*)

Figure 4.3. Relationships: (*a*) one-to-one, (*b*) one-to-many, and (*c*) many-to-many.

in Figure 4.3. The question that we must now ask is, "How easily can we store data involving the two kinds of associations and three kinds of relationships in independent linear files?"

Roughly speaking, unary associations and one-to-one relationships are handled well by such files. After all, a key field and a simple non-key field in a record represent such a case, as shown in Figure 4.4. But when it comes to multiple associations and their resulting relationships, simple files leave something to be desired.

A multiple association can be represented "horizontally" with variable length records, as illustrated in Figure 4.5*a*. Unfortunately, that can cause program logic and space management headaches. Usually, if a programmer accesses a single record of a file, there is an action to be taken on the single value in one or more of its fields. In Figure 4.4, the programmer might read the record for employee 2186 and then perform some action with the single social security number found in it. But what if that programmer accesses the record for manager Smith in Figure 4.5*a*, with the intention of acting on the serial numbers of the people in that man-

EMPLOYEE SERIAL NO	SOCIAL SECURITY NO	MANAGER	・・・
1234	111-000-2222	Smith	
1572	111-22-3333	Jones	
2186	222-11-5432	Jones	
4522	522-52-5221	Smith	
4991	333-55-9999	Doe	
5283	123-45-6789	Smith	
5542	654-32-1234	Smith	
・	・	・	
・	・	・	
・	・	・	

Figure 4.4. Simple file.

MANAGER	EMPLOYEE SERIAL NO'S		. . .
Doe	4991		
Jones	1572 2186		
Smith	1234 4522 5283 5542		
.			
.			
.			

Figure 4.5*a*.   Multiple relationship representation: Horizontal representation.

MANAGER	EMPLOYEE SERIAL NO	. . .
Doe	4991	
Jones	1572	
Jones	2186	
Smith	1234	
Smith	4522	
Smith	5283	
Smith	5542	
.	.	
.	.	
.	.	

Figure 4.5*b*.   Multiple relationship representation: Vertical representation.

ager's employ? He or she must, under program control, manage the list of employee serial numbers found in it, performing the desired action on each one. That makes for a more complex, error-prone program. Also, working with variable length records can be a tricky business from a space management point of view. If a new employee is added to a manager's record in the file in Figure 4.5*a*, the new, larger size of the record may preclude its being stored in its previous disk location. Placing it somewhere else can cause performance problems in future retrievals.

A multiple association can also be represented "vertically," with each participant being repeated once for each of the other related participants, which is the situation illustrated in Figure 4.5*b*. But that introduces a form of redundancy: The name "Smith" appears once for each of Smith's employees. (It will turn out that when processed with "relational" constructs, files of the type in Figure 4.5*b* will qualify as the foundation of a legitimate database solution. Under these circumstances, the kind of redundancy found in Figure 4.5*b*, which concerns the key fields of two entities involved in a multiple association, will be acceptable. More about that later, in Chapter 6.)

Finally, a multiple association can be represented with interspersed record types, as shown in Figure 4.5*c*, but this requires some fancy software devices to maintain the integrity of what are really two different files (represented by the two different record types) and still show the one-to-many (manager name to employee number) relationship shown in Figure 4.5*c*. (Once again, going to all of that trouble forms a kind of a database solution to be discussed later.)

One of the capabilities of database management systems is that they provide the means, naturally, easily, and for all types of applications, of representing multiple associations and their attendant one-to-many and many-to-many relationships.

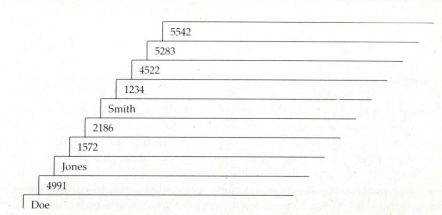

Figure 4.5c. Multiple relationship representation: Interspersed records.

Data Management Control Topics

There are several concerns about the way we manage data that must be considered in any data processing environment, regardless of the file structures in use. These control topics are inherent in storing, managing, and accessing data. The areas are:

Security
Backup and Recovery
Concurrency
Auditability

Security

There are actually many aspects of security in a data processing environment, only some of which deal immediately and directly with access to data, which is our concern in this book. For example, sign-on passwords are often used to prevent an unauthorized person from gaining access to the system itself. In a different vein, locked doors and armed guards are sometimes used to stop someone from blowing up the computer. There are several aspects of security which are specifically data related, however, and thus are of interest here. The two key points involved are preventing people from seeing data that they are not entitled to see and preventing them from changing data that they are not entitled to change.

It is certainly possible to design and build systems that can protect the data in independent linear files. The problem is that unless everyone agrees to use this system, every programmer is left to his or her own devices, either omitting such security considerations or reinventing the wheel for each application.

Backup and Recovery

Suppose an accident or an act of nature causes some unspeakable tragedy that mangles one of your disk packs. Or suppose that an error in input is discovered that took place 10 minutes ago and, in the real-time environment, affected other data as well.

Clearly, it is always advisable to have more than one copy of every data file. Furthermore, the copies must be kept in different buildings, or even different cities, to prevent a catastrophe from destroying all copies of the data. The process of copying a file, which must be done on a periodic basis to reflect changes in the data, is known as "backup," or "backing-up" the file. The process of using the file copy, plus other data, to correct either of the kinds of problems mentioned previously is known as "recovery."

Here again, as with the security case, it is certainly feasible to have backup and recovery systems for independent linear file based data processing. But, again, this means that everyone in the environment must use the same system, which is often contrary to the independent nature of the applications in such environments.

Concurrency

In a multiuser application, such as an airline reservations system with many reservations agents, a particular problem can surface regardless of the file structure in use, involving changing field values. When two users try to update the same record simultaneously (or as simultaneously as a multiprogrammed system allows), they have a rather nasty way of interfering with each other so that one of those two updates may wind up being ignored.

A common solution to this problem involves a technique called "lock-out." Unfortunately, as so often happens, the use of this technique itself causes other problems that did not previously exist and that have to be handled.

Once again, there is an important concern: Who and what software system should be responsible for implementing these protective devices?

Auditability

As more and more of an enterprise's data is stored and processed in automated data processing systems, it becomes an increasingly important focus of the auditing function. There is an endless list of reasons for management, accountants, and others to ask who had access to or made changes to what data, and when—not to mention what the new and old values of the data were.

The primary tool of the auditor is the audit trail: a permanent record of the nature of the changes made to the data. But here, as in the other three situations discussed, who or what should be responsible for the audit function?

Independent Files and General Data Management Issues

In all four of the above cases, the key concept is that it makes sense to have a common way to deal with these areas built into the Database Management System (DBMS). This means that when a new application program is written, we can avoid the expense of the programmer having to write from scratch routines for security, recovery, and so forth, or trying to use specialized but unconnected software packages for these functions. It means that we can be confident that the routines work, since they are standard, tested components of the DBMS. It means that the functions are standard for all application programs in the environment, which leads to easier management of them and economies of scale in assigning and training personnel to be responsible for these aspects. This kind of commonality is a hallmark of the database approach.

Data Independence

In the independent linear file data processing environment, decisions involving the way that the application program is written are usually made in concert with the choice of file organization and access method. The program logic itself is dependent on the way in which the data is stored. In fact the dependence is often so strong that if for any reason the storage characteristics of the data should be changed in the future, the program itself must be modified, often extensively. That is a very undesirable characteristic because of the time and expense involved in such efforts. In practice, storage structures do and/or should change to reflect improved storage techniques, new hardware, attempts at sharing data, and performance tuning, to name a few reasons. One of the reasons for the massive amounts of time spent on program maintenance is the typical level of dependency between programs and data.

What we would like to be able to do is separate out storage and access considerations from programming to as great an extent as possible. Today's DBMSs have been somewhat successful in solving certain aspects of this problem.

Conclusion

The use of independent linear files during the early days of automated data processing should be looked back upon as a starting point and, historically, as a stopgap measure. It is clear that the independent linear files method of data storage, combined with individual applications implemented in a vacuum, carries with it a host of undesirable side effects. The solution, as we shall see more and more, is the database approach.

References

Date, C. J., *An Introduction to Database Systems,* 4th ed., vol. I, Addison-Wesley, Reading, MA; 1986.

Inmon,W. H., and Bird, T. J. Jr., *The Dynamics of Data Base,* Prentice-Hall, Englewood Cliffs, NJ; 1986.

Kroenke, D. M., and Dolan, K. A., *Database Processing,* 3rd ed., Science Research Associates, Chicago, IL; 1988.

Pratt, P. J., and Adamski, J. J., *Database Systems,* Boyd & Fraser, Boston, MA; 1987.

Questions and Exercises

4.1. Should data be considered a true corporate resource? Why or why not? Compare and contrast data to other corporate resources (capital, plant and equipment, personnel, etc.) in terms of importance, intrinsic value, and modes of use.

4.2. Defend or refute the following statement: "Data is the most important corporate resource because it describes all of the others."

4.3. How does the database environment change the way that we treat and think about data?

4.4. What are the two kinds of data redundancy, and what problems do they cause in the data processing environment?

4.5. Devise an example that demonstrates the problem of data redundancy within one file.

4.6. Describe the apparent trade-off between data redundancy and data integration in simple linear files.

4.7. In your own words, describe the key quality of a DBMS that sets it apart from other data handling systems.

4.8. Describe the situation in which data is held redundantly across several files.

4.9. Do you think that the single-file redundancy problem is more serious, less serious, or about the same as the multifile redundancy problem? Why?

4.10. Choose a functional part of a corporation and describe a few one-to-one, one-to-many, and many-to-many relationships among its entities.

4.11. In your own words, describe the problems involved in trying to handle multiple associations in simple linear files.

4.12. How important do you think it is to be able to handle multiple associations for data processing applications? Why?

4.13. Describe the "general data management issues" outlined in this chapter. How important is it for a database management system to be able to handle them?

4.14. What is data independence? Why is it desirable?

5

Database Management Systems Characteristics

The Nature of a Database Management System

Grasping the concept of a database management system requires some thought about the idea of a "middleman." There are many examples of middlemen in the world, with a number of variations.

Consider, for example, the idea of shopping for goods through a mail-order company, a process diagramed in Figure 5.1. On one side is the consumer who wants to buy some merchandise, while on the other side is the company's warehouse containing the merchandise. In the middle is a combination of the catalog describing the merchandise and the people and facilities of the company's catalog ordering department. The consumer cannot reach the merchandise in the warehouse without going through the catalog ordering department. This is an important point, because it allows the company to maintain strict inventory and accounting control over the goods in the warehouse; to allow the consumers direct access to the warehouse might well cause some serious control problems. Focusing on the catalog brings up another interesting point about this situation. The catalog is, of course, not the merchandise itself, but a description of it. There may be 300 Brand X fishing reels in the warehouse, but, since they're all identical, a single catalog description of a Brand X fishing reel, together with the fact that there are 300 of them, is sufficient to describe the warehouse's stock. The consumer and the catalog ordering department both use the catalog as a means of knowing something about the fishing reels without actually going over to the shelf in the warehouse and touching them. That's important too. Eventually, the consumer places an order with the catalog ordering department. The department, consult-

Figure 5.1. Mail-order department as middleman.

ing the catalog and other directory information, such as what aisle and shelf in the warehouse the goods are on, causes the goods to be shipped to the consumer, handling all of the accounting details along the way. The consumer receives his or her order, having dealt only with the "middleman" organization and its descriptive catalog.

Another example of a middleman is a long-distance telephone information operator, who serves as the interface between a person seeking a telephone number and the distant telephone directories unavailable to the caller (see Figure 5.2). There are several noticeable differences between this example and the catalog buying example. For one thing, the "merchandise" in this case (the telephone numbers in the directories) is data. It is not exhaustible, unlike fishing reels on a shelf. An operator could give out the same telephone number an unlimited number of times and it could still be given out again. Also, we could give everyone in the country direct access to every telephone book in the country by giving them each a copy of every telephone book. Without belaboring the physical problems involved in doing that, we will simply say that that solution would create a tremendous amount of redundancy. There is no need to give everyone a copy of every telephone book if the long-distance information operators can serve as middlemen and funnel the information in their copies of the telephone books to those customers who need it, when they need it.

A third example of a middleman is a stockbroker, connecting potential buyers of stock with potential sellers through the mechanism of the stock markets, shown in Figure 5.3. One difference between this example of

Figure 5.2. Long-distance telephone information operator as middleman.

Figure 5.3. Stockbroker as middleman.

a middleman and the two previous ones is that in this case the two parties on either side of the interface are functional equals, passing equally
important data across the interface between each other. Also, this instance
presents the clearest case of the three for keeping both sides strictly separated across the middleman interface. Can you imagine the anarchy of
having all of the thousands of potential buyers and sellers of stock in one
room together?

A DBMS is also a middleman. In the data processing environment it
serves as the interface between data files and the people who seek the
data in those files (see Figure 5.4). Whether access to the files is sought in

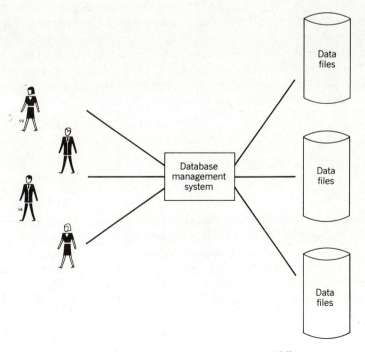

Figure 5.4. Database management system as middleman.

the form of an ad hoc query, typed in at a display terminal, or in the form of a formal printed report, the request must go through the DBMS, and the response must be passed back through the DBMS. A bit more formally, a DBMS is a sophisticated piece of software that specifies how data may be structured, controls all access to the data, and provides certain other essential data services. The data structure, in some cases in concert with the way that the data is manipulated, must provide for data integration, reduction of data redundancy, and the expression of multiple relationships in the data. Access to the data is provided via a query facility, through calls embedded in a higher level language, or both. Other DBMS-supplied data services include security, backup and recovery, and concurrent update control.

Database management systems usually run under the control of a general purpose operating system, often taking careful advantage of the facilities of the operating system. They may have an entire computer system dedicated to them, or they may share a central processing unit (CPU) with other kinds of software facilities. A DBMS and its associated application programs may operate in a batch mode, in an on-line, multiterminal environment using an additional data communications facility, or in both of these environments concurrently.

The DBMS is the consummate middleman. As in the catalog buying example, the DBMS is the only means of accessing its "merchandise," that is, the data in the files. Like the long distance telephone information example, it avoids a proliferation of copies of the same data. Like the stockbroker example it passes data in both directions across its interface, allowing data to be read from its files and allowing new data to be inserted or existing data to be modified. As in all of the examples, it provides a degree of security to the "materials" (data) that it is responsible for and creates order out of what might have been chaos.

Let's take a look at some of these ideas in a little more detail.

Data Definition Languages

Introduction

The term "data definition (or description) language" (DDL) is a broad label for the aspect of the DBMS that specifies the *way* that data may be stored. As basic as that statement sounds, there are really two views of the "way" that data is stored, stemming from the apparent conflict between the following two goals. One is the desire to have the data appear to the programmer to be stored in a relatively simple way. The other is the desire to have the data, as actually stored on the disk devices, take the fullest advantage of the complexities of the hardware and of the theories of database technology to accomplish all of the advertised benefits of the database approach. That distinction is important enough to warrant DBMS designers, at considerable expense, to create the capability of having two "views" of the data. We speak of the **logical view** of the data as the form that the programmer perceives it to be in, while the **physical view** reflects the way that it is actually stored on disk.

For this distinction to work, there must be a component of the DBMS that can convert requests for data coming from terminals or application programs based on the logical view into the physical view form, which is the way that the data is really stored on the disk. For the DBMS to accomplish that, it must have at its disposal descriptions that it can "understand" of the way that the data is stored on the disk and the way that the users or programmers perceive it. Such information is stored in special groups of records known as **control blocks**.

The Four Approaches to Structure

Introduction. Any particular DBMS is based on a data structure and data access mechanism. Whatever that structure and mechanism are, they must be able to store data in a nonredundant way, to handle multiple associations among the data, to integrate the data, and to provide direct as well as sequential access to the data. Over the years, many DBMSs have been developed for environments ranging from the largest mainframe computers to the smallest microprocessors. Yet every one of them is based on one of four fundamental approaches to DBMS data structure and data access mechanisms:

The relational approach
The pseudo-relational or flat-file integrated approach
The hierarchical approach
The network approach

Explaining each of these four approaches will be the focus of a large part of the rest of this book. Nevertheless, a few introductory remarks are appropriate here.

Relational Databases. Figure 5.5 shows a relational database. At first glance it appears to consist of a few independent linear files, and, from a structural point of view that's true. Notice also, reading across the files from left to right, that since the BRANCH OFFICE, CAR, EMPLOYEE, and MAINTENANCE DATE (plus CAR) fields are unique, there is only one record for a given branch office (and it is in the Branch file), one record for a given car (in the Car file), and so on. This, of course, means that there is no data redundancy. No fact about the real world environment appears more than once. For example, since there is only one record for a

Figure 5.5. A relational database.

particular branch office, all of the fields dependent on it, such as BRANCH MANAGER, BRANCH ADDRESS, and so on appear only once.

But what about the fact that the BRANCH OFFICE field appears in the Car file? Is that redundant with the BRANCH OFFICE field in the Branch file? The answer is, "Absolutely not!" Since the records in the files in the relational database are not structurally interconnected, the only way to provide for integration of the files is to repeat the identifying field of one file in the other. If we didn't have the BRANCH OFFICE field in the Car file, how else would we know which cars were assigned to which branch offices? The car *assignments* constitute a one-to-many relationship, indicating that a branch office may be assigned several cars. Since the assignments are themselves individual, specific facts about the real world environment that we have to store, there is no introduction of data redundancy. Later on we will see how many-to-many relationships are handled in relational database structures.

Although the files in the relational database concept are independent, there must be a way to integrate the data in them—to bring together related data from different files. There is such a concept and, as we shall see later, its power comes from execution time procedures involving the fields that appear in more than one file.

Pseudo-Relational Databases. Figure 5.6 shows a pseudo-relational or flat-file integrated database. First, notice that the Branch file, Car file, Employee file, and Maintenance file are identical to the files of the relational database in Figure 5.5. The foregoing comments about eliminating data redundancy in the flat files of the relational database apply here as well.

But the execution time procedures for integrating the data in the relational files do not exist here. There must be some physically built-in way of connecting the files. The lower half of Figure 5.6 shows three additional "match" files of two fields each. Such files indicate which records of one file are related to which records of the other file, effectively integrating the two files. For example, Match File A indicates which records of the Branch Office File and which records of the Car File are related, which really means which records of these two files have the same branch office numbers. This, in effect, allows the combining of detail data about a given branch office with detail data about the cars assigned to it. Thus the pseudo-relational database combines the flat-file data structure of the relational database with the *concept* of accomplishing data integration with some kind of prestored, physical construction.

Hierarchical Databases. Figure 5.7 shows a hierarchy of record types, representative of the type of structure found in a hierarchically based DBMS. The four record types in Figure 5.7 represent a firm's branch

Figure 5.6. A pseudo-relational database.

Figure 5.7. A data hierarchy.

offices, cars assigned to each branch office, employees authorized to drive a particular car, and maintenance dates at which the car was serviced. Although not shown in the figure, each of these boxes really represents a collection of fields, as any record must. For example, each Branch Office record contains a BRANCH OFFICE NUMBER field, a BRANCH OFFICE NAME field, a BRANCH OFFICE CITY field, and so on. The Branch Office, Car, and Employee records are identified by unique identifying fields (e.g., the BRANCH OFFICE NUMBER field for the Branch Office record type).

A basic tenet of the hierarchical data structure is that each link connecting two record types represents a one-to-many relationship, in the downwards direction. Thus the structure in Figure 5.7 indicates that each branch office has several cars assigned to it, each car has several employees authorized to drive it, and each car has a multiple maintenance date history. Many-to-many relationships can be handled with a combination of hierarchies, as we shall see later.

The potential reduction of redundancy with this arrangement comes first from the fact that the details of a particular superior record (e.g., a Branch Office record) are stored only once and can be integrated with the details of any occurrences of its subordinate records (e.g., CAR). For example, we would be able to combine the branch office address— which is stored only once in the one Branch Office record occurrence for that branch— with details about any of the cars assigned to that branch. Also, it will turn out that the way that many-to-many relationships are accommodated through connected hierarchies also saves on redundancy.

Network Databases. Figure 5.8 shows a network. As in the hierarchical case, each link between two record types in the network represents a one-to-many relationship between them. The direction of the relationship

Figure 5.8.   A data network.

is shown by the double arrowheads in the figure. Again, many-to-many relationships require some additional constructs. Unlike the hierarchical case, it is common in networks, as we shall see in more detail later, to consider two connected record types and the link connecting them to be a substructure called a "set," which has certain valuable properties.

Database management systems that are based on the hierarchical or the network approaches are often called **navigational** systems. In both cases, data is stored as records of different types that are interconnected by physical address pointers. Programmers, using either the hierarchical or network forms, can "navigate" through their structures. This means, for instance, that a program call to the database can be designed to find a particular branch office or a particular car in that branch and to produce a list of the people authorized to drive it.

Data Manipulation Languages

The term "data manipulation language" refers broadly to the mechanism used for retrieving data stored in a database. There are two basic ways of accessing the data in a database. One way is to have an application program issue an instruction to the DBMS to find certain data in the database and return it to the program. We speak of these instructions as being "embedded statements." The other way of accessing the data is for the person seeking the data to sit down at a display terminal and issue a command in a special language directly to the DBMS to find certain data and return it to the screen. We speak of that as a "query" operation.

Either the embedded statement or query language approach to accessing data can be used with any of the four approaches to database structure.

Embedded Statements

The logic of a computer program, whether it's written in COBOL, PL/I, Assembler Language, or any other procedural language dictates that at various points in the execution of that program, data must be brought in from and sent out to appropriate stored files. Thus, *embedded* in the program, at the proper logical places among the GOTO, IF-THEN-ELSE, and A = B + C statements, are other statements that, when executed, cause the system to reach out to the disk drives (or tape drives, etc.) and transfer data into and out of the running program. When the program operates in the database environment, those I/O statements must be specially constructed to conform to the rules of the DBMS, which will serve as the middleman between the program and the database.

Query Languages

There are situations that call for simply looking something up in the database. At such times, one would like to be able to send a command directly to the DBMS, instructing it to find and return the desired data, as opposed to having to plan, write, debug, and finally execute a program to accomplish the same thing. Such direct interaction with the DBMS through a terminal is the nature of a **query language**. Logic to interpret and carry out the query requests is packaged as a part of or an adjunct to the DBMS. The queries generally must be constructed according to a planned syntax.

Comparing Embedded Statements to Query Languages

There is a crucial point to be made in understanding the nature of data manipulation languages, and now is not too soon to make it. The concept of exactly what constitutes a "query" is partially dependent on from whose point of view we are approaching the situation. In a query language situation there is a general purpose processor capable of searching for and retrieving any data, as long as it is stored according to the prescribed DBMS structure and as long as the construction of the query itself follows the proper conventions. Anyone using a query language should feel as if they are making a "query."

Now let's look at the embedded statement situation. Modern programming techniques in general, and DBMSs in particular, certainly permit on-line, terminal-oriented operations. It is quite usual for executing programs with I/O statements written as embedded DBMS calls to accept requests for data from terminal devices and update the database from data values typed in at these devices. The point is that the *programmer* was well aware, when writing the program in the first place, that he or she was not dealing with what we have been calling a "query language"; but, if during execution of the program, you ask what the *end user* is doing, the reply will be, "Querying the database." Any operation on data from a terminal can be termed a query, but one has to look at what is supporting it to determine if it is in the embedded statement or query language category.

Later in this book, we will look at some examples of both embedded statements and query language calls.

Security, Backup and Recovery, and Concurrency

There are certain concerns about stored data that we should have regardless of the storage structure used and whether or not a DBMS is involved. One concern is the security of the data. As more and more of a company's business procedures are performed with the use of computers, the security of the data becomes ever more crucial. In addition to the need to keep all of its internal and customer records accurate, there are issues of protecting its new products and ideas, keeping its personnel and customer data confidential, and keeping its corporate budget and strategic planning information strictly within the company, to name a few.

We might ask such systems-oriented questions as: Is the data protected against unauthorized access and changes? Are the programs that do have legitimate access to the data protected against unauthorized modifications that could affect the data? Are the people who have legitimate access to some of the data in the database blocked from purposely or accidentally accessing the rest of the data?

Another concern is the ability to reconstruct the data if any part of it is inadvertently destroyed. The process of making a copy of a file for such purposes is referred to as a backup operation. The process of repairing a relatively small amount of damage to a file or recreating a totally destroyed file is called a recovery operation.

A third concern is the issue of concurrency. As we shall develop later, problems can arise when two or more users or programs attempt to update a particular piece of data simultaneously (concurrently). Without protections, the final result may not include all of the intended changes.

Since all three of these concerns are common to all data, and since the procedures needed to handle them can be constructed in a very general manner, it is clear that such procedures should be built into any DBMS. To do otherwise would be to return to the earlier days of data processing, when programmers were on their own for such issues with each new application they developed.

Data Communications Interface

Earlier in this chapter, we discussed queries and query operations; taking the necessary details for granted, we just assumed that interaction with the database was possible through a display terminal.

In fact, all of the detailed material discussed thus far in this book, and most of what is yet to come, concern the data, the DBMS, and directly related topics of accessing the data. All of this *could* be done in a batch environment, but most DBMS environments today operate primarily in an on-line mode for fast access to data, immediate posting of changes to the data, and access to the data over a wide geographical range. The users and their terminals may all be clustered near the computer itself, or they may be in far-flung locations across the country or the world.

The mechanisms needed to permit such an array of terminals, and in general the entire on-line environment, are not trivial and do not come free. Whether the data is in a database or not, such on-line terminal access to it requires a complex piece of software, usually called a "data communications driver," together with additional interfaces to the DBMS and the application programs. (Note that the comment about "database or not" is in the same spirit as the similar comment about security, etc., in the last section.)

In the query language form of access, the DBMS must be prepared to receive messages from terminals and send messages to them. In the embedded statement form, the application programs must not only have the capability of using special instructions for database access, but must also have the capability of using other special instructions to interact with the terminals. These instructions, inserted at appropriate places in the code according to the program logic, must be able to accept messages from the terminals through the communications driver and send messages back out. The incoming messages, in their most basic form, will be requests for data in the database and instructions to change data in the database, and the outgoing messages will be the data being sent out to the terminals that requested it.

We will look at the issues of security, backup and recovery, and concurrency in more detail later in this book.

References

Date, C. J., *An Introduction to Database Systems*, 4th ed., vol. I, Addison-Wesley, Reading, MA; 1986.

Inmon, W. H., and Bird, T. J., Jr., *The Dynamics of Data Base*, Prentice-Hall, Englewood Cliffs, NJ; 1986.

Kroenke, D. M., and Dolan, K. A., *Database Processing*, 3rd ed., Science Research Associates, Chicago, IL; 1988.

Pratt, P. J., and Adamski, J. J., *Database Systems*, Boyd & Fraser, Boston, MA; 1987.

Questions and Exercises

5.1. As described in this chapter, a database management system is a middleman between data and users. Think of another example of a middleman outside of data processing. Does it provide a total separation between the two parties? Do the two parties consider the middleman to be a help or a hindrance?

5.2. What do you think are the benefits of having a middleman between data and its users in a data processing environment? Are there any disadvantages?

5.3. In your own words, what is a database management system?

5.4. Outline the capabilities that a database management system is expected to have.

5.5. What is the difference between the logical and the physical views of data stored in a database? What are the reasons for making the distinction?

5.6. What is the difference between a data definition language and a data manipulation language? How closely is each tied to the other?

5.7. What are the four approaches to database management system structure? At first glance, do you think that some of them are better than the others? Why or why not?

5.8. At first glance, do you think that all four of the database management system approaches are capable of fulfilling all of the promises of database?

5.9. What is the difference between an embedded data manipulation language and a query type data manipulation language?

5.10. In your own words, describe the circumstances under which someone might perceive an application that uses embedded statements to be in the realm of the query type language.

5.11. Give an introductory description of security, backup and recovery, and concurrency. How important do you think it is for a database management system to handle these concerns?

6

The Relational Approach to Database

Introduction

In 1970, Dr. Edgar F. Codd of IBM published a paper entitled "A Relational Model of Data for Large Shared Data Banks." This paper marked the beginning of the field of relational database. During the ensuing years the relational approach to database received a great deal of publicity. Yet only since the early 1980s have commercially viable relational database management systems been available. Relational database was always very tempting in concept, but for a long time it remained elusive when it came to applying it in a real-world environment. Today there is intense interest in this approach to database management, with the general feeling being that this approach is the one that holds the greatest promise for the future.

The saga of relational DBMSs is one of the most fascinating stories in this still young field of database. How they compare with hierarchical and network DBMSs in terms of operation, performance, and overall philosophy is not only interesting, but highly instructive for a true understanding of some of the most basic concepts in database.

In this chapter we will provide an easy to understand, basic foundation in relational database concepts and operations. In Chapter 7 we will describe SQL, the major commercial relational language. In Chapter 8 we will take a look at some other commercial products and variations. Later, after we have discussed the navigational approaches to database management, we will make some comparisons between them and the relational approach.

SALESPERSON NUMBER	· · ·	SALESPERSON NAME	· · ·
137		Baker	
186		Adams	
204		Dickens	
361		Carlyle	
· · ·		· · ·	

(a)

CUSTOMER NUMBER	· · ·	SALESPERSON NUMBER	· · ·
0121		137	
0839		186	
0933		137	
1047		137	
1525		361	
1700		361	
1826		137	
2198		204	
2267		186	
· · ·		· · ·	

(b)

Figure 6.1.   (a) Salesperson file and (b) Customer file.

Review of the Database Premise

We began the discussion of database in Chapter 4 with the separate simple linear files of Figure 4.1 and the combined file of Figure 4.2. For convenience, those two figures have been repeated as Figures 6.1 and 6.2. Let's review the situation concerning the files in those figures. The two files represented in Figure 6.1 are simple linear files. SALESPERSON NUMBER is the unique key field of the Salesperson file; CUSTOMER NUMBER is the unique key field of the Customer file. There is one record for each salesperson in the Salesperson file and one record for each customer in the Customer file. These two files have the highly desirable properties of being conceptually simple and having no data redundancy among their non-key fields. A given salesperson's number and

SALESPERSON NUMBER	CUSTOMER NUMBER	SALESPERSON NAME	· · ·
137	1021	Baker	
137	0933	Baker	
137	1047	Baker	
137	1826	Baker	
186	0839	Adams	
186	2267	Adams	
204	2198	Dickens	
361	1525	Carlyle	
361	1700	Carlyle	
· · ·	· · ·	· · ·	

Figure 6.2. Combined file.

name (and presumably address, telephone number, etc.) are listed exactly once in the Salesperson file. The same can be said for the customer data in the Customer file.

The problem with these two files is the seeming inability to integrate data in any way short of brute force application programming. In order to find the *name* of the salesperson responsible for a given customer, the application programmer must find the record for that customer in the Customer file, pick up the salesperson number in it, and use that piece of data as entry to the Salesperson file to find the record for that salesperson, which contains the salesperson's name.

The other choice, the combined file of Figure 6.2, solves the data integration problem—the above query can be answered with the retrieval of a single record—but introduces extensive and unacceptable data redundancy. Yet we asserted in Chapter 4 that a true DBMS must both provide a data structure that allows data to be stored nonredundantly and also makes the data appear highly integrated to the application programmer. In the rest of this chapter, we will demonstrate that the relational database approach is truly capable of providing data integration while maintaining data nonredundantly. We will also show how the approach handles that other important database concept, multiple relationships.

The Relational Approach

What is a Relation?

In spite of the apparent conflict between nonredundant, linear file storage and data integration shown above, the concept of having the relative simplicity of simple linear files in a true database environment is rather compelling. After all, the linear file arrangement is the most basic and commonly used data structure there is. This is precisely the driving force behind the idea of relational database.

To begin with, let's consider the data structure used in relational databases. That's easy. As implied previously, the data appears to be stored in what we have been referring to as simple linear files. Whether or not the actual physical storage is arranged that way or just makes it appear so is unimportant. Following the conventions of the area of mathematics on which relational database is founded, we will begin calling those simple linear files **relations** or **tables**. We will assume that no two rows, records, or **tuples** of a relation are identical. Technically, the columns, fields, or **attributes** of a relation can be arranged in any order without affecting the meaning of the data.

A relation always has a unique key, a field or a group of fields whose values are unique throughout all of the tuples of the relation. The number of fields involved in the key is always the minimum number of fields that provide the uniqueness quality. For example, if a company assigns each employee a unique employee number, then the employee number field could be the key of the personnel relation. On the other hand, if a company does not use employee numbers, then the first name field, middle name field, and last name field may have to be taken as a group to provide a unique key for the relation. A relation always has a unique key, since we know that no two tuples can be identical, and so, as a worst case, all of the relation's fields could serve as the key if necessary (but that situation is rare in practice). If a relation has more than one unique key then they are each called **candidate keys** and the one that is chosen as "the key of the relation" is called the **primary key**. If in a collection of relations that make up a relational database a field or group of fields serves as the primary key of one relation and also appears in another relation, then it is called a **foreign key** in that other relation. The concept of a foreign key is an important one that we shall explore shortly. Assuming that the relations, like those in Figure 6.1 (we'll start referring to those two files as relations now), are designed well, there is no redundancy among the non-key fields.

A relational database is simply a collection of relations. In terms of the way that we think about the data, the relations are quite independent, physically, as opposed to the tightly pointer-connected structures in the hierarchical- and network-based approaches that we shall discuss later. The question of how to design relational databases will be deferred until Chapter 11, but we will make appropriate comments about it as needed in this chapter as well.

By the way, as with any database approach, there is the issue of sequential and direct access to the individual records. Since a relation is fundamentally thought of as a simple linear file, any of the access methods that we've discussed in this book are potentially applicable. The tuples of a relation can be stored with a hashing algorithm, with an index, or in a simple sequential arrangement (without an index). We will see shortly that the nature of relational operations would render the exclusive use of a sequential access method unacceptable in practice. As will also become clear, efficiency in relational DBMSs usually depends on direct access to a number of the attributes of a relation. Thus relational DBMSs typically allow for indexes to be created over several or even all of the attributes of a relation.

Extracting Data from a Relation

Given a relational database consisting of one or more relations, we have to begin to think about how to extract data from it. Without any special tools for extracting data from a relation, the problem reverts to simply writing a program in some programming language to retrieve data from a simple linear file. If that was as far as we could go, then there would be no discipline of relational database to talk about! But the crucial point is that an inherent feature of a relational DBMS is the capability to accept high-level data retrieval commands aimed at relations and to process them, *even to the extent of matching related records in different files* (integrating data), as in the earlier example of finding the name of the salesperson on a particular customer account. Let's see what relational retrieval might look like, first in terms of single relations and then across multiple relations.

Since a relation is fundamentally a rectangular arrangement of data values, it would seem to make sense to want to approach data retrieval horizontally, vertically, or in a combination of the two. To take a horizontal slice of a relation implies retrieving one or more tuples or rows of the relation. In effect, that's nothing more than an expression for retrieving one or more records of a file. Taking a vertical slice of a relation means retrieving one or more attributes or columns of the relation for all of its tuples or rows. In combination, we can retrieve one or more attributes of one or more tuples, the minimum of which is a single attribute of a single tuple, or a single field value of a single record. That's as fine a sense of retrieval as we would ever want.

Using terminology from a database formalism called "relational algebra" and a relaxed, free-form command style for now, let's look at two commands called Select and Project, which are capable of the kinds of horizontal and vertical manipulations that we just discussed. For a database we'll use the relations in Figure 6.3, which are the same two relations as those in Figure 6.1, except that we have now added some more non-key fields and eliminated the ellipses that indicated additional unknown

SALESPERSON NUMBER	SALESPERSON NAME	COMMISSION PERCENTAGE	YEAR OF HIRE
137	Baker	10	1975
186	Adams	15	1971
204	Dickens	10	1963
361	Carlyle	20	1963

(a)

CUSTOMER NUMBER	SALESPERSON NUMBER	CITY
0121	137	New York
0839	186	Hartford
0933	137	Boston
1047	137	Boston
1525	361	Newark
1700	361	Washington
1826	137	New York
2198	204	New York
2267	186	New York

(b)

Figure 6.3. *(a)* Salesperson relation and *(b)* Customer relation.

attributes and tuples. To begin with, suppose that we want to find the record for salesperson number 204. In a very straightforward way, our command might be:

```
Select tuples from the Salesperson relation in which
SALESPERSON NUMBER = 204.
```

The result would be:

SALES-PERSON NUMBER	SALES-PERSON NAME	COMMISSION PERCENTAGE	YEAR OF HIRE
204	Dickens	10	1963

Notice that the result of the Select operation is itself a relation, in this case consisting of only one tuple. *The result of a relational operation will always be a relation,* whether it consists of many tuples with many attributes or one tuple with one attribute (i.e., a single value).

Perhaps we want all of the records with a common value in a particular (nonunique) field:

```
Select tuples from the Salesperson relation in which
COMMISSION PERCENTAGE = 10.
```

The result of that operation is:

SALES– PERSON NUMBER	SALES– PERSON NAME	COMMISSION PERCENTAGE	YEAR OF HIRE
137	Baker	10	1975
204	Dickens	10	1963

Of course we might want to retrieve the entire file, perhaps with a command like

```
Select all tuples from the Salesperson relation.
```

To retrieve what we referred to earlier as a vertical slice, we will use the Project operator. To retrieve the number and name of each salesperson in the file we issue:

```
Project the SALESPERSON NUMBER and SALESPERSON NAME over
the Salesperson relation.
```

The result will be a long, narrow relation:

SALES– PERSON NUMBER	SALES– PERSON NAME
137	Baker
186	Adams
204	Dickens
361	Carlyle

If we project a nonunique field, then a decision must be made at some level as to whether or not we want duplicates (although, since the result is itself a relation, technically we can't have any duplicates). For example, whether:

```
Project the YEAR OF HIRE over the Salesperson relation
```

produces:

YEAR OF HIRE
1975
1971
1963
1963

or

YEAR OF HIRE
1975
1971
1963

would depend on the particular implementation involved.

More powerful still is the combination of the Select and Project operators. Suppose we apply them serially, with the relation that results from one operation being used as the input to the next operation. Let's say that we want the number and name of the salespersons working on a 10% commission. We would issue the following two commands:

```
Select tuples from the Salesperson relation in which
COMMISSION PERCENTAGE = 10. Project the SALESPERSON
NUMBER and SALESPERSON NAME over that result.
```

This produces:

SALES–PERSON NUMBER	SALES–PERSON NAME
137	Baker
204	Dickens

The following combination illustrates the ability to retrieve a single value. Suppose that we want to know the year of hire of salesperson number 204. Since we know that SALESPERSON NUMBER is a unique field, we know that we will be dealing with only one tuple. Since we are seeking one attribute from that tuple, we know that we will wind up with a single value:

```
Select tuples from the Salesperson relation in which
SALESPERSON NUMBER = 204. Project the YEAR OF HIRE over
that result.
```

The result is the single value:

```
YEAR
 OF
HIRE
```
```
┌──────┐
│ 1963 │
└──────┘
```

Extracting Data across Multiple Relations: Data Integration

We will discuss data integration in the relational database approach within the context of extracting data across multiple relations. Look at the relations in Figure 6.3 and think back to the earlier example of data integration: Find the name of the salesperson on a particular account. The suggested solution to that problem thus far has been to find the account record in the customer file, read the salesperson number in that record, and use that number to find the record for the salesperson in the salesperson file.

Wouldn't it be nice if the same system that is capable of retrieving data from a single relation, based on the kinds of Select and Project commands that we've looked at, is also capable of doing automated, multiple relation searches? In fact, using an operator called Join, we can solve the multiple relation data integration problem, after which we can further refine the result with Select and Project.

Continuing with our relaxed command style, let's issue commands to find the name of the salesperson responsible for customer number 1525:

```
Join the Salesperson relation and the Customer relation,
using the SALESPERSON NUMBER of each as the join field.
Select tuples from that result in which CUSTOMER NUMBER
= 1525. Project the SALESPERSON NAME over that result.
```

Let's examine the first sentence, which represents the Join command. Remember how we had picked up the SALESPERSON NUMBER attribute value in one relation and used it to search for the needed record in the other relation? We were able to do that precisely because that field existed in both relations! (Even if the two attributes had had different names, like "SALESPERSON NUMBER" in one relation and "EMPLOYEE NUMBER" in the other relation, we still could have performed the same operation because they represent the same *kind* of information. Technically we would say that they have the same "domain of values.") The Join operation will take advantage of the common SALESPERSON NUMBER field, which for this purpose is called the **join field** in both relations, and look for tuples in the two relations that have the same value for the join field. When it finds such a pair of tuples, it takes all of the fields from both and creates a single new tuple out of them in the resultant relation. In its most basic form, as shown here, it is truly an exhaustive operation, comparing every tuple of one relation against every tuple of the other relation, and looking for a match in the join fields. So the result of the Join command, the first of the three commands in the example command sequence we're executing, is:

SALES-PERSON NUMBER	SALES-PERSON NAME	COMMISSION PERCENTAGE	YEAR OF HIRE	CUSTOMER NUMBER	SALES-PERSON NUMBER	CITY
137	Baker	10	1975	0121	137	New York
137	Baker	10	1975	0933	137	Boston
137	Baker	10	1975	1047	137	Boston
137	Baker	10	1975	1826	137	New York
186	Adams	15	1971	0839	186	Hartford
186	Adams	15	1971	2267	186	New York
204	Dickens	10	1963	2198	204	New York
361	Carlyle	20	1963	1525	361	Newark
361	Carlyle	20	1963	1700	361	Washington

Notice that the first and sixth attributes are identical. They represent the SALESPERSON NUMBER attribute from the Salesperson and Customer relations respectively. Remember that two tuples would not be combined together to form a tuple in the resultant relation unless those two join field values were identical in the first place. This type of join is called an "equijoin." If, as seems reasonable, we eliminate one of the two identical columns in the process, we call the result a "natural join."

To continue with the command sequence to eventually find the name of the salesperson responsible for customer number 1525, first we issue the Select command portion of the example, using the relation that resulted from the join as input. This produces:

SALES-PERSON NUMBER	SALES-PERSON NAME	COMMISSION PERCENTAGE	YEAR OF HIRE	CUSTOMER NUMBER	SALES-PERSON NUMBER	CITY
361	Carlyle	20	1963	1525	361	Newark

Finally, we issue the third command, the Project, and get:

SALES-PERSON NAME
Carlyle

Notice that we could have streamlined the process. We were dealing with only a single customer, and there is only one tuple for each customer in the Customer relation, with CUSTOMER NUMBER as the unique key field. Also, there is only one tuple for each salesperson in the Salesperson relation. Thus, we really only needed to look at one tuple in the Customer relation and one tuple in the Salesperson relation to solve the problem (which assumes, at a practical level, that we had means of direct access into the relations). We'll talk about the use of information like that to increase the overall efficiency of the process in Chapter 7, within the context of the Structured Query Language.

A variation on the join concept is called the "outer join" (as opposed to the previously mentioned operation, which is "inner join"). In an outer join, all of the tuples of one of the relations appear in the resultant relation regardless of the presence or absence of a join field match in the other relation. If a particular tuple's join field doesn't match that of any tuple in the other relation, then in the resultant relation that tuple will appear with null values where the value from the matching tuple in the other relation, had there been one, would have gone.

Foreign Keys and Multiple Relationships

Now, what about the ability of the relational database approach to handle one-to-many and many-to-many relationships? In fact, not only are relational databases quite capable of handling multiple relationships, but as we shall see, the way that they do so is intimately related to their data integration capability! The first case is the one-to-many relationship.

The SALESPERSON NUMBER field in the Customer relation of Figure 6.3 serves as the link between the salesperson and customer entities. It is the presence of a salesperson number in a customer record that indicates with which salesperson the customer is associated. Fundamentally, that is why the SALESPERSON NUMBER field is in the Customer relation and that is the essence of its being a foreign key in that relation. Let's show the one-to-many relationship between salespeople and customers diagramatically as:

```
Salesperson <——>> Customer
```

In building that one-to-many relationship into the relational database, it will always be the case that the unique identifier of the entity on the *unary side* of the relationship (SALESPERSON NUMBER, in this example) will be placed as a foreign key in the relation representing the entity on the *multiple side* of the relationship (the Customer relation, in this example).

Next, let's take a look at the issue of multiple relationships in the context of an example. We will need an example that is a bit more complex than the one we've been using, so we will change the ground rules of the

Salesperson/Customer environment: Let's now assume that the customers can range in size from very small to very large companies. A salesperson who works with the small companies will still be responsible for servicing several of them, but now, in order to properly service the large companies, we will allow the situation in which several salespeople can be assigned to one customer. Furthermore, there can be a mixture of duties in that a salesperson may service several small companies and also be part of the sales teams that service one or more large companies. Clearly, what we have now defined is a many-to-many relationship. A salesperson can be associated with several customers, and a customer can be associated with several salespeople:

Salesperson <<——>> Customer

Figure 6.4*a* shows the Salesperson relation as it appeared in Figure 6.3*a*. Figure 6.4*b* shows the Customer relation with a field added that stores the name of the president of each company. Note that PRESIDENT is a nonunique field; different people whose last name is Smith can, of

SALES-PERSON NUMBER	SALES-PERSON NAME	COMMISSION PERCENTAGE	YEAR OF HIRE
137	Baker	10	1975
186	Adams	15	1971
204	Dickens	10	1963
361	Carlyle	20	1963

(*a*)

CUSTOMER NUMBER	CITY	PRESIDENT
0121	New York	Smith
0839	Hartford	Jackson
0933	Boston	Johnson
1047	Boston	Williams
1525	Newark	Smith
1700	Washington	Jones
1826	New York	Smith
2198	New York	Taylor
2267	New York	Jones

(*b*)

Figure 6.4.   (*a*) Salesperson relation and (*b*) Customer relation.

SALES- PERSON NUMBER	CUSTOMER NUMBER	YEARS
137	0121	6
137	0933	3
137	1047	2
137	1826	5
137	2198	4
186	0839	2
186	1047	3
186	2198	2
186	2267	1
204	2198	3
361	1047	4
361	1525	2
361	1700	3

(c)

Figure 6.4. (c) Services relation.

course, be the presidents of different companies. But also note that the SALESPERSON NUMBER field does not appear in the Customer relation as it did in Figure 6.3b, where it was used to represent the one-to-many relationship. Representing a many-to-many relationship in a relational database requires the creation of an additional relation. That relation will consist of fields which serve one or the other of two purposes. First, it will have as its key the combined unique identifiers of the two entities in the many-to-many relationship. In addition, it will have fields that constitute **intersection data**, that is, attributes or fields that describe not one entity or the other alone, but the *relationship* between the two entities. (Note that the additional table is required even if there is no intersection data and the only fields in the additional table are the unique identifiers of the two entities.) Attempting to account for the many-to-many relationship in the original tables without creating the additional table will always result in the creation of redundant data, whether or not there is any intersection data involved. The situation would be somewhat akin to what happened when we tried to combine the files in Figure 4.1 and wound up with the redundant file in Figure 4.2.

Thus, the many-to-many relationship between salespeople and customers requires an additional relation, the Services relation, as shown in Figure 6.4c. The key of the Services relation is the combination of the unique identifiers of the two entities involved in the many-to-many relationship: the SALESPERSON NUMBER and CUSTOMER NUMBER fields.

Notice that salesperson 137, alone or in a group, services five customers. Reading down the CUSTOMER NUMBER column, you can see that customer 2198 is serviced by three salespeople: numbers 137, 186, and 204. The number of years that a salesperson and a customer have been associated with each other is intersection data that further describes the many-to-many relationship. Years becomes an additional attribute in the Services relation. For example, salesperson 137 has been servicing customer 0121 for 6 years.

Adding, Deleting, or Updating Data: Referential Integrity

As we have noted, a relational database is composed of independent relations that are related to each other only by the equivalence of specific fields that appear in them and then only by identical values in those fields. Thus far, we have been concerned only with retrieving data from the relations. Certainly, we should expect that, as with any data storage scheme, in addition to retrieving data we must be prepared to add new records, delete existing records, or update existing records. Unfortunately, the logically related but physically independent nature of the relations in a relational database exposes the database to the possibility of a data integrity problem of a particular kind. This type of problem has come to be known as **referential integrity** because it revolves around the circumstance of trying to refer to data in one relation based on values in another relation in the database.

Let's say that our example company, represented in Figure 6.3, gets a new customer account, and it is assigned to a particular salesperson. Naturally, we would expect a new record to be inserted into the Customer relation, which would include the SALESPERSON NUMBER for the salesperson responsible for that account. But in the relations of Figure 6.3, there is nothing inherent in the data structure to force a tuple for a particular salesperson to exist in the Salesperson relation just because someone inserts a customer record into the Customer relation with that salesperson recorded in it.

For example, what if a record for customer 1950 is inserted into the Customer relation, the record shows a value of 275 as the salesperson number, and there is no record for salesperson number 275 in the Salesperson relation? Then, what if someone tried to find the name of the salesperson on account number 1950 by joining the two relations? Obviously, that would cause a problem. Similarly, a salesperson record can be deleted, leaving the value referring to it in the customer record with nothing to reference. Or a salesperson's number can be changed in the Salesperson relation without the salesperson's references being changed in the SALESPERSON NUMBER field of the Customer relation.

Referential integrity, ultimately, is an issue in the philosophy of how a particular relational database management system is designed. If there are no built-in controls on referential integrity, then the responsibility falls to the application programmer or end-user who is working with the data. The work of application programmers can be monitored, but it is unrealistic to expect that an end-user who has unrestricted access to the database will always be careful about referential integrity: Some kind of control must be established and built.

By the way, note that under certain application circumstances you may want to modify one relation without modifying logically related relations. For example, you might want to add a new customer to our Customer file without yet specifying who the salesperson is. Or, you might want to specify a salesperson in that new customer record who for some reason does not yet exist in the Salesperson file. A well-designed relational database management system will provide for automated referential integrity maintenance, but will allow an application designer to invoke it or not, depending on the nature of a particular application.

Performance Characteristics

At last it's time to answer the question of why relational DBMSs have only recently become commercially viable. Recall the explanation of the Join command earlier in this chapter and the example in which we joined the two relations of Figure 6.3. As sample relations, the Salesperson relation has only four tuples and the Customer relation has only nine tuples. The thought of comparing every tuple of one of those relations with every tuple of the other to accomplish the join seemed so reasonable that you probably didn't give it a second thought. But what if we attempted to join a 1 million tuple relation with a 3 million tuple relation. How long do you think that would take—even on a large, fast computer? It might well take much longer than a person waiting for a response at a terminal would tolerate.

On the other hand, in a typical relational database application environment, many queries to the database will deal with only one relation and will not require a Join operation at all. It is certainly reasonable to assume that such single file queries should not take any longer in a relational database system than they would in any other kind of file management system. Still, what about the queries that do involve joins? Modern, sophisticated relational database systems rely either on special hardware devices for performance enhancement or on clever software techniques to speed up the join process by, for example, reducing the scope of the join in terms of the number of tuples involved. They also take advantage of the general increase in speed of computer processors that has developed continually over the years. We will discuss the hardware devices in Chapter 16 and the software techniques in Chapter 7, under the Structured Query Language heading.

References

Brown, R. G., "Referential Integrity Checking and SQL," *Database Programming and Design* **1** (3); (March, 1988): 36–45.

Date, C. J., *An Introduction to Database Systems*, 4th ed., vol. I, Addison-Wesley, Reading, MA; 1986.

Date, C. J., *Relational Database: Selected Writings*, Addison-Wesley, Reading, MA; 1986.

IBM Corporation, *IBM DATABASE 2 Relational Concepts*, IBM Form No. GG24-1581 (1983).

Kroenke, D. M., and Dolan, K. A., *Database Processing*, 3rd ed., Science Research Associates, Chicago, IL; 1988.

Questions and Exercises

6.1. What is a relation? What are primary, candidate, and foreign keys?

6.2. What is the distinction between a relational database and an ordinary set of independent linear files?

6.3. How would you compare a relational database management system with a set of application programs that process a set of independent linear files?

6.4. How would you compare a set of application programs that process data within a relational database management system environment with a set of application programs that process a set of independent linear files?

6.5. In your own words, describe the essence of how a relational database management system works.

6.6. Describe the Select operation. What does it accomplish?

6.7. Describe the Project operation. What does it accomplish?

6.8. Refer to the Customer relation in Figure 6.3B and, using the relational command style shown earlier in the chapter, indicate the results of the following commands:

    a. Select tuples from the Customer relation in which CUSTOMER NUMBER = 1047.

    b. Select tuples from the Customer relation in which SALESPERSON NUMBER = 361.

    c. Project the CUSTOMER NUMBER and CITY over the Customer relation.

    d. Project the CITY over the Customer relation.

    e. Select tuples from the Customer relation in which SALESPERSON NUMBER = 137. Project the CUSTOMER NUMBER and CITY over that result.

6.9. Describe the Join operation. What does it accomplish?

6.10. Consider *only the first three rows* of both the Salesperson relation and the Customer relation of Figure 6.3. Using the relational command style shown earlier in the chapter, indicate the results of the following command sequences.

    a. Join the Salesperson relation and the Customer relation, using the SALESPERSON NUMBER of each as the join field. Select tuples from that result in which SALESPERSON NUMBER = 137. Project the SALESPERSON NUMBER, SALESPERSON NAME, CUSTOMER NUMBER, and CITY over that result.

    b. Join the Salesperson relation and the Customer relation, using the SALESPERSON NUMBER of each as the join field. Select tuples from that result in which CITY = Hartford. Project SALES-PERSON NAME over that result.

6.11. Consider the Salesperson relation and the Customer relation of Figure 6.3. Using the relational command style shown earlier in the chapter, write relational statements to answer the following questions.

    a. Find the Salesperson record for Carlyle.

    b. Find the Customer records for all customers in Boston.

    c. Produce a list of all of the customers (by customer number) with the city in which each is located.

    d. Produce a list of the customers (by customer number and city) for which salesperson 186 is responsible.

    e. Produce a list of the customers (by customer number and city) for which salesperson Adams is responsible.

    f. What are the names of the salespersons who have accounts in New York?

7

Structured Query Language (SQL)

SQL Concepts

Introduction

Of the early attempts at creating a relational database language, one has clearly emerged as the industry standard: Structured Query Language, or SQL. SQL is derived from an early IBM research project in relational database called "System R." Many manufacturers have produced versions of SQL that are all quite similar, at least at the level at which we will look at it in this book. SQL has been declared a standard for relational data retrieval languages by the American National Standards Institute (ANSI) and by the International Standards Organization (ISO). Among the many relational database systems incorporating the SQL language are IBM's DB2 and SQL/DS, ORACLE by the company of the same name, Relational Technology's INGRES, and Ashton-Tate's dBASE IV.

As a rule, the systems (at least the mainframe-oriented ones) that incorporate the SQL language are full-fledged DBMSs, with provisions for backup and recovery operations, security checks, and so forth, but these topics will be discussed in general in later chapters, not here. We will concentrate on the language aspects in this chapter. Comprising an introductory chapter in a general database book, the SQL syntax presented here is sufficiently basic to conform to the SQL standard and to all major implementations. In preparation for the SQL language discussion, some structural and processing comments follow.

The SQL Data Structure

There are only a couple of points to mention about the SQL data structure, beyond repeating what by now should be obvious: The data appears to be stored as simple linear files or relations. In the SQL terminology they're called "tables."

Typically, the tables are accessed either sequentially or through indexes. An index can reference one or a combination of columns (in SQL the term "column" is used instead of "field") of a table. A table can have several indexes built over it. An index can reference a column whose values are or are not unique. When the data in a table changes, SQL automatically updates the corresponding data in any indexes that are affected by that change.

The concept of logical versus physical view is implemented in SQL. A physical table is called a "base table." A logical view is called a "view" and is derived from one or more base tables. A view may consist of a subset of the columns of a single table or of two or more joined tables. As is typical of implementations of the concept of a logical view, the creation of a view in SQL does not entail the creation of a new table by physically duplicating data in a base table. Instead, information describing the nature of the view is kept in one of several system "catalogs." If a query references a view (queries can be issued to either base tables or views), the information about the view in the catalog will map it onto the base table where the required data is actually stored.

Also, the latest versions of several of the SQL-based database management systems include some level of system-managed referential integrity checking and protection.

SQL Performance and Query Optimizer Concepts

Many SQL implementations include a query optimizer. Using a query optimizer, SQL attempts to figure out the most efficient way of answering a query, prior to actually responding to it. Clearly, a query that involves only one table should be evaluated to take advantage of aids such as indexes on pertinent fields. But the most compelling and interesting reason for a query optimizer in a relational database system is the goal of executing a multiple table, join-type of operation without having to go through the very time-consuming, exhaustive search process that was described in the previous chapter. In this section, we will discuss SQL performance concepts and relate them to the idea of query optimization.

The performance of a relational system in responding to a query involves a number of factors about the query itself, as well as factors about the data structure, the relational processor, and the computer system. Several of the major factors include whether or not a join operation will be required, whether only a few or most of the records of a particular table will be involved in answering the query, the presence or absence of indexes, the ability of the system to efficiently sort the records of a table, and the availability of a choice of different join algorithms.

Perhaps the foremost and most obvious device for improving performance is the index. SQL implementations are geared towards taking maximum advantage of their indexes. That, of course, makes it incumbent upon the person designing the SQL tables to include an appropriate set of indexes based on the anticipated types of queries. Let's digress for a moment on that point. First of all, remember that SQL will answer queries regardless of whether or not indexes that might speed up the process exist. Secondly, bear in mind that the helter-skelter creation of a large number of indexes may adversely impact performance. If an SQL database is at all volatile, that is, if it has a significant amount of insert, delete, and update activity, then the automatic facility in SQL that updates the indexes will tend to slow down the overall system: The more indexes, the more overall system performance is likely to suffer.

An index may be "clustered" or not. A clustered index is similar in concept to the index in an indexed-sequential file organization. Records with closely spaced values of the clustered indexed field are also located physically near each other on the disk. It should be clear that there can be only one clustered index for a given table because the records can only be physically stored in one order, while the values of the different fields of a table will, in general, exist in a variety of orders. There may, of course, be any number of nonclustered indexes, in addition to the clustered one.

An optimizer should check to see if a query involves columns that have indexes built over them and, if so, note other factors about the column values, such as whether or not they are unique. For many select-type operations it will clearly take advantage of those indexes, going directly to only those records that are required. If a join is involved in the query, the system tries to figure out the way that it can take the greatest advantage of any appropriate indexes. For example, if the query calls for a join operation, and the join columns (join fields) in each table are either in sorted order or have indexes built over them, then comparing every record of one table against every record of the other is unnecessary. The system can simply start at the top of each table (or index, if the table is not in order by the join column) and move downward, keeping track of the current value in each, as if performing a merge operation. In fact, this algorithm is called a "Merge-Scan Join." Another example involves the case where a join requires only a single record from one table, which must be matched against one or many records of another table. Clearly, if that single record from the first table can be found directly with an index, then the system is saved from having to go through all of the records of that table, as it would have to in a brute force join. Our original example of finding the name of the salesperson responsible for a particular customer account is an instance of that case.

A "Nested-Loop Join" can be used when appropriate indexes are not available. One of the two tables is selected for the outer loop, as it were, and the other for the inner loop. Each of the records of the outer loop that are involved in the query are chosen in succession and, for each, the inner loop table is scanned for matches on the join field. The optimizer should take into account the relative lengths (number of records) of the two tables and, if possible, the number of records of each table actually involved in the query, in deciding which table is to be the outer loop table and which the inner.

Note in passing that an SQL system also should check over a query to make sure that it is legitimate in a number of respects. For example, it should check to see that the specified columns are in fact in the specified tables, that the user is authorized to see that data, that numeric columns are not being compared to alphabetic columns, and so forth. All of that information is stored in the collection of system catalogs.

The SQL Language

Introduction

In this section we will explore many of the commands in the SQL language in the context of an example involving a baseball league. The mode of operation will be the ad hoc query mode, as opposed to the embedded language mode, which we will discuss later. So, the situation here is one in which an end user enters these commands directly into a terminal. We also note in passing that any of the commands to be discussed in this section can be "canned" for later use, that is, they can be written, debugged as necessary, stored on disk under a unique name, and then called up by that name for use, when needed. Before we begin the SQL commands, let's take a look at the Baseball League database.

The Baseball League database contains data about baseball teams and players in the major (professional) leagues. Actually, with minor alterations to the data structure, any sport and league could be substituted for baseball. The entities that we are interested in maintaining data about are teams, coaches, coach prior work experiences, bats, and players. A team may have several coaches, a coach may have several prior work experiences, and a team may own several bats (in general, any kind of equipment that a team uses). All three of those situations are one-to-many relationships. Also, a player may have played on several teams during his years in the league, while, naturally, a team will have had many players playing for it over the years. That situation is a many-to-many relationship. The six tables in Figure 7.1 represent the database.

The Teams table contains one record for each team in the league. TEAMNUM is a unique, team number field and serves as the key; the

TEAMNUM	TEAMNAME	TEAMCITY	TEAMMGR
12	Dodgers	Los Angeles	Wilson
15	Giants	San Francisco	Johnson
20	Yankees	New York	Simpson
24	Tigers	Detroit	Corbin

TEAMS Table

TEAMNUM	COACHNAM	COACHPH
12	Adams	555-1524
12	Baker	555-3690
15	Taylor	555-4820
20	Jackson	555-2444
24	Victor	555-9327
24	Dooley	555-7321

COACHES Table

TEAMNUM	COACHNAM	EXPTYPE	EXPYRS
12	Adams	High School Coach	5
12	Adams	College Coach	10
12	Baker	College Coach	3
12	Baker	Japan League Coach	2
12	Baker	Minor League Coach	4
15	Taylor	College Coach	15
24	Victor	Minor League Coach	12

WORKEXP Table

TEAMNUM	BATNUM	MANUF
12	B01	Acme
12	B09	General
12	B13	Acme
15	B01	Acme
20	B03	United
20	B04	Modern
24	B18	General
24	B21	United

BATS Table

Figure 7.1.   The Baseball relational database.

PLAYNUM   PLAYNAME   AGE

PLAYNUM	PLAYNAME	AGE
358	Stevens	21
523	Doe	32
1131	Johnson	28
1779	Jones	25
2007	Dobbs	27
4280	Cohen	25
4319	Ross	24
5410	Smith	27
6564	Linton	24
8093	Smith	21
8366	Gomez	33

PLAYERS Table

PLAYNUM   TEAMNUM   YEARS   BATAVG

PLAYNUM	TEAMNUM	YEARS	BATAVG
358	15	5	0.300
358	20	3	0.320
523	12	10	0.257
1131	20	1	0.283
1779	12	1	0.223
1779	15	7	0.246
1779	24	2	0.240
2007	24	3	0.290
4280	15	1	0.195
4280	20	3	0.227
4319	15	4	0.298
5410	12	6	0.307
6564	20	12	0.310
6564	24	3	0.280
8093	12	5	0.250
8093	20	2	0.240
8093	24	8	0.265
8366	20	7	0.283

AFFILIATION Table

Figure 7.1.   (*continued*) The Baseball relational database.

other three fields are attributes representing the name, home city, and manager of each team.

The Coaches table contains one record for each coach in the league. It is assumed that a coach must be associated with a team. The only identifier for a coach is his last name, which may not be unique. Thus, with the assumption that a team will not have two coaches with the same last name, TEAMNUM is included as a field in the Coaches table so that the combination of TEAMNUM and COACHNAM serves as a unique identifier or key for the records of the table. Since the TEAMNUM field is the key of the Teams table, it is said to serve as a foreign key in the Coaches table. In fact, its presence in the Coaches table is what establishes the one-to-many relationship between teams and coaches. An additional attribute is the coach's telephone number.

The Workexp table lists the work experiences that each coach had before going to work for a major league team. Carrying forward the reasoning from the Coaches table, the unique identifier or key is the combination of the fields for team number, coach name, and experience type. The key of the COACHES table, which is the combination of the TEAMNUM and COACHNAM fields, is a foreign key in the Workexp table and establishes the one-to-many relationship between coaches and their prior work experiences. The number of years that a coach had a particular type of experience is an additional attribute.

The Bats table lists the bats used by each team. BATNUM is a bat serial number that is unique only within a given team. Thus, TEAMNUM is again included to form a unique identifier or key with BATNUM and to establish the one-to-many relationship between teams and bats. The manufacturer of the bat is an additional attribute.

The Players table lists the players in the league, independently of any team that they might be playing on now or have played on in the past. PLAYNUM is the unique, player number key field while the player's name and age are additional attributes.

The many-to-many relationship between teams and players requires an additional table, the Affiliation table. The key of the Affiliation table is the combination of the unique identifiers of the two entities involved in the many-to-many relationship: the PLAYNUM and TEAMNUM fields. The number of years that a player played on a team and the batting average that the player compiled during those years are intersection data that further describe the many-to-many relationship. They become additional attributes in the Affiliation table.

SQL Simple Single Table Retrievals

Let's begin with some simple select- and project-type commands. Actually, all of the retrieval type commands in SQL, including those that we have previously spoken of as "Select," "Project," and "Join," will be performed with the SELECT command. For clarity we will indent and place different parts of the commands on different lines, although SQL commands can be written as a continuous string at a display terminal. To retrieve the entire Teams table you would issue:

```
SELECT *
  FROM TEAMS
```

Literally translated this says "Display all (*) columns in the Teams table." By default, since no further restrictions are specified, all of the records of the table are involved. The result would look exactly like the Teams table in Figure 7.1 (which is reasonable, since the result of a relational query is a relation itself):

TEAMNUM	TEAMNAME	TEAMCITY	TEAMMGR
12	Dodgers	Los Angeles	Wilson
15	Giants	San Francisco	Johnson
20	Yankees	New York	Simpson
24	Tigers	Detroit	Corbin

To select a single record by identifying a value of a unique column, for example, "Find the record for team number 12," you would issue:

```
SELECT *
  FROM TEAMS
  WHERE TEAMNUM = 12
```

The WHERE clause is used to limit the horizontal slice through the table, causing a subset of the records to be retrieved. In this case, the column whose value is specified is a unique column, and so only one record will be retrieved:

TEAMNUM	TEAMNAME	TEAMCITY	TEAMMGR
12	Dodgers	Los Angeles	Wilson

A simple project operation, "List the team number and team name of all teams," would look like this:

```
SELECT TEAMNUM, TEAMNAME
  FROM TEAMS
```

The column names immediately after the SELECT key word are the columns that are to be retrieved:

TEAMNUM	TEAMNAME
12	Dodgers
15	Giants
20	Yankees
24	Tigers

To combine a simple select and project, for example, "Find the player number and player name of all players who are over 30 years of age," you would issue:

```
SELECT PLAYNUM, PLAYNAME
   FROM PLAYERS
   WHERE AGE>30
```

Notice that the WHERE clause is quite flexible, allowing the full range of comparison operators. Incidentally, if this statement were embedded in a program, we could replace the constant "30" with a variable whose value would have been set earlier in the program. The result in this case is:

PLAYNUM	PLAYNAME
523	Doe
8366	Gomez

Multiple conditions can be combined in a SELECT statement. If you want a list of the coaches who have been college coaches for more than 5 years, you would issue:

```
SELECT TEAMNUM, COACHNAM
   FROM WORKEXP
   WHERE EXPTYPE = 'College Coach'
   AND EXPYRS > 5
```

The result is:

TEAMNUM	COACHNAM
12	Adams
15	Taylor

Similarly, if you want a list of the work experience records that either involve college coaching or reflect a period of more than ten years (or both), you would issue:

```
SELECT *
  FROM WORKEXP
  WHERE EXPTYPE = 'College Coach'
  OR EXPYRS > 10
```

The result is:

TEAMNUM	COACHNAM	EXPTYPE	EXPYRS
12	Adams	College Coach	10
12	Baker	College Coach	3
15	Taylor	College Coach	15
24	Victor	Minor League Coach	12

Projecting over a nonunique column may yield duplicate entries in the result. For example, if you want a list of the teams, by team number, that use bats manufactured by the Acme Company you would issue:

```
SELECT TEAMNUM
  FROM BATS
  WHERE MANUF = 'Acme'
```

and the result would be:

TEAMNUM
12
12
15

In a case like this you are clearly not interested in duplicates so you add the word "distinct":

```
SELECT DISTINCT TEAMNUM
  FROM BATS
  WHERE MANUF = 'Acme'
```

and get:

TEAMNUM
12
15

Next is an example that demonstrates that the records selected can be limited by a range of column values and ordered by the values of any column. To get the player records of those players between the ages of 25 and 29 and order those records by age, you would issue:

```
SELECT *
  FROM PLAYERS
  WHERE AGE BETWEEN 25 AND 29
  ORDER BY AGE
```

The result is:

PLAYNUM	PLAYNAME	AGE
1779	Jones	25
4280	Cohen	25
2007	Dobbs	27
5410	Smith	27
1131	Johnson	28

Records can be selected based on the values of one of their columns being in a specified set. If you want a list of the bats that were manufactured by either the General Company or the United Company and the teams that use them, you would issue:

```
SELECT *
  FROM BATS
  WHERE MANUF IN ('General', 'United')
```

and get as a result:

TEAMNUM	BATNUM	MANUF
12	B09	General
20	B03	United
24	B18	General
24	B21	United

Records also can be retrieved based on the commonality of only a part of the values of a column. For instance, to satisfy the query, "Find the records for all of the players whose last names begin with the letter "S," you would issue:

```
SELECT *
  FROM PLAYERS
  WHERE PLAYNAME LIKE 'S%'
```

The result is:

```
PLAYNUM   PLAYNAME      AGE
-------   --------      ---
    358   Stevens        21
   5410   Smith          27
   8093   Smith          21
```

The above result is based on the percent sign substituting for an arbitrary-length string beyond the leading "S." If one or more underscores (_) are used instead of the percent sign, then the match is based on exactly as many unknown characters as there are underscore characters.

SQL Built-In Functions

Numeric Functions.   A number of built-in functions give the SQL language additional capabilities. To get a count of the number of records in a table—for example, to find the number of teams in the league—you would issue:

```
SELECT COUNT(*)
  FROM TEAMS
```

The result is shown as:

```
COUNT(EXPRESSION 1)
-------------------
         4
```

Another variation on that theme is to count the number of distinct values in a particular column in a table. For example, if you want to find the number of different manufacturers of bats who supply the league, you would issue:

```
SELECT COUNT(DISTINCT MANUF)
  FROM BATS
```

which produces:

```
COUNT(DISTINCT MANUF)
---------------------
          4
```

A count can be guided by a WHERE clause, too. To satisfy the query, "Find the number of players over age 30," you would issue:

```
SELECT COUNT(*)
  FROM PLAYERS
  WHERE AGE>30
```

which produces:

```
COUNT(EXPRESSION 1)
_____

         2
```

Other special features of the same general type as COUNT include finding the sum of several numbers, their average, and the maximum and minimum values among them. For example, to find the total number of years of experience that coach Adams of the Dodgers (team number 12) has, you would issue:

```
SELECT SUM(EXPYRS)
  FROM WORKEXP
  WHERE TEAMNUM = 12
  AND COACHNAM = 'Adams'
```

The system would reply:

```
SUM(EXPYRS)
_____

     15
```

Grouping.   You might want to perform one of these operations on several *subsets* of the records of a table *independently*. For example, you might want to know the total number of years of prior experience of each of the coaches in the league. That is, you want to divide the records of the table into several groups (each group representing a different coach) and make some kind of calculation (sum the values of the EXPYRS field) within each group. To accomplish that, you would use the "Group By" feature and issue:

```
SELECT TEAMNUM, COACHNAM, SUM(EXPYRS)
  FROM WORKEXP
  GROUP BY TEAMNUM, COACHNAM
```

The result would be:

TEAMNUM	COACHNAM	SUM(EXPYRS)
12	Adams	15
12	Baker	9
15	Taylor	15
24	Victor	12

Note that the resultant table contains one record for each coach, as expected.

Just as the WHERE clause can be used to choose certain records from a table, the HAVING clause can be used to choose certain groups from the result of a GROUP BY operation. For example, to list the coaches who have more than 10 years of experience, you would modify the last command to read:

```
SELECT TEAMNUM, COACHNAM, SUM(EXPYRS)
   FROM WORKEXP
   GROUP BY TEAMNUM, COACHNAM
   HAVING SUM(EXPYRS)>10
```

The result would be:

TEAMNUM	COACHNAM	SUM(EXPYRS)
12	Adams	15
15	Taylor	15
24	Victor	12

SQL Multiple Table Retrievals

Introduction to Joins. Let's present a join operation and then discuss it. The command for a join between the Coaches and Teams tables would be written as:

```
SELECT COACHES.*, TEAMS.*
   FROM COACHES, TEAMS
   WHERE TEAMS.TEAMNUM = COACHES.TEAMNUM
```

and would produce:

TEAMNUM	COACHNAM	COACHPH	TEAMNUM	TEAMNAME	TEAMCITY	TEAMMGR
12	Adams	555-1524	12	Dodgers	Los Angeles	Wilson
12	Baker	555-3690	12	Dodgers	Los Angeles	Wilson
15	Taylor	555-4820	15	Giants	San Francisco	Johnson
20	Jackson	555-2444	20	Yankees	New York	Simpson
24	Victor	555-9327	24	Tigers	Detroit	Corbin
24	Dooley	555-7321	24	Tigers	Detroit	Corbin

Notice the following points about the command: The expression FROM COACHES, TEAMS indicates that there are two tables involved in this command. The expression WHERE TEAMS.TEAMNUM = COACHES. TEAMNUM defines the join column to be the team number column in each of the two tables. The use of the syntax "table.column" distinguishes exactly which column is being referred to in the case where columns in different tables have the same column name. The expression SELECT COACHES.*, TEAMS.* indicates that the join will be an equijoin: all of the columns from both tables (the join column twice) will appear in the result. In fact, we could simply have written SELECT *.

As another variation, a join can involve all of the columns of both tables, but only a subset of the records. For example, you can join the Coaches and Teams tables for just those records that involve the Dodgers:

```
SELECT COACHES.*, TEAMS.*
  FROM COACHES, TEAMS
  WHERE TEAMS.TEAMNUM = COACHES.TEAMNUM
  AND TEAMNAME = 'Dodgers'
```

The result of this command is:

```
TEAMNUM COACHNAM COACHPH    TEAMNUM TEAMNAME TEAMCITY      TEAMMGR
─────── ──────── ───────    ─────── ──────── ───────────── ───────
     12 Adams    555-1524        12 Dodgers  Los Angeles  Wilson
     12 Baker    555-3690        12 Dodgers  Los Angeles  Wilson
```

Practical Use of Joins.   Let's begin to look at some practical examples of the use of the join facility. The query, "Find the names of the coaches on the Dodgers," is similar to the earlier, "Find the name of the salesperson on a particular account." The difference is that there was just one salesperson, but there may be several coaches. In this example, the coach names appear in a different table from the one with the "Dodgers" reference, which is the same sort of situation that we had in the salespersons and customers files. Your command would be:

```
SELECT COACHNAM
  FROM COACHES, TEAMS
  WHERE TEAMS.TEAMNUM = COACHES.TEAMNUM
  AND TEAMNAME = 'Dodgers'
```

which would result in:

```
COACHNAM
────────
Adams
Baker
```

How about, "List the league's coaches, their telephone numbers, and the *names* of the teams that they're on"?

```
SELECT COACHNAM, COACHPH, TEAMNAME
   FROM COACHES, TEAMS
   WHERE TEAMS.TEAMNUM = COACHES.TEAMNUM
```

The result is:

COACHNAM	COACHPH	TEAMNAME
Adams	555–1524	Dodgers
Baker	555–3690	Dodgers
Taylor	555–4820	Giants
Jackson	555–2444	Yankees
Victor	555–9327	Tigers
Dooley	555–7321	Tigers

Here's one that involves the join of three tables: Suppose you are asked to list the player numbers and names of the players who have played on the Dodgers, and include the number of years that they played on the Dodgers and the batting average they compiled. The information about which players have played on which teams exists only in the Affiliation table. This is reasonable, since it involves a many-to-many relationship and would introduce redundancy if there was an attempt to combine it into either the Teams or Players tables. The years and batting average data, describing the relationship between a particular player and a particular team, also belongs in the Affiliation table. But the player names appear only in the Player table and the team name, Dodgers, appears only in the Teams table. What you have to do in this situation is join the Teams and Affiliation tables using the TEAMNUM column as the join column and join the Players and Affiliation tables using the PLAYNUM column as the join column. Your command would look like this:

```
SELECT PLAYERS.PLAYNUM, PLAYNAME, YEARS, BATAVG
   FROM PLAYERS, AFFILIATION, TEAMS
   WHERE PLAYERS.PLAYNUM = AFFILIATION.PLAYNUM
   AND AFFILIATION.TEAMNUM = TEAMS.TEAMNUM
   AND TEAMNAME = 'Dodgers'
```

and the result would be:

PLAYNUM	PLAYNAME	YEARS	BATAVG
523	Doe	10	0.257
1779	Jones	1	0.223
5410	Smith	6	0.307
8093	Smith	5	0.250

As a final example of a join, suppose you were asked to find the age of the oldest player on the Dodgers. Again, this request requires a three table join to satisfy it. The name "Dodgers" appears only in the Teams table, the age data appears only in the Players table, and the connection between those two is maintained in the Affiliation table. You would issue:

```
SELECT MAX(AGE)
  FROM PLAYERS, AFFILIATION, TEAMS
  WHERE PLAYERS.PLAYNUM = AFFILIATION.PLAYNUM
  AND AFFILIATION.TEAMNUM = TEAMS.TEAMNUM
  AND TEAMNAME = 'Dodgers'
```

which produces:

```
MAX(AGE)
————————
     32
```

Subqueries.   Another syntax variation is known as a "subquery." It allows the nesting of SQL commands so that the table that results from one SQL command can then be queried by another SQL command. For example, take the query, "Find the names and telephone numbers of the coaches on the Dodgers." As you are now aware, this could be accomplished by issuing a join-type command. But it could also be answered with a subquery-type command. In the following subquery-type command, the second SELECT statement will be executed first, because it is within the innermost set of parentheses. It will find the team number for Dodgers. This result will then be operated on by the first SELECT statement, which will find the name and telephone number of the coaches on that team (the Dodgers).

```
SELECT COACHNAM, COACHPH
  FROM COACHES
  WHERE TEAMNUM IN
  (SELECT TEAMNUM
    FROM TEAMS
    WHERE TEAMNAME = 'Dodgers')
```

The result of this query is:

```
COACHNAM   COACHPH
————————   ————————

Adams      555-1524
Baker      555-3690
```

What about a query that requires a comparison to a value that is derived from all of the records of the table? For example, "Find the players who are older than the average age of all of the players." Such a query requires a subquery. The average age must be determined first and then used in the comparison:

```
SELECT *
  FROM PLAYERS
  WHERE AGE>
  (SELECT AVG(AGE)
    FROM PLAYERS)
```

The result of this query is:

PLAYNUM	PLAYNAME	AGE
523	DOE	32
1131	JOHNSON	28
2007	DOBBS	27
5410	SMITH	27
8366	GOMEZ	33

The average age is, in fact, 26 and a fraction.

There are several other variations involving subqueries, one of which uses the keyword ANY. In this case, the query checks to see if there is *any* (i.e., at least one) record among those with a common value in a particular field that satisfies a particular condition. Using this kind of formulation, the syntax for the query, "Find the names and numbers of the players who played on at least 1 team for 5 years or more," looks like this:

```
SELECT PLAYNUM, PLAYNAME
  FROM PLAYERS
  WHERE PLAYNUM = ANY
  (SELECT PLAYNUM
    FROM AFFILIATION
    WHERE YEARS>=5)
```

The result of this query is:

PLAYNUM	PLAYNAME
358	STEVENS
523	DOE
1779	JONES
5410	SMITH
6564	LINTON
8093	SMITH
8366	GOMEZ

Notice that the above query triggers the selection of a record with a particular player number from the Players table, based on the presence of at least one record with that player number in the Affiliation table satisfying some condition.

SQL Update, Delete, and Insert Operations

The three data manipulation operations are straightforward, except for the question of data integrity. For example, remember that the system will not stop you from entering a record in the Coaches table with a team number for which there is no corresponding team record in the Teams table. It is up to the users of the system to maintain their own data integrity in this sense.

Update.   The first of the data manipulation commands is UPDATE. If the Dodgers move back to Brooklyn and change their manager to Malloy, you would issue the following to update the Teams table:

```
UPDATE TEAMS
   SET TEAMCITY = 'Brooklyn',
   TEAMMGR = 'Malloy'
   WHERE TEAMNAME = 'Dodgers'
```

The Teams table would then look like:

TEAMNUM	TEAMNAME	TEAMCITY	TEAMMGR
12	Dodgers	Brooklyn	Malloy
15	Giants	San Francisco	Johnson
20	Yankees	New York	Simpson
24	Tigers	Detroit	Corbin

Several records can be changed at once through such an operation too. If the Acme Company changes its name to the Royal Company and you want to reflect this change in the Bats table, you would issue:

```
UPDATE BATS
   SET MANUF = 'Royal',
   WHERE MANUF = 'Acme'
```

The Bats table would then look like this:

TEAMNUM	BATNUM	MANUF
12	B01	Royal
12	B09	General
12	B13	Royal
15	B01	Royal
20	B03	United
20	B04	Modern
24	B18	General
24	B21	United

Delete.   Suppose the Dodgers dissolve and you want to delete them from the Teams table (here again, you yourself have to manage what happens to references to them in other tables). You would issue:

```
DELETE
 FROM TEAMS
 WHERE TEAMNAME = 'Dodgers'
```

The remainder of the Teams table would be:

TEAMNUM	TEAMNAME	TEAMCITY	TEAMMGR
15	Giants	San Francisco	Johnson
20	Yankees	New York	Simpson
24	Tigers	Detroit	Corbin

If the WHERE clause had specified a nonunique value, then several records would have been deleted.

Insert.   To insert the Cardinals into the Teams table you would issue:

```
INSERT
 INTO TEAMS
 VALUES (17, 'Cardinals', 'St. Louis', 'Gregory')
```

The Teams table (assuming that it appeared as in Figure 7.1 at the time you issued this command) would then look like:

TEAMNUM	TEAMNAME	TEAMCITY	TEAMMGR
12	Dodgers	Los Angeles	Wilson
15	Giants	San Francisco	Johnson
20	Yankees	New York	Simpson
24	Tigers	Detroit	Corbin
17	Cardinals	St. Louis	Gregory

While this table is no longer in sorted order, remember that if (as would probably be the case) there was an index over the TEAMNUM column, the system would automatically insert the value 17 (with a pointer to the Cardinals record in the Teams table) into that index in sorted order. The index would then provide properly sorted access to the file.

SQL Maintenance Commands

A variety of other database maintenance-type commands fill out the SQL language. Some of the more prominent ones are discussed in this section.

Table Creation. CREATE TABLE creates the structure for a new table. The command must include the table name, the names of the fields that are to make up the table, and the data types of the fields. For example, to initially create the Players table, you would issue:

```
CREATE TABLE PLAYERS
    (PLAYNUM SMALLINT,
    PLAYNAME CHAR(12),
    AGE SMALLINT)
```

This example illustrates the "small integer" and "character" data types. There are several others, depending on the implementation, usually including FLOAT for "floating point."

Table Deletion. DROP TABLE destroys existing tables. To delete the entire Teams table you would issue:

```
DROP TABLE TEAMS
```

View Creation. CREATE VIEW creates a logical view of a base table or of a joined combination of base tables. Once the base table or tables to be involved in the view are chosen, there are three further kinds of choices to make: the columns of the base table(s) to be included in the view, whether those columns are to have the same names in the view as they do in the base table(s) or different names, and whether all or only a subset of the records of the base table(s) are to be accessible through the view. The syntax of CREATE VIEW is similar to that of the SELECT command. For example, suppose you want to create a view over the Players base table, called YOUNG_PLAYERS. The only columns to be visible in the view are PLAYNUM, which is now to be called NUMBER, and AGE. The only player records to be visible are those of players under 25 years of age. The command would be:

```
CREATE VIEW YOUNG_PLAYERS (NUMBER, AGE)
    AS
    SELECT (PLAYNUM, AGE)
        FROM PLAYERS
        WHERE AGE<25
```

Granting Authority to Others. GRANT is a command that gives you the latitude to allow others to work with tables that you have created. Exactly how the SQL system identifies you and others in the environment is an implementation-specific detail that we will not address here. Nevertheless, the GRANT command allows you to specify *what* can be done to *which* tables, by *whom*. For example, if you want a user named Miller to be able to retrieve and update data in the Teams table, you would issue:

```
GRANT SELECT, UPDATE ON TEAMS TO MILLER
```

Index Creation. CREATE INDEX creates an index on one or a combination of columns of a table. For example, to create an index called Numbers on the TEAMNUM column of the Teams table, you would issue:

```
CREATE INDEX NUMBERS
   ON TEAMS(TEAMNUM).
```

Embedded SQL

We have been discussing the use of SQL commands as ad hoc query commands, but SQL commands can also be issued as data access commands embedded in COBOL, FORTRAN, PL/I, or Assembler Language programs. The concept is straightforward. At the appropriate point in the logic of the program when data from a file must be brought into the program for processing, an SQL command is issued to accomplish it. SQL's powerful retrieval capabilities can thus be used even within a traditional type of programming language. The command syntax in the embedded mode is basically the same as in the query mode, except that some additional devices are required to compensate for the differences between the nature of SQL ad hoc queries and the programming language environment.

The main point regards SQL's "set-at-a-time" retrieval style, as opposed to a traditional application programming language's "record-at-a-time" processing style. Traditional applications process one record, then another record, and so on, through a collection of like-structured records. But since the result of an SQL query is a relation, SQL is capable of retrieving what in effect are several, possibly many, records with one command. In the ad hoc query mode that seems quite natural, as the end user can peruse the resultant relation on the screen. However, a traditional program that uses SQL as a means of retrieving data must be able to separate the individual records retrieved by a single SQL command and process each one individually.

To accomplish the processing of the result of an SQL query in an application program, a new command called FETCH is added. Using a new device called a "cursor," FETCH is capable of accessing one record of a resultant relation (the "active set" of the records), at a time for processing, normally within a loop in an application program. A sample of the syntax for such a FETCH statement is:

```
EXEC SQL FETCH cursor INTO variable-1, variable-2, ...
```

Each time this statement is executed, the cursor (a uniquely named variable) is moved to point to the next record in the active set and that record is prepared for processing by having its field values assigned to application program variables variable-1, variable-2, ...

References

Ageloff, R., *A Primer on SQL*, Times Mirror/Mosby, St. Louis, MO; 1988.

Cheng, J. M.; Loosley, C. R.; Shibamiya, A.; and Worthington, P. S., "IBM Database 2 Performance: Design, Implementation, and Tuning," *IBM Systems Journal* **23** (2), (1984): 189–210.

Date, C. J., and White, C. J., *A Guide to DB2*, 2nd ed., Addison-Wesley, Reading, MA, 1988.

Date, C. J., and White, C. J., *A Guide to SQL/DS*, Addison-Wesley, Reading, MA; 1989.

Date, C. J., *A Guide to the SQL Standard*, Addison-Wesley, Reading, MA; 1987.

Haderle, D. J., and Jackson, R. D., "IBM Database 2 Overview," *IBM Systems Journal* **23** (2), (1984): 112–125.

IBM Corporation, *IBM DATABASE 2 General Information*, IBM Form No. GC26-4073 (1986).

IBM Corporation, *IBM DATABASE 2 Reference*, IBM Form No. SC26-4078 (1986).

IBM Corporation, *IBM DATABASE 2 Relational Concepts*, IBM Form No. GG24-1581 (1983).

IBM Corporation, *IBM DATABASE 2 SQL Learner's Guide*, IBM Form No. SC26-4082 (1987).

IBM Corporation, *IBM DATABASE 2 SQL Reference*, IBM Form No. SC26-4346 (1987).

IBM Corporation, *IBM DATABASE 2 VERSION 2 SQL User's Guide*, IBM Form No. SC26-4376 (1988).

Trimble, J. H. Jr., and Chappell, D., *A Visual Introduction to SQL*, Wiley, New York; 1989.

Wiorkowski, G., and Kull, D., "The Optimizer: Invisible Hand of the DBMS," *Database Programming and Design* **1** (9), (September, 1988): 26–33.

Questions and Exercises

7.1. Outline the concepts behind the optimizer in the IBM SQL system. Are there other ways you can think of to improve relational database performance?

The following four relations, which constitute an appliance repair company's database, will be used in all of the following questions about SQL. The company maintains data on its technicians (employee number, name, and title); the types of appliances that it services, along with the hourly billing rate to repair each; the specific appliances (by serial number) for which it has sold repair contracts; and which technicians are qualified to service which types of appliances (including the number of years that a technician has been qualified on a particular appliance type).

TECHNUM	TECHNAME	TITLE
062	Regan	Senior
297	Mercer	Trainee
553	Hewitt	Senior
718	Stein	Staff

Technicians relation.

APPLTYPE   CATEGORY   RATE

APPLTYPE	CATEGORY	RATE
Washer	Major	20
Dryer	Major	20
Toaster	Minor	10
Blender	Minor	8
Freezer	Major	25

Types relation.

APPLNUM   APPLTYPE   AGE   OWNER

APPLNUM	APPLTYPE	AGE	OWNER
00730	Toaster	5	M. Peters
08331	Freezer	7	R. Carr
16365	Freezer	3	S. Small
22770	Blender	1	C. Ramos
40034	Washer	10	S. Small
47222	Dryer	12	S. Small
49371	Freezer	9	N. Rice
58449	Toaster	7	L. Shaw
60558	Washer	3	M. Peters
72589	Washer	7	S. Bauer

Appliances relation.

TECHNUM   APPLTYPE   YRSQUAL

TECHNUM	APPLTYPE	YRSQUAL
533	Dryer	15
062	Washer	18
297	Toaster	1
297	Dryer	1
718	Washer	5
553	Freezer	12
062	Blender	14
062	Freezer	10
062	Dryer	12

Types relation.

7.2. Using the appliance repair company database, translate the following SQL commands to English (or your national language) and indicate their results with the data shown.

a. SELECT *
        FROM TECHNICIANS
        WHERE TITLE = 'Senior'

b. SELECT APPLNUM, OWNER, AGE
        FROM APPLIANCES
        WHERE APPLTYPE = 'Freezer'
        ORDER BY AGE

c. SELECT APPLTYPE, OWNER
        FROM APPLIANCES
        WHERE AGE BETWEEN 5 AND 10

d. SELECT COUNT(*)
        FROM TECHNICIANS

e. SELECT AVG(RATE)
        FROM TYPES
        WHERE CATEGORY = 'Major'

f. SELECT CATEGORY, AVG(RATE)
        FROM TYPES
        GROUP BY CATEGORY

g. SELECT APPLNUM, OWNER
        FROM TYPES, APPLIANCES
        WHERE TYPES.APPLTYPE = APPLIANCES.APPLTYPE
        AND CATEGORY = 'Minor'

h. SELECT APPLNUM, OWNER
   FROM TECHNICIANS, QUALIFICATION, APPLIANCES
   WHERE TECHNICIANS.TECHNUM = QUALIFICATION.TECHNUM
   AND QUALIFICATION.APPLTYPE = APPLIANCES. APPLTYPE
   AND TECHNAME = 'Hewitt'

7.3. Formulate SQL commands to answer the following requests for data from the appliance repair company database. Use good judgment in deciding which fields are required in the response.

a. Which are the major appliances?

b. Who owns freezers?

c. What are the serial numbers and ages of the toasters on service contracts?

d. What is the average age of the washers on service contracts?

e. Whose homes might Stein have to visit?

f. How many different job titles are represented?

g. What is the average age of each owner's major appliances?

h. Whose freezers are over 6 years old?

i. What is the average billing rate for the major appliances that Regan is qualified to fix?

j. What is the name of the technician who is most qualified to fix freezers?

8

Other Relational Tools

Introduction

Even though SQL is now the clear standard in relational query languages, the story of query interfaces to relational databases is not over. There are several practical reasons for this situation. One is historical: There were relational query products that were commercially available either before SQL or at the same time as its early, limited commercial use. Another is ease of use: There are those who argue that other relational query interfaces are easier to use than SQL, at least by some people in certain circumstances. Still another is that there is a class of products that go beyond SQL's ability to pleasingly format output. Such products are capable of taking the results of an SQL query and reformatting them for presentation purposes.

In this chapter we will look at three products, each of which represents one or more of the three classes just described. Query-by-Example (QBE) is a two-dimensional query interface to relational databases. It was originally developed by the IBM Corporation, but the basic idea has now been incorporated into the products of a number of software vendors. While QBE was originally marketed by IBM as a stand-alone product, we will focus our discussion of it in this chapter on its implementation within the QMF umbrella. Query Management Facility (QMF) is an IBM product that serves as a report writing umbrella over both its SQL and QBE interfaces. dBASE III+ and dBASE IV are products of Ashton-Tate Corporation. They are personal computer database software products that contain a variety of query, report writing, and other facilities. dBASE IV includes an implementation of SQL. (A fourth relational database product, the database component of the IBM AS/400 computer system, will be discussed in Chapter 9 because of its historical derivation from an earlier pseudo-relational database product.)

Query-by-Example (QBE)

Introduction

Query-by-Example was IBM's first commercially offered relational query language and was one of the first in the industry. Its highly innovative user interface also sets it apart from other relational systems. In fact, over time, other vendors have produced query languages that look similar to QBE in interface style. The version of QBE that we will look at in this chapter is the one found in IBM's Query Management Facility (QMF) product.

The user interface, designed for technical and nontechnical people alike, is a two-dimensional, on-line, video display terminal oriented query facility. In fact, as you begin to look at the QBE format, you will note the difference between its pictorial approach and SQL's linear, more textual approach. (In practice, it has been found that some people prefer one and some the other style.) The user begins by specifying which table(s) is needed for a particular query. If the user is not sure about that, then the system can provide him or her with a list of the available tables and their descriptions. Once a table(s) is chosen, the system displays an outline of that table, showing the table name and the names of its fields. To issue a query, the user gives an *example* of the required information, which amounts to specifying a variable name in the column of the desired information. The user also specifies any limiting factors in that and other columns, either in the same table or, in certain circumstances, in a special "condition box." To execute a join operation, the user brings the required tables onto the screen simultaneously and identifies the join fields by specifying the same variable name under the appropriate join field columns. The query results can either be displayed and scrolled or printed.

We will describe QBE further in the context of our familiar baseball example in Figure 7.1. In fact, we will follow the same sequence of queries that we used in discussing SQL. As you read through this section, you might want to refer back to the SQL section to see the comparison of how the same queries are handled in QBE and SQL.

QBE Simple Single Table Retrievals

To begin, let's retrieve the entire Teams table. To do this in QBE, you must have a skeleton of the Teams table on the screen. You can accomplish this by simply typing the name of the table into a blank skeleton. If you didn't know the name of the table you were interested in, QBE would present you with a list of the tables that you have access to and you could peruse them as necessary. The skeleton of the Teams table looks like this:

TEAMS	TEAMNUM	TEAMNAME	TEAMCITY	TEAMMGR

Notice that the first "column" heading is not a field but indicates the name of the table, Teams.

To display the contents of the entire table you enter "P." (which originally stood for "print") under the table name (all of the QBE commands begin with a command letter followed by a period):

TEAMS	TEAMNUM	TEAMNAME	TEAMCITY	TEAMMGR
P.				

The result is shown as:

TEAMNUM	TEAMNAME	TEAMCITY	TEAMMGR
12	Dodgers	Los Angeles	Wilson
15	Giants	San Francisco	Johnson
20	Yankees	New York	Simpson
24	Tigers	Detroit	Corbin

To find just the record for team number 12, you would limit the search in the table, quite literally by specifying that you are interested only in that team number:

TEAMS	TEAMNUM	TEAMNAME	TEAMCITY	TEAMMGR
P.	12			

The result would then be:

TEAMNUM	TEAMNAME	TEAMCITY	TEAMMGR
12	Dodgers	Los Angeles	Wilson

To project out only the team numbers and names, you specify the P. command under just those fields that you're interested in, instead of under the table name:

TEAMS	TEAMNUM	TEAMNAME	TEAMCITY	TEAMMGR
	P.	P.		

Then you get:

TEAMNUM	TEAMNAME
12	Dodgers
15	Giants
20	Yankees
24	Tigers

To find the numbers and names of the players who are over 30 years of age you would specify in the skeleton for the Players table:

PLAYERS	PLAYNUM	PLAYNAME	AGE
	P.	P.	>30

This yields:

PLAYNUM	PLAYNAME
523	Doe
8366	Gomez

Switching to the work experience (Workexp) table, you can get a list of the coaches who have been college coaches for more than 5 years by specifying:

WORKEXP	TEAMNUM	COACHNAM	EXPTYPE	EXPYRS
	P.	P.	College Coach	>5

Since writing two conditions on the same row of a skeleton table requires that they both be satisfied (an "AND" condition), this yields:

TEAMNUM	COACHNAM
12	Adams
15	Taylor

On the other hand, if you want a list of the work experience records that either involve college coaching or reflect a period of more than 10 years, or both, you would specify:

WORKEXP	TEAMNUM	COACHNAM	EXPTYPE	EXPYRS
P.			College Coach	
P.				>10

Writing two conditions on different rows of a skeleton table in this fashion yields an "OR" effect with the result here being:

TEAMNUM	COACHNAM	EXPTYPE	EXPYRS
12	Adams	College Coach	10
12	Baker	College Coach	3
15	Taylor	College Coach	15
24	Victor	Minor League Coach	12

To find the teams that use bats manufactured by the Acme Company, you would specify:

BATS	TEAMNUM	BATNUM	MANUF
UNQ.	P.		Acme

The UNQ. operator (which is the default) eliminates duplicate tuples in a result and so this query yields:

TEAMNUM
12
15

If you did want to get an indication of all of the records involving the Acme Company, again with only the team number in the output (although that doesn't make all that much sense in this example) you would have specified:

BATS	TEAMNUM	BATNUM	MANUF
ALL.	P.		Acme

and gotten:

TEAMNUM
12
12
15

Remember the query in the SQL section of this chapter that involved finding the players between the ages of 25 and 29 and ordering the results by age? Since both of these specifications involve age, and writing them under the AGE column in the Players skeleton would be somewhat complex, you may form part of the query in a special "Conditions Box":

PLAYERS	PLAYNUM	PLAYNAME	AGE
P.			AO._OLD

CONDITIONS
_OLD BETWEEN 25 AND 29

Notice that the "P." command has returned to a position under the table name because the result must include all of the columns in the table. The "AO." indicates ascending order of the resulting tuples by age ("DO." would indicate descending order). The specification in the CONDITIONS box is connected to the AGE column by the common and arbitrary variable "_OLD" (the leading "_" is required). The result is:

PLAYNUM	PLAYNAME	AGE
1179	Jones	25
4280	Cohen	25
2007	Dobbs	27
5410	Smith	27
1131	Johnson	28

To produce a list of the bats manufactured by either the General Company or the United Company you would specify:

BATS	TEAMNUM	BATNUM	MANUF
P.			IN (General, United)

which results in:

TEAMNUM	BATNUM	MANUF
12	B09	General
20	B03	United
24	B18	General
24	B21	United

The QBE form for retrieving all occurrences of a field that have a common portion is similar to the SQL form. It uses the term "LIKE," the "%" character to replace an arbitrary number of unknown characters, and the "_" (underscore) character to replace a specific number of unknown characters. To find the players whose last names begin with the letter "S," you would specify:

PLAYERS	PLAYNUM	PLAYNAME	AGE
P.		LIKE S%	

The result is:

PLAYNUM	PLAYNAME	AGE
358	Stevens	21
5410	Smith	27
8093	Smith	21

QBE Built-In Functions

Numeric Functions. QBE has commands equivalent to the built-in functions that we discussed in SQL. For example, to find the number of records in the Teams table, you would specify:

TEAMS	TEAMNUM	TEAMNAME	TEAMCITY	TEAMMGR	
	_X				P.CNT._X

Notice the use of the arbitrary, connective variable _X and the additional column placed at the end of the skeleton table. The result is presented as:

CNT(TEAMNUM)
4

To find the number of different manufacturers who supply bats to the league, you would use the "UNQ" (unique) key word, which is the QBE equivalent of the SQL "DISTINCT" key word:

BATS	TEAMNUM	BATNUM	MANUF	
			_Y	P.CNT.UNQ._Y

which yields:

CNT(MANUF)
4

You can get a count of the number of players over age 30 by specifying:

PLAYERS	PLAYNUM	PLAYNAME	AGE	
	_Z		>30	P.CNT._Z

Remember that the variable "_Z" is arbitrary. The result is:

CNT(PLAYNUM)
_____

2

To find the total number of years of experience coach Adams of team number 12 has, you would use the Work Experience table and specify:

WORKEXP	TEAMNUM	COACHNAM	EXPTYPE	EXPYRS	
	12	Adams		_X	P.SUM._X

The result is:

SUM(EXPYRS)
_____

15

Grouping. The equivalent of the "GROUP BY" specification in SQL is the "G." key word in QBE. To find the total number of years of experience of each coach in the league (remembering that a coach is identified by the combination of TEAMNUM and COACHNAM), you would issue:

WORKEXP	TEAMNUM	COACHNAM	EXPTYPE	EXPYRS	
	G.P.	G.P.		_X	P.SUM._X

which would yield:

TEAMNUM	COACHNAM	SUM EXPYRS
12	Adams	15
12	Baker	9
15	Taylor	15
24	Victor	12

To list the number of years of experience only for those coaches who have more than 10 years of experience requires the QBE equivalent of the SQL HAVING clause:

WORKEXP	TEAMNUM	COACHNAM	EXPTYPE	EXPYRS	
	G.P.	G.P.		_X	P.SUM._X

CONDITIONS
SUM._X > 10

With the CONDITIONS box limiting the output to those groups that satisfy the condition, this yields:

TEAMNUM	COACHNAM	SUM EXPYRS
12	Adams	15
15	Taylor	15
24	Victor	12

QBE Multiple File Retrievals (Joins)

Introduction to Joins.   To specify a command that requires a join in QBE, you must display all of the involved tables simultaneously. The join fields are indicated by placing the same (arbitrary) variable name under the matching join columns in the different tables. Fields are added to and deleted from one of the tables to create the model for the desired output. As a first example, as it was in the SQL section, here is the join between the Coaches and Teams tables:

COACHES	TEAMNUM	COACHNAM	COACHPH			
P.	_TEAM			_X	_Y	_Z

TEAMS	TEAMNUM	TEAMNAME	TEAMCITY	TEAMMGR
	_TEAM	_X	_Y	_Z

The Coaches table, with the P. in the lead column, serves as the model for the output. Notice the way that the (arbitrary) variable names _X, _Y, and _Z, specified in the Teams table and added to the Coaches table, add the TEAMNAME, TEAMCITY, and TEAMMGR fields to the output. The variable _TEAM sets up the two join fields and carries their result to the output table as well. The result is:

TEAMNUM	COACHNAM	COACHPH	TEAMNAME	TEAMCITY	TEAMMGR
12	Adams	555–1524	Dodgers	Los Angeles	Wilson
12	Baker	555–3690	Dodgers	Los Angeles	Wilson
15	Taylor	555–4820	Giants	San Francisco	Johnson
20	Jackson	555–2444	Yankees	New York	Simpson
24	Victor	555–9327	Tigers	Detroit	Corbin
24	Dooley	555–7321	Tigers	Detroit	Corbin

To find the coach and team data for only those coaches on the Dodgers you would specify:

COACHES	TEAMNUM	COACHNAM	COACHPH			
P.	_TEAM			_X	_Y	_Z

TEAMS	TEAMNUM	TEAMNAME	TEAMCITY	TEAMMGR
	_TEAM	_X	_Y	_Z

CONDITIONS
_X = Dodgers

The result is:

TEAMNUM	COACHNAM	COACHPH	TEAMNAME	TEAMCITY	TEAMMGR
12	Adams	555-1524	Dodgers	Los Angeles	Wilson
12	Baker	555-3690	Dodgers	Los Angeles	Wilson

Practical Use of Joins. Continuing to follow the pattern of queries from the SQL section, the next query is, "Find the names of the coaches on the Dodgers." Remember this requires a join, because the coach names appear in a different table from the one with the "Dodgers" reference. You specify:

COACHES	TEAMNUM	COACHNAM	COACHPH
	_TEAM	P.	

TEAMS	TEAMNUM	TEAMNAME	TEAMCITY	TEAMMGR
	_TEAM	Dodgers		

Again the _TEAM variable sets up the join fields, and the constant Dodgers satisfies the query limitation. The result is:

COACHNAM
Adams
Baker

Next, "List the league's coaches, their telephone numbers, and the *names* of the teams that they're on" is specified as:

COACHES	TEAMNUM	COACHNAM	COACHPH	
	_TEAM	P.	P.	P._N

TEAMS	TEAMNUM	TEAMNAME	TEAMCITY	TEAMMGR
	_TEAM	_N		

The result is:

COACHNAM	COACHPH	TEAMNAME
Taylor	555-4820	Giants
Adams	555-1524	Dodgers
Baker	555-3690	Dodgers
Victor	555-9327	Tigers
Dooley	555-7321	Tigers
Jackson	555-2444	Yankees

Now for the three-table join. The query directs you to list the player numbers and names of the players who have played on the Dodgers and to include the number of years that they played on the Dodgers and the batting average they compiled. The tables needed are Players, Teams, and Affiliation. The player information appears in the Players table, the "Dodgers" reference is in the Teams table, and the connection between them is in the Affiliation table:

PLAYERS	PLAYNUM	PLAYNAME	AGE		
	P._PL	P.		P._A	P._B

AFFILIATION	PLAYNUM	TEAMNUM	YEARS	BATAVG
	_PL	_TNUM	_A	_B

TEAMS	TEAMNUM	TEAMNAME	TEAMCITY	TEAMMGR
	_TNUM	Dodgers		

_PL ties the Players and Affiliation tables together; _TNUM ties the Affiliation and Teams tables together. The result is:

PLAYNUM	PLAYNAME	YEARS	BATAVG
523	Doe	10	0.257
1779	Jones	1	0.223
5410	Smith	6	0.307
8093	Smith	5	0.250

The final join example called for the age of the oldest player on the Dodgers. Here again, the age information is in the Players table, the "Dodgers" reference is in the Teams table, and the connection between them is in the Affiliation table:

PLAYERS	PLAYNUM	PLAYNAME	AGE	
	_PL		_A	P.MAX._A

AFFILIATION	PLAYNUM	TEAMNUM	YEARS	BATAVG
	_PL	_TNUM		

TEAMS	TEAMNUM	TEAMNAME	TEAMCITY	TEAMMGR
	_TNUM	Dodgers		

Since the result consists of the age only, the result is:

MAX(AGE)
32

One of the SQL subquery examples that we looked at is interesting in QBE too. The query is, "Find the players who are older than the average age of all of the players."

PLAYERS	PLAYNUM	PLAYNAME	AGE	
P.			> AVG._A	

PLAYERS	PLAYNUM	PLAYNAME	AGE
			_A

The two tables taken in tandem find the average age of all employees and then compare each age to that average. The result is:

PLAYNUM	PLAYNAME	AGE
523	Doe	32
1131	Johnson	28
2007	Dobbs	27
5410	Smith	27
8366	Gomez	33

QBE Update, Delete, and Insert Operations

The QBE data manipulation operations are straightforward and follow the same general syntax that we've been working with.

Update. To update the Teams table to reflect the Dodgers moving back to Brooklyn and hiring Malloy as their manager, you specify:

TEAMS	TEAMNUM	TEAMNAME	TEAMCITY	TEAMMGR
		Dodgers	U.Brooklyn	U.Malloy

Obviously, "U." is the update command. If we now specify a P. command in the Teams skeleton, we would see that it looks like:

TEAMNUM	TEAMNAME	TEAMCITY	TEAMMGR
12	Dodgers	Brooklyn	Malloy
15	Giants	San Francisco	Johnson
20	Yankees	New York	Simpson
24	Tigers	Detroit	Corbin

To change the name of the Acme Company to the Royal Company in all of Acme's records in the Bats table, issue:

BATS	TEAMNUM	BATNUM	MANUF
			Acme U.Royal

TEAMNUM	BATNUM	MANUF
12	B01	Royal
12	B09	General
12	B13	Royal
15	B01	Royal
20	B03	United
20	B04	Modern
24	B18	General
24	B21	United

Delete. To delete the Dodgers record, you specify:

TEAMS	TEAMNUM	TEAMNAME	TEAMCITY	TEAMMGR
D.		Dodgers		

Of course, D. is the delete command. Teams now shows:

TEAMNUM	TEAMNAME	TEAMCITY	TEAMMGR
15	Giants	San Francisco	Johnson
20	Yankees	New York	Simpson
24	Tigers	Detroit	Corbin

Insert. Finally, you use the I. command to insert a record for the Cardinals into the original Teams table:

TEAMS	TEAMNUM	TEAMNAME	TEAMCITY	TEAMMGR
I.	17	Cardinals	St. Louis	Gregory

Displaying the Teams table yields:

TEAMNUM	TEAMNAME	TEAMCITY	TEAMMGR
12	Dodgers	Brooklyn	Malloy
15	Giants	San Francisco	Johnson
20	Yankees	New York	Simpson
24	Tigers	Detroit	Corbin
17	Cardinals	St. Louis	Gregory

While the placement at the end of the table reflects the physical position, any future output can be ordered by any field with the proper ascending and descending sequence commands.

Query Management Facility (QMF)

Introduction

Query Management Facility (QMF) is IBM's front-end relational query and report generating product. It runs in both of IBM's mainframe relational database environments, DB2 and SQL/DS. QMF is designed to be both a query product and a report generator, but rather than creating a new query language, QMF incorporates both SQL and QBE as its query languages. QMF provides an environment in which SQL and QBE queries can be created, tested, run, stored, and called back for future use. In addition, QMF includes a report generator that is capable of taking the output of an SQL or QBE query, performing certain types of additional calculations on that output, and formatting it in a business-like presentation style. SQL was discussed in the previous chapter of this book and QBE was discussed in the previous section of this chapter. Our purpose here is to provide a brief overview of QMF's report generation capability.

The QMF Report Generator

The QMF Report Generator or "Forms" facility is a screen-oriented tool for describing how the results of an SQL or QBE query are to be presented. Figure 8.1 shows the essential portion of the primary forms screen, known as FORM.MAIN. There are a number of "backup panels" that can provide additional detail for a complex report, but FORM.MAIN includes all of the primary concepts and will be sufficient for our discussion here.

Looking at the empty FORM.MAIN in Figure 8.1, you can begin to get an idea of what QMF is capable of doing with the output of an SQL or QBE query. Under the heading "COLUMNS:" will be a list of the fields in the query output. Included will be layout instructions as well as "USAGE" instructions. One of the USAGE facilities is the ability to form subgroups of records and perform calculations on the numeric fields in those subgroups. Among the numeric functions included in QMF are maximum, minimum, sum, average, standard deviation, and others. The "PAGE:" specification permits titles to be entered at the tops and bottoms of the pages of the report. "FINAL:" is the heading that goes with the final totals from the USAGE functions. "BREAK1:," "BREAK2:," "OPTIONS:," and "DE-

FORM.MAIN

COLUMNS: Report Width is now:
   NUM   COLUMN HEADING   USAGE   INDENT   WIDTH   EDIT

PAGE: HEADING →
          FOOTING →
FINAL: TEXT →
BREAK1: NEW PAGE FOR BREAK? →
          FOOTING →
BREAK2: NEW PAGE FOR BREAK? →
          FOOTING →
OPTIONS: OUTLINE? →   DEFAULT BREAK TEXT? →

Figure 8.1. QMF FORM.MAIN.

FORM.MAIN

COLUMNS:		Report Width is now:			
NUM	COLUMN HEADING	USAGE	INDENT	WIDTH	EDIT
1	TEAM_NUMBER	BREAK1	2	7	L
2	COACH_NAME	BREAK1	2	8	C
3	EXP_TYPE		4	20	C
4	EXP_YEARS	SUM	2	6	L

PAGE: HEADING → SUMMARY OF PRIOR COACH EXPERIENCE
        FOOTING → LEAGUE HEADQUARTERS   PAGE &PAGE
FINAL: TEXT → LEAGUE TOTAL
BREAK1:   NEW PAGE FOR BREAK? → NO
        FOOTING → COACH &1 &2 TOTAL
BREAK2:   NEW PAGE FOR BREAK? →
        FOOTING →
OPTIONS: OUTLINE? →   DEFAULT BREAK TEXT? →

Figure 8.2.   QMF FORM.MAIN for the Workexp table.

FAULT BREAK TEXT?" are all related to the subgrouping capability. Let's
take a closer look at this screen in the context of an example.

Figure 8.2 shows a FORM.MAIN panel that is designed to display the
output from the SQL command:

```
SELECT *
  FROM WORKEXP
```

where Workexp is, of course, one of the tables in the baseball example.
Specifically, recall that Workexp indicates the type and number of years
of experience that each coach had prior to joining the league. The four
columns in the output from that SQL query are clearly shown in FORM.-
MAIN, except that the old column names have been replaced with terms
that will look more pleasing on a report. The USAGE specifications indicate that the team number and coach name fields will be used for BREAK1.
That means that the output will be displayed in groups, one group for each
coach (recall that TEAMNUM and COACHNAM must be taken together in
the Workexp table to form a unique key). Furthermore, the term SUM on
the line for the years of experience column indicates that the total number
of years of experience will be recorded *for each group* (i.e., for each coach),
as well as for the entire league. The INDENT column indicates how many
spaces will be left blank between a column and the one to its left. WIDTH
is the column width on output and EDIT is the field type (L for numeric
and C for character).

The PAGE specification indicates that titles will appear at the top and
bottom of the pages. Note the term &PAGE, which will display successive
page numbers. FINAL shows the heading that will be displayed with the
grand total of the number of years of experience. BREAK1 shows the title

SUMMARY OF PRIOR COACH EXPERIENCE

TEAM NUMBER	COACH NAME	EXP TYPE	EXP YEARS
12	Adams	High School Coach	5
		College Coach	10
COACH 12 Adams TOTAL			15
12	Baker	College Coach	3
		Japan League Coach	2
		Minor League Coach	4
COACH 12 Baker TOTAL			9
15	Taylor	College Coach	15
COACH 15 Taylor TOTAL			15
24	Victor	Minor League Coach	12
COACH 24 Victor TOTAL			12
LEAGUE TOTAL			51

LEAGUE HEADQUARTERS   PAGE 1

Figure 8.3 Workexp report generated by QMF FORM.MAIN.

to be displayed with each group total. Note that &1 and &2 will be the values of column 1 and column 2, respectively, for a given group (the team number and coach name for the group).

Figure 8.3 shows the result of applying the FORM.MAIN panel in Figure 8.2 to the result of the given SQL SELECT statement. Notice how the four new column names in the FORM.MAIN panel are displayed in the report. The coach experience records are grouped by coach. The total number of years of experience is shown for each group and for the league. Headings appear at the top and bottom of the page, with each group's total for years and the league total for years.

This example shows some of the basic facilities of QMF. One obvious enhancement would have been to group the teams and then the coaches within the teams. Then there would have been a total on years for each coach, for each team, and for the league.

dBASE III+ and dBASE IV

Introduction

It wasn't long after the advent of personal computers that people became excited about the possibilities of having their own personal databases on their desks. Over the last few years, a wide range of personal computer database applications have been developed that for a variety of reasons would have been impractical on mainframes. Of course, while the fundamental concepts of database are the same regardless of the size of the computer involved, the nature of personal computer hardware does give us cause to make some specific comments here about databases and database management systems in the personal computer environment. Compared to mainframes, personal computers are slower in processing speed and are limited in data storage capacity.

There are a large number of personal computer database management software products on the market today. These products vary greatly from vendor to vendor in capability and form. Most, but not all, are based on a simple linear file structure, due to the processing limitations of the machines and the fact that most of the users of these products are not data processing professionals. Some follow the definition of database developed in this book and include a join capability, while others do not; the term database is used a bit more freely with personal computers than with larger computers.

Personal computers are generally capable of communicating with large, mainframe computers. The nature of the relationship between the two, as relates to data and database, varies. Perhaps the simplest is the use of the personal computer as a dumb terminal. In this mode the personal computer can access data in the mainframe's database, just as an unintelligent terminal can. The use of the personal computer as a dumb terminal contrasts with its use as an independent, albeit small, data processing system communicating with a mainframe. The simplest form in this mode is one in which the personal computer can download (get data from) and upload (send data to) the mainframe, with no particular commonality existing between the database systems of the two. For example, the personal computer can bring data into its main memory from the mainframe's database, convert its format, and then store or process it with its own DBMS, as shown in Figure 8.4. In a more advanced form, the same database software might be running in both the personal computer and the mainframe. These two database systems might or might not "know about each other" and be set up to work closely together, but in either case they will have their data formats in common.

Figure 8.4. Mainframe to personal computer link.

We will spend the rest of this section looking at the command structure of one particular personal computer DBMS. dBASE III + and dBASE IV are the latest in a series of popular personal computer DBMSs from Ashton-Tate Corporation. These products include a variety of query interface tools, report generation capabilities, a mailing label production capability, and tailorable input screen capabilities.

dBASE III + includes three different facilities for using relational data. One is called the Assistant and is a user-friendly, menu-driven, interactive screen based approach. It is particularly useful for the novice. Another facility is referred to as command files and is a form of programming in the embedded language style of database interaction. The third is the interactive entry of commands at the "dot prompt" on the screen. It is this last mode that we shall discuss in this chapter.

dBASE IV, which also runs the dot prompt commands discussed here, includes a new facility called the Control Center. The dBASE IV Control Center replaces the dBASE III + Assistant and greatly expands the capabilities of the menu-driven, on-line interface concept. dBASE IV also includes an implementation of SQL.

dBASE Simple Single File Retrievals

The following commands illustrate the native dBASE language. Once again, we will follow the sequence of queries and the baseball example of Figure 7.1 that we used to describe SQL. To retrieve the entire Teams file using the dBASE commands, you must first make it the "active" file. To accomplish this in the Dot Prompt mode you would issue:

USE TEAMS

Once Teams has been established as the "active" file, you merely issue:

LIST

to print the entire file:

```
TEAMNUM   TEAMNAME   TEAMCITY         TEAMMGR
     12   Dodgers    Los Angeles      Wilson
     15   Giants     San Francisco    Johnson
     20   Yankees    New York         Simpson
     24   Tigers     Detroit          Corbin
```

(Note that as a default, dBASE includes record numbers as part of its output, but we will not include them in this chapter.)

To find the record for team number 12 you would ensure that Teams is the active file and then issue:

```
LIST FOR TEAMNUM = 12
```

resulting in:

```
TEAMNUM   TEAMNAME   TEAMCITY      TEAMMGR
     12   Dodgers    Los Angeles   Wilson
```

In dBASE, the simple project operation, "List the team number and team name of all teams," would be written like this:

```
LIST TEAMNUM, TEAMNAME
```

which yields:

```
TEAMNUM   TEAMNAME
     12   Dodgers
     15   Giants
     20   Yankees
     24   Tigers
```

To combine a simple select and project, you specify both the fields of interest and the search condition. To find the names and player numbers of the players over 30 years old, you would make Players the active file and issue:

```
LIST PLAYNUM, PLAYNAME FOR AGE > 30
```

The result is:

```
PLAYNUM   PLAYNAME
    523   Doe
   8366   Gomez
```

Multiple conditions can be combined in a LIST command in a manner similar to that which we saw in SQL. If you want a list of the coaches who have been college coaches for more than 5 years, you would make Workexp the active file and issue:

```
LIST TEAMNUM, COACHNAM FOR EXPTYPE = 'College Coach' .AND.
EXPYRS > 5
```

The result is:

```
TEAMNUM   COACHNAM
     12   Adams
     15   Taylor
```

Similarly, to obtain a list of the work experience records that either involve college coaching or reflect a period of more than 10 years (or both), you would issue:

```
LIST FOR EXPTYPE = 'College Coach' .OR. EXPYRS > 10
```

The result is:

```
TEAMNUM  COACHNAM  EXPTYPE                EXPYRS
    12   Adams     College Coach             10
    12   Baker     College Coach              3
    15   Taylor    College Coach             15
    24   Victor    Minor League Coach        12
```

Projecting over a nonunique column may yield duplicate entries in dBASE as it did in SQL. For example, to ask for a list of the teams, by team number, who use bats manufactured by the Acme Company you would make Bats the active file and issue:

```
LIST TEAMNUM FOR MANUF = 'Acme'
```

which yields:

```
TEAMNUM
    12
    12
    15
```

To eliminate the duplicates with dBASE you can issue the following sequence of commands:

```
SET UNIQUE ON
INDEX ON STR(TEAMNUM,2)+MANUF TO BATINDEX
LIST TEAMNUM FOR MANUF = 'Acme'
```

and get:

```
TEAMNUM
    12
    15
```

Basically, the first two of these statements create an index on the Bats file, singling out unique combinations of team number and manufacturer name. Using that index to list only the records of the file that involve Acme as the manufacturer produces the desired result.

Next is the example that demonstrates that the records selected can be limited by a range of column values and ordered by the values of any column. To find the records of those players between the ages of 25 and 29 and order those records by age, you would make Players the active file and issue:

```
INDEX ON AGE TO AGEINDEX
LIST FOR AGE >= 25 .AND. AGE <= 29
```

The result is:

```
PLAYNUM   PLAYNAME      AGE
   1779   Jones          25
   4280   Cohen          25
   2007   Dobbs          27
   5410   Smith          27
   1131   Johnson        28
```

Note that retrieving the data based on the index on the age field accomplishes the ordering on age in the result.

Using dBASE, records can be selected based on their having a field value in a specified set. To retrieve a list of the bats that were manufactured by either the General Company or the United Company and the teams that use them, you would make Bats the active file and using the .OR. parameter issue:

```
LIST FOR MANUF = 'General' .OR. MANUF = 'United'
```

and get as a result:

```
TEAMNUM   BATNUM   MANUF
     12   B09      General
     20   B03      United
     24   B18      General
     24   B21      United
```

In SQL we issued a query to find the records for all of the players whose last names begin with the letter 'S.' In dBASE, with Players as the active file, you would issue:

```
LIST FOR PLAYNAME = 'S'
```

The result is:

```
PLAYNUM   PLAYNAME      AGE
    358   Stevens        21
   5410   Smith          27
   8093   Smith          21
```

dBASE Built-In Functions

Numeric Functions. To get a count of the number of records in the Teams file (to find out how many teams there are in the league), as we did previously using SQL, you would set Teams as the active file and issue the dBASE command:

```
COUNT
```

The result is shown as:

```
4 records
```

Counting the number of distinct values in a particular field in a dBASE file requires the creation of a unique index. With that in place, the count can be made for all values of the subject field. For example, to find the number of different manufacturers of bats who supply the league, you would make Bats the active file and issue:

```
SET UNIQUE ON
INDEX ON MANUF TO MANINDEX
COUNT FOR MANUF = ''  TO TEMP
? TEMP
```

which yields the result:

```
4
```

Counts can also be restricted to specific records. To satisfy the query, "Find the number of players over age 30," you would make Players the active file and issue:

```
COUNT FOR AGE > 30
```

which yields the result:

```
2 records
```

To find the total number of years of experience that coach Adams of the Dodgers (team number 12) has, you would make Workexp the active file and then issue:

```
SUM EXPYRS FOR TEAMNUM = 12 .AND. COACHNAM = 'Adams'
```

The system would indicate that the result is 15 years by replying:

```
2 records summed
EXPYRS
      15
```

Grouping. In SQL, we looked at the issue of performing an operation on several subsets of the records of a table independently. The example involved determining the total number of years of prior experience of each of the coaches in the league. One way of accomplishing that in dBASE is to use its report generation facility. Recalling that a coach is identified by his name and the team number of the team that he works for, we can set two grouping levels in the dBASE report generator, as follows:

```
Group on expression        TEAMNUM
Sub-group on expression    COACHNAM
```

Generating the report correctly shows that the total years for the coaches are:

```
               YEARS

12 Adams       15
12 Baker        9
15 Taylor      15
24 Victor      12
```

dBASE Multiple File Retrievals (Joins)

Introduction to Joins. dBASE III+ had two ways of integrating data from multiple files, even before the SQL capability was introduced in dBASE IV. One way was with a command known as SET RELATION. The other, which we will use in the following discussion, is with the JOIN command. Let's present a JOIN command and then discuss it. To join the Coaches and Teams files, you would issue:

```
CLEAR ALL
SELECT 2
USE COACHES
SELECT 1
USE TEAMS
JOIN WITH COACHES TO TCJOIN FOR TEAMNUM = COACHES -> TEAMNUM
  FIELDS COACHES -> TEAMNUM, COACHES -> COACHNAM, COACHES ->
  COACHPH, TEAMS -> TEAMNAME, TEAMS -> TEAMCITY, TEAMS ->
  TEAMMGR
USE TCJOIN
LIST
```

which produces:

```
TEAMNUM COACHNAM COACHPH   TEAMNAME  TEAMCITY       TEAMMGR
     12 Adams    555-1524 Dodgers   Los Angeles    Wilson
     12 Baker    555-3690 Dodgers   Los Angeles    Wilson
     15 Taylor   555-4820 Giants    San Francisco  Johnson
     20 Jackson  555-2444 Yankees   New York       Simpson
     24 Victor   555-9327 Tigers    Detroit        Corbin
     24 Dooley   555-7321 Tigers    Detroit        Corbin
```

Here is the explanation. We opened the Coaches file in work area 2, then we opened the Teams file in work area 1. (Teams is the active file because it was the last one opened.) The JOIN command (reading its parameters from the beginning) joins the active file (Teams) with the Coaches file and creates a new file arbitrarily named here Tcjoin. The join fields, TEAMNUM of the active Teams file and TEAMNUM of the Coaches file (note how the -› symbol specifies a field of a particular file) are set equal to each other. Then, all of the fields from the two files that are to be included in the result are identified after the parameter FIELDS. Finally, notice that we did not bother repeating the TEAMNUM field twice in the result, even though, as the join field, it appears in each of the two original files.

Now, with the resultant file, Tcjoin, safely stored on the disk, we can issue other commands against it. For example, to retrieve just those records that involve the DODGERS, make Tcjoin the active file and issue:

```
LIST FOR TEAMNAME = 'Dodgers'
```

The result of this command is:

```
TEAMNUM COACHNAM COACHPH   TEAMNAME  TEAMCITY       TEAMMGR
     12 Adams    555-1524 Dodgers   Los Angeles    Wilson
     12 Baker    555-3690 Dodgers   Los Angeles    Wilson
```

Practical Use of Joins. To find the names of the coaches on the Dodgers you would type USE Tcjoin and then issue:

```
LIST COACHNAM FOR TEAMNAME = 'Dodgers'
```

which would result in:

```
COACHNAM
Adams
Baker
```

How about, "List the league's coaches, their telephone numbers, and the *names* of the teams that they're on"?

```
LIST COACHNAM, COACHPH, TEAMNAME
```

The result is:

Adams	555–1524	Dodgers
Baker	555–3690	Dodgers
Taylor	555–4820	Giants
Jackson	555–2444	Yankees
Victor	555–9327	Tigers
Dooley	555–7321	Tigers

Here's the example that we had in SQL involving the join of three tables: Players, Affiliation, and Teams. The goal is to list the player numbers and names of the players who have played on the Dodgers and include the number of years that they played on the team and the batting average they compiled. To do that in dBASE, we will join the Players file with the Affiliation file, then join the result of that operation with the Teams file, and finally, execute an appropriate LIST command:

```
CLEAR ALL
SELECT 2
USE AFFILIAT
SELECT 1
USE PLAYERS
JOIN WITH AFFILIAT TO PAJOIN FOR PLAYNUM = AFFILIAT -> PLAYNUM
   FIELDS PLAYERS -> PLAYNUM, PLAYERS -> PLAYNAME, PLAYERS ->
   AGE, AFFILIAT -> TEAMNUM, AFFILIAT -> YEARS, AFFILIAT ->
   BATAVG

CLEAR ALL
SELECT 2
USE PAJOIN
SELECT 1
USE TEAMS
JOIN WITH PAJOIN TO TPAJOIN FOR TEAMNUM = PAJOIN -> TEAMNUM
   FIELDS TEAMS -> TEAMNUM, TEAMS -> TEAMNAME, TEAMS -> TEAMCITY,
   TEAMS -> TEAMMGR, PAJOIN -> PLAYNUM, PAJOIN -> PLAYNAME,
   PAJOIN -> AGE, PAJOIN -> YEARS, PAJOIN -> BATAVG

USE TPAJOIN
LIST PLAYNUM, PLAYNAME, YEARS, BATAVG FOR TEAMNAME = 'Dodgers'
```

and the result would be:

PLAYNUM	PLAYNAME	YEARS	BATAVG
523	Doe	10	0.257
1779	Jones	1	0.223
5410	Smith	6	0.307
8093	Smith	5	0.250

In the final example of a join in SQL, we tried to find the age of the oldest player on the Dodgers. In dBASE, we will use the Tpajoin file created in the last example. We will create an index on its age field, restricting entries (with a SET FILTER command) to records involving the Dodgers. We will then move to the "bottom" of that ordered (indexed) file and request the age:

```
USE TPAJOIN
SET FILTER TO TEAMNAME = 'Dodgers'
INDEX ON AGE TO AGEINDEX
GO BOTTOM
? AGE
```

The result is shown, simply, as:

```
32
```

At this point in the discussion of SQL, we discussed subqueries. The equivalent in dBASE would be either an appropriate single command, or several commands issued in sequence. For example, the query, "Find the names and telephone numbers of the coaches on the Dodgers," is answered by using the Tcjoin file (which we have already, conveniently created and saved) and issuing:

```
LIST COACHNAM, COACHPH FOR TEAMNAME = 'Dodgers'
```

The result of this query is, of course:

```
COACHNAM   COACHPH
Adams      555-1524
Baker      555-3690
```

What about the query that required a comparison to a value that was derived from all of the records of the file? "Find the players who are older than the average age of all of the players." Using the single file, Players and the dBASE command AVERAGE, we issue:

```
AVERAGE AGE TO AVGAGE
LIST FOR AGE > AVGAGE
```

AVGAGE is an arbitrarily named variable, created for this query. The result of this query is:

```
PLAYNUM   PLAYNAME      AGE
    523   DOE           32
   1131   JOHNSON       28
   2007   DOBBS         27
   5410   SMITH         27
   8366   GOMEZ         33
```

dBASE Update, Delete, and Insert Operations

As in SQL, the three data manipulation operations are straightforward, except for the question of data integrity. Recall again that the system will not stop you from entering a record in the Coaches file with a team number for which there is no corresponding team record in the Teams file. It is up to the users of the system to maintain their own data integrity in this sense.

Update.   The equivalent of SQL's UPDATE command is dBASE's REPLACE command. To change the Dodgers' city and manager fields, you would set Teams up as the active file and issue:

```
REPLACE TEAMCITY WITH 'Brooklyn', TEAMMGR WITH 'Malloy' FOR
   TEAMNAME = 'Dodgers'
```

The Teams file would then look like:

TEAMNUM	TEAMNAME	TEAMCITY	TEAMMGR
12	Dodgers	Brooklyn	Malloy
15	Giants	San Francisco	Johnson
20	Yankees	New York	Simpson
24	Tigers	Detroit	Corbin

To change the Acme Company's name to the Royal Company and have that change reflected in all of the affected records in the Bats file, you would activate the Bats file and issue:

```
REPLACE MANUF WITH 'Royal' FOR MANUF = 'Acme'
```

The Bats file would then look like this:

TEAMNUM	BATNUM	MANUF
12	B01	Royal
12	B09	General
12	B13	Royal
15	B01	Royal
20	B03	United
20	B04	Modern
24	B18	General
24	B21	United

Delete.   Suppose the Dodgers dissolve and you want to delete them from the Teams file (here again, you yourself have to manage what happens to references to them in other files). You would make Teams the active file and issue:

```
DELETE FOR TEAMNAME = 'Dodgers'
```

but that would only "logically" delete the record and it would still appear in the file with a flag indicating logical deletion attached. At this stage, the record could be brought back with a RECALL command. To "physically" delete the flagged record, you would issue the PACK command.

The remainder of the Teams file would then be:

```
TEAMNUM   TEAMNAME   TEAMCITY        TEAMMGR
     15   Giants     San Francisco   Johnson
     20   Yankees    New York        Simpson
     24   Tigers     Detroit         Corbin
```

Insert.   A simple insertion of a new record at the end of a dBASE file can be accomplished with the APPEND command. The INSERT command permits insertion into the middle of a file. Issuing these commands with a particular file active takes you into a full-screen editing mode in which there is a clearly defined entry space for each field of this new record of the file. Note that additional screen formatting facilities allow the user to create a customized screen for inputting new records.

Other dBASE Commands

dBASE includes a large number of other commands and facilities which we will not discuss here. These include file creation and maintenance commands, index creation and maintenance commands, a report generation facility (of which we had a small sample earlier in grouping), and an input screen format generation facility, also mentioned above.

References

Brownstein, M., *Using dBASE IV*, Wiley, New York; 1989.

Graham, S. L., Jr., *Using Query Management Facility: Advanced Topics*, Science Research Associates, Chicago, IL; 1985.

Graham, S. L., Jr., *Using Query Management Facility: Basic Topics*, Science Research Associates, Chicago, IL; 1985.

IBM Corporation, *Query Management Facility: Learner's Guide*, IBM Form No. SC26-4094 (1985).

IBM Corporation, *Query Management Facility User's Guide and Reference*, IBM Form No. SC26-4096 (1985).

Jones, E., *dBASE IV Programmer's Reference Guide*, Howard W. Sams, Indianapolis, IN; 1989.

Jones, E., *Using dBASE III Plus*, Osborne McGraw-Hill, Berkeley, CA; 1987.

Questions and Exercises

The following four relations, which constitute an appliance repair company's database, will be used in the following questions about QBE and dBASE III + . The company maintains data on its technicians (employee number, name, and title); the types of appliances that it services, along with the hourly billing rate to repair each, the specific appliances (by serial number) for which it has sold repair contracts, and which technicians are qualified to service which types of appliances (including the number of years that a technician has been qualified on a particular appliance type).

TECHNUM	TECHNAME	TITLE
062	Regan	Senior
297	Mercer	Trainee
553	Hewitt	Senior
718	Stein	Staff

Technicians relation.

APPLTYPE	CATEGORY	RATE
Washer	Major	20
Dryer	Major	20
Toaster	Minor	10
Blender	Minor	8
Freezer	Minor	25

Types relation.

APPLNUM	APPLTYPE	AGE	OWNER
00730	Toaster	5	M. Peters
08331	Freezer	7	R. Carr
16365	Freezer	3	S. Small
22770	Blender	1	C. Ramos
40034	Washer	10	S. Small
47222	Dryer	12	S. Small
49371	Freezer	9	N. Rice
58449	Toaster	7	L. Shaw
60558	Washer	3	M. Peters
72589	Washer	7	S. Bauer

Appliances relation.

TECHNUM	APPLTYPE	YRSQUAL
533	Dryer	15
062	Washer	18
297	Toaster	1
297	Dryer	1
718	Washer	5
553	Freezer	12
062	Blender	14
062	Freezer	10
062	Dryer	12

Qualification relation.

8.1. Using the appliance repair company database, translate the following QBE commands to English (or your national language) and indicate their results with the data shown.

a.

TYPES	APPLTYPE	CATEGORY	RATE
	P.		>18

b.

APPLIANCES	APPLNUM	APPLTYPE	AGE	OWNER
P.		Freezer	<6	

c.

APPLIANCES	APPLNUM	APPLTYPE		AGE	OWN
	P.	IN (Washer,Dryer)			P.

d.

TECHNICIANS	TECHNUM	TECHNAME	TITLE	
	_Y		Senior	P.CNT.ALL._Y

e.

APPLIANCES	APPLNUM	APPLTYPE	AGE	OWNER	
			_Z	P.G.	P.AVG._Z

f.

TECHNICIANS	TECHNUM	TECHNAME	TITLE
	_NUM	P.	

QUALIFICATION	TECHNUM	APPLTYPE	YRSQUAL
	_NUM	Dryer	>10

g.

TYPES	APPLTYPE	CATEGORY	RATE		
	P._APPL	P._CAT		P._NUM	P._OWN

APPLIANCES	APPLNUM	APPLTYPE	AGE	OWNER
	_NUM	_APPL	>9	_OWN

h.

TECHNICIANS	TECHNUM	TECHNAME	TITLE
	_NUM	P.	

QUALIFICATION	TECHNUM	APPLTYPE	YRSQUAL
	_NUM	_APPL	

TYPES	APPLTYPE	CATEGORY	RATE
	_APPL		>19

8.2. Formulate QBE or dBASE III+ commands to answer the following requests for data from the appliance repair company database. Use good judgment in deciding exactly which fields are required in the response.

    a. Which are the major appliances?

    b. Who owns freezers?

    c. What are the serial numbers and ages of the toasters on service contracts?

    d. What is the average age of the washers on service contracts?

    e. Whose homes might Stein have to visit?

    f. How many different job titles are represented?

    g. What is the average age of each owner's major appliances?

    h. Whose freezers are over 6 years old?

    i. What is the average billing rate for the major appliances that Regan is qualified to fix?

    j. What is the name of the technician who is most qualified to fix freezers?

8.3. How do you feel about the difference between the two-dimensional QBE interface in comparison with the SQL interface?

8.4. Describe the concepts and advantages of a report generators, such as QMF.

9

The Pseudo-Relational Approach to Database

Introduction

Many of those who work in the field of database consider the hierarchical, network, and relational models of database system design to be the only ones in existence. In this book we will speak of a fourth approach to database, which has been labeled in the literature as the "pseudo-relational," "flat-file integrated," "semi-relational," or "relational-like" approach.

The pseudo-relational approach is really a hybrid, composed of several of the features of the database approaches that we have already examined. The fundamental data structure is that of simple linear files, a feature it shares with the relational approach. But as a general rule, pseudo-relational database systems are not geared towards performing execution-time joins the way relational systems are. Like the hierarchical and network approaches, they require that some form of physical linkage between related records of different files be constructed and stored with the database in advance of any on-line query.

There is no formal definition for the pseudo-relational approach to database management system construction. A description of the pseudo-relational approach is really a statement of the basic concept, such as we have given, coupled with the variations in the implementation of the concept that various database system developers have actually incorporated into their designs—there are several such variations. We will make more comparisons between the pseudo-relational approach and the other approaches as this chapter progresses. As an aside, one occasionally sees the term "inverted file structure" used to describe a data storage form consisting of simple linear files that have indexes built over all or many of their fields. Whether or not systems based on such structures qualify as database systems fundamentally depends, as should be evident to you by now, on whether or not they have some kind of join capability.

Pseudo-Relational Database Concepts

Figure 9.1 is a repetition of Figure 6.3, the Salesperson and Customer files (we will drop the term "relation" in this chapter) that we used in the last chapter. Note that on the left we have added relative record numbers, which simply indicate the serial order in which the records are placed.

Once again we are faced with the now familiar dilemma of wanting to maintain the nonredundant nature of the data, while at the same time integrating the data between the two files. We've seen how the hierarchical and network approaches structure the data and develop integration with physical pointers within those structures. We've also seen how the relational approach integrates data stored in relations on the fly (at execu-

	SALESPERSON NUMBER	SALESPERSON NAME	COMMISSION PERCENTAGE	YEAR OF HIRE
1	137	Baker	10	1975
2	186	Adams	15	1971
3	204	Dickens	10	1963
4	361	Carlyle	20	1963

(a)

	CUSTOMER NUMBER	SALESPERSON NUMBER	CITY
1	0121	137	New York
2	0839	186	Hartford
3	0933	137	Boston
4	1047	137	Boston
5	1525	361	Newark
6	1700	361	Washington
7	1826	137	New York
8	2198	204	New York
9	2267	186	New York

(b)

Figure 9.1. (a) Salesperson file and (b) Customer file.

tion time) through the join fields. Let's try something else for the pseudo-relational approach.

Figure 9.2 shows a "link file" that indicates which records of the Salesperson and Customer files are related to each other. Of course, the way that the records are related is in the spirit of the join concept. For example, record 1 of the Salesperson file has a SALESPERSON NUMBER field value of 137. Record 1 of the Customer file also has a SALESPERSON NUMBER value of 137. Thus, appropriate to the join concept, a record is created in the link file in Figure 9.2 (the first record in that link file) that indicates that record 1 of the Salesperson file and record 1 of the Customer file are related. In fact, this link file contains a record for every combination of records of the Salesperson and Customer files that have identical SALESPERSON NUMBER field values. But this, in a sense, is just what we have described as a join.

So in the pseudo-relational approach the data remains in independent, simple linear files, but additional link files are created—normally well in advance of any queries being posed to the data—that indicate how the records of the different files relate to each other in the sense of the join concept.

The advantages and disadvantages of the pseudo-relational approach parallel those aspects of the other database approaches from which it is derived. The pseudo-relational approach has what many would consider to be the relative simplicity of simple linear files. It also has the performance boost of joins being done in advance, with the results of those joins being stored for future use by queries. On the other hand, it has the disadvantage of not having the true relational on-the-fly join capability. Also, at the time that data values are changed in a file, the system must take the time to update any affected indexes. If those index updates are postponed, then the system must go through extra processing to do an indexed search

SALESPERSON RECORD	CUSTOMER RECORD
1	1
1	3
1	4
1	7
2	2
2	9
3	8
4	5
4	6

Figure 9.2.   Link file between the Salesperson and Customer files.

for records based on those changed values. Another drawback is that, as with the hierarchical and network approaches, decisions must be made at the time the database is designed as to which files must be prejoined, and the results stored in link files.

But as we said at the outset of this chapter, there is no hard and fast definition of the pseudo-relational approach. For example, some such systems may allow link files to be created dynamically, at the time at which a query that requires one is posed. What the performance implications of such an action would be clearly depends on the intricacies of the particular system involved. Another variation would be a system that permits pre-created link files to exist *and* has a true, on-the-fly join capability. Such systems would more likely be classed as relational rather than pseudo-relational, but at this point the labels that we give to the systems become unimportant; there is no harm in the boundaries between the different approaches blurring. Nevertheless, there are enough database systems that are linear file oriented and have only the link file type of join capability that we feel they deserve to be considered in a class by themselves, with the label "pseudo-relational."

IBM AS/400-System/38 Database

Introduction

The IBM AS/400 is the recent follow-on to the IBM System/38. Like its predecessor, the AS/400 is a medium-scale computer system that is architecturally novel in a number of ways. One such aspect is of concern to us here: As an integral part of its design philosophy the AS/400 is designed to create a legitimate user-friendly database environment for all of its users. The AS/400 database is a legitimate relational database. The data structure is based on linear files and it has a run-time join capability. *We include the AS/400 database in this chapter on pseudo-relational database largely because of the way that it evolved from the original System/38 pseudo-relational database, several aspects of which it retains.*

Moving quickly over already familiar territory, let's begin with some basic concepts. Data in the AS/400 is stored in what we have been referring to as simple linear files. In keeping with standard database terminology, these files are called "physical files." Indexes can be built over any field or combination of fields of the physical files. (The indexes are built, as they were in the System/38, in the form of structures called "binary trees"; we shall defer discussion about these until the end of this chapter.) New records are added to a file at the end of the file, an arrangement known as "arrival sequence." When a record is added to a file, the system automatically adds corresponding index records to all indexes that reference that file and naturally places those new index records in their proper sorted positions in the indexes. So while the file itself may not be in order by any set of field values, the indexes effectively provide such orderings.

Records can be retrieved from the files in the physical sequence in which they are stored, directly using an appropriate index built over the file, in field-value sequence via any of the indexes built over the file or directly by relative record number. Notice that retrieving a record by its relative record number implies that on an earlier retrieval of the record we noted and somewhere maintained its relative record number for future use.

Data Retrieval and Manipulation

There are several modes of retrieving and manipulating data in the AS/400 environment. One is with what we referred to earlier in this book as embedded commands. In fact, AS/400 files can be accessed and modified with data retrieval, insert, delete, and update operations in the RPG, COBOL, PL/I, BASIC, and PASCAL languages.

Another data access tool is called the Data File Utility (DFU), which, as its name implies, is a special purpose program for inquiring into and modifying the data in AS/400 files. Very importantly, in terms of database, the AS/400 includes an implementation of SQL, called SQL/400.

The AS/400 also includes a query facility called AS/400 Query, which is designed for both ad hoc and stored queries. It is a menu-driven tool that leads the user through a series of questions to describe to the system the data for which the user is looking. Also available is the AS/400 Business Graphics Utility, which can easily produce line graphs, bar graphs, pie charts, and the like.

Physical and Logical Files

Just as the AS/400 term "physical file" follows standard database usage, so does the AS/400 term "logical file." A logical file is a programmer's view of the data: a mapping onto one or more of the physical files.

Logical File Based on One Physical File.   A logical file based on a single physical file can present the programmer with a view of the data that differs significantly from the original physical file. It may contain only a subset of the fields of the physical file, a subset of the records, or both. It may present the file with the order of the fields rearranged. It may present the records of the file in a different sequence, based on an index existing over the field that is to provide that sequence.

Figure 9.3 shows the original Players file from Figure 7.1. Let's assume that file is the AS/400 physical file for the players in the league. Figure 9.4*a* shows a logical file based on that physical file, in which the records appear in ascending order by age and within age by the players' last names.

	PLAYNUM	PLAYNAME	AGE
1	358	Stevens	21
2	523	Doe	32
3	1131	Johnson	28
4	1779	Jones	25
5	2007	Dobbs	27
6	4280	Cohen	25
7	4319	Ross	24
8	5410	Smith	27
9	6564	Linton	24
10	8093	Smith	21
11	8366	Gomez	33

Figure 9.3.   The Players physical file.

This implies that there is a binary index tree based on the concatenation of the AGE and PLAYNAME fields. Figure 9.4*b* shows a logical file in which the AGE field has been left out and the order of the PLAYNUM and PLAYNAME fields has been reversed. Figure 9.4*c* shows a logical file in which only the records for those players 27 years of age or younger appear. In addition, the PLAYNAME field does not appear, and the other two fields are in reversed order.

Descriptions of the physical and logical files are specified in the Data Description Specifications (DDS). In addition to the usual specifications of characteristics of the fields, the DDS can contain column headings and other textual information, range bounds for numeric fields, and validity checking specifications. When a programmer wants to write code to access a field or file from his program, he can just reference the DDS entry for the appropriate (logical or physical) file, instead of coding the field or file description from scratch. At program compile time, the system will copy the pertinent information about the fields and files from the DDS into the program and compile it with the rest of the program. Other data in the DDS, such as the range checking and validity checking information, is kept with the files.

Another feature of the AS/400 is the Field Reference File (FRF), which is a form of control block. This facility maintains information about the domain of values of the field. An important data feature of the AS/400 is that, through the FRF, different fields with different names can be controlled by the same domain definition. The domain information is taken from the FRF and used to control the validity of the data entered into and displayed from the files. The result is a high level of data integrity.

PLAYNUM	PLAYNAME	AGE
8093	Smith	21
358	Stevens	21
6564	Linton	24
4319	Ross	24
4280	Cohen	25
1779	Jones	25
2007	Dobbs	27
5410	Smith	27
1131	Johnson	28
523	Doe	32
8366	Gomez	33

(a)

PLAYNAME	PLAYNUM
Stevens	358
Doe	523
Johnson	1131
Jones	1779
Dobbs	2007
Cohen	4280
Ross	4319
Smith	5410
Linton	6564
Smith	8093
Gomez	8366

(b)

AGE	PLAYNUM
21	358
25	1779
27	2007
25	4280
24	4319
27	5410
24	6564
21	8093

(c)

Figure 9.4 (a) A Players logical file sorted on AGE and PLAYNAME, (b) a Players logical file with the AGE field missing, and (c) a Players logical file consisting of only those records in which the AGE value is 27 or less, with one field left out and the other fields reordered.

Logical Files Based on More than One Physical File: The Join. In the original System/38 implementation, a limited form of a join took place when a logical file was created over more than one physical file. Normally, a join operation combines the fields of the records of two different files into records of a new resultant file based on like values in the join fields. In the original System/38, a logical file based on two physical files logically interleaved the records of these two physical files with an ordering based on what, in effect, were the values of the join fields. Let's look at an example.

Figure 9.5 shows the Teams and Coaches files from Figure 7.1. The join fields—the fields of those two files that relate the records of one to the other—are, clearly, the two TEAMNUM fields. The TEAMNUM field in the Coaches table indicates which team a particular coach works for. Figure 9.6 shows a System/38 logical file based on the Teams and Coaches physical files. The records are arranged (with the indentation of the Coaches records for emphasis in that figure) so that the records of the coaches for a particular team follow that team's record. All of the teams' records can be retrieved in order, all of the coaches' records can be retrieved in order, or the teams' and coaches' records, even though they represent two different record types, can be retrieved in the order shown in Figure 9.6, with the records for the coaches on a team following that team's record.

During the life of the System/38, the database mechanism gradually evolved to one that looked more and more relational, with a true, run-time join capability. The foregoing discussion of the System/38 pseudo-

	TEAMNUM	TEAMNAME	TEAMCITY	TEAMMGR
1	12	Dodgers	Los Angeles	Wilson
2	15	Giants	San Francisco	Johnson
3	20	Yankees	New York	Simpson
4	24	Tigers	Detroit	Corbin

(a)

	TEAMNUM	COACHNAM	COACHPH
1	12	Adams	555-1524
2	12	Baker	555-3690
3	15	Taylor	555-4820
4	20	Jackson	555-2444
5	24	Victor	555-9327
6	24	Dooley	555-7321

(b)

Figure 9.5. (a)The Teams physical file; (b) the Coaches physical file.

12		Dodgers		Los Angeles		Wilson
	12		Adams		555-1524	
	12		Baker		555-3690	
15		Giants		San Francisco		Johnson
	15		Taylor		555-4820	
20		Yankees		New York		Simpson
	20		Jackson		555-2444	
24		Tigers		Detroit		Corbin
	24		Dooley		555-7321	
	24		Victor		555-9327	

Figure 9.6. Logical file based on the Teams and Coaches physical files.

relational database capability is important both for historical reasons and because it may still be in use in many installations. But it is important to note, as we said earlier, that the AS/400 does have a truly relational, run-time join capability. That join capability is still dependent on the unique binary index tree structure that was developed for the System/38.

The Binary Index Tree

Introduction. The indexes in AS/400 are constructed in the form of binary trees (or, more precisely, full binary trees). A (full) binary tree is a tree in which every node either has two branches emanating downward from it or is a terminal node with no branches emanating downward from it. As the AS/400 binary index tree is an interesting idea and is quite different from the indexing structures that we described in Chapter 3, we will digress and describe it in the context of an example.

Figure 9.7 is a portion of the Players file of our baseball league. For illustrative purposes it includes some of the records from the Players table in Figure 7.1 as well as some other Players records. Also notice that it is not in sequence by the PLAYNUM (or any other) field, which makes the point that a file in AS/400 need not be in any physical sequence.

	PLAYNUM	PLAYNAME	AGE
1	1779	Jones	25
2	1732	Blake	22
3	4319	Ross	24
4	6564	Linton	24
5	4802	Turner	33
6	4809	Norton	28

Figure 9.7. A portion of the Players file.

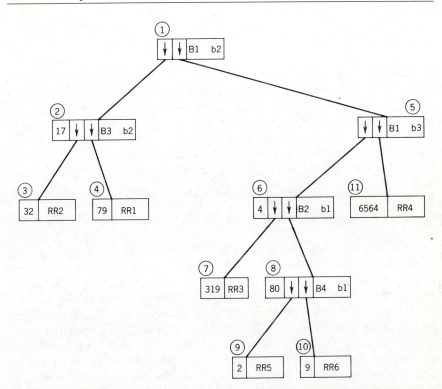

Figure 9.8. Binary index tree over the PLAYNUM field of the Players File in Figure 9.7.

Figure 9.8 is a binary index tree that is built over the PLAYNUM field of the Players file in Figure 9.7. First, we will describe the strange looking data in that tree, then we will discuss how to conduct a search through it, and finally we will explain how to construct it.

Structure of the Tree. First of all, the circled numbers that label the nodes in Figure 9.8 are simply there for our convenience in this explanation. The downward pointing arrows are pointers to other nodes in the tree. Since the structure is a full binary tree, there must be exactly two such arrows in every nonterminal node. The numbers at the left end of some of the nodes are either partial or full values of the data field(s) (also referred to as the "key field") being indexed, in this case the PLAYNUM field of the Players file. A partial value, which may only appear in a non-terminal node, is known as "common data" and, as we will explain, forms part of the value of all of the keys represented below it in the tree. The RR values refer to the relative record numbers of the records of the Play-ers file. For example, notice that node 11 indicates that the record with PLAYNUM value 6564 exists at relative record number position 4 in the Players file. Refer back to Figure 9.7 to confirm this. Remember that this means that Linton's record was the fourth to be added to that file and is physically the fourth record in the linear file. Some of the field values are built up progressively, starting from the root of the index tree downwards. For example, moving from node 1 through node 2 to node 3, you construct field value 1732 and, in the terminal node, find that the record with that PLAYNUM value is the second in the Players file. RR pointers to the physical file may only appear in terminal nodes. The capital and small "b"s represent bits within bytes of the field values to be tested in guiding the traversal through the tree (which is our notation and is not found in the AS/400 literature). The capital "B" stands for "byte," counting from the left and starting with 1. The small "b" stands for "bit," counting from the left and, for simplicity, starting with 1 as the leftmost bit of the four bits that represent the digits 0–9 in binary. Of course, these represent only the four righthand bits of the byte, but the four lefthand bits are identical for all of the digits and so do not affect the outcome, as we shall see.

Searching the Tree. Remember that the purposes of an index are to allow direct access to a record in a file through the value of one of its fields and to permit the sequential retrieval of the records of a file according to the values of one of its fields. Let's demonstrate a direct access through the binary index tree with an example. Suppose we are searching for the record in the Players file with PLAYNUM value 4802. We enter the index at the root node (node 1). This node tells us to test byte 1, bit 2. (We will discuss how we established this test in the next section.) On such a bit test, the general rule is that a 0 sends us to the left and a 1 sends us to the right. Since byte 1 of 4802 is a 4, and bit 2 of a 4 (0100) is a 1, we move down to the right. There we encounter node 5. The test on byte 1 (the same 4), bit 3, yields a 0, and we move down and to the left. This brings us to node 6 where, for the first time, we find common data: a 4. This means that all of the nodes from that point downward in the tree involve PLAYNUM values with a 4 in their leftmost byte position. Why the leftmost byte position? Because that 4 is the first common data that we've come upon in tracing down from the root. If the common data does not correspond to the data in the same byte position(s) in the field value that we are searching for, then we are not permitted to make the specified bit test, we declare a "not found" condition for that field value, and we end the search through the index. But in fact, the first byte of 4802 is a 4, and so we test byte 2 (an 8), bit 1, find a 1, and move down and to the right. At node 8 we find 80 as common data and note that it corresponds to the 80 in the second and third byte positions of the search field value 4802. The test on byte 4 (a 2), bit 1, yields a 0, which sends us down and to the left to terminal node 9. The 2 that we find there completes the value 4802. Since node 9 is a terminal node, if the 2 were not there we would have registered a not found condition. At node 9 we are told that the record with PLAYNUM value 4802 is at relative record position 5 in the Players file, and so it is. This process may sound rather complex, for what is supposed to be a fast, indexed, direct search, but remember that at each nonterminal node the test made is a single bit test, and the stored instructions on which bit to test were put there at the time that the binary index tree was created.

To use the binary index tree to retrieve all of the records in sequence we merely traverse it in a top-to-bottom, left-to-right fashion, which happens to be the order in which the nodes were numbered. Convince yourself that such a traversal will find the PLAYNUM field values (and the corresponding records in the Players file through the relative record numbers) in ascending sequence.

Constructing the Tree. Finally, there's the question of how the binary index tree was built in the first place. Constructing a AS/400 binary index tree is really a matter of performing multiple inserts of new key field values into new nodes. Basically, to perform an insert, the system starts at the root and searches through the tree as if assuming that a node with that value is already in the tree and it is trying to retrieve it. When it reaches a terminal node, it replaces that terminal with a nonterminal node that has the old terminal value and the new value to be inserted at the two terminals emanating downward from it. As we shall see, there's a bit more to it than that.

Let's assume that we are going to start building the Players file in Figure 9.7 and the binary index tree on the PLAYNUM field from scratch. First, the record for player Jones is added to the (new) Players file, and the binary index tree looks like the simple structure in Figure 9.9*a*. It is a single node that indicates that the record with PLAYNUM value 1779 (the record for Jones) is at relative record position 1 in the Players file. Next, the record for Blake is added to the file. Its PLAYNUM value, 1732, is compared to the single index record of Figure 9.9*a*. Starting from the left, 1732 shares two byte values in common with the value 1779 in the tree. So, Figure 9.9*b* shows that a new root is created with 17 as common data. The first byte from the left not common to 1732 and 1779 is byte 3. Comparing the bit representations for the 3 of 1732 (0011) and the 7 of 1779 (0111), the first bit from the left that is different is bit 2. So the value that has the

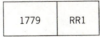

Figure 9.9*a*. The development of the binary index tree: Binary index tree for the first record.

Figure 9.9*b*. The development of the binary index tree: After adding the second record.

0 bit is sent off to the left, and the value that has the 1 bit is sent off to the right. That's why the partial key 32, which completes the value 1732 with the relative record 2 indication, is down and to the left, and 79, for 1779, is down and to the right in Figure 9.9*b*. The B3b2 test information and the common data are stored in the nonterminal node that separates them. Next, the record for Ross, with PLAYNUM value 4319, is added to the Players file. To find the proper place to add it in the tree in Figure 9.9*b*, we would do what we did in a somewhat trivial way in the construction of Figure 9.9*b*. That is, we would trace through the tree as if conducting a search for the value that we have to add, and then actually add it when we reach a terminal node, as we described earlier (the single node in Figure 9.9*a* was a terminal node, in a trivial sense). So we try to do the same thing with the value 4319 and the tree of Figure 9.9*b*. But we can't move down from the root node because the common data specified in it (17) does not correspond to the first two byte positions of the value 4319 that we are trying to add to the tree. When that happens on an insert attempt, the tree is built *upwards* from that point. Thus the tree of Figure 9.9*c* shows a new root that differentiates between the 1 of the common data 17 of the old root and the 4 of the new value 4319, and so on through the rest of the records to be added.

There's more to it than that, but that's the basic idea. It turns out that the algorithm just described may place some values out of sequential order in the top-to-bottom, left-to-right traversal sense. When this happens, the AS/400 invokes other instructions that force a change in the ordering so that the proper sequence is preserved. Also, you might wonder how efficient the index search process is if the entire tree is not in main memory during the search, which is a good bet for a large file. The answer lies in a clever method of paging portions of the tree into main memory as needed.

Implementing a Join with the Tree. Figure 9.10 shows a simplified view of the binary index tree that makes the logical file in Figure 9.6

Figure 9.9c. The development of the binary index tree: After adding the third record.

Figure 9.10. Binary index tree for the logical file in Figure 9.6.

possible. Once again, the circled node labels are just for our own reference purposes. We have left out the bit test information at the nonterminal nodes for simplicity. In the terminal nodes, the "T" and "C" adjuncts to the RR numbers refer to the Teams and Coaches files, respectively. The fields involved in this tree are the TEAMNUM fields of both the Teams and Coaches physical files and the COACHNAM field of the Coaches file. Let's trace through part of this tree. Node 2 shows common data of 1, indicating that all of the nodes below it will eventually lead to teams and coaches records involving teams whose team numbers begin with the value 1. Node 3 shows common data of 2 in the second of the team number byte positions. Combining the information in nodes 2 and 3 we realize that all of the nodes below node 3 have something to do with team 12, the Dodgers. Node 4 is a terminal node and shows a null (the hyphen here) where a whole or partial coach name might be. This means that node 4 refers to the record for team 12 itself, and, sure enough, that node has a pointer to relative record position 1 of the Teams file (TRR1), which is where the record for team 12 resides. Backing up from terminal node 4 and continuing in the usual top-to-bottom, left-to-right order of node traversal, we find that node 5 leads to nodes 6 and 7, which do indeed represent and contain pointers to the coach records for Adams and Baker, the two Dodger coaches. The next node in order is node 8, which leads to the specific nodes for team number 15 and its coach, and so on.

References

Conte, P., "SQL/400: Is It SQL Yet?" *Database Programming and Design* **1** (12), (December, 1988): 40–45.

Hoskins, J., *IBM AS/400 A Business Perspective*, Wiley, New York; 1989.

IBM Corporation, *IBM AS/400 Programming: Structured Query Language/400 Programmer's Guide*, IBM Form No. SC21-9609 (1988).

IBM Corporation, *IBM AS/400 Programming: Structured Query Language/400 Reference*, IBM Form No. SC21-9608 (1988).

IBM Corporation, *IBM System/38 Control Program Facility Concepts Manual*, IBM Form No. GC21-7729 (1981).

IBM Corporation, *IBM System/38 Control Program Facility Programmer's Guide*, IBM Form No. SC21-7730 (1981).

IBM Corporation, *IBM System/38 Introduction*, IBM Form No. GC21-7728 (1983).

Questions and Exercises

9.1. Explain the statement, "The pseudo-relational approach to database is a hybrid between the relational and the hierarchical and network approaches."

9.2. What is a link file in the pseudo-relational approach? What are the advantages and disadvantages associated with them?

9.3. How does the AS/400 distinguish between stored files and programmer views of those files? What is the significance of that distinction?

9.4. Construct a logical view of the AS/400 physical file in Figure 9.3 in which the player name comes first, the player age comes second, the player number is left out, the records are in alphabetic order by player name, and only those players older than 27 are included.

9.5. In your own words, describe how a AS/400 binary index tree is constructed.

9.6. What are the advantages of the binary index tree approach?

9.7. Build a AS/400 binary index tree with the following key values in the order shown.

    a. 5527

    b. 8326

    c. 5528

    d. 1274

    e. 1500

    f. 5524

    g. 7231

9.8. Describe how the AS/400 would find the record for Dooley in the binary index tree of Figure 9.10.

10

The Hierarchical
Approach to Database

Introduction

The next approach to database management systems that we will look at is the hierarchical approach. Since one of the oldest and most widely used DBMSs is based on that approach, the thrust of this chapter will be to examine that system: IBM's Information Management System (IMS).

IMS is actually composed of two parts. One part, Data Language/I (DL/I), is the database facility itself, including the data structure rules and the programming language interface. The second part, called the Data Communications Facility, is the communications driver (the software that defines an interactive environment) and allows messages and requests for data to be sent from terminals to the central computer and replies to be sent back to the terminals. IMS is not its own operating system, but runs under IBM's OS/MVS family of large-scale operating systems. DL/I can also use the Customer Information Control System (CICS) as a communications driver in either the OS or DOS (a medium-scale operating system) environments, or it can run as a batch-only system, although that is not common today. In practice, the acronyms IMS and DL/I are used interchangeably to refer to the database portion of the system. This is the portion that will be discussed in this chapter.

IMS is a full-scale database management system capable of handling very large files and a very large number of simultaneous users. Of course, it has the ability to integrate data, reduce redundancy, and handle multiple relationships in the data. It also includes facilities for backup and recovery, security, and concurrent processing protection.

Hierarchies

Before looking at IMS, we should set a firm foundation in what a **hierarchy,** or **tree** (we'll use the words interchangeably) is. Figure 10.1 shows an abstract tree or hierarchy. It is simply an arrangement of points called **nodes** (numbered 1–11 in the figure) connected by **branches** or **edges** (the straight lines in the figure) with the following restrictions. There is one special node called the **root** which is always drawn at the top of the diagram (node 1 is the root node in the tree in Figure 10.1). The tree branches downward from the root; each node is capable of branching into several nodes at the next level downward. As a result, every node (with the exception of the root) is connected upward to one and only one node in the tree. For example, node 3 is connected upward only to node 1. Node 9 is connected upward (immediately) only to node 6.

The nodes that come downward directly out of a given node are called its **child nodes**. Conversely, for any child nodes, the node from whence it came is called its **parent node**. For example, in Figure 10.1, nodes 2, 3, and 4 are child nodes of node 1, and nodes 5 and 6 are child nodes of node 2. Looked at the other way, node 1 is the parent of nodes 2, 3, and 4, and node 2 is the parent of nodes 5 and 6. We might speak of all of the nodes below a given node as its **descendants**. Thus the descendants of node 1 are nodes 2 through 11. The descendants of node 2 are nodes 5, 6, 8, 9, 10, and 11. A node with no branches coming out of it downward (e.g., nodes 3, 5, and 8) is called a **leaf** or **terminal node**, as distinguished from

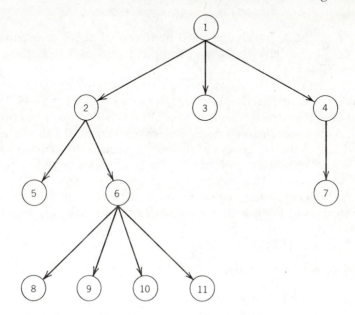

Figure 10.1. A tree or hierarchy.

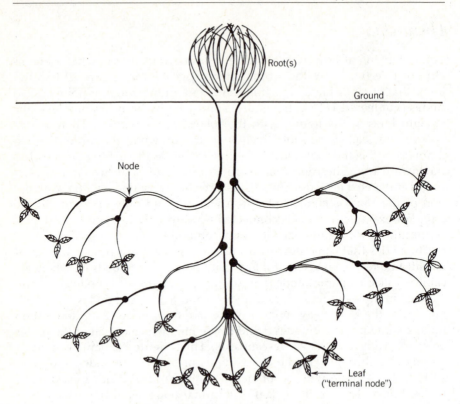

Figure 10.2.   A real tree upside-down.

nodes 1, 2, 4, and 6, which are called **nonterminal nodes** or **intermediate nodes**. Nodes that have the same parent (e.g., nodes 5 and 6) are called **twins** or **siblings**.

Actually, the use of the word "tree" here and some of the accompanying terminology, derive directly from trees in everyday life. Figure 10.2 shows a picture of a tree turned upside down. On top is the root and branching downward are the branches, nodes, and leaves. Figure 10.3 shows a family tree, with all of the concepts of children, descendants, parents, and so forth. George and Mary (née Smith) Jones have three children: John, Susan, and Marsha, and so on.

That the concept of the tree can be used to manage stored data may be a bit mysterious at this point, but we shall gradually develop that idea in the succeeding pages.

IMS Physical Structure

Now that you know what a hierarchy is, let's begin the discussion of IMS by describing how data can be stored in that form and what the advantages are of doing so. We'll continue to use the baseball teams

Figure 10.3.   The Jones family tree.

example. Remember, we have to maintain information about each team in the league, including information about all of the players on the team, all of the coaches on the team, the various prior work experience that each coach has, and the bats (each bat has a team-unique serial number) that each team has. For the moment, we will disregard the many-to-many relationship between teams and players and will instead associate players with a single team in a one-to-many relationship. We will pick up the many-to-many relationship again later in the chapter.

Simple Hierarchies

The Baseball Teams Hierarchy. Figure 10.4 shows the Baseball Teams hierarchy. The first thing to realize is that each node of this tree represents a different *record type*, called a **segment** in IMS. The Teams record or segment, like any record, consists of a number of fields that describe the team: team number, team name, etc. The words in the boxes in Figure 10.4, for example Teams, Players, etc., are record or segment names; it will be convenient in several of the IMS diagrams in this chapter to omit the field names and show only the segment names.

Figure 10.5 shows the Baseball Teams hierarchy with its field names included. The segment names (shown outside of the segment boxes) are,

Figure 10.4. The Baseball Teams hierarchy.

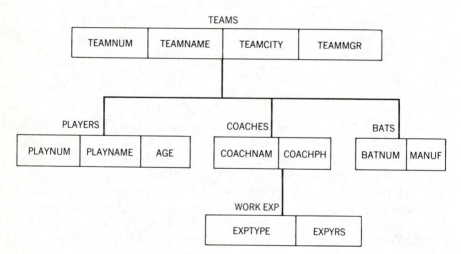

Figure 10.5. The Teams hierarchy showing segment names and field names.

of course, identical to those shown in Figure 10.4. Every branch in the tree in Figure 10.4 represents a one-to-many relationship. Thus, for a given team there are many players, many coaches, and many bats; for a given coach there are many pieces of work experiences. (By the way, "many" in this context really means 0, 1, or more than 1; for example, a coach might have no applicable pieces of work experience, one, or more than one.)

How does the Baseball Teams hierarchy of Figure 10.5 compare with the relational database of Figure 7.1? The record type of the Teams table in the relational database becomes the Teams (root) segment type of the hierarchy. As we know, there is a one-to-many relationship between teams and coaches. That was reflected in the relational database by the TEAM-NUM field appearing in the Coaches table as a foreign key. In the hierarchy, Coaches becomes a subordinate segment type to Teams, reflecting that one-to-many relationship in the hierarchical manner. But notice, very importantly, that *the TEAMNUM field does not appear in the Coaches segment in the hierarchy.* The connection between teams and coaches in the hierarchy (which we shall demonstrate shortly) removes the need for the foreign key to appear in the "many" side of the one-to-many relationship. Bats is connected under Teams and Workexp is connected under Coaches in a similar manner. Caution: Remember that, for the moment, we have changed the relationship between Teams and Players from the many-to-many relationship in the relational database of Figure 7.1 to a one-to-many relationship in Figure 10.5. Accept, for now, that Players is placed under Teams in the hierarchy of Figure 10.5 in the style of the one-to-many relationship. Again, we will handle the many-to-many relationship a bit later in this chapter.

Figure 10.5 shows just the overall outline of how we are going to store information about baseball teams. It does not show the details of what the storage for one specific team would look like. Figure 10.6 shows the *occurrence* of the Teams hierarchy for the Dodgers. Each segment occurrence is represented, informally at this point, with the value of an identifying field, for example, Dodgers, Doe, etc. Such a hierarchical occurrence, which is called a "database record" in IMS, consists of a single occurrence of the root node and all of its related subordinate segment occurrences. All of the database records of the same hierarchy put together are called a "database." Carrying that definition one step further, several databases spoken of together are often informally also called a "database" or "data-bank."

Thus in Figure 10.6 we find the Dodgers occurrence of the Teams record on top, the Doe, Jones, and Smith occurrences of the Players record attached underneath it, and so on. Coach Adams has high school and college coaching experience; Coach Baker has college, Japan League, and minor league coaching experience. (The connecting lines in Figure 10.6 are intended only to·show the one-to-many relationships, not the physical storage arrangements—that will come next.) Although it's not shown, we understand that the Doe record really includes fields that describe his player serial number, his name, his hometown, and so forth. (If seeing the whole picture will make you more comfortable at this point, look ahead to Figure 10.24.)

Something else to notice about this hierarchical arrangement, which may not be immediately apparent, is the savings in what would otherwise be redundant data. Whatever information we have about the Dodgers that is stored in the Dodgers segment (e.g., the name of the team manager) *applies to all of its subordinate segments.* For example, at one time or another we may want to know the name of Doe's manager, Jones' manager, or

Figure 10.6. The Dodgers occurrence of the Baseball Teams hierarchy.

Smith's manager. Since they're all on the same team, they all have the same manager, and in fact we do not have to store his name redundantly with each player precisely because each of those player occurrences is connected to the Dodgers team occurrence up above. The information is kept once, in the Dodgers segment above. Correspondingly, part of the sense of data integration in the hierarchical arrangement is that, within a database record, data in a superior segment applies to all of the occurrences of its subordinate segments. As we will see later, this interlinking of records also provides a sense of data integration in that a programmer can take advantage of the structure by navigating through it with the proper commands in an application program.

Once again this brings us to one of those places where the logical must give way to the physical. The previous discussion *sounds* good, but how do you convince a computer that bunches of record occurrences of different types are arranged in the tree-like form we've been describing? That's neither obvious nor trivial, but it is very important. Here are two fundamental methods.

Sequential Storage of Hierarchies. One way of storing IMS hierarchical occurrences is to "flatten them," in a controlled way, and store them sequentially. Figure 10.7 shows a schematic of a section of computer memory (it could be either primary or disk memory) containing the Dodgers database record of Figure 10.6. The segment occurrences are laid out in a particular sequence, which is a variation of a technique known as "pre-order sequential traversal." Essentially, it's a top-to-bottom, left-to-right, and front-to-back listing. Notice that we start at the top of the tree and store the Dodgers segment first. Then we travel downward and to the left and pick up the segment for player Doe. With nothing below Doe, we move "back" through Jones and Smith. Then we move towards the right and get coach Adams and his subordinate segment occurrences, and so on. Could we reconstruct the tree from the stored form in Figure 10.7? Yes, but we would have to include some other information along the way, such as the segment type and segment length of each stored occurrence. (By the way, the empty spaces at the end of each line in Figure 10.7 are not directly germane to this discussion but add some realism to it. They indicate that there may be space boundaries in the disk storage medium and only records that entirely fit in a storage unit may do so. If not, they must be placed in the next "line.")

This seems like a workable arrangement for storing a database record, and in fact it is quite appropriate for certain kinds of applications. Unfortunately it has a couple of drawbacks that make it inappropriate for use in most database applications, especially those requiring fast, on-line response to queries. One problem is that the way the segment occurrences are laid out in so tight a sequence makes it difficult to insert new data into the middle of a database record. For example, if a new player joins the team, there is no space left to insert his segment occurrence among those of the players already on the team.

The other problem has to do with rapid access to a specific segment occurrence. Let's assume for the moment that we can get to all of the root segment occurrences on some kind of a direct basis (we'll further develop this later). With the sequential storage arrangement, there is no way to get to any of the subordinate segment occurrences (i.e., all of the nonroot segment occurrences in the database record) except by methodically and slowly moving sequentially through the stored segments, starting with the root, until you find the segment for which you are looking. For example, in Figure 10.7, if you know that Baker is one of the coaches on the Dodgers, and you want to find out about his prior experience, you have to read

Figure 10.7. Sequential storage of the Dodgers team occurrence.

through the segments for Dodgers, Doe, Jones, and so on, until you finally reach Baker and his experience segments. There has to be a better way!

Pointer-Based Storage of Hierarchies. The better way for achieving rapid access to a specific segment occurrence is based on the use of pointers to connect the different segment occurrences of a database record. Figure 10.8 shows the Dodgers database record stored physically with two kinds of pointers, known as **child pointers** and **twin pointers**. Those terms follow the usage for the words child and twin that we developed earlier. A child pointer (called "physical child first" pointer in IMS) points from a

Figure 10.8. Child and twin pointer storage of the Dodgers team occurrence.

given node to the first occurrence of one of its child segment types. Thus in Figure 10.8, there is a child pointer from Dodgers to Doe, the first of its players, to Adams, the first of its coaches, and to B01, the first of its bats. Also there is a child pointer from Adams to High School Coaching, and from Baker to College Coaching, in each case the first of their pieces of work experience. Each collection of segment occurrences of the same kind *that belong to the same occurrence of the parent segment type* are connected by twin pointers ("physical twin forward" pointers in IMS). Doe, Jones, and Smith are all players on the Dodgers, and so are connected together by twin pointers (the arrangement is called a **twin chain**). Coaches Adams and Baker are chained together under Dodgers, as are all of the Dodgers' bats. Similarly, the High School Coaching segment and the (first) College Coaching segment are chained together under coach Adams, as are the (second) College Coaching segment, the Japan League Coaching segment, and the Minor League Coaching segment under coach Baker.

New segment occurrences can be added physically anywhere on the disk, as long as the appropriate pointers are updated and added to maintain the proper logical structure of the database record. Incidentally, it does help, for performance reasons based on minimizing the amount of travel of the disk access arm mechanism, to insert the new segment in an open space as close to the other members of its twin chain as possible.

This arrangement is much better for fast access of the subordinate segments. Again assuming that we can get to the Dodgers segment directly, locating Baker's pieces of experience is readily accomplished. First we follow a child pointer from Dodgers to Adams (the system can distinguish one child pointer from another, so with the proper command it will get to Adams and not to Doe or to bat B01). Then we follow a twin pointer from Adams to Baker, a child pointer from Baker to the first of his pieces of work experience, and a series of twin pointers to the rest of his pieces of work experience.

For performance reasons, IMS also provides as options pointers that go backward through a twin chain and pointers that go from a segment occurrence to the last segment occurrence on its subordinate twin chains.

Logical Relationships

Introduction. We have seen that a single hierarchical structure can be a very powerful data storage form. But it also can be limiting, both in the degree of data integration that it permits, and in the fact that it cannot directly handle many-to-many relationships.

Figure 10.9 shows two hierarchical structures. The one on the left is the Teams hierarchy that we have been looking at. The one on the right is another hierarchy, the Players hierarchy. The Players hierarchy has one database record (remember, that means one root occurrence and all of its subordinate occurrences) for every player in the league. Stored with each player are his annual statistics, arranged as one segment occurrence

Figure 10.9. The Teams and Players hierarchies.

per year, and information about the positions he is qualified to play. This additional data did not appear in the earlier, relational example.

As you look at those two hierarchies side by side, it might strike you as strange that a Players segment appears in both hierarchies. On the left it represents the players on a given team, while on the right it is an independent list of all of the players in the league. Let's assume that the fields in each of those two Players segments are identical (PLAYER SERIAL NUMBER, PLAYER NAME, PLAYER HOME ADDRESS, etc.). Then it might seem that an alternative to the two hierarchies in Figure 10.9 would be the single hierarchy in Figure 10.10 with the players' annual statistics and position information folded in under the Players segment in the Teams hierarchy. Is that a better solution?

It turns out that there are advantages to the storage arrangements of both Figure 10.9 and Figure 10.10. (For the following discussion, remember that the assumption made earlier in this chapter—direct access can only be made to the root of each database record—still holds).

There are a couple of advantages to the two-hierarchy arrangement in Figure 10.9. It may well be necessary, for some applications, to be able to reach Players segment occurrences directly. In the two-hierarchy arrangement of Figure 10.9, Players can be reached directly, since the Players segment is the root of its own database. In the single hierarchy of Figure 10.10, Players cannot be reached directly (although later on we shall see an embellishment to the system that would allow that). Also in Figure 10.9, a player in the league who is not currently affiliated with a team can still exist quite comfortably in the Players hierarchy, which is independent of teams. In the single hierarchy of Figure 10.10, a player can

Figure 10.10.   The combined Teams and Players hierarchies.

only exist if he is affiliated with a team. (We might fix that by having a special team called "unaffiliated players," but in general you can see that that sort of situation might be a problem.)

On the other hand, there are a couple of advantages to the single hierarchy arrangement in Figure 10.10. The most obvious is the one that we have already alluded to: By moving the player annual statistics and position information over to the Teams hierarchy we eliminate the redundancy of having each Players segment appear twice, once in each of the two hierarchies. And with the single hierarchy arrangement we achieve a higher degree of data integration. Suppose we want a report detailing all of the player position information for all of the players for a given team. Even though we have not gone into data accessing in IMS yet, you can see that in the two-hierarchy arrangement of Figure 10.9, we would have to use the Teams hierarchy to find out who all of the players are on that team and then use that information to inquire about the position information for those players in the Players hierarchy. In the single hierarchy of Figure 10.10, we can gather all of that information in a much more direct manner.

So which arrangement do we use? What we would really like are the strengths of both and the weaknesses of neither. We would like the more flexible access and less restrictive storage benefits of the two-hierarchy case and, at the same time, the reduced redundancy and higher degree of data integration of the single hierarchy case. In fact, there is a facility in IMS that brings together the best of both of those worlds; it is called **logical relationships**.

Figure 10.11 shows what is known as a unidirectional logical relationship. We have replaced the Players segment in the Teams hier-

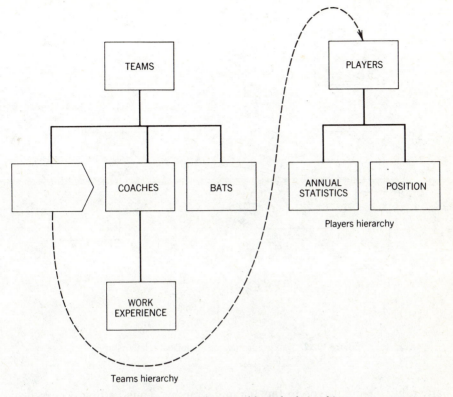

Figure 10.11. A unidirectional logical relationship.

archy with a special kind of pointer segment known as a **logical child segment**. We can jump from that logical child segment in the Teams hierarchy to the Players segment in the Players hierarchy, effectively finding all of the players on a given team, just as we could with the old Players segment in the Teams hierarchy. Have we accomplished what we aimed to? Since the Players hierarchy remains as it was we can find players directly (it's still the root of its own hierarchy) and handle the case of a player not currently on a team. Since the player information only appears in one of the two hierarchies we have eliminated the players redundancy that we were concerned about. Finally, using the logical relationship we can start at the Teams segment of the Teams hierarchy and cross over to the Players hierarchy, picking up all of the player, annual statistics, and position information that we desire. That takes care of the broader level of data integration that we talked about before.

Implementation. How does that really work on the disk? Figure 10.12 shows part of the Dodgers database record from the Teams database, together with the root portions of the Doe, Jones, and Smith database records from the Players database. The logical child segment behaves like

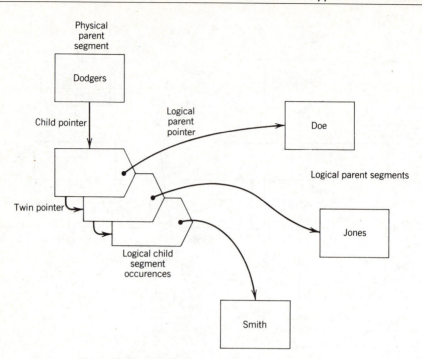

Figure 10.12.   An occurrence of the logical relationship.

any other segment type in the Teams hierarchy. Thus its first occurrence under a given team is reached via a child pointer, and the rest are reached via a twin chain as shown. But there is now an additional pointer, housed in the logical child segment (called a **logical parent pointer**) which jumps over to the other database. Incidentally, because the logical child segment is really a part of the Teams hierarchy, we refer to its parent segment, Teams, as its **physical parent**, and the segment that it points to in the other hierarchy, PLAYERS, as its **logical parent**.

As an aside, why did we bother setting up an entire new segment type, the logical child segment, to effect the logical relationship? In going from Dodgers to the logical child occurrences and over to the Players occurrences aren't we just following one pointer (the child pointer out of Dodgers) to another pointer (the logical parent pointer) to finally get to the destination? Why not just have one pointer in Dodgers that points directly over to its players? The answer is that we can't do that because we don't know how many players there are on the Dodgers, and so we wouldn't know how much room to leave for all of the pointers that we would have to put in the Dodgers segment. Setting up the logical child segments as we have done allows for any number of players, lets the system use its normal methods for insertions and deletions, and simplifies the application programming. It also allows for intersection data.

Intersection Data.   At this point we will re-introduce the concept of intersection data that we explored in Chapter 6 and see how it fits into IMS hierarchical structures.

We long ago settled the matter that simple attribute data, like a team's manager, is stored as a field in the appropriate segment. But there is another kind of attribute data. Often there is descriptive information about a relationship *between* two entities, and that kind of information cannot go into either of their segments. Consider, for example, the number of years that a player has played on a particular team. Could that information be stored in the team's segment? No, because there are many players on that team and it would be impractical to store such information in its segment. What about in the player's segment? If we now consider this database to hold historical data, we have the same problem: A player may have played on several different teams over many years. The answer is to take advantage of the logical child segments. One of the things that Figure 10.12 shows is that there is a different occurrence of the logical child segment *for every combination of a related team and player.* Thus the logical child occurrence that connects two entity occurrences is the natural place to store such intersection data. Figure 10.13 shows how we would

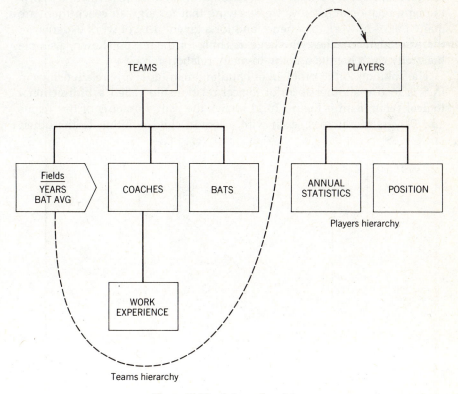

Figure 10.13.   Intersection data.

represent intersection data in the general structure. By the way, that's the first time that we've seen fields—intersection data is represented as fields—in any of this series of figures. (BAT AVG is that player's batting average calculated over all of the years that he played for that team.)

Many-to-Many Relationships. Hierarchies, as we have shown, are quite adept at handling one-to-many relationships. But as it turns out, a single simple hierarchy cannot handle many-to-many relationships. Look at Figure 10.6 once again. Both coaches Adams and Baker had college coaching experience. Let's assume for the moment that there are no fields other than the EXPERIENCE NAME field in those Work Experience segments, making the two College Coaching segments identical. If that's the case, then isn't it redundant to carry the identical College Coaching segment under two different coaches?

Yes, it is. But what is the alternative? If we had both Adams and Baker, either through child or twin pointers, point to a single College Coaching segment, then we would get all mixed up over whether the Japan League Coaching and Minor League Coaching segments, connected to the College Coaching segment via a twin chain, belonged to Adams or to Baker. The reason that happens is that the situation described really involves a many-to-many relationship. Now we're saying that for a given coach there are many pieces of work experience and for a given piece of work experience, there are many coaches who have it. Thus, for the reason shown, a simple hierarchy can't handle a many-to-many relationship.

The solution to the problem of handling many-to-many relationships in IMS is to use another form of logical relationship called a **bidirectional logical relationship**. Figure 10.14 shows the root segments of the Teams and Players hierarchies, each with a logical child pointing to the other.

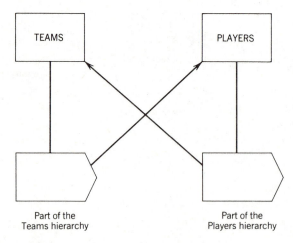

Figure 10.14.   A bidirectional logical relationship for a many-to-many relationship.

Again, consider the data to be historical in nature so that we are interested in keeping track of all of the teams that a particular player has ever played on, and of all of the players who have ever played on a particular team. This is a many-to-many relationship, which can be implemented in IMS by the dual or bidirectional logical relationship structure shown.

Once again moving to a view of the actual storage, Figure 10.15 shows an occurrence of that bidirectional logical relationship. The Dodgers have had Doe and Jones on their team. The Giants have had Jones and Smith on their team. Conversely, Doe has played for the Dodgers, Jones has played

Figure 10.15. An occurrence of the bidirectional logical relationship.

for the Dodgers and the Giants, and Smith has played for the Giants. The child, twin, and logical parent pointers operate as before, but in both directions.

With this arrangement, there are two logical child occurrences for every match-up between a player and a team, specifically one under the player involved and one under the team involved. The two boxes labeled "A" in Figure 10.15 both connect the Dodgers with Doe. We will note in passing that if intersection data exists, such as the number of years that a player has played for a team in this example, it is stored in both of the appropriate logical child segments, and if it ever changes in one place, the IMS system automatically updates it in the other.

Figure 10.16 shows the entire Teams and Players hierarchies connected by the "physically paired" bidirectional logical relationship. It also includes the YEARS and BAT AVG fields as sample intersection data. You should refer back to the baseball relational database of Figure 7.1 to recognize that this IMS bidirectional logical relationship serves the same purpose here that the Affiliation table did in the relational case. Each is capable of handling the many-to-many relationship and the associated intersection data in its respective environment. Finally, note in passing that there is another, structurally more complex form of bidirectional logical relationship (called "virtually paired") in which intersection data resides on only one side of the relationship.

Logical versus Physical Databases

Incidentally, did it sound strange a little while ago when we were talking about a logical child segment's "logical" and "physical" parents? Were we saying that the logical child segment can have *two* parent segment types, a physical parent and a logical parent? Doesn't that violate the fact that in a tree a node can have only one parent? Yes and no.

Each of the two separate structures in Figure 10.9 is clearly a hierarchy. The combined structures shown in Figures 10.11, 10.14, and 10.16 are, technically, restricted networks. We will discuss networks as a database storage form in Chapter 11. Suffice it to say for now that a network is a more complex form than a hierarchy (in fact, a hierarchy is a limited kind of network). What is important about this in terms of IMS is that while, technically, the use of logical relationships creates networks in the underlying physical structure, *programmers always write their programs based on hierarchies.*

All of the IMS database structures that we have looked at thus far are known as IMS **physical databases**. Programmers (we will look at IMS programming shortly) write their code based on IMS **logical databases**. Logical databases and their derivatives are really the logical view mechanism in IMS, merely descriptions of what the programmers should consider the data to look like. Segments of logical databases map onto

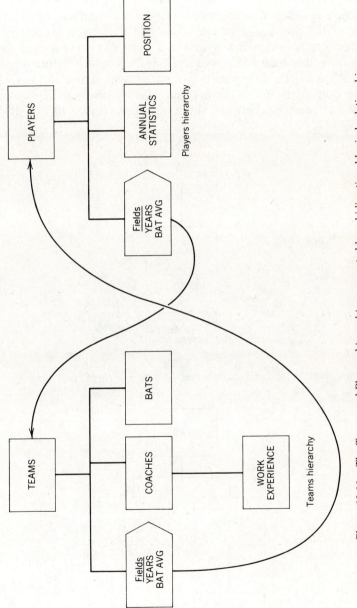

Figure 10.16. The Teams and Players hierarchies connected by a bidirectional logical relationship.

segments of physical databases, which contain the actual data. An IMS logical database, in the simplest case, is a subtree of an IMS physical hierarchy; that is, it consists of a node and some or all of its descendants. The starting node, that is, the root of the logical database, must be either the root of the physical database or a node that has a secondary index (to be discussed later) pointing into it. Figure 10.17 is a logical database derived from the Teams physical database. Compare Figure 10.17 with Figure 10.9 to see the mapping between the two. Figure 10.18 is a logical database derived from the Teams and Players physical hierarchies and the logical relationship between them. Compare Figure 10.18 with Figure

Figure 10.17.   A logical database derived from a single physical hierarchy.

Figure 10.18.   A logical database derived from two physical hierarchies connected by a logical relationship.

10.11 and see how the logical relationship connecting the two physical databases becomes a branch in the logical database.

There are a couple of advantages to the concept of logical databases. One is simplicity, in that the programmers always work with hierarchies, not networks. Another is the ability to have different programs access data from the same physical database(s), with each program being restricted to only those segments (and even only those fields) that it really needs.

Access Methods

In Chapter 3, we discussed access methods for simple linear files. Several times thus far in this chapter there has appeared the expression, "assuming that we can reach the root occurrences directly." The time has come to make some meaning out of that expression and discuss access methods in the hierarchical context.

There are four main "IMS Access Methods." They are:

1. Hierarchic Sequential Access Method (HSAM)
2. Hierarchic Indexed Sequential Access Method (HISAM)
3. Hierarchic Indexed Direct Access Method (HIDAM)
4. Hierarchic Direct Access Method (HDAM)

The choice of IMS Access Method really determines two things. One is whether the individual database records will be stored using the sequential or pointer-based storage techniques. The second is the type of access that the system will construct to the root occurrence of each database record. Figure 10.19 outlines all of the possibilities.

In HSAM the database records are constructed using the sequential storage technique. As far as access to the root occurrences goes, there is no direct access capability. The database records are simply stored one after the other on the disk in sequence based on the key field in the root segment. Lacking any direct access capability, HSAM is used, for example, for archival storage.

As in HSAM, the database records in HISAM are constructed using the sequential storage technique. But in HISAM, the database records are

	Access to Root	Database Record Structure
HSAM	Sequential	Sequential
HISAM	Indexed	Sequential
HIDAM	Indexed	Pointer-Based
HDAM	Hashed	Pointer-Based

Figure 10.19. IMS Access Methods.

directly accessible via an index that points to the key field of the root occurrences, as shown in Figure 10.20. The index used today is usually the VSAM-KSDS index that we discussed in Chapter 3. Since that is really an indexed-sequential structure, not only are the database records directly accessible by the key of the root segment, but they are also stored in physical sequence by that field, too.

In HIDAM the database records are constructed using the child pointer–twin pointer arrangement (or another method known as hierarchic pointers). Here, as in HISAM, the VSAM-KSDS index is used to access the roots. The combination of direct, indexed access to the roots, plus pointer-based construction of the database records makes HIDAM a candidate for use in on-line, fast response systems.

In HDAM the database records are constructed using the pointer-based method. The root occurrences are directly accessible, but this time using a hashing-based access method. That means that with HDAM, access to the root occurrences is normally faster than with HIDAM, but since hashing is used, the database records are in no particular order, sequential or otherwise, on the disk. The fastest access method is generally considered to be HDAM.

One final note about this topic: Figure 10.20 is really a rather profound diagram. It shows the use of the tree concept *both for index construction and for data storage simultaneously*. The VSAM-KSDS index is based on the tree concept, as is the method of storing the actual data in the IMS database records. The distinction between those two uses of the tree and the fact that they can be used in tandem are important, interesting, and often overlooked.

Secondary Indexes

Using the IMS Access Methods, direct access to database records can be achieved through the key field of the root segment. But there are many circumstances in which additional direct access is required. This can either take the form of direct access to the root segment via a field other than the key or direct access to any field of any other segment. For example, going back to the Teams hierarchy in Figure 10.9, we might want direct access to the Teams segment via the MANAGER NAME field or direct access to the Coaches segment via the COACH NAME field.

Such additional direct access can be accomplished by the use of a **secondary index**. While the values of the key fields used in the IMS Access Methods must be unique, the fields on which secondary indexes are built need not be. Figure 10.21 shows the Teams hierarchy with secondary indexes pointing to the two fields suggested. The secondary indexes themselves are organized as additional VSAM-KSDS indexes.

A side effect of the use of secondary indexes is additional flexibility in the creation of logical databases. We mentioned earlier that without the use of secondary indexes, the root of a logical database must be

Figure 10.20. The index concept in HISAM or HIDAM.

211

the root of a physical database. However, with the use of secondary indexes, the root of a logical database may be either the root of a physical database or a segment pointed to by a secondary index. Loosely speaking, the root of a logical database must map onto a physical segment that can be accessed directly. If the root of a logical database is a segment pointed to by a secondary index, the structure of the logical database must conform to certain rules. Figure 10.22 shows a logical database based on the physical database of Figure 10.21. Relying on the Coach Name secondary index, the Coaches segment is set up as the root of the logical hierarchy. The subordinate segments in the logical hierarchy fall into two classes. They may be any of the logical root's descendants in the physical hierarchy (the Work Experience segment in this case). Or they may be the segments in the unique path of segments from the indexed segment (Coaches) back to the root of the physical database (which qualifies only the Teams segment in this example). In this arrangement, the system uses an optional pointer called the "physical parent" pointer to point upward in the physical hierarchy, for example, from Coaches to Teams in Figure

Figure 10.21. Secondary indexes.

Figure 10.22.   A logical database based on a secondary index.

10.21, so that logically Coaches can have Teams as a subordinate segment type in Figure 10.22.

Let's note in passing that since a secondary index orders the values of the field that it indexes, it can be used for sequential retrieval too. For example, the COACH NAME field secondary index of Figure 10.21 could be used to retrieve all of the league's coaches in alphabetic order, regardless of what teams they are working for. The problem with that is performance: Since the coaches were stored relative to the teams that they work for, their storage was done without regard to keeping coach names that are close in alphabetic order near each other on the disk. Using the secondary index to retrieve them sequentially will cause a great deal of disk access arm movement, and poor performance will result.

Control Blocks

We're about to discuss how programmers use IMS and its data (the "data manipulation language"). But first, we must mention the link within the IMS system between the data structures and the application programs that will use them.

It's well and good to talk about hierarchies, logical relationships, and so on, and about how they are physically stored and accessed. But how does the IMS system, as the middleman between the data and the programs, know what the nature of the data is and how it is stored? The answer is with a set of instructions given to IMS, known as *control blocks*.

There are several kinds of control blocks in IMS, and it is interesting to see how they mesh with the concepts and structures that we have been discussing. One is called the Physical Data Base Description (Physical DBD). Physical DBDs describe the physical storage structures, including what the segments are, how they are arranged in hierarchies, key fields, logical relationships, secondary indexes, IMS Access Methods, and optional pointer choices. Interestingly, the way that the hierarchical structure is specified is by indicating the parent of each listed segment. Since one of the characteristics of the tree structure is that every node has exactly one parent (except for the root, which has none), that method is an unambiguous way of specifying to the system what the tree structures look like.

There are also several kinds of control blocks that describe what we have called the logical databases, that is, data the way that programmers perceive it. First there is the Logical Data Base Description (Logical DBD) control block. It selects those segments of individual or logical relationship–connected physical hierarchies that will form the programmers' hierarchical views. The Program Communication Block (PCB) is a control block that picks out subtrees from the Logical DBDs (the rules about which segments may be roots in the logical structures hold here, too) for specific program uses. Any given IMS program ties to one Program Specification Block (PSB), which lists all of the PCBs needed by that program.

DL/I Language Interface

Introduction

In terms of data manipulation, DL/I is what we referred to earlier as an "embedded" language. DL/I statements that access the data in the IMS database are embedded in COBOL, PL/I, or Assembler language application programs. In effect, the DL/I statements function as macro or subroutine calls to the IMS database management system, instructing it to retrieve or store data in the IMS databases. Let's take a look at how this works.

The Calling Mechanism

The DL/I call statement contains a number of parameters, each designed to perform a specific function in communicating between the program and the database during the data transfer operation. The parameter that sets the tone for this call statement is the "Function Code," which specifies what kind of data transfer statement it is. It distinguishes among the four basic kinds of such operations—retrieval, update, insertion, and deletion—and among some variations within them, as we shall soon see.

Once you have specified what kind of operation this is to be, you must indicate what portion of the database it is to operate on. For that purpose, the DL/I call statement includes a PCB name. Remember a PCB is a control block that defines a portion of the database from the programmer's point of view.

Also, there must be a defined storage area in main memory that serves as the actual transfer point for data. When a retrieval operation is specified, the defined storage area is where the program knows the requested data will be placed after it is found in the database. On an insertion or update operation, that is where the program is to put the new data for the system to pick up and transfer to the database. In DL/I this is called the "Input/Output Area" or "I/O Area."

In addition, there is other information that the system passes back for the program's use after a call is made. This includes a list of the key field occurrences of the segments that the system encounters from the root segment down to the segment being sought. The list of key field occurrences is placed in a designated storage area (called the "Key Feedback Area.") The system also sends back a status code providing further information about the result of the call.

Last but not least in the call statement are the "Segment Search Arguments" (SSAs). These are parameters that guide the system through the hierarchy specified by the PCB, to the place where the desired operation is to take place. In the following example we will further explain all of these parameters and concepts.

Figure 10.23 is a logical database that encompasses the entire Teams physical database (thus, making it identical with Figure 10.5). It not only shows the segments in the hierarchy but also the fields in the segments. The leftmost field in each segment is a unique key field. In DL/I the root segment must have a unique key field, but the subordinate segments may or may not have one. Figure 10.24 is the occurrence of the Teams hierarchy for the Dodgers (the Dodgers database record) first shown in Figure 10.6, but this time including the field occurrences. As shown, it is structured with child and twin pointers. We will assume that the IMS Access Method chosen is either HIDAM or HDAM, so that the key field of the root segment is either indexed or hashed for direct access.

Direct Retrieval

The simplest kind of DL/I statement is the GET UNIQUE statement, which has a function code of "GU." It is designed to find a specific segment occurrence directly and return it or several of its fields to the calling

Figure 10.23. The Teams hierarchy showing segment names and field names.

Figure 10.24. Field occurrences in the Dodgers database record.

program. The nature of the direct retrieval is based on locating the root segment of a logical hierarchy. Again, this means that that segment either maps to a segment that is the root of a physical hierarchy (and is accessible by either a hashing algorithm or an index) or is a segment that has a secondary index pointing to it. Let's take a look at it in the context of our baseball example.

Suppose you want to find the root occurrence of the Dodgers database record because you want to find its home city and manager's name. Assume that at the point you need the information you know that the Dodgers are team number 12. At the appropriate point in your program's logic, you would issue the following DL/I call: (Note: for simplicity, all of the following examples will show only the function code and segment search arguments).

GU TEAMS (TEAMNUM = 12)

The expression "TEAMS (TEAMNUM = 12)" is called a Qualified SSA. Remember that the PCB denoted in the call (not shown in this example) specifies which *hierarchy* you are interested in. The segment name (TEAMS) in the SSA specifies which *segment type* in that hierarchy you are interested in. The field name and value (TEAMNUM = 12) in the SSA specifies which *occurrence* of that segment type in that hierarchy you are interested in. Thus the expression "GU TEAMS (TEAMNUM = 12)," with the Teams hierarchy specified in the PCB, says to the system, "Go to the Teams hierarchy and find the occurrence of the Teams segment that has a TEAMNUM field value of 12, and return that segment to the program." In this case, since the field involved in the SSA (the "search field") is a unique key field, then of course, there will only be one segment involved.

Since TEAMNUM is a unique key field, and in fact, is the key field of the root segment, this call will be quite straightforward. The system will determine which IMS Access Method the database is stored with, and thus determine whether the database records are stored with an index based on the key of the root (TEAMNUM) or are stored directly with a hashing algorithm based on the key of the root. The system will find the Teams segment for Dodgers and return

```
12  Dodgers  Los Angeles  Wilson
```

to the designated I/O Area.

You can also issue a GET UNIQUE call with a search field that is not the key of the root segment (and is not a field that has been indexed with a secondary index). In that case the system will do a sequential search through the database records of that database looking for the requested segment. Obviously, this can be a very time-consuming process, therefore the database design and the DL/I calls must take it into account.

The following is an example with multiple SSAs. Suppose you know that Baker, a coach on the Dodgers, used to be a minor league coach, and you want to find out how many years he coached in the minors. You would issue the following DL/I call:

```
GU TEAMS (TEAMNUM = 12)
   COACHES (COACHNAM = Baker)
   WORKEXP (EXPTYPE = Minor League Coach)
```

Look at Figure 10.23 and notice that each of the three SSAs refers to a record type at a successive level downwards in the hierarchy. Again, since the first SSA refers to the key field of the root segment, the system will find the Dodgers root directly. Then, following the instructions in the succeeding SSAs, it will move from the Dodgers database record, following along the child and twin pointers, to the Coaches occurrence for Baker, then to the Workexp occurrence for Minor League Coach. Note that if any of the search fields in the lower level SSAs are not unique, the system will choose the first occurrence it comes to that satisfies the condition within the higher level SSA constraints. It will return the last segment named in the SSA list to the I/O Area:

Minor League Coach   4

The Key Feedback Area will contain:

12 Baker   Minor League Coach

which are the key fields of the three segments designated by the SSAs and accessed during the search. The EXPYRS field in the retrieved segment has the value 4, and that is the answer to the question.

SSAs can also be "unqualified." Suppose we know that each coach's set of work experiences are ordered from earliest to most recent, and you want to find Baker's earliest work experience, not knowing in advance what type it is. You would issue:

GU TEAMS (TEAMNUM = 12)
   COACHES (COACHNAM = Baker)
   WORKEXP

The system would home in on Baker under Dodgers and pick up his first work experience with no qualification.

What if you issue a GET UNIQUE and the segment that you specify in the SSAs is not there? This is where the status code comes in. For each DL/I function code, there are a number of status codes that can be returned by the system after a call with that code is issued. In the situation of the missing segment described here, a status code indicating "Not Found" would be returned. After every DL/I call the application program must include instructions to test for the status codes that are appropriate possibilities for the function code used in that call.

Sequential Retrieval

IMS is also capable of conducting sequential searches through the database. In their simplest form, such sequential searches consist of retrieving all or some of the segments on a twin chain. However, sequential searches can involve occurrences of different segment types in a database record and even segment occurrences in more than one database record. It is important to note that when the latter happens, the order of retrieval is preorder sequential: top to bottom, left to right, and front to back, regardless of whether the actual storage of the segment occurrences is accomplished physically sequentially in preorder sequential order or is accomplished with child and twin pointers.

In the direct retrieval situations that we just saw the search always started at the beginning of the database. In sequential retrieval we will establish a position at a particular record in the database and work from there. That position, which can be set with either a GU call or with one of the sequential type calls, that we are about to look at, is held with a "current position" pointer, which the system takes responsibility for maintaining. Loosely speaking, it means the system always keeps track of exactly "where it is in the database" at any given time.

As a final note before looking at a few examples, let's consider how a program can use the data returned to it as the result of IMS sequential retrievals. In the direct retrieval case, the program issued a single request and got back a single segment occurrence. In an in-line fashion, the program's logic could make whatever use of the data it was supposed to. But in the sequential retrieval case, the program must plan to process multiple occurrences of the same segment type (on a twin chain) or even occurrences of different segment types. Thus the IMS calls involving sequential retrieval statements must be in the midst of some kind of loop in the program logic to process one occurrence, then another, then another, until all of the intended occurrences have been processed.

Suppose you wanted to retrieve all of the occurrences of all types of segments under the Dodgers root. You would first issue:

```
GU TEAMS (TEAMNUM = 12)
```

which would accomplish two things. First of all it would get you the information in that root segment occurrence, and second it would establish the system's current position pointer at that segment occurrence. Then to get all of the subordinate segment occurrences, you would issue the "GET NEXT" statement in some kind of a program loop:

```
GN
```

Each time that (very simple) GN call statement is executed in the loop, the system will return another segment in preorder sequential order. First will be the Players segment for Doe, then Jones, then Smith, then the Coaches segment for Adams, followed by his two Workexp segments, then Baker, followed by his three Workexp segments, then the three Bats segments. If the GN call was executed one more time, the next segment occurrence to be returned would be the root segment of *the next database record*. To stop that from happening, the program must continually check the status code returned by the system. After GN calls, the system will indicate whether the current position pointer has moved up a level in the database record, retrieved a segment type different than the last one, or reached the end of the database. Of course, the program can also check to see the type of segment retrieved, which would also answer the question of whether it has gone on to the next database record (i.e., if the segment type retrieved is a root).

For example, as a variation on this theme, if you issue

GN COACHES

in a loop, you will retrieve all of the Coach segment occurrences starting from the point that the current position pointer is at, to the point that your program ends the execution of the loop.

While the GN statement is obviously useful, it may have struck you that it seems a bit uncontrolled in the way that it can jump from segment type to segment type. What is needed is a way to more carefully limit the range of a sequential retrieval call. In fact, it is quite common to have application situations in which we want to focus on a single, particular segment occurrence and consider only its subordinate occurrences and no other record occurrences in the database. To accomplish this in DL/I there is another function code called "GET NEXT WITHIN PARENT" (GNP).

Let's say that you want to find all of the players on the Dodgers. First you would "establish parentage" (which can be done with either a GU or GN call) by issuing:

GU TEAMS (TEAMNUM = 12)

Then you would loop through:

GNP PLAYERS

After you have retrieved the last of the players on the Dodgers (Smith), the next pass through that loop will produce a status code indicating that there are no more occurrences of that segment type within the parentage setting (no more players on the Dodgers).

If you want to find all of the subordinate segment occurrences of all types under the Dodgers root, you would again establish parentage at Dodgers and then loop through

GNP

This time, in preorder sequential order, you will pick up all of the subordinate segment occurrences under Dodgers, from Doe to bat number B13, and then on the next pass through the loop the system would return the status code indicating that you have reached the end of the parentage bounds.

Insertion, Deletion, and Update

Insertion. When a new segment occurrence is to be inserted, the program must place it in the I/O Area. Then a DL/I INSERT call must be issued, with the lowest level SSA left unqualified. For example, if you want to insert a new player under Dodgers, you would place the new segment occurrence in the I/O Area and issue:

```
ISRT TEAMS (TEAMNUM = 12)
     PLAYERS
```

If the segment occurrence being inserted is a root, then the system uses the appropriate indexing or hashing technique to insert it into the correct place in the database. If it is not a root, then the system will insert it into the appropriate twin chain in one of several ways. If the segment type has a unique key field on which sequence is being maintained, then the system will insert the segment into the place that will maintain that sequence based on the inserted segment's key field value. If the segment type has no key field, then it will be placed either at the beginning of the twin chain (referred to as "first" in the syntax), the end of the twin chain ("last"), or wherever in the twin chain the system's current position pointer happens to be ("here"), depending on specifications made in the control blocks. If the segment has a nonunique key field, then the same "first, last, or here" rules apply within the equi-key value segments on that twin chain.

Deletion. Deletion is simply a matter of specifying a particular segment occurrence by having the system's current position pointer point to it and then issuing a DLET call. That pointer would ordinarily be positioned with a retrieval call: GU, GN, or GNP. However, there is a potential problem, not just with IMS, but with any shared data situation in which multiple users may try to simultaneously change a record. It requires the use of slightly different function codes in this context. We will discuss that problem later under the heading of "concurrency." Suffice it for now to say that there is a set of commands parallel to GET UNIQUE, GET NEXT, and GET NEXT WITHIN PARENT, known as "GET HOLD" commands, which are used when that situation may be a factor. They are GET HOLD UNIQUE (GHU), GET HOLD NEXT (GHN), and GET HOLD NEXT WITHIN PARENT (GHNP). Thus to delete the segment occurrence for bat number B09, you would issue:

```
GHU TEAMS (TEAMNUM = 12)
    BATS (BATNUM = B09)
DLET
```

There is a potential complication on a delete operation, which has to do with logical relationships. First let's look a little bit closer at deletions within our single physical hierarchy example. If we delete the segment for coach Adams, we should reasonably expect the system to also automatically delete his experience segments, and it will. There's no point in keeping around a coach's experience segments if he no longer exists. In fact, this is a characteristic of the hierarchical structure: Other than a root occurrence, every segment occurrence must be attached to a parent occurrence at all times.

But what if the DL/I call refers to a logical database that involves two physical databases connected by a logical relationship? Refer back to the logical hierarchy in Figure 10.18 and to the two connected hierarchies in Figure 10.13 on which that logical hierarchy is based. If we delete the Dodgers root segment occurrence, should all of the players on the Dodgers be deleted from the database too? After all, they are connected under Dodgers in the logical hierarchy in Figure 10.18. On the other hand, in the physical hierarchies of Figure 10.13, they stand alone as occurrences of a physical root segment type. The answer depends on the application situation. We might want them to be deleted or we might not. The system is general enough to allow for that decision to be made in advance in the control blocks. In IMS this is called "rules coding," and there are such "rules" for insertion and update as well as for deletion.

Update.   The update operation in DL/I is called "REPLACE" and has a function code of REPL. The mode of operation is a cross between those of INSERT and DELETE. The updated segment is placed in the I/O Area (as in Insert). The segment to be updated is located in the database with the current position pointer, and the GET HOLD commands are used (as in Delete).

Additional Topics

Command Codes.   Certain parameters (called "command codes") can be added to DL/I call statements. They are capable of expanding the range of function of the DL/I calls. Here are two examples.

As we have seen, a multi-SSA call retrieves only the segment named in the last SSA. There is a parameter that signals a "path call," which retrieves all (or any additional specified) segments in the unique path of segments between the first and last specified SSAs. For example, the call:

```
GU TEAMS*D (TEAMNUM = 12)
   BATS (BATNUM = B09)
```

would return

```
12  Dodgers  Los Angeles  Wilson  B09  General
```

in the I/O Area. "D" is the parameter for the path call and is not required on the last SSA since it is always returned.

The parameter "L" will find the last occurrence on a twin chain. For example:

```
GU TEAMS (TEAMNUM = 12)
    BATS*L
```

will return

```
B13   Acme
```

in the I/O Area.

Multiple "Current Position Pointers."   We have described the current position pointer as a place keeper within a database. There are application situations in which one such pointer is not enough. For instance, a program may need to keep track of the last occurrence of each of several different segment types that it accessed. Two techniques, known as "multiple positioning" and "multiple PCBs," allow for a range of options in having the system maintain multiple current position pointers. Those options include a separate such pointer for each segment type in a hierarchy and even multiple positions within the segment type.

Application Development Facility (ADF)

The Application Generator Concept.   A **transaction** in IMS is a message sent by a user from a terminal into the computer, which triggers a program to begin some processing and eventually return the results to the terminal. Some transactions are associated with complex and protracted processing, but many transactions are simple requests to display the data in a segment, insert or delete a segment, or update the data in a segment. Certainly the program logic and code needed to perform those simple functions will differ little from one such request to another, albeit different data, hierarchical structures, and screen displays will be involved. It seems a shame to have to have programmers write such code from scratch every time a new program that must process such simple transactions is written.

This situation is common to any database (and in general to any large-scale file processing) environment. One response to it has been the development of **application generators**. An application generator allows a programmer to implement simple display, insert, delete, and update application functions at a simpler, higher level than that provided by ordinary COBOL or other standard language code. Typically, an application generator contains standard routines for performing those simple functions. The generator plugs a description of the database involved and a description of the nature of the output required (such as the screen layout) for a specific application into those standard routines and produces code to accomplish the requested functions.

For DL/I applications, IBM originally offered the Application Development Facility (ADF) for the IMS/DC environment, and the functionally similar Development Management System (DMS) for the CICS environment. DMS has since been replaced by the Cross Systems Product (CSP), which may eventually subsume ADF, too.

Application Development with ADF. Application development with ADF is an alternative to writing programs in COBOL, PL/I, or Assembler that access IMS databases. It is important to understand at this point that ADF has absolutely nothing to do with designing or creating IMS databases. Like a COBOL program with embedded DL/I calls in it, ADF is strictly a vehicle for accessing existing DL/I databases and displaying or manipulating the data in them.

ADF contains standard processing routines for database manipulation that are tailored by the application developer for the particular application. The tailoring is done by supplying the system with descriptive specifications called "rules." The rules describe the structure of the databases to be accessed; the nature of the transactions; security considerations of which users can perform what functions on what data; edit and audit functions, which check to make sure that data being input into the database fall within expected value ranges; and error messages for given situations. The rules are specified as lines in tables, and thus ADF is called a "table driven" system.

In addition, for more complex functions, users can execute COBOL, PL/I, or Assembler code in a "special processing" mode while remaining under the ADF umbrella.

Using ADF. Figure 10.25 is the first image that the ADF user sees on the display screen (after a simple sign-on screen). This "Primary Menu" screen is a system-generated, standard screen that presents the user with several options. For database access the user would select option "D," indicating that he or she wants to execute an IMS transaction. The user would then also select a transaction mode. The transaction modes on the Primary Menu screen represent the four simple functions that we have been discussing. The reason that there are six modes listed is that a distinction is made between deleting or inserting a root segment ("delete" and "initiate") and a nonroot segment ("remove" and "add"). The term "retrieve" indicates a simple display of data, while "update" means display and permit changes.

Having indicated the type of operation to be performed, the system then moves the user to the "Secondary Option Selection" screen, shown in Figure 10.26. Using this screen the user selects the desired transaction from among those transactions he or she is authorized to execute. The transaction includes directions both on what is to be done, and on which segment *type* of which database it is to be done to.

```
                      P R I M A R Y     M E N U
    OPTION:       TRANSACTION MODE:      IDENTIFIER:
                  KEY:

      OPTIONS                          TRANSACTION MODES
  A - PROJECT MESSAGE SENDING           1 - DELETE
  B - PROJECT MESSAGE DISPLAY           2 - INITIATE
  C - SESSION TERMINATION               3 - REMOVE
  D - TRANSACTION SELECTION             4 - ADD
  F - PROJECT / GROUP SWITCH            5 - UPDATE
  H - USER MESSAGE SENDING              6 - RETRIEVE
  I - USER MESSAGE DISPLAY

                        FOR OPTION  - IDENTIFIER IS
                             D      - TRANSACTION ID
                             F      - PROJECT/GROUP
                      A,B,C,H,I     - (NOT USED)
```

Figure 10.25. ADF Primary Menu. (Reprinted by permission from *IMSADF GIM* (GB21-9869-2) by IBM Corporation.)

Figure 10.27 shows the "Primary Key Selection Screen," which is the next one that the user sees. It specifies what the key field(s) are of the segment type that will be accessed by the requested transaction and allows the user to enter values for those key fields. This tells the system which *occurrence* of that segment type the user wants to see or work on.

Finally, the segment occurrence in question is displayed, as shown in Figure 10.28. If the segment occurrence exists already, the display will

```
     S E C O N D A R Y   O P T I O N   S E L E C T I O N   PAGE:
                                                            LAST
INITIATE  SELECT:      KEY:
ACTION:                SELECT 'C' TO RETURN TO PRIMARY MENU
P3 - PAY/PERS YTD
P5 - PAY/PERS YTD
P7 - PAY/PERS SAVINGS BOND
P8 - PAY/PERS MISC.LEAVE
PA - PAY/PERS PERS+EDUC
PB - PAY/PERS POSITION
PC - PAY/PERS APPOINTMENT
PD - PAY/PERS SEPARATION
C2 - CLASS/COMP GRADE
C4 - CLASS/COMP POSN+HOLDER
T3 - TIME+ATTEND ACCT CHG
T4 - TIME+ATTEND LEAVE
M2 - PAYROLL PROCESS
D2 - DEPT/PAYR PROCESS
A1 - PAY CHK RECON
EA - EMPLOYEE APPOINTMENT
```

Figure 10.26. ADF Secondary Option Selection Menu. (Reprinted by permission from *IMSADF GIM* (GB21-9869-2) by IBM Corporation.)

```
                              PRPS PAYROLL/PERSONNEL APPLICATIONS
                                 PRIMARY KEY SELECTION SCREEN
        INITIATE      TRANSACTION:  EMPLOYEE APPOINTMENT
        OPTION:       TRX:  2EA  KEY:

      *** ENTER THE FOLLOWING KEY INFORMATION ***
          EMPL SOC-SEC NUMBER-----------
          PAY-PERS KEY PERSONNEL--------
          PAY-PERS KEY EDUCATION--------
          PAY-PERS KEY POSITION---------
          PAY-PERS KEY APPOINT----------
```

Figure 10.27. ADF Primary Key Selection Menu. (Reprinted by permission from *IMSADF GIM* (GB21-9869-2) by IBM Corporation.)

```
              PRPS PAYROLL/PERSONNEL APPLICATIONS

                  EMPLOYEE APPOINTMENT (PAGE 1 OF 2)
      INITIATE          TRANSACTION:  EMPLOYEE APPOINTMENT
      OPTION:      TRX:   2EA  KEY:    548586513B5B5B5B5
      *** ENTER DATA FOR UPDATE ***
      SOCIAL SECURITY NUMBER:  _____
      POSITION NUMBER:  _____
      TITLE CODE:   GRADE:__   STEP:__   SALARY:      .00  HOW-PAID:  _____
      EMPLOYEE NAME LAST:_____  FIRST:_____  MI:__  JRSR:  _____
      PRIOR SERVICE:    0      YEAR LAST WORKED:  _____
      PROBATION CODE:____     DATE PROBATION END:_____   FLAS:_____
      TYPE APPOINTMENT:_____   FULLPART TIME:  ____   HIRE DATE:_____  MAIN:_____
      PAY-PERS KEYS: :  PERSONNEL(P9):  B5    EDUCATION(PA)  :  B5
                        POSITION (PB):  B5    APPOINTMENT(PC):  B5
        NEXT SCREEN:ENTER,OR STOP PROCESS:E,OR RETURN TO BEGINNING:R  1
```

Figure 10.28. ADF Data Display. (Reprinted by permission from *IMSADF GIM* (GB21-9869-2) by IBM Corporation.)

show the actual field values along with the field names. If not, then it will show just the field names (in preparation for an insert operation, for example). The format of this final display can be a system default arrangement or specified by the application developer in a very easy way.

References

IBM Corporation, *IMS Application Development Facility (IMSADF) General Information Manual*, IBM Form No. GB21-9869 (1980).

IBM Corporation, *DL/I Functions for Application Design*, IBM Form No. SR20-4680 (1981).

IBM Corporation, *IMS/VS Version 1 Application Programming*, IBM Form No. SH20-9026 (1987).

IBM Corporation, *IMS/VS Version 1 Data Base Administration Guide*, IBM Form No. SH20-9025 (1986).

IBM Corporation, *IMS/VS Version 1 General Information Manual*, IBM Form No. GH20-1260 (1984).

Kapp, D., and Leben, J. F., *IMS Programming Techniques*, 2nd ed., Van Nostrand Reinhold, New York; 1986.

Walsh, M. E., *Information Management Systems / Virtual Storage*, Reston Publishing, Reston, VA; 1979.

Questions and Exercises

10.1. Describe a hierarchy. Describe an example of a hierarchy in a corporation.

10.2. Describe the basic form of an IMS hierarchy. What do the nodes represent? Conceptually, how are multiple associations handled? How does it provide for the reduction of data redundancy?

10.3. How would we modify the Baseball Teams hierarchy in Figure 10.4 to maintain information on each team's season ticket holders?

10.4. Carefully explain the difference between a segment type and a segment occurrence.

10.5. Compare the advantages and disadvantages of pointer-based storage and sequential storage of data in IMS hierarchies.

10.6. In the Baseball Teams hierarchy of Figure 10.4, is it necessary to have a team number field in the Players segment? Why or why not?

10.7. Redraw the Dodgers occurrence of the Baseball Team hierarchy in Figure 10.8 to reflect the following. (Note: players and coaches are kept in alphabetic order.)

    a. The addition of coach Doogan, who has been a high school and college coach.

    b. The addition of player Evans.

    c. The addition of player Turner.

10.8. Describe the meaning of the hierarchy shown in the following figure in terms of the real-world environment that it represents (what is the nature of the data that can be stored in it, what kinds of applications might use it?).

10.9. In your own words, describe the advantage of a logical relationship in reducing redundancy, promoting data integration, and so on.

10.10. Why are the combined Teams and Players hierarchies in Figure 10.10 an incomplete solution to the redundancy of the two Player segment types in the hierarchies of Figure 10.9?

10.11. What are the advantages of the unidirectional logical relationship in Figure 10.11?

10.12. Define and describe the purpose of a logical child segment. What is intersection data? Why does it belong in the logical child?

10.13. How can logical relationships be used to represent many-to-many relationships in IMS databases?

10.14. Describe the meaning of the database shown in the following figure in terms of the real world environment that it represents (what is the nature of the data that can be stored in it, what kinds of applications might use it?).

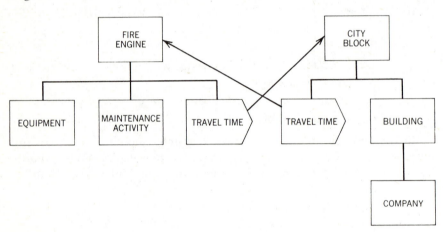

10.15. What is the difference between an IMS logical and physical database? What are the advantages of making the distinction?

10.16. What is an IMS Access Method? Describe Figure 10.20 in your own words.

10.17. What are secondary indexes and what do they accomplish? If there is already direct access to the root segment, what is the purpose of having a secondary index based on a field in the root segment?

10.18. What is a control block? What kind of information do control blocks contain?

10.19. What are the major IMS data manipulation statements? Do they cover all of the types of data manipulation functions that you might need?

10.20. Refer to the IMS database record in Figure 10.24 (an occurrence of the hierarchy shown in Figure 10.23) and indicate the results of each of the following IMS calls.

    a. GU TEAMS (TEAMNUM = 12)
              PLAYERS (PLAYNUM = 5410)

    b. GU TEAMS (TEAMNUM = 12)
              BATS (BATNUM = B09)

    c. GU TEAMS (TEAMNUM = 12)
              BATS (MANUF = Acme)

    d. GU TEAMS (TEAMNUM = 12)
              COACHES (COACHNAM = Adams)
              WORKEXP (EXPYRS = 10)

    e. GU TEAMS (TEAMNUM = 12)
              COACHES (COACHNAM = Adams)
              WORKEXP (EXPYRS = 13)

10.21. Refer to the IMS database record in Figure 10.24, which is an occurrence of the hierarchy shown in Figure 10.23.

    a. Write a DL/I call to find out how many years coach Adams of team 12 was a college coach.

    b. Write a DL/I call to find out if a player named Murray is on team 12.

10.22. Refer to the IMS database record in Figure 10.24 (an occurrence of the hierarchy in Figure 10.23) and indicate the results of each of the following IMS calls or call sequences. In each case, assume that

GU TEAMS (TEAMNUM = 12)

has just been executed. Loop indications are for COBOL or PL/I programs.

    a. Start of loop
            GN PLAYERS
        end of loop

    b. Start of loop
            GNP PLAYERS
        end of loop

    c. Start of loop
            GNP BATS (MANUF = Acme)
        end of loop

    d. GN COACHES
            start of loop
       GNP WORKEXP
          end of loop

10.23. Refer to the IMS database record in Figure 10.24, which is an occurrence of the hierarchy shown in Figure 10.23. Write DL/I calls with loops, if necessary (see the style in the previous exercise), to get:

    a.   All of the coaches on team 12

    b.   All of team 12's coach Adams' coaching experience

    c.   All of the coaching experience of each of the coaches on team 12

10.24. Refer to the IMS database record in Figure 10.24, which is an occurrence of the hierarchy shown in Figure 10.23. Write DL/I calls with loops if necessary to:

    a.   Insert new coach, Turner, into the team 12 database record.

    b.   Delete all of coach Adams experience.

    c.   Update player Jones' age to 26.

10.25. What is an application generator? What are the advantages of using one? Are there any disadvantages?

11

The Network Approach to Database

Introduction

Another approach to database management systems is based on structures called networks. Over the last two decades many DBMSs have been developed that are implementations, to a greater or lesser extent, of the network-oriented DBMS specifications developed by the Conference on Data Systems Languages (CODASYL) and its Data Base Task Group (DBTG) and Data Description Language Committee (DDLC). The Conference on Data Systems Languages is "an organisation composed of volunteer representatives of computer manufacturers and users in industry and the Federal Governments of Canada and the United States of America" (the reason for the unusual spelling of the word "organization" is that the specifications are published by the EDP Standards Committee of the Secretariat of the Canadian Government).

The CODASYL work on uniform specifications for a DBMS began in the late 1960s. Reports or sets of CODASYL specifications have been produced from time to time; some of the most notable came out in 1971, 1973, 1978, and 1982. The different commercially available "CODASYL DBMSs" are based on some percentage of the specifications in one or more of the CODASYL reports.

In keeping with the spirit of this book to provide a thorough and accurate understanding of the *fundamental concepts* of database, we will discuss the CODASYL approach to database management systems as a general topic. We will not differentiate between the different CODASYL specification versions or the different commercial implementations. What we will do is describe the general features and objectives of the CODASYL approach.

Networks

To begin with, let's take a look at what is meant by the term **network**. A network is really a very general kind of a structure: in the abstract, it is simply a set of **points** connected in some way. For convenience we will refer to the connection between two points as an **edge**. Didn't the concept of a tree fit that definition? Yes, it did, but with further restrictions. In fact, a tree is merely a restricted kind of a network.

In practice we deal with networks frequently in everyday living. Figure 11.1 shows one such common network: a network of highways connecting cities. Another example is the telephone network. We also speak of a "network of friends" in which the people interact with each other.

Defining the following terms now will help later. Two points are **adjacent** if they are connected by an edge. Thus, Chicago and Denver are adjacent in Figure 11.1, since they are connected by Highway 25. An edge is **incident** to a point if it touches it. Highway 15 is incident to Dallas. The **degree** of a node is the number of edges incident to it. The degree of Atlanta is 4 because Highways 70, 55, 50, and 75 are all incident to it. A **path** is a serially connected series of edges, such as Highways 10, 25, and 80, connecting Los Angeles to New York. A **cycle** is a path that begins and ends at the same point. The path of Highways 25, 55, 75, and 40 is a cycle because it begins and ends at Denver.

Understanding the differences between trees and more general networks is important to the coming discussion. There are a couple of ways

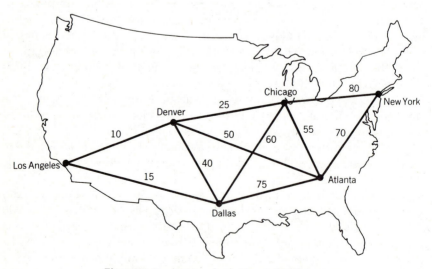

Figure 11.1.   A network of cities and highways.

of distinguishing a tree from a more general network, and while such a discussion can quickly become rather complex, we will try to keep it as simple as possible.

Ordinarily, a tree is a network that has no cycles. Refer back to Figure 10.1 and convince yourself that for each and every point on that network, which we call a tree, there is no way to begin a path at a point, to traverse a series of edges, and to return to the starting point without having to back track over at least one edge at least once. Contrast that with the structure of Figure 11.2, which shows a cycle connecting nodes 1, 2, and 3.

But it is also possible to have a network that *is not a tree and yet has no cycles*. In talking about the trees of Chapter 6, we established the root as the node at the "top" of the structure and always worked downward from it. In effect, we established a *direction* on the branches or edges namely downward (which also corresponded very conveniently to a one-to-many relationship in that same direction for DL/I). Once we have established such a downward direction on the edges of a tree, another characteristic of the tree is that *a node may not have more than one parent*. Figure 11.3 is a copy of Figure 10.1 with a new node added (number 12). It represents a network that is not a tree but that has no cycles. If all of the edges are considered to point downward on the page, then node 2 clearly has two "parent" or superior nodes, rendering that structure invalid as a tree, but still perfectly valid as a network.

Now, just as we did for linear files in relational databases and hierarchies in IMS, let's see how networks can be used to store data in the CODASYL DBMS concept.

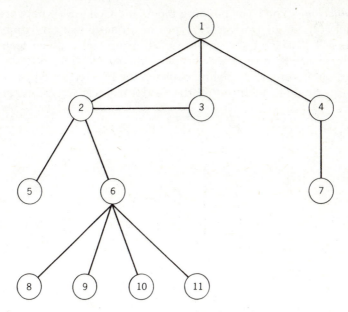

Figure 11.2. A network with a cycle.

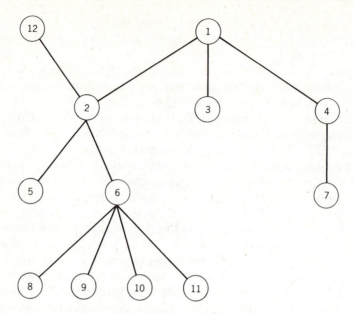

Figure 11.3.   A network with no cycles.

CODASYL Physical Structure

To describe how data can be stored in the form of a network, we will continue to use our baseball example.

The Set Concept

Introduction. The basic building block of a CODASYL network is the **set**. A set consists of two record types in a one-to-many relationship to each other. Figure 11.4 shows the Coach Team set; a given team has a number of coaches on it. We will follow the convention, often found in CODASYL literature, that the link between the two record types of a set is shown as a single-headed (rather than a double-headed) arrow, although

Figure 11.4.   A CODASYL set.

it represents a one-to-many relationship. Unlike our description of IMS, we will leave the arrow heads in here because as we shall soon see, the direction of the one-to-many relationship will not always be downward in the diagrams as it is in IMS.

The record type on the "one" side of the one-to-many relationship (Teams) is called the **owner record type**, while the record on the "many" side (Coaches) is called the **member record type**.

Storage of Sets. Just as we have previously spoken of record occurrences and hierarchical occurrences, here we can speak of set occurrences. A set occurrence consists of one occurrence of the owner record type of the set and all of the occurrences of the member record type associated with it. Figure 11.5 shows an occurrence of the Coach Team set. The Dodgers have three coaches, Adams, Baker, and Carter. Figure 11.5 also shows the usual way that CODASYL set occurrences are stored: with pointers. The main (and the only required) pointer is the "next" pointer, shown as solid lines in Figure 11.5. With next pointers, the owner record occur-

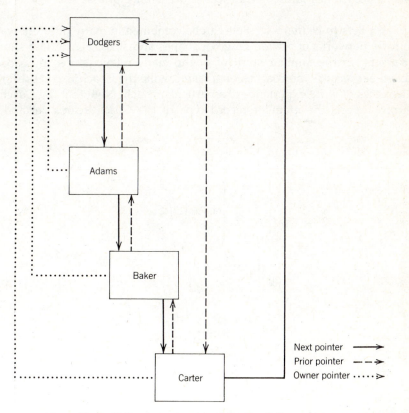

Figure 11.5. An occurrence of the Coach Team set.

rence (Dodgers) points to the first member record occurrence (Adams). That member record occurrence points to the next one, and so on, until the last member record occurrence (Carter) of the set points back to the owner record occurrence.

Notice that except for that last next pointer going from the last member record occurrence back to the owner record occurrence, the chain of next pointers looks just like the child-twin pointer arrangement in IMS. By the way, you might be tempted to look at the chain of next pointers and yell "cycle," and you would be right: They do form a cycle. Just remember that here we have a cycle of *record occurrences* within a set occurrence, while the essence of the discussion about cycles earlier in this chapter was geared towards cycles of *record types*, a discussion we will come back to a little later on.

There are two optional types of pointers illustrated in Figure 11.5, which in practice are used for some of the more complex network arrangements and processing. The "prior" pointer (shown as dashed lines) operates the same way that the next pointer does, but it goes in the opposite direction. The "owner" pointer (shown as dotted lines) points from each member record occurrence to the owner record occurrence of that set.

From Sets to Networks.   Sets can be combined in many different ways to form networks of a wide range of shapes and sizes. Figure 11.6 shows two sets. In the familiar spirit of one-to-many relationships, the Coach Teams set records the coaches on a team, while the Coach Exp set records the pieces of work experience of a particular coach. Note that the Coaches record type is the member record type of the Coach Teams set and at

Figure 11.6.   A record as the member record type of one set and the owner record type of another.

the same time is the owner record type of the Coach Exp set. Figure 11.7 shows two sets that have the same owner record type: Players.

Notice that the networks shown in Figures 11.4, 11.6, and 11.7 (Figure 11.4 can be looked upon as a network consisting of one set) appear on the surface to be indistinguishable from trees. Now look at Figure 11.8, which shows three sets. The College set indicates all of the players in the league who came from a particular college, the On Team set shows all of the players on a team, and the Home set shows all of the players in the league who were born in a particular state. In that structure, all three sets have the same member record type, Players. Borrowing from the IMS terminology we might say that the Players record has three "parent" record types (which, of course, can't happen in IMS). Thus the structure is not a tree, but a more general network.

Figure 11.9 shows the pointer arrangement for an occurrence of each of those three sets. A record occurrence participates in (and must have a "next" pointer slot for) one chain of record occurrences for each set it is in. In the structure in Figure 11.8, the Players record is the member record type of each of the three sets, meaning that a player can be shown to have graduated from one college, to be playing for one team (presumably

Figure 11.7. A record as the owner record type of two different sets.

Figure 11.8. A record as the member record type of three different sets.

COLLEGES

HOME STATES

TEAMS

PLAYERS

Figure 11.9. An occurrence of each of the three sets of Figure 11.8. In player occurrences: Left pointer slot is for college chain; middle pointer slot is for team chain; and right pointer slot is for home state chain.

currently), and to have been born in one state. In the Players occurrences in Figure 11.9, the leftmost of the three pointer slots is for the College set, the middle is for the On Team set, and the rightmost is for the Home set. The diagram shows that Jones and Taylor graduated from Harvard; Doe, Jones, and Smith play for the Dodgers; and Smith, Taylor, and Turner were born in New York. If all of the data was shown, we would see what

Figure 11.10. Another network structure.

college chain Doe is on, what home state chain Jones is on, and so forth.

Figure 11.10 shows another network structure that is not a tree. It can maintain the players on a team in the Team Player set, the coaches on a team in the Team Coach set, and the coaches who coach a particular player in the Coached By set. But if we also wanted to maintain the opposite of the Coached By set, that is, the players whom a coach is responsible for coaching, then the two together would form a many-to-many relationship, which leads to the following discussion on "juncture records."

Juncture Records

Thus far we have not said anything about storing data in many-to-many relationships in CODASYL networks. In fact (in a way similar to the situation in IMS), CODASYL network structures cannot directly represent many-to-many relationships. We would say that within one set a member record occurrence can be associated with a single owner record occurrence. In Figure 11.4 a coach can only be associated with one team; there can be no historical data on all of the teams that a coach has worked for during his career. Many-to-many relationships are developed in CODASYL networks through the introduction of a new record type, variously known as a **juncture**, "link," "intersection," or "connection" record. Instead of a single many-to-many linkage between two record types being represented in one set, there will be two sets. One set will have one of those two record types as its owner record type and a newly created juncture record as its member record type. The other set will have the other of the two record types as its owner record type and that same juncture record as its member record type. The arrangement is actually quite similar in spirit to the logical relationship structure in IMS.

Figure 11.11 shows the many-to-many relationship between Teams and Players, on the same historical basis that we dealt with in the last chapter,

Figure 11.11.   A many-to-many relationship in CODASYL.

represented in the CODASYL network form. The Team Roster set and
the Player Roster set taken together form the many-to-many relationship.
There will be a Roster record occurrence for each instance of a particular
player having played on a particular team or vice versa. Figure 11.12
(which demonstrates the same relationships shown in Figure 10.15) shows
occurrences of the two sets described in Figure 11.11. The Roster record
occurrences and the pointers are labelled for reference in the following
discussion. The Roster record occurrences, drawn in the middle of Figure
11.12, each have two next pointer slots, since the Roster record type is the
member record type of both of the sets involved. In each occurrence, the
left-hand pointer is for the Team Roster set, while the right-hand pointer
is for the Player Roster set. The Dodgers have had both Doe and Jones
as players, at one time or another, while the Giants have had Jones and
Smith. Conversely, Doe has only played on the Dodgers, Smith only on
the Giants, and Jones on both.

Figure 11.12 also provides a good illustration of the need for the optional
"owner" pointer. Remember that all of the pointers shown in Figure 11.12
are next pointers. Suppose you start out at the Jones occurrence and want
to find out which of the teams he has played on and other information
about those teams stored in the Teams record occurrences. Pointer 8 from
Jones leads the system to Roster occurrence B. The system could at that
point, loosely speaking, hold its place at B and follow pointer 2 to Dodgers,
yielding one of the teams that Jones has played on. But this is only because
B happens to be the last of the players on the Dodgers chain and thus
points over to Dodgers. The more general and problematic case is illustrated by following pointer 9 to the next roster record occurrence on the
Jones chain, roster record C. In order to get to the teams record associated with roster record C (the Giants), the system must follow pointer
11 and then pointer 4 (and in general, possibly many more pointers on a
longer chain). In so doing it passes through Roster occurrence D, which
has absolutely nothing to do with Jones. On the other hand, if the Roster occurrences had owner pointers, then from C it could simply use an
owner pointer to directly find the Giants, which is the owner record of
that occurrence of the Team Roster set.

Figure 11.13 (including the Roster record of Figure 11.11) shows the
full Teams and Players network. Remember that intersection data will be
stored in the juncture record. This network is the CODASYL equivalent
of the IMS structure shown in Figure 10.16.

Figure 11.12. Occurrences of the two sets shown in Figure 11.11.

Schemas and Subschemas

Following commonly used DBMS conventions, the CODASYL specifications allow for a distinction to be made between the actual stored data and the view of it that the programmer sees. In addition, they suggest another intermediate level of view. Described as the "conceptual level," this view describes the overall database and can involve several physically separate networks.

In CODASYL, the description of the actual stored data is called the **internal schema**. The description at the conceptual level is called the **logical schema**. The description of a program or programmer's view of the

Figure 11.13.   The Teams and Players example in network form.

data is called a **subschema**. For purposes of security and clarity a connected portion of a CODASYL network can be described in a subschema and presented to a programmer for a particular application. The programmer need not be aware of the rest of the actual stored network defined in the schemas.

Access Methods

Options. The various versions of the CODASYL specifications and various implementations of them have provided a variety of ways to store and access record occurrences. As we look at the alternatives, bear in mind that in CODASYL every record type may, although need not, be treated independently in terms of access from all of the other record types. We shall now explain this further.

One common CODASYL file organization stores the occurrences of a record type using a hashing algorithm based on their keys. When stored in this way access is said to be "via calc." As is usual for a hashing driven organization, this method provides very fast direct access but no physical sequencing of the data.

Another method of storage and access for the occurrences of a record type is referred to as "via set." The record type involved must be the member record type of a set. The point of this method is to store the member record occurrences of a set occurrence physically near the owner record occurrence of the set. Access to those member record occurrences must be through the owner record occurrence of that set. Those occurrences cannot be retrieved independently.

Another method, known in CODASYL as "direct," has been dropped from the latest set of specifications but may still be found in some implementations. In this arrangement all record occurrences are assigned a relative address called a "data base key." A program can discern and maintain data base key values and, at a later time, refer directly to a record occurrence by its data base key. This method is also a convenient way of creating a sequential file.

Some implementations permit indexed-sequential storage. Some also include secondary indexes as options.

Usage Comments. Remember that each record can be treated independently in terms of access if that makes sense for the application set that will use the data. In theory, every record type of a network can be stored "via calc" using a hashing method. The record occurrences of the different record types will be scattered over a wide physical range of disk cylinders and packs, but will be related to each other in the usual CODASYL set-oriented way with (at least) next pointers. In this arrangement fast direct access can be had to any occurrence of any record type. However, navigating through the network from occurrence to occurrence will be relatively slow because of the scattering of data characteristic of hashing.

The way to avoid that problem is to store one of the record types with a hashing algorithm and to store the others connected to it, and in turn others connected to them, "via set." This will allow fast direct access to one of the records and then, since they are stored physically close by on the disk, relatively fast sequential access to the occurrences connected to it in the network. However, in so doing, we give up direct access to those other records (unless secondary indexes are permitted). Referring back to Figure 11.6, if Coaches records are stored via set relative to Teams records and Work Experience records are stored via set relative to Coaches records, then a team and its descendants will be stored physically near each other, which may well be a plus for performance depending on the nature of the applications using the data.

This is a standard, common sense kind of trade-off situation. Similar arguments can be made in other systems, including IMS.

CODASYL Language Interface

Introduction

The CODASYL organization is responsible for maintaining standards for the COBOL language. As a result of this orientation, the intention of the

CODASYL database specifications was for the databases to be accessible by COBOL programs. While a variety of methods of language access have been built into and around various CODASYL database implementations, they are fundamentally intended to be embedded type functions in COBOL programs. We will explore the various statements involved in such access, but first we must look at a few preliminary topics.

Preliminary Topics

Set Membership Class. An occurrence of a record type that is the member record type of a particular set can exist in the database without being in an occurrence of that set (i.e., without being associated with an occurrence of the owner record type of the set). For example, referring back to Figure 11.4, a coach can have a record in the database without being in an occurrence of the Coach Team set; it simply means that he or she is temporarily unemployed.

For that reason, the CODASYL database designer must specify certain characteristics of the record types relative to the sets of which they are the member record type. Those characteristics will guide the system in whether or not certain record and set manipulation statements can act on the particular records and if so, how. There are two "storage class" options and three "removal class" options. A given record type can have any combination of storage class and removal class options for a given set in which it is the member record type. In general, it can have different such combinations for each set of which it is the member record type. It will be necessary to look at those options now before we look at the data manipulation statements a little later.

Storage Class. A record's "storage class" (also called "insertion class") guides the DBMS in inserting a new occurrence of a record into the database when that record acts as the member record occurrence of a set.

One possibility is for a record type to be declared **automatic** relative to a set of which it is the member record type. Then, when an occurrence of that record is inserted into the database, the system will automatically link it to an occurrence of that set (associate it with—that is, connect it to— an occurrence of the owner record type). Of course, the program must indicate with which occurrence of that set it is to be associated. The other choice is **manual**. If a member record type of a set is declared to be manual, then when an occurrence of it is inserted into the database it will not be linked into an occurrence of the set; if it subsequently becomes necessary, this will have to be done by a separate command, which we will describe later.

Removal Class. A record's "removal class" (also called "retention class") gives or denies the system permission to obey application program commands to move member record occurrences already associated with a set occurrence out of that set occurrence.

If a record type that is the member record type of a particular set is declared **fixed** for that set, then it must always stay in the occurrence of that set in which it was originally inserted. It cannot be moved to a different occurrence of that set unless, as a brute force measure, it is deleted from the database entirely and reinserted with a new set occurrence association.

If a record type is **mandatory** for a particular set, then it must always be in the chain of some occurrence of that set, but not necessarily the one with which it was originally associated.

If a record type is **optional** with regard to a given set, then it can be disassociated (disconnected) from the occurrence of the set that it was in, remain in the database, and not be reassociated with another occurrence of that set.

Currency. In the discussion on IMS we developed the concept of the system place-keeper or internal pointer, which always maintains a sense of current position in the database. This concept is highly developed in the CODASYL specifications, and a fairly large number of such current position pointers, each referring to a different substructure of the network, can be maintained. Remember that the system simultaneously maintains a different set of position pointers for each user of each program.

The CODASYL equivalent of the basic IMS current position pointer is called the **current of run-unit**. It always indicates the last record occurrence (of any record type) reached in the network. The **current of record** indicates the last occurrence of a particular record type reached. There is such an indicator for each different record type. The **current of set** is for the last record occurrence reached in a given set. Again there is one such pointer for each set, all simultaneously maintained. The **current of realm** is for the last record occurrence reached within a large subset of the network known as a "realm" or "area."

The FIND Statement

The first CODASYL statement that we will look at is the FIND statement. We will discuss it and all of the other CODASYL language statements with an example network that parallels the IMS example used in Chapter 6. Figure 11.14 is a network structure that represents the same data as the Teams hierarchical structure that appeared in Figure 10.4. Figure 11.15 shows the fields in the records of that network structure, just as Figures 10.5 and 10.23 did for the hierarchical case. Figure 11.16 shows the same actual data in the network as Figure 10.24 did in the hierarchy. The pointers in Figure 11.16 are all next pointers.

One word of caution before we begin: Different versions of the CODASYL specifications and different CODASYL implementations have used

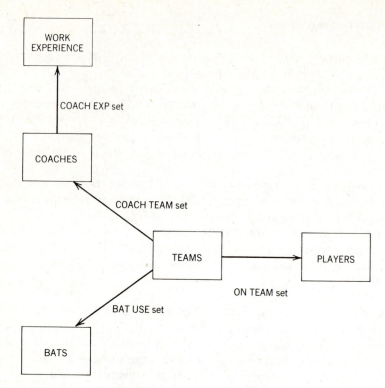

Figure 11.14. A CODASYL network.

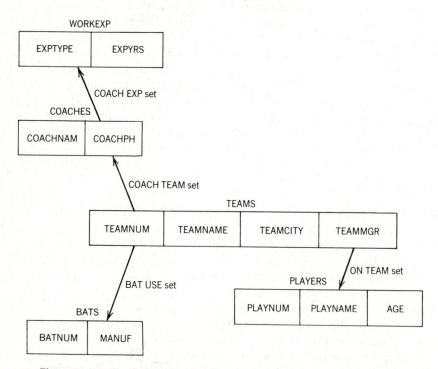

Figure 11.15. The CODASYL network in Figure 11.14 showing field names.

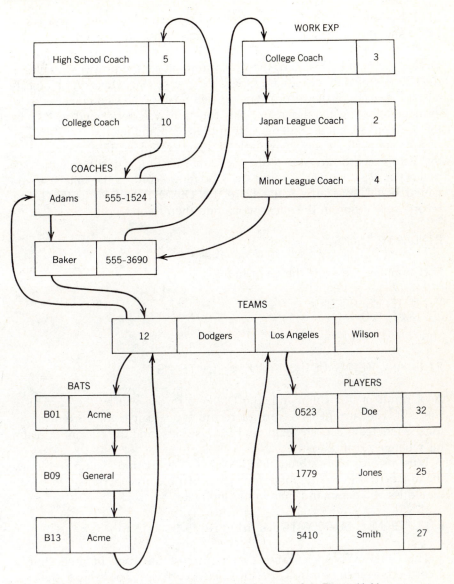

Figure 11.16. A partial occurrence of the network in Figure 11.14.

somewhat different command syntax constructions. There are two main families of such syntax constructions. We will try to stick to one of them but will mention the other occasionally as well.

Informally stated, the purpose of the FIND statement is to locate and have the system point to a particular record occurrence in the database. More formally, the FIND statement locates a particular record occurrence and sets the current of run-unit indicator to it. (It normally also sets the current of record for the record type involved, the current of set for the set involved, and the current of realm for the realm involved.) The FIND statement does not retrieve the record from storage—that requires a GET statement after the FIND statement, as we will discuss. Before a FIND statement is executed, the program must set the proper variables in the subschema defined in the COBOL program's Data Division to indicate *which occurrence* of the record type written in the FIND statement is to be located. By way of comparison, this function was performed in IMS by the segment search arguments within the command itself.

Let's start with a simple example of direct record location. Assume that the Teams records are stored directly with a hashing algorithm, which we called the "calc" mode. To find the Dodgers record in the database you would first "move" the value 12 to the TEAMNUM field in the Teams record description in the subschema, and then issue:

```
FIND ANY TEAMS
```

Variations on the same theme include:

```
FIND TEAMS RECORD
```

and

```
FIND ANY TEAMS USING TEAMNUM IN TEAMS
```

As a result of this command, the Dodgers record will be the current of run-unit, the current of record for record type Teams, the current of set for the On Team, Coach Team, and Bat Use sets, and the current of realm for whatever realm it is in.

If the records were stored in CODASYL's "direct" mode, and you know the unique positional identifier for a particular record occurrence, then you would issue a command that would look like:

```
FIND TEAMS; DB—KEY IS identifier
```

The CODASYL specifications also support the concept of finding a record occurrence within a specified set occurrence. To do that, the first thing that has to be done is to establish the set occurrence involved. The easiest way to do this is to specify the owner record occurrence of the desired set. If a particular record type is the owner record type of a particular set, then each occurrence of that owner record type establishes an occurrence of the set.

For example, suppose you want information about the bats that the Dodgers use. The first thing you would do is select the occurrence of the Bat Use set in which Dodgers is the owner record occurrence. You can do that by doing a simple FIND of the Dodgers record, which among other things establishes the (one and only) set occurrence of the Bat Use set that

Dodgers is in as the current of set. Having done this, if, for instance, you wanted the first Bats record associated with Dodgers, you would issue:

```
FIND FIRST BATS RECORD WITHIN BAT USE
```

where Bats is the name of the record type and Bat Use is the name of the set. If you wanted the last of the bats associated with Dodgers you would replace FIRST with LAST. NEXT would get you the next one on the chain (compare with the IMS GET NEXT command); PRIOR would get you the previous one; and an integer represented as a constant or an integer variable would get you that number occurrence (first, second, third, etc.), counting from the first member record occurrence of the set (and going backwards if the number is negative).

You can also find a record occurrence within a set occurrence based on the value of one of the fields of that record occurrence. For example, if you wanted to find the record for Dodger's bat B09, you would first establish the Bat Use set occurrence that has Dodgers in it as the owner record, as the current of set, and then you would issue:

```
FIND BATS WITHIN BAT USE USING db-id
```

where db-id would identify B09 as the search key.

What if you wanted to find all of the Dodger's bats manufactured by the Acme Company? You can't use the command form just discussed, because if several Bats record occurrences have the same search field value, then *every time* you issue that command you will find the *first* occurrence with that field value. Another command form is needed, and obviously, the command must be set up within a program loop to process all of the record occurrences with the specified search key value (e.g., all of the Dodgers' bats made by the Acme Company). First you establish the proper set occurrence (again, the occurrence of the BAT USE set with Dodgers in it) as the current of set. Then you FIND the first Acme manufactured Dodgers' bat using one of the command structures discussed. To find the rest of the Dodger's Acme bats, you issue within a program loop:

```
FIND DUPLICATE WITHIN BAT USE USING db-id
```

where db-id again establishes the search key.

Another FIND variation within a set is to locate the owner record occurrence of the current of set as:

```
FIND OWNER WITHIN BAT USE
```

For systems supporting the realm concept there are similar commands for finding record occurrences within a realm as opposed to within a set. Included in these are commands to find the FIRST, LAST, NEXT, PRIOR, or integer identified record occurrence of a given record type within a realm.

Finally, it may be necessary to reestablish a record occurrence as the current of run-unit. The term reestablish is used because in this case the record was previously "found" and is at the moment the current of some record, set, or realm. But due to subsequent FIND statements, which involved other records, it is not at the moment the current of run-unit. For example, to find the last referenced bat in the Bat Use set you would issue

```
FIND CURRENT BATS WITHIN BAT USE
```

or

```
FIND CURRENT OF BAT USE SET
```

As a final note remember that, as was the case with IMS, exception conditions must be tested for after a CODASYL command is issued. Examples of these conditions include end of set or realm reached, no record found (which matches the selection criteria specified), current of run-unit is not correct record type, and so forth.

The GET Statement

The GET statement brings a record occurrence or selected fields of a record occurrence into the user's "user work area" (UWA) in main memory. If you simply issue:

```
GET
```

then the system retrieves the record occurrence that is the current of run-unit. If, for example, to retrieve a Teams record, you issue:

```
GET TEAMS
```

then the system not only retrieves the current of run-unit, but also checks to see if it is in fact an occurrence of the Teams record type. While there are different capabilities and limitations among the different systems, it is fair to make the broad comparison that in CODASYL a FIND statement followed by a GET statement accomplishes the same thing that a GET UNIQUE or GET NEXT (depending on the circumstances) statement does in IMS.

Record Maintenance Statements

The STORE, ERASE, and MODIFY statements serve as maintenance commands for records in the database (although, as you will see, there are side effects of these commands that do affect set membership). After this section we will discuss maintenance commands for sets.

The STORE Statement. The STORE statement inserts new records into the database. The program must first move the appropriate data for the new record into the user work area (UWA), and then, for example, issue:

```
STORE TEAMS
```

to insert a new Teams record. Of course, the system will handle the necessary details of insertion depending on whether the records of the record type involved are stored with a hashing algorithm, an index, or a relative address.

Remember too, that the system will automatically add that record occurrence to the sets in which that record type participates (the Coach Team, Bat Use, and On Team sets, to continue the example) *if* the storage class for that record in those sets was declared to be "automatic" in the schema (see the earlier discussion on storage classes). A word of caution: For those automatic set connections to be made to the correct occurrences of those sets, those set occurrences must be specified before the STORE statement is issued. There are variations on how this can be done (it comes under a heading known as "Set Selection"), but generally it can be done by setting variables in the schema or by issuing FIND statements to set the current of set indicators.

The ERASE Statement. The ERASE statement deletes records from the database. In the various versions and implementations of the CODA-SYL specifications there have been a number of variations of the ERASE statement with various restrictions. We will discuss two such variations.

Suppose a team drops out of the league entirely. In addition to the TEAMS record, and depending on the circumstances, you might or might not want to delete the descendants of that record, namely the Bats, Players, Coaches, and Workexp records as shown in Figure 11.15. If, for example, you make Dodgers the current of run-unit, and then issue:

```
ERASE ALL TEAMS
```

then the Dodgers and all of its descendant record occurrences—that is, everything shown in Figure 11.16—will be erased from the database.

If, on the other hand, you issue:

```
ERASE Dodgers
```

(without the parameter "ALL"), then the rules for the removal class of a record type in a set will be considered. For example, let's say that Bats in the Bat Use set are fixed. This means that the bats assigned to the Dodgers can never be used by another team and, as common sense would dictate, they will be deleted with the Dodgers. Assume that Players in the On Team set is optional. Then the players can exist independently in the database, without having to be assigned to a team, so they will be taken out of the On Team set, but otherwise left alone. And what if Coaches in the Coach Team set is mandatory? Then coaches may move from team to team but must always be in *some* team. Since the ERASE Dodgers statement doesn't say which team to reconnect the coaches to, this causes a problem, and in fact, would invalidate this entire command, leaving the database as it was before.

The MODIFY Statement.   Updates to stored records are accomplished using the MODIFY statement. For example, if you want to change some data in a Teams record, you issue a FIND and then a GET statement to bring the record into the UWA, you change the appropriate data fields, and then you issue:

MODIFY TEAMS

Set Maintenance Statements

The CONNECT, DISCONNECT, and RECONNECT statements serve as set maintenance commands as follows.

The CONNECT Statement.   The CONNECT statement links an existing record occurrence that is the current of run-unit into the set occurrence that is the current of set (for the desired set type). For example, what do you do if Stanton, a currently unemployed player, joins the Dodgers? First you would issue a FIND statement to set the current of set indicator to the occurrence of the On Teams set that has Dodgers as its owner record occurrence. Then you would issue a FIND statement to make Stanton the current of run-unit. Finally, you would issue:

CONNECT PLAYERS TO ON TEAMS

The DISCONNECT Statement.   If a record is currently a member record occurrence of some set occurrence, it can be removed from that set by using Disconnect, but still remain in the database, whether or not it is involved in any other sets. For example, to fire Stanton from the Dodgers, you would first make Stanton the current of run-unit and then issue:

DISCONNECT PLAYERS FROM ON TEAMS

Remember the removal class rules: For the foregoing statement to make sense, it must have a removal class of optional specified for that set.

The RECONNECT Statement.   The RECONNECT statement allows you to move a record occurrence from one occurrence of a set to another occurrence of the same set. For example, suppose that Stanton is currently on the Dodgers, but is traded to the Giants. First you would identify the occurrence of the On Teams set with the Giants as the owner record occurrence as the target set occurrence (based on the "set selection" rules). Next you would make Stanton the current of run-unit. Then you would issue:

```
RECONNECT PLAYERS WITHIN ON TEAMS
```

Here again, the removal class option specified must be taken into account. Obviously, a RECONNECT statement would be in direct contradiction with a removal class of fixed for that record type in that set. It must be either mandatory or optional.

Comparison between the Relational and the Other Approaches

Points of Comparison

Now that we have had the opportunity to explore the relational and navigational approaches to database management, it is appropriate to make some comparisons between them. One way of comparing the relational approach with the others is through the concept of data integration and the join. A second way is in the comparative effort to design a database and to modify it after it is in use. A third way of comparing the relational and nonrelational approaches is by their performance characteristics. (This discussion will also explore the reasons why relational database has only relatively recently become commercially viable.) And a fourth mode of comparison involves potential integrity exposures at the time of insertion and deletion operations.

A Join Is a Join Is a Join

Figures 11.17 *a* and *b* repeat the Salesperson and Customer files from Figure 6.3. Figure 11.18 shows the same Salesperson and Customer data model set up in a hierarchical or network form. The comparison between the relations of Figure 11.17 and the structure of Figure 11.18 is very important and drives to the heart of the database concept.

Regardless of what the underlying structure is in the DBMS being used for a particular application, one fundamental concept of data integration remains the same: Records describing different, but related, entities in the application environment must in some way be capable of being associated each with another. Fundamentally, this is not a deep concept in computer science, but rather the way the world around us works. A salesperson is responsible for several customers; a customer is assigned a sales-

SALESPERSON NUMBER	SALESPERSON NAME	COMMISSION PERCENTAGE	YEAR OF HIRE
137	Baker	10	1975
186	Adams	15	1971
204	Dickens	10	1963
361	Carlyle	20	1963

(a)

CUSTOMER NUMBER	SALESPERSON NUMBER	CITY
0121	137	New York
0839	186	Hartford
0933	137	Boston
1047	137	Boston
1525	361	Newark
1700	361	Washington
1826	137	New York
2198	204	New York
2267	186	New York

(b)

Figure 11.17. (a) Salesperson relation. (b) Customer relation.

SALESPERSON NUMBER	SALESPERSON NAME	COMMISSION PERCENTAGE	YEAR OF HIRE

SALESPERSON record/segment

CUSTOMER NUMBER	CITY

CUSTOMER record/segment

Figure 11.18. Salesperson–Customer hierarchy or network.

person with whom to place an order. The world revolves around such relationships. And yet, when we try to model the world in a data directed, automated data processing environment, those relationships translate into the concept of data integration.

Return to Figure 11.17 and think about how such relationships leading to data integration are maintained in the relational (or for that matter, the simple linear file) environment. With independent relations, the information recording which tuple(s) of a relation have a meaningful association with which tuples(s) of another relation must exist explicitly. The SALES-

PERSON NUMBER attribute obviously belongs in and, in fact, does appear in the Salesperson relation. In addition, while it may be something that at first glance we might take for granted, the fact that SALESPERSON NUMBER also appears as a foreign key in the *Customer* relation is crucial to making sense out of the application environment. That's how we know which customers a salesperson is responsible for and which salesperson a customer contacts to place an order. That the SALESPERSON NUMBER attribute was in fact placed in the Customer relation when these structures were being designed is a nontrivial point, which will be discussed under the heading of "database design" in Chapter 12 of this book.

Now focus your attention on the hierarchical or network equivalent in Figure 11.18. There too, salespersons are associated with customers but in a different way. They are related implicitly by the design of the hierarchical structure, and explicitly by the child and twin or next pointers, which are created when data is actually loaded according to the defined structure. Notice that the Customer Record in Figure 11.18 is missing the SALESPERSON NUMBER field. It's not needed because when the data is loaded according to that structural form *physical pointers* will be created that will tie the customers to their responsible salespersons.

But that leads to another crucial question: Does the concept of the join exist in hierarchical and network databases? The answer, as you should be able to surmise at this point, is *yes* (at least informally). And now, here is a key point in the comparison between relational and nonrelational databases:

In hierarchical and network databases, joins are performed implicitly at the time that the hierarchies and networks are designed, and explicitly with pointers when the data is loaded according to those structures. The power of data integration is primarily a function of the data structure.

In relational databases joins are performed "on the fly" at execution time by the DBMS according to commands given to the system at that time. The data structure, that is, the relations, must have join fields present in the right places, but the power of data integration is fundamentally an execution-time function of the DBMS.

Data integration is *the* fundamental concept in database, and one way or another, the join is the implementation vehicle for it.

Flexibility in Design and Modification

As we will see in Chapter 12, there are several prominent methods for designing a database. Each method has proponents who feel that the one that they favor is easier to use. This is really a part of a larger argument that often flares up about which approach to database is more "natural" in terms of the way that it models real world application situations. Database experts have been known to go on for hours arguing that question to no agreement, because it is a matter of opinion. "Natural" is not a technical term and we will not pursue that argument here.

Nevertheless, we will note in passing that there are many people who feel that relations are easier to design and inherently simpler to manage than hierarchies or networks. One result of the design process of a relational database is the proper distribution of join fields in the relations, based on the way the application environment operates. This assures that any semantically correct query (that is, one that makes sense in terms of the application) that requires a join will find the join fields in the right places when it needs them. But join operations, particularly brute force joins that require full file scans of one or both files, can be painfully slow for large files.

When designing a hierarchical or network database, decisions must be made as to which of the integrating associations are actually designed into the structure. In the hierarchical and network environments, the performance of join-oriented accesses based on relationships that have been designed into the structure (and are ultimately implemented with pointers) can be very fast, although accesses based on relationships that have not been designed into the structure can be extremely slow.

Later modifications to the database, depending on their nature, can often be made more easily in a relational database, too. We're not talking about adding additional record or tuple occurrences to a database, but rather changing or expanding the number of record *types*. For example, an entirely new relation can be added to a relational database without affecting existing query forms or the existing relations. Adding new record types to hierarchical or network databases may require fitting them into existing structures, reloading the data into the database, and resetting pointers. It may also affect queries in existing application programs.

But it is also important to note that if the nature of the change involves an underlying change in the application, such as the salesperson number no longer being unique or more than one salesperson now being responsible for a customer, then the database may have to be redesigned regardless of which approach to database was taken.

Performance Characteristics

At last it's time to answer the question of why relational DBMSs have only recently become commercially viable. As sample relations, our Salesperson relation has only four tuples and our Customer relation has only nine tuples. The thought of performing even a brute force join, comparing every tuple of one of those relations with every tuple of the other seemed so reasonable that you probably didn't give it a second thought. But what if we attempted to join a 1 million tuple relation with a 3 million tuple relation. How long do you think that would take even on a large, fast computer? It might well take much longer than a person waiting for a response at a terminal would tolerate.

On the other hand, in a typical relational database application environment, many queries to the database will deal with only one relation and will not require a join operation at all. Still, what about the queries that do? Modern, sophisticated relational database systems rely either on special hardware devices for performance enhancement (see Database Machines in Chapter 16), or on query optimization techniques, as we discussed in Chapter 7. They also take advantage of the general increase in speed of computer processors that has developed continually over the years.

And what is the comparative situation with hierarchical and network databases? The key point here revolves around the fact that data integration is accomplished at the time the data is loaded and is maintained by all of the physical pointers that interconnect the records. Hierarchies and networks may appear to be complex structures and may present problems in future database structure modifications, but their physical pointers provide speedy retrieval. That's the other side of the coin—the reason, at least vis-à-vis performance, that hierarchical- and network-based DBMSs have been commercially successful from the advent of the database era.

While still the subject of heated debate, it appears that relational query optimizers will eventually close the performance gap between relational and hierarchical database management systems.

Integrity Exposure on Insertion and Deletion

Let's say that our example company gets a new customer account and it is assigned to a particular salesperson. If IMS is our DBMS, and the data structure is as represented in Figure 11.18, then we can only add the new Customer segment as an attached segment to the applicable Salesperson segment, which makes sense in the overall scheme of things. In the network environment we can force the situation with the specification of "automatic" as a set insertion parameter. But in the relations of Figure 11.17, there is nothing inherent in the data structure to force a tuple for a particular salesperson to exist in the Salesperson relation just because someone inserts a customer record into the Customer relation with that salesperson recorded in it. That is a potential integrity exposure that the system or the application program must handle. As defined in Chapter 6, the formal term involved is "referential integrity." Similarly, a salesperson record can be deleted, leaving the value referring to it in the customer record with nothing to reference.

By the way, note that under certain application circumstances the ability to add a tuple to a relation without regard to referential integrity considerations can be an advantage. For example, we might want to add a new customer to our Customer file either without specifying who the salesperson is or specifying a salesperson who for some reason does not yet exist in the Salesperson file. Nevertheless, there are many who feel that for a relational DBMS to address a full spectrum of operational application systems, referential integrity as a system function is a necessary requirement. In fact, it is beginning to be made available in commercially available relational DBMSs, as we discussed earlier in the book.

References

CODASYL Data Description Language Committee, *CODASYL Journal of Development* (January, 1978). (May be ordered from: Materiel Data Management Branch, Department of Supply and Services, 4th Floor, Core B1,Place du Portage, Phase III, 11 Laurier Street, Hull, Quebec, K1A 0S5, Canada.)

Date, C. J., *An Introduction to Database Systems*, 4th ed., vol. I, Addison-Wesley, Reading, MA, 1986.

Gourley, D. I., *IDMS Theory & Practice*, TechWest, Danville, CA, 1987.

Husband, R. W., McHenry, T. J., and Wooten, J. C., *IDMS/R Systems Desk Reference*, Wiley, New York, 1987.

Kroenke, D. M., and Dolan, K. A., *Database Processing*, 3rd ed., Science Research Associates, Chicago, IL, 1988.

Olle, T. W., *The Codasyl Approach to Data Base Management*, Wiley, New York, 1978.

Questions and Exercises

11.1. Describe a network. Describe some portion of or activity in a corporation that can be described as a network.

11.2. What is the distinction between a tree and a network? Which is a subcategory of the other?

11.3. What is a CODASYL set? What kind of data and data relationships is a set capable of holding? What are the pointer options for storing occurrences of sets?

11.4. Describe the basic form of a CODASYL network. What do the nodes represent? How are sets incorporated into the structure? Conceptually, how are multiple associations handled? How does it provide for the reduction of data redundancy.

11.5. Redraw the partial network occurrence in Figure 11.9 to reflect the following. (Note: Players are kept in alphabetic order.)

    a. Doe and Smith attended Stanford.

    b. Doe's home state is New York.

    c. Taylor and Turner play for the Giants.

11.6. What is a juncture record? How are many-to-many relationships handled in CODASYL networks?

11.7. Why are juncture records really necessary? Can't many-to-many relationships be handled in CODASYL networks without them? Explain.

11.8. What are schemas and subschemas in CODASYL database management systems? What is the distinction between them, and what are the advantages of making that distinction?

11.9. What are the access method options for storing CODASYL networks? For a given node in a network, what are the trade-offs between those options?

11.10. How would you modify the Teams and Players network in Figure 11.13 to:

    a. Maintain information on each team's season ticket holders?

    b. Maintain information on each coach's skills?

    c. Maintain a variety of data about the colleges that players attended? (Several players may have attended a particular college, and a given player may have attended more than one college.)

11.11. Describe the meaning of the CODASYL network in the following figure in terms of the real-world environment that it represents. (What is the nature of the data that can be stored in it? What kinds of applications might use it?)

11.12. Discuss the concepts of storage class and removal class in CODASYL networks. What are they? How do they relate to each other? Why are they necessary?

11.13. What are the major CODASYL data manipulation statements? Do they cover all of the types of data manipulation operations that you might need?

11.14. Refer to the occurrence of the CODASYL network of Figure 11.15, which is shown in Figure 11.16. Indicate the results of each of the following CODASYL statement sequences.

    a. MOVE 12 to the TEAMNUM field in the TEAMS record
        FIND ANY TEAMS
        GET

    b. MOVE 12 to the TEAMNUM field in the TEAMS record
        FIND ANY TEAMS
        FIND FIRST COACHES RECORD WITHIN COACH TEAM SET
        GET

    c. MOVE 12 to the TEAMNUM field in the TEAMS record
        FIND ANY TEAMS
        FIND COACHES WITHIN COACH TEAM USING Adams
        GET

    d. MOVE 12 to the TEAMNUM field in the TEAMS record
        FIND ANY TEAMS
    start of loop
        FIND NEXT PLAYERS RECORD WITHIN ON TEAM
        GET
    end of loop

11.15. Refer to the occurrence of the CODASYL network of Figure 11.15, which is shown in Figure 11.16. Write CODASYL calls, with loops if necessary (see the style in the previous exercise), to:

    a. Get the record for coach Baker.

    b. Get coach Baker's first experience record.

    c. Get all of the coaches on the Dodgers.

    d. Get all of coach Baker's pieces of experience.

    e. Add a new player, Turner, to the Dodgers.

    f. Delete player Jones from the database.

    g. Update player Jones' age to 26.

    h. Remove player Jones from the Dodgers.

    i. Transfer player Jones from the Dodgers to the Giants.

11.16. What are the CODASYL record maintenance statements? Do they cover the full range of record maintenance activities?

11.17. Discuss the CODASYL set maintenance statements. What do they do? Why are they necessary?

11.18. In your own words, compare the ways that data integration (the join concept) is accomplished in the relational versus the hierarchical and network database management systems.

11.19. In your own words, compare the flexibility in design and modification afforded by the relational versus the hierarchical and network database management systems.

11.20. What are the major factors that influence the performance of relational versus hierarchical and network database management systems.

11.21. What is referential integrity? Discuss it in terms of relational and hierarchical and network database management systems.

12

Database Design

The Concept of Database Design

Introduction

Database design refers to the process of arranging the data fields needed by one or more applications into an organized structure. This structure must foster the required relationships among the fields while conforming to the physical constraints of the particular database management system in use. There are two parts to the process that people usually associate with the term "database design." One is "logical database design," which in turn has two components. The first involves organizing the data fields into nonredundant groupings based on the data relationships. The second involves an initial arrangement of those logical groupings into structures based on the nature of the DBMS and the applications that will use the data. There are several techniques for performing logical database design, each with its own emphasis and approach. The second part of database design is "physical database design," which refers to refitting the previously described derived structures to conform to the performance and operational idiosyncrasies of the DBMS, again guided by the application's processing requirements.

But the preparation for database design really begins at a much earlier stage of the data processing life cycle. Put another way, how did we know what the fields and relationships to be incorporated in the database by the database design process were in the first place? The story begins at a stage called "Information Systems Strategic Planning."

Information Systems Strategic Planning

The history of data processing has been such that applications have usually been developed quite independently of each other. We've already discussed one result of this: large-scale redundancy of data in scattered files,
instead of data sharing where applicable. There should come a stage in the
growth of every company's data processing activities when it recognizes
that the helter-skelter mode of application development must yield to a
well-planned approach. As a first step, the company must make a serious
study of its current data processing environment, its future data processing needs, and the ways that its various corporate components interact in
terms of passing data back and forth.

One available methodology designed to accomplish those purposes is
IBM's Business Systems Planning (BSP) technique. Figure 12.1 shows the
flow of steps in a BSP study. The scope of the study might be an entire
company, a division, or some other well-defined operating unit, depending on size. The study, which ideally takes about 6 weeks to complete,
should be conducted by a group of 8–12 people representing the major
functional areas of the company, as well as key systems analysts and,
very importantly, one major corporate executive. In terms of the eventual
database design, the key parts of the BSP process are the steps in Figure
12.1 labeled "Defining business processes," "Defining data classes," and
"Defining Information Architecture."

"Defining business processes" refers to a thorough study of the company to determine its component operations. "Defining data classes" refers
to a study that defines the major types of data (*not* down to the field level)
required by the company and thus by the company's business processes.
Figure 12.2 shows a sample matrix that relates a company's business processes, shown on the left, to its data classes, shown across the top. At the
individual intersection points the "C" label indicates that the process is
responsible for "creating" the data in that data class, while the "U" label
indicates that the process "uses" the data in the data class. The groupings
delineated by the dark-edged rectangles are based on processes that are
related to each other (e.g., the third group down is composed of manufacturing processes).

From the "U" boxes that fall outside of the dark-edged rectangles in Figure 12.2, it is evident that in a large number of instances processes belonging to one of the major groupings use data created by processes belonging
to another one of the major groupings. For example, the material requirements process of the manufacturing grouping uses product data created
by the design and development process of the requirements (research and
development) grouping. Such cross involvements of data among the different business process groupings is natural, and their discovery is a crucial result of the BSP work. Figure 12.3 (with the business process and
data class axes switched) continues the development of the matrix in Figure 12.2 through the "Defining information architecture" stage. At this

Figure 12.1. The steps in the BSP process. (Reprinted by permission from *Information Systems Planning Guide* (GE20-0527-3) IBM Corporation.)

PROCESS \ DATA CLASS	Planning	Financial	Product	Parts master	Bill of material	Vendor	Raw material inventory	Fin. goods inventory	Facilities	Work in process	Machine load	Open requirements	Routings	Customer	Sales territory	Order	Cost	Employee
Business planning	C	U	U						U					U			U	U
Organization analysis	U																	
Review and control	U	U																
Financial planning	C	U								U								U
Capital acquisition		C																
Research			U												U			
Forecasting	U	U												U	U			
Design and development			C	C	U									U				
Product specification maintenance			U	C	C	U												
Purchasing						C											U	
Receiving						U	U											
Inventory control							C	C		U								
Workflow layout			U						C			U						
Scheduling			U						U	C	U				U			
Capacity planning									U		C	U	U					
Material requirements			U		U	U						C				U		
Operations										U	U	U	C					
Territory management			U											C		U		
Selling			U											U	C	U		
Sales administration															U	U		
Order servicing			U											U		C		
Shipping			U					U								U		
General accounting		U				U								U			U	U
Cost planning						U										U	C	
Budget accounting	U	U								U							U	U
Personnel planning		U																C
Recruiting/development																		U
Compensation		U																U

Figure 12.2. Sample data class versus business process matrix in BSP. (Reprinted with permission from *Information Systems Planning Guide*, (GE20-0527-3) IBM Corporation.)

point we have a good idea of the organization's data classes and business processes and the data-oriented relationships among them.

With this strategic level information architecture defined, we can now turn our attention to individual application development efforts. We will divide the processes into smaller subprocesses and arrange them on a priority basis for computer implementation. The information architecture will serve as a permanent record of how all of the computer applications relate to each other in the strategic plan.

Systems Analysis

Deciding to implement one of the subprocesses that we identified in the BSP study, we move into the application development cycle. The application development cycle begins with the all-important systems analysis

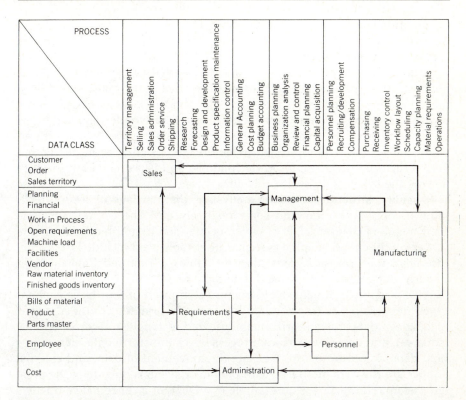

The table shows PROCESS columns and DATA CLASS rows:

| Territory management | Selling | Sales administration | Order service | Shipping | Research | Forecasting | Design and development | Product specification maintenance | Information control | General Accounting | Cost planning | Budget accounting | Business planning | Organization analysis | Review and control | Financial planning | Capital acquisition | Personnel planning | Recruiting/development | Compensation | Purchasing | Receiving | Inventory control | Workflow layout | Scheduling | Capacity planning | Material requirements | Operations |

DATA CLASS rows:
- Customer / Order / Sales territory — Sales
- Planning / Financial — Management
- Work in Process / Open requirements / Machine load / Facilities / Vendor / Raw material inventory / Finished goods inventory — Manufacturing
- Bills of material / Product / Parts master — Requirements
- Employee — Personnel
- Cost — Administration

Figure 12.3. Sample BSP information architecture. (Reprinted with permission from *Information Systems Planning Guide*, (GE20-0527-3) IBM Corporation.)

phase. Systems analysis is the detailed study of how the business process (really what we were calling "subprocess" in the last section) being considered for computer implementation works. Systems analysis is an implementation-independent exercise and does not involve the mention of tapes, disks, CPUs, or any other computer components. It is truly foolhardy to proceed with a computer implementation of a process that is not thoroughly understood. Any misconceptions of how the process works are sure to become embedded in the application code. The later in the application development cycle these errors are discovered, the more expensive it will be to fix them.

The systems analyst serves as an interface between the people responsible for carrying out the business process (the users) and the people responsible for the computer implementation of it (the programmers). The systems analyst will interview the users and study documentation about the business process, reformulate this information in an appropriate form, and pass it on to the programmers. A systems analysis methodology should support the systems analyst in performing this task. The methodology and its forms for recording the business process information must be detailed enough for the programmers to work with. But at the same time, it must be unintimidating enough for the nonanalytically oriented users to be able to read and understand for the purpose of providing feedback on its accuracy. One such methodology is called "Structured Systems Analysis."

Structured systems analysis is a data-directed, engineering-oriented approach to systems analysis that was developed in the mid-to-late 1970s. Since the term "structured" has become one of the most overused words in data processing, one is immediately drawn to wonder about the use of the term here. In fact, as will be shown, this approach *is* structured in the sense that it is top-down in nature, is designed to be integrated with structured program design techniques, and is a unified approach to solving the systems analysis problem.

In reality, structured systems analysis is the marriage of several techniques, some fairly new and some relatively old. The central vehicle is the Data Flow Diagram (DFD), which is intended to graphically show the movement of data through a system. Other tools used include Data Structure Diagrams, decision trees, decision tables, structured English, tight English, data normalization, and data dictionaries.

A DFD is a two-dimensional structure composed of four basic element types: process boxes (represented by vertically oriented, rounded-edged rectangles), data stores (horizontally oriented rectangles), external entities (squares), and data flow arrows. Process boxes transform data, data stores hold data, data flow arrows facilitate the movement of data, and external entities are the data interfaces with people or systems outside of the present system. Figure 12.4 is an example of a DFD for a car rental company's reservation and billing system.

Data Flow Diagrams are intended to be nonphysical, showing only the flow of information among processes, stores, and external entities, and not showing disks, tapes, CPUs, or any other potential physical implementation vehicles. They are designed to be understandable not

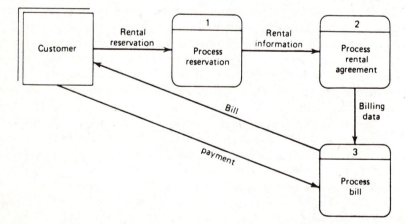

Figure 12.4. Structured systems analysis: Data flow diagram for the car rental reservation system.

only to programmers, but to users as well, in order to facilitate the user feedback process. To that end, one feature of the DFD concept is that the diagrams are drawn in a top-down fashion. Admittedly, the diagram in Figure 12.4 is a high-level view of the system. But it does fulfill two needs. For one thing, it outlines the entire system, and for another, it provides an easy to understand entry vehicle for a nonanalytically oriented user.

The diagram in Figure 12.5 is an "explosion" of the "Process Reservation" process box in Figure 12.4. The process boxes in Figure 12.5, when taken together, describe in further detail the function outlined in the process box in Figure 12.4. The intention is that the process boxes be repeatedly exploded down, creating a hierarchy of process box levels, until each lowest-level process box represents an amount of function implementable

Figure 12.5. Structured systems analysis: Detail of the "Process Reservation" box.

by a module of code (about 50 to 100 lines in a higher-level language) in a structured design sense. Thus, all of the DFDs taken together describe the application in a top-down, comprehensive, and yet easy to understand manner.

The DFDs will eventually be used by program designers and programmers for the implementation of the application. Therefore it follows that there must be yet another level of logic detail to describe the details of the functions in the lowest-level process boxes. For that need, structured systems analysis turns to several well-known, detail-level techniques: decision trees, decision tables, structured English, and tight English. One problem that arises from the choice of any one of these techniques is that the more formal tools—decision tables and structured English—can more readily be converted to code by programmers, but are more difficult for uninitiated users to comment on for feedback. Conversely, the less formal tools—decision trees and tight English—make user feedback more of a real possibility, but require more work on the part of the programmers. An attempt by the systems analyst to solve that dilemma by using two methods to describe a single lowest-level process box unfortunately raises the possibility of an integrity problem.

The data stores are collections of fields of information. Exactly what fields belong in a given store can be discerned from a study of the data flows into and out of the data store. A further question about the fields in a data store is the manner in which they should be passed on to the file or database designers after the systems analysis phase. The stated philosophy of structured systems analysis is that the fields in a data store should be passed in a form in which they are grouped into simplified sets (which would contain nonredundant data if implemented directly as physical files). It is felt that this is the clearest form for the designers to use in the eventual design phase. The suggested technique for accomplishing this is data normalization. Data normalization has usually been associated with database design as opposed to systems analysis (and will be discussed in detail shortly). There are two arguments for data normalization being performed as part of structured systems analysis. For one thing, data normalization requires a thorough understanding of the true semantic meaning of the fields and the relationships of the fields to each other in the application, and it is the systems analyst who has the earliest and deepest understanding of that. In addition, one of the standard techniques for database design requires data normalization as its first step regardless of the eventual physical structure used. Thus, if it has to be performed unconditionally, it might as well be done at this stage, even if the eventual physical vehicle has not yet been selected.

Since all of the DFDs and associated information must be recorded and maintained, a suggestion is made for a recording method. This method is the use of a data dictionary (discussed in detail in Chapter 11), which dictates that the systems analysts be the originators of the items in the dictionary. These would include the process boxes, data flows, data stores, and external entities, as well as field descriptions. The latter would presumably be used and enhanced by the physical design people at a later time.

Another aspect of structured systems analysis is its potential interface to structured system design techniques. As stated earlier, each lowest-level process box is intended to become a module of code in a structured design sense. Thus, the program designer is expected to convert the DFD lowest-level process boxes (and overall logic) into a top-down modular design. Clearly, the program designer's job is not eliminated. Not only does the program designer have to do the stated conversion, but in addition the functions in some process boxes may have to be combined into a single program module, or alternately, the function in a single process box may have to be divided among several program modules, all to accommodate the realities of the physical system.

Several items can be noted in terms of the usage of the structured systems analysis techniques relative to standard systems development phases. The most significant of these is that the systems analysts should first develop a DFD of the existing system (if one does not already exist from when that system was created) and then later, as the analysis phase progresses and further management approvals are obtained, develop a DFD of the proposed system. Another point is that a DFD can be subdivided to reflect that a particular physical implementation may only encompass part of the studied application, for economic or other reasons. A third item is that further information can be put into the DFDs even after the analysis phase is over, in the form of notes in the process boxes that indicate where or how the function was eventually implemented.

The Need for Database Design

A variety of reasons make careful database design essential. These include data redundancy, application performance, data independence, data security, and ease of programming. All are important factors in the data processing environment, and all can be adversely affected by a poor database design.

Intrafile and Multifile Redundancy

Proper database design is essential in avoiding both the intrafile and multifile redundancies that were discussed earlier. Strictly speaking, the amount of apparent redundancy (key and non-key fields) varies with the type of DBMS for which the files are being designed. In all cases, at least in the early stages of design, the goal is to eliminate all redundancy among the non-key fields. In the later stages of design, as the data takes on the form of the particular DBMS structures, there may or may not be overt redundancy among the key fields. Specifically, the relational approach requires certain fields to appear as attributes of different relations, while in the navigational cases this field duplication is replaced by pointers.

Performance

Performance, the operational speed of applications and systems, can be affected or influenced by a number of factors in the database environment. Several of these factors are common data processing issues that are beyond the control of database design. The latter items include CPU processing speed, disk data transfer rate, channel speed, the contention of different applications sharing the same hardware system, and of course, the efficiency of the techniques embodied in the DBMS itself.

However, there are many elements of the database environment that affect performance and that *are* under the control of the database designer. Many of them are product specific; that is, they depend on quirks of the particular DBMS. But others are general enough in nature to deserve mention here and further discussion later. Most of these are directly or indirectly related to the scourge of database performance: the number and nature of accesses to the data on the direct access, secondary storage devices, commonly known as "disk I/Os."

One common example of a performance-related choice is which access method to use and exactly how to implement it for the application at hand. The designer may have to decide whether to use a hashed access method or an indexed method, how many fields to index, which data placement or hashing method to use (in the hashed case), and so on. There may be a variety of types of pointers to link various records together, each with different performance ramifications for different types of applications. There may be a variety of ways to design the juxtaposition of various record types in a hierarchy or network, and in addition, several options for grouping occurrences on the same direct access device. Further comments on specific systems will be made later.

Data Independence

Data independence, the ability to modify data structures without affecting existing programs, is fundamentally a function of the data model used by a particular DBMS. All such systems provide an enhanced degree of data independence when compared to ordinary file processing. Nevertheless, there are database design choices that can be made, particularly when dealing with hierarchical and network DBMSs, that can affect the degree of independence achieved. The intricacy of the matter does not end there, because beyond the specifics of the data structure and the database design, the way that a program is written can affect data independence.

Data Security

Database management systems generally have a variety of built-in data security safeguards. These range from passwords associated with a given user, to passwords associated with particular data, to various ways of prohibiting all but certain users from performing certain operations on certain data. Data security becomes an issue in database design when the minimum amount of data that the system is capable of returning from the database on a program call is greater than the amount that the person who executed the program has the right to see. In that case, the structure may have to be designed so that data that otherwise would have been placed together into a retrievable unit is split over several units.

Ease of Programming

While the use of database management systems requires programmers to learn new concepts and protocols, the overall effect of the use of DBMSs is to decrease programming complexity and the attendant programming error rates. One reason for this is the standardization that results from using the same protocol for data manipulations in all programs. Another reason involves the integrated nature of the data structures, which allows a programmer to obtain data from physically separate files or distinct record types (depending on the data model used) with one call from the high-level programming interface. Without the use of a DBMS, and assuming the avoidance of unacceptable levels of data redundancy, the alternative would be accessing data in one file, using it to access data in another file, and so on through as many files as necessary to satisfy the query. This latter method is clearly much more error prone, not to mention more time consuming to write.

Within the improved level of programming that the use of DBMSs affords, certain decisions in database design can make the programmer's job somewhat harder or easier. Unfortunately, the decisions that can simplify programming specifications usually have an adverse effect on data redundancy, system performance, or both. For example, combining fields within one data structure unit may allow a programmer to simplify the specifications needed to retrieve that data, but will usually result in an increase in data redundancy. Adding additional indexes into the data structure creates more flexibility in on-line retrieval and simplifies program retrieval specifications at the expense of performance when the data must be updated. A highly volatile file with a large number of indexes connected to it may degrade the performance of the entire system.

Database Design Methodologies

This section will present three of the most common database design techniques. In all of the cases, we will begin with the data-oriented information generated as output from systems analysis and proceed to relational, pseudo-relational, hierarchical, and network database models. The method of explanation will be by example with appropriate commentary along the way.

The first method, "data normalization and data structuring," is representative of the class of methods that takes as input a list of fields and the associations among those fields. The second method, the "entity-relationship" method, and the third method, the "Date-Wilson" method, are representative of the class of methods that takes entities and relationships as input.

Data Normalization and Data Structuring

The Example.   This first method of database design requires one major step for the relational approach and two major steps for the other three approaches. Fortunately for convenience of explanation, the one major step for the relational approach is the first of the two steps for the other three approaches.

Figure 12.6 shows an example set of fields that concern the personnel information system of a nationwide chain of automobile repair shops. It is clear from this list of fields that the goal of the system is to keep track of the company's mechanics, their skills, their locations, and other associated information. The MECHANIC'S SKILL PROFICIENCY LEVEL field is intended to store a particular mechanic's proficiency level in a particular skill. (This set of fields was chosen for this example to make certain database design points. As we shall see, a much higher percentage of the fields in this collection will participate as key fields than would be the case in most actual situations.) Figure 12.7 shows the associations among our example fields. The single-headed arrows indicate unique identifications. Thus, Association number 2 indicates that for a given mechanic number, there is exactly one name associated with it (mechanic numbers are unique), and Association number 10 indicates that for a given shop number there is exactly one city associated with it. If I give you mechanic number 81, you can uniquely give me back John Smith; if I give you shop

MECHANIC NUMBER (MECH NO)
SKILL NUMBER (SKLL NO)
SKILL CATEGORY (SKLL CAT)
MECHANIC NAME (MECH NAME)
MECHANIC AGE (MECH AGE)
SHOP NUMBER (SHOP NO)
SHOP CITY
SHOP SUPERVISOR (SUPV)
MECHANIC'S SKILL PROFICIENCY LEVEL (PROF)

Figure 12.6.   Example set of fields.

1. MECH NO ⟶⟶ SKLL NO
2. MECH NO ⟶ MECH NAME
3. MECH NO ⟶ MECH AGE
4. MECH NO ⟶ SHOP NO
5. MECH NO ⟶ SUPV
6. SKLL NO ⟶⟶ MECH NO
7. SKLL NO ⟶ SKLL CAT
8. SHOP NO ⟶⟶ MECH NO
9. SHOP NO ⟶ SUPV
10. SHOP NO ⟶ SHOP CITY
11. MECH NO, SKLL NO ⟶ PROF

Figure 12.7. Associations between the fields.

number 12, you can uniquely give me back Chicago. Note that unless explicitly stated, the inverse cannot be assumed to hold true. Thus, there may be several John Smiths in the company, and there may be several shops in Chicago. The double-headed arrows in Figure 12.7 indicate multiple associations: An instance of the item on the left may be associated with several instances of the item on the right. Association number 1 says that a mechanic may have several skills. Association number 8 says that a shop may have several mechanics working in it.

Potential Database Problems. Before beginning the database design process, it is instructive to revisit the problems that poor database design can cause in the context of this example. Figure 12.8 shows seven sample records of a file made up of all of the fields listed in Figure 12.6. It assumes that no database design effort was made, and thus all of the fields were just lumped together in one file. MECHANIC NUMBER and SKILL NUMBER were chosen as a compound (multifield) key, since the two taken together can uniquely identify a record in the file. Note that it follows that since a key value can uniquely identify a record in a file, the key value uniquely determines the values of the non-key fields of that record (conversely the non-key values are "dependent" on the key value).

It is evident that there is a great deal of redundancy in the file in Figure 12.8. Mechanic number 35 has three skills. To represent this requires three records, since MECHANIC NUMBER and SKILL NUMBER must be taken together to form a legitimate key. In fact, each MECHANIC NUMBER–SKILL NUMBER pair must appear in a separate record in order to be associated with a PROFICIENCY LEVEL number, which is dependent on the combination of who the mechanic is and what skill is under discussion. As a result of that situation, one example of redundancy is that the mechanic's age, name, shop number, shop city, and supervisor must be carried in the file as many times as the number of skills the mechanic has. Another example is that the information about who the supervisor is at a particular shop must be carried at least once for each mechanic who works at that shop. These facts bring with them all of the standard problems of

MECH NO	SKLL NO	SKLL CAT	MECH NAME	MECH AGE	SHOP NO	SHOP CITY	SUPV	PROF
21	113	Body	Adams	55	52	NYC	Brown	3
35	113	Body	Baker	32	44	LA	Green	5
35	179	Engn	Baker	32	44	LA	Green	1
35	204	Tran	Baker	32	44	LA	Green	6
50	179	Engn	Cody	40	44	LA	Green	2
77	148	Tire	Doe	47	52	NYC	Brown	6
77	361	Engn	Doe	47	52	NYC	Brown	6
. . .								

Key { MECH NO, SKLL NO }

Figure 12.8. Sample records.

redundancy: extra storage space, extra time spent on update, and potential integrity problems.

Another potential problem with the file involves the deletion and addition of data. Suppose Adams and Doe are the only two mechanics in shop number 52. If they quit and, as might reasonably be expected, we delete the records concerning them, then we have also deleted the fact that Brown is the supervisor of shop number 52 from the file. These two fundamentally different pieces of information cannot exist separately in the current design. A similar, but reversed, situation exists in adding data to the file. Ordinarily, if we add a new mechanic to the file we would expect to find the shop city and supervisor information from records already in the file that involve that shop. But if the new mechanic is the first one in the shop, then the shop city and supervisor data will not exist in the file and will have to be sought elsewhere. Adding a mechanic who does not yet possess any skills could have serious implications in terms of the key. Thus it is clear that simply putting all of the fields into one file leaves a great deal to be desired.

Data Normalization. Data normalization is a methodology for arranging fields into tables (or files or relations) so that redundancy among the non-key fields is eliminated. Each of the resultant tables deals with a single area of knowledge, as opposed to the mixture seen in Figure 12.8. The input required by the normalization process is a list of the set of data fields and the associations among them, as for instance in Figures 12.6 and 12.7. Nevertheless, it is easier to explain the process in the context of an example that includes sample records, so we shall continue with the example we have been using. We stress again that the lists of data fields and associations, which are the required inputs here, are parts of the output of the systems analysis phase.

Unnormalized Data. Figure 12.9 shows the example data in a somewhat loosely structured arrangement called "unnormalized" form. Unnormalized data may include situations such as a multivalued field. For instance, the second record in Figure 12.9 refers to mechanic number 35 and notes, within that single record, that he has three skills. This form of data has certain distinct disadvantages, including the need for some form of variable-length records and additional complexity for the programmer, which would invariably lead to increased programming errors. Furthermore, in the case of mechanic number 35's record, we happen to know that skill number 113 matches up with skill category "body," and so on through all of the listed pairs of skill numbers and categories, but such matches may not always exist in all similar situations, causing incredible confusion.

First Normal Form. First normal form data requires that every data entry, or field value, must be nondecomposable. Figure 12.10 is the

MECH NO	SKLL NO	SKLL CAT	MECH NAME	MECH AGE	SHOP NO	SHOP CITY	SUPV	PROF
21	113	Body	Adams	55	52	NYC	Brown	3
35	113	Body	Baker	32	44	LA	Green	5
	179	Engn						1
	204	Tran						6
50	179	Engn	Cody	40	44	LA	Green	2
77	148	Tire	Doe	47	52	NYC	Brown	6
	361	Engn						6

Figure 12.9. Unnormalized data.

MECH NO	SKLL NO	SKLL CAT	MECH NAME	MECH AGE	SHOP NO	SHOP CITY	SUPV	PROF
21	113	Body	Adams	55	52	NYC	Brown	3
35	113	Body	Baker	32	44	LA	Green	5
35	179	Engn	Baker	32	44	LA	Green	1
35	204	Tran	Baker	32	44	LA	Green	6
50	179	Engn	Cody	40	44	LA	Green	2
77	148	Tire	Doe	47	52	NYC	Brown	6
77	361	Engn	Doe	47	52	NYC	Brown	6

Key { MECH NO, SKLL NO

Figure 12.10. First normal form.

first normal form representation of the data in Figure 12.8. Every field entry of every record consists of only one piece of nonsubdivisible data. Essentially, the unnormalized records with multivalued fields were cloned to produce several records with some data repeated, as necessary. Except for the fact that the data shown in Figure 12.8 is meant to represent only part of a file, while the data in Figure 12.10 is meant to represent an entire file (for illustrative purposes), the two are identical. Clearly, the first normal form representation of data is not, in and of itself, helpful as a redundancy-controlling arrangement, but is merely a jumping-off point for further work.

Second Normal Form.   We have already established that the data in Figure 12.10 (like Figure 12.8) is highly redundant. At this point the methodology turns to the question of what to look for and change in the data structure to begin to alleviate the redundancy.

The fact that the MECHANIC NUMBER SKILL NUMBER combination of fields is a valid key for this file has already been established. Again, this means, among other things, that every non-key field in the file is dependent on the key, which can be verified by the single-arrow associations in Figure 12.7. While both parts of the compound key are necessary to define the PROFICIENCY FIELD (association number 11 in Figure 12.7), only one or the other of the two parts of the key is needed to define each of the other non-key fields. This fact is a clue to the redundancy and its at least partial elimination.

Figure 12.11 shows the same data in second normal form. It has been divided into three tables, each of which has the property that its entire key is needed to define each of its non-key fields. Within a given table, no nonkey field is defined by part of the key alone. Several fields were duplicated in this process. MECHANIC NUMBER, which appeared only once as a field in first normal form, now appears both in the Mechanic Table and in the Proficiency Table. As we shall see, this kind of field duplication is necessary at this stage (and for the relational case in general) among those fields participating as key fields. In fact, the total number of field value occurrences has decreased from 63 in Figure 12.10 to 55 in Figure 12.11, indicating a net decrease in redundancy. Also notice that individually identifiable areas of knowledge are represented in each of the tables (although not to the final degree, as we shall soon see).

Third Normal Form.   The Skill Table and the Proficiency Table in Figure 12.11 are both completely free of non-key redundancy at this point. In fact, they are both already in third normal form. But a glance at the Mechanic Table will reveal some residual redundancy. For example, both records 1 and 4 indicate that shop number 52 is in New York City and is supervised by Brown; likewise for records 2 and 3 and shop number 44. Yet according to the list of relationships, the key of that table, MECHANIC NUMBER, identifies each of its other fields, and since the key consists of only one

Key

MECH NO	MECH NAME	MECH AGE	SHOP NO	SHOP CITY	SUPV
21	Adams	55	52	NYC	Brown
35	Baker	32	44	LA	Green
50	Cody	40	44	LA	Green
77	Doe	47	52	NYC	Brown

Mechanic table

Key

SKLL NO	SKLL CAT
113	Body
148	Tire
179	Engn
204	Tran
361	Engn

Skill table

Key

MECH NO	SKLL NO	PROF
21	113	3
35	113	5
35	179	1
35	204	6
50	179	2
77	148	6
77	361	6

Proficiency table

Figure 12.11. Second normal form.

field, the second normal form rule of non-key dependence on the entire key is, of course, met.

The problem has to do with the associations between SHOP NUMBER and SHOP CITY, and between SHOP NUMBER and SUPERVISOR (Associations number 9 and number 10 in Figure 12.7). SHOP NUMBER defines SHOP CITY and SUPERVISOR, but is clearly not a valid key of the entire table (it does not define MECHANIC NUMBER, MECHANIC NAME, or MECHANIC AGE). Thus the situation is one of a non-key field defining other non-key fields. This kind of incestuous relationship, which is another kind of indication of fundamentally different kinds of information being mixed together in the same table, is what is causing the remaining redundancy.

Figure 12.12 shows the third normal form representation of the data. Notice that a new table, the Shop table, has been created to separate out the shop-related data. Also notice that in splitting off the Shop table, a copy of the SHOP NUMBER column was left behind in the Mechanic table. This is done because it was the only way to continue to indicate with which shop a mechanic was associated.

So in third normal form we can say that in each table no situation exists where a non-key field defines another non-key field. There is a fairly common exception to this when there are two fields that *could* be the key, such as an employee identification number and a social security number. The field not chosen as the key would seem to be a non-key field that then defines other non-key fields, but in this specific case it is not a violation of the stated rule. The third normal form data in Figure 12.12 contains no redundancy among the non-key fields. This is the goal that we sought.

Other Normal Forms.   As further research continues to be done in this field, new problems and solutions arise. Two exceptions have been identified that involve third normal form data but still contain redundancy. Both involve combinations of multiple associations. Named fourth and fifth normal forms, they are encountered infrequently in practice and are beyond the scope of this book.

The Value of Normalized Tables.   Two major statements can be made about normalized data. One is that this form of data, free of redundancy among the non-key fields, is an intermediate plateau in the design of data structures for hierarchical and network databases.

The other point is that normalized data, subject to possible structural modifications for performance reasons, *is* the final design for relational databases. In fact, the normalization process assures that join fields will appear in all of the tables they should appear in, based on the given relationships among the fields. That is a very strong statement and a fact that is central to the use of normalization for the design of all of the types of databases.

The same remarks about normalization producing the database design, subject to performance modifications, applies to pseudo-relational databases, subject to the addition of tables or indexes that prejoin the normalized tables based on the data relationships and application needs. In fact, the same basic remark also applies to ordinary, nondatabase flat files, for which normalization is also an ideal design technique.

Data Structuring—Hierarchical Databases.   Generally, in converting from a set of normalized tables to a hierarchical data structure, the normalized tables are transformed into nodes in the hierarchy. Occurrences of the same and different record types are connected by a variety of types

Key

MECH NO	MECH NAME	MECH AGE	SHOP NO
21	Adams	55	52
35	Baker	32	44
50	Cody	40	44
77	Doe	47	52

Mechanic table

Key

SKLL NO	SKLL CAT
113	Body
148	Tire
179	Engn
204	Tran
361	Engn

Skill table

Key

SHOP NO	SHOP CITY	SUPV
44	LA	Green
52	NYC	Brown

Shop table

Key

MECH NO	SKLL NO	PROF
21	113	3
35	113	5
35	179	1
35	204	6
50	179	2
77	148	6
77	361	6

Proficiency table

Figure 12.12. Third normal form.

of pointers. In effect, certain of the normalized tables are chosen to have their records prejoined to each other, to physically realize a selected set of relationships. The primary advantage of this technique is superior performance during execution of accesses based on those relationships.

The procedure for designing a hierarchical database, such as for a DL/I system, begins with a set of normalized tables. We will continue following the example we have been using and resume with the normalized tables in Figure 12.12.

The Structuring Process.   The process begins by noting the multiple associations in Figure 12.7, the original list of associations among the fields. A multiple association whose inverse multiple association does not appear on the list is recorded as a one-to-many relationship. There is one such relationship in Figure 12.7:

SHOP NO ———>> MECH NO

which is association number 8. A multiple association whose inverse does appear on the list is recorded as a many-to-many relationship. There is one such relationship in Figure 12.7:

MECH NO <<———>> SKLL NO

which is formed by the combination of associations number 1 and number 6.

Next, hierarchies are formed from the one-to-many relationships. Since every branch of a hierarchical data structure represents a one-to-many relationship, this step is quite straightforward. Figure 12.13 shows a hierarchy built out of the one one-to-many relationship in the example. The Mechanic and Shop nodes in the hierarchy are directly derived from the normalized Mechanic and Shop tables of Figure 12.12. Note that the SHOP NO field in the Mechanic table in Figure 12.12 does not appear in the MECHANIC record in Figure 12.13. In the normalized tables the only way to indicate which shop a mechanic works at is to include SHOP NO as a field in the Mechanic table. In a sense, the fact that SHOP NO also

SHOP NO	SHOP CITY	SUPV

SHOP record

MECH NO	MECH NAME	MECH AGE

MECHANIC record

Figure 12.13.   Hierarchy representing the one-to-many relationship.

appears as a field in the Shop table seems to be a form of redundancy involving a field that serves, at least in one table, as the key. But when these tables are converted into records in a hierarchy that represents the one-to-many relationship between shops and mechanics, the SHOP NO field is not included in the Mechanic record. The point is that the knowledge of which shop a mechanic works at is now stored by means of the pointers, which connect a particular shop to all of the mechanics who work there.

A many-to-many relationship cannot be built directly in a hierarchical data structure. It must be simulated by two one-to-many relationships, each of whose target, or "many" side record type, is the same specially created new record. When the data is eventually loaded using this structure there will be one occurrence of this new special record *for every occurrence of the relationship* (for every connection between two entities in the relationship). Figure 12.14 shows the hierarchy of Figure 12.13 on the left, with a new (single record type) hierarchy on the right consisting of just the Skill record type. Mechanic and skill, which have a many-to-many relationship to each other, are both in a one-to-many relationship with a specially created record type labeled Proficiency. The Skill node, forming the new hierarchy on the righthand side, is derived from the Skill table in Figure 12.12. The Proficiency node is derived from the Proficiency table in Figure 12.12. Remember that the many-to-many relationship being implemented links Mechanic occurrences to Skill occurrences. The Proficiency table in Figure 12.12 not only indicates these linkages, but gives additional information (the proficiency of a particular mechanic in a particular skill) about them.

DL/I. Figure 12.15 shows substantially the same hierarchical structure as shown in Figure 12.14, except that it has been modified to conform

Figure 12.14. Two hierarchies connected to represent the many-to-many relationship.

Figure 12.15.   DL/I representation including logical relationship.

to DL/I conventions. The term "record" is replaced by "segment." The special record type serving as the connector for the many-to-many relationship is called a "logical child" segment. The fact that it appears in both hierarchies (with the proficiency data duplicated in both places in one variation) indicates that the many-to-many relationship can in fact be exercised in both directions. That is, for a given skill we can find all of the mechanics who have that skill, and for a given mechanic we can find all of the skills he has. If the logical child appeared in only one of the hierarchies, then the relationship could only be traversed from that side.

Access and Performance Modifications.   Substantial work remains after normalization and structuring. The tentative hierarchical structure has to be adjusted for access, performance, and occasionally, security reasons. This process is what we referred to earlier as physical design.

In terms of access, the designer must specify which fields of which segments must be directly accessible. This will be based on the systems analysis results for the set of applications slated to use the database. Ordinarily, only the root segments can be directly accessed and only by their key fields at that (and even the provision of that capability is a decision that has to be made). But suppose that an application requires direct access to a field in a nonroot segment. For instance, say that in the current example there is a need to find mechanics directly by mechanic number. Or, suppose that an application requires direct access to a non-key field in a root segment, for example a need to find shops directly by city. Then either secondary indexes must be employed or the structure must be rearranged so certain nonroot segments become roots of new hierarchies, with logical relationships employed to connect the new and the old hierarchies to maintain the appropriate relationships.

Another example of an application-dependent decision is the choice of access methods. Access to the root segments can be either sequential, both direct (specifically indexed) and sequential, or direct (via hashing methods). Of course, such a decision is based on the needs of the applications that will use the data.

A wide variety of factors must be taken into account in DL/I in terms of performance, many of which are interrelated: A change in one may require a balancing or compensating change in another. For example, long twin chains (e.g., a large number of mechanics working in one shop) can have a deleterious effect on performance, because the system does not permit direct access into the middle of such a chain when access is being made from the superior segment. Starting from the beginning of the chain, access can only be made by sequentially traversing the pointer-connected segment occurrences. Depending on the length of the chain and the number of segment occurrences that can be brought into main memory from disk at one time, traversing such a chain can mean an unacceptable number of time-consuming disk accesses. Among the solutions to this problem are inserting a new dummy-level segment type above the one with the long twin chains and increasing the number of occurrences that can be read into main memory at one time.

Another example of a performance consideration that should affect the design concerns the number of occurrences of a hierarchy's root segment. Again using the structure in Figure 12.15, assume that there is a fairly small number of shops, but that there are a substantial number of mechanics in each shop. Also assume that most program references will be to Mechanic and will presume the knowledge of the mechanic's name or number and shop location. Under these circumstances it makes little sense to have a Shop segment root. The capability provided by the IMS access methods of accessing a root segment directly, and particularly the speed of such access using the hashed organization facility, is extremely powerful and is wasted on a root that has few occurrences. In the case described, the Mechanic segment should be made the root, with the SHOP NUMBER field appended to the MECHANIC NUMBER field to form a two-field key. This would create some redundancy in the SHOP NUMBER field, but that kind of key field redundancy has to be considered acceptable under the circumstances. The SHOP CITY and SUPERVISOR information can be held, still nonredundantly, in a small, separate file.

Other performance considerations, which become more or less important depending on the particular case, include the number of levels (depth) of the hierarchy, the distance from the root of particular segments, relative segment sizes, the use of variable length segments, and so on.

Data Structuring—Network Databases. The basic principles of database design, using the normalization and structuring approach, are the same in the design of CODASYL network databases as they are in the design of DL/I hierarchies. The set of normalized relations together with a list of the one-to-many and the many-to-many relationships among the entities is the starting point.

Figure 12.16 shows a network constructed from the third normal form relations of Figure 12.12 and the one-to-many relationship

(SHOP NO ———>> MECH NO)

and the many-to-many relationship

(MECH NO <<———>> SKLL NO)

of Figure 12.7. Notice the specification of the three sets involved. Also notice the link record connecting the Mechanic and Skill records, which realizes the many-to-many relationship. Just as in the construction of the DL/I database in Figure 12.15, the one-to-many relationship was drawn first, followed by the many-to-many relationship. In the network case, when the time came to draw the many-to-many relationship, the Skill record was added to the network structure, which had already been started with the one-to-many relationship between the Shop and the Mechanic records. That contrasts, technically, to the DL/I case, in which a second hierarchy had to be created when the Skill record (or segment) had to be added to the picture.

Figure 12.16. CODASYL network representation.

As for further modifications based on performance issues, the same remarks, in principle, that applied to DL/I, apply here. Factors such as chain lengths, access method types, pointer options, network complexity, and so on, must be considered in the atmosphere of the particular application requirements and the specific DBMS being used. Modifications in the network must then be made based on these factors.

Data Structuring—Pseudo-Relational Databases. Again in the pseudo-relational case, the normalized relations and the one-to-many and many-to-many relationships constitute the jumping off point to structuring. Structuring basically consists of three steps.

First, a decision has to be made concerning the viability of creating files in the exact form of the normalized relations (since the fundamental data structure in such systems is simple linear files). There is no question that keeping the files in the same form as the normalized relations is the optimum in terms of minimizing data redundancy. However, in specific instances, the normalization process may produce a large number of relations, each containing a relatively small number of fields. This situation could have an important negative impact on performance and/or on application programming complexity. In this case it may be necessary to tolerate a certain amount of redundancy in combining the fields from some of the normalized relations to create larger files.

Second, data structures logically linking (actually "joining") various files to each other must be designed. Such structures may take the form of either matched linear lists or binary index trees based on concatenated file keys, as in IBM's System/38.

Third, the designer must study the data requirements of the set of applications and determine which fields of each particular file must be accessible on a direct basis. Such systems have the capacity to have some kind of an index built for each field that has such a requirement.

The Entity-Relationship Model

Introduction. Another major method of database design involves the entity-relationship model. Database design using the entity-relationship model begins with a list of the entity types involved and the relationships among them. The philosophy of assuming that the designer knows what the entity types are at the outset is significantly different from the philosophy behind the normalization-based approach. Both methods assume that a thorough systems analysis has been done; however, the entity-relationship approach asserts that one of the results of systems analysis is a clear understanding of what the entities involved are. The normalization-based approach takes the view that systems analysis produces a list of the applications' data fields and the relationships among them and that it is then the responsibility of the normalization process to separate the fields

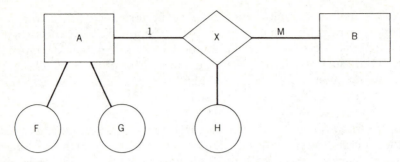

Figure 12.17. The entity-relationship diagram.

that identify entities from those that merely further describe entities, as we have seen.

The entity-relationship approach uses "entity-relationship" diagrams, a hypothetical example of which is shown in Figure 12.17. The rectangular boxes represent entity types, the diamond-shaped box represents a relationship between entities, and the circular figures represent attributes. Thus Figure 12.17 shows two entities, A and B, which have a one-to-many relationship X to each other (note the "1" and "M" on either side of X). Entity A has two attributes (fields describing it), F and G. The relationship X has further descriptive information about it, H. H represents information about the relationship X, that is, about pairs of As and Bs, that does not apply to either an A occurrence by itself or a B occurrence by itself.

Figure 12.18 is an entity-relationship diagram for the fields and relationships shown in Figures 12.6 and 12.7 (the same example used in the normalization-structuring discussion). Shop, mechanic, and skill have been recognized as the three entities in the application. The one-to-many relationship between Shop and Mechanic and the many-to-many relationship between Mechanic and Skill are both clearly displayed. Notice the fields (including the key fields), which describe the entities, and the PROFICIENCY data, which further describes the relationship between Mechanics and Skills.

Other embellishments can be added to entity-relationship diagrams. One such device is a notation to show that occurrences of a particular entity cannot exist with an occurrence of another entity. Another is an indication that an entity does not have a unique key associated with it and must depend on another entity for proper identification.

From Entity-Relationship Diagrams to CODASYL Network Structures. Finally, the entity-relationship diagram must be converted to a form that corresponds to the data structure of the particular DBMS in use. To convert from an entity-relationship diagram to a CODASYL network representation is straightforward: The entity-relationship diagram is, in fact, itself a network. Compare the entity-relationship diagram of Figure 12.18 with the CODASYL network of Figure 12.16. The two figures are virtu-

Figure 12.18. Entity-relationship diagram for the sample data.

ally identical, with the recognition that the connector in the middle of the many-to-many relationship must be converted into a record type and serve as the target of the two one-to-many relationships, which replace the many-to-many relationship.

From Entity-Relationship Diagrams to Hierarchical Structures. Converting from an entity-relationship diagram to a set of DL/I hierarchies requires a bit more effort, but is still basically direct. The one-to-many relationships shown in the entity-relationship diagram simply become parent-child segment combinations in the DL/I hierarchies. The many-to-many relationships form the basis for DL/I logical relationships. The diamond-shaped box between the two entities in the many-to-many relationship becomes the logical child in the DL/I logical relationship, and any fields attached to the diamond-shaped box become intersection data. Thus the entity-relationship diagram of Figure 12.18 can be converted to the DL/I hierarchies of Figure 12.15.

From Entity-Relationship Diagrams to Relational and Pseudo-Relational Structures.   To convert from an entity-relationship diagram to a set of relational structures—or ordinary flat files, for that matter—is, in a manner of speaking, a reversal of the design effort using the normalization-based approach. The set of attributes of each entity in the entity-relationship diagram becomes a relation or file, with the unique identifying attribute becoming the key. But in addition, the identifying attribute of the entity on the "one" side of the one-to-many relationship must be duplicated and made one of the attributes of the relation based on the entity on the "many" side of that relationship. Once the network-like diagram is dismantled that is the only way of keeping track of which occurrence of the entity on the "one" side is related to an occurrence on the "many" side. If there is a multilevel hierarchy of entities, then such duplication must be propagated throughout the hierarchy when converting it to relations or files. In addition, relations or files must be created from the many-to-many relationships found in the entity-relationship diagram. The key of such a relation will consist of the identifying or key fields of the two entities involved, and the non-key fields will be the relationship modifiers (the fields attached to the diamond-shaped box).

Consider a conversion of the entity-relationship diagram in Figure 12.18 back to the third normal form relations in Figure 12.12. Notice that the shop, mechanic, and skill entities each form the basis for a relation. The Mechanic relation must contain a copy of the key (SHOP NO) of the Shop relation because it was the target in the one-to-many relationship. The Proficiency relation in Figure 12.12 is derived from the many-to-many relationship between Mechanic and Skill in Figure 12.18. Note that the key, MECH NO SKLL NO, is formed from the identifying fields of the mechanic and skill entities, and the non-key field, PROFICIENCY, was formerly the field connected to the diamond-shaped relationship connector.

The Date-Wilson Technique

A third database design technique is based on the ideas of Chris Date and Max Wilson, two researchers who worked at IBM's Santa Teresa, CA, laboratory in the early 1980s. In a broad sense, this technique is a hybrid: a cross between the data normalization and entity-relationship techniques. It shares with the data normalization technique its tabular, relational orientation. It shares with the entity-relationship technique the philosophy that the database designer has a thorough understanding of what the entity types are at the outset of the design process.

The Date-Wilson technique begins by assuming that the entities and their unique identifying fields are readily recognizable. In the current example of Figures 12.6 and 12.7, they are mechanics (MECH NO), skills (SKLL NO), and shops (SHOP NO). Furthermore, the technique makes the assumption that the designer understands the nature of foreign keys in conjunction with one-to-many relationships and of many-to-many relationships and intersection data.

So in this example, we start out with three "base" tables, each consisting initially of only an entity identifier, as shown in Figure 12.19a. There are then basically four other operations to perform in constructing the relational database. They are: adding simple attribute fields to those tables, adding foreign keys to those tables to satisfy the one-to-many relationships, constructing additional tables to handle the many-to-many relationships, and adding intersection data to those latter tables. Continuing with the example in the order of operations stated above, the simple attributes are inserted, as shown in Figure 12.19b.

What remains is the handling of the multiple relationships. In the next step, we recognize that the one-to-many relationship between mechanics and shops requires a foreign key to interrelate the currently very separate relations 1 and 3. The way to do that is to add the field that is the identifier of the entity on the "one" side of the one-to-many relationship to the table representing the "many" side of the one-to-many relationship. In this case, since for a given shop there are many mechanics, it means adding the shop identifier (SHOP NO) to the mechanics table (relation 1), as shown in Figure 12.19c. Finally, we take care of the many-to-many relationship between mechanics and skills by creating a new table with their identifiers as the compound key and adding the intersection data (proficiency) as a non-key field, as shown in relation 4 of Figure 12.19d.

Notice that the result of the data normalization technique in Figure 12.12 and the result of the Date-Wilson technique in Figure 12.19d are the same. The data normalization technique arrives at the result from a set of rules

1)	MECH NO			
2)	SKLL NO			
3)	SHOP NO			

(a)

1)	MECH NO	MECH NAME	MECH AGE
2)	SKLL NO	SKLL CAT	
3)	SHOP NO	SHOP CITY	SUPV

(b)

1)	MECH NO	MECH NAME	MECH AGE	SHOP NO
2)	SKLL NO	SKLL CAT		
3)	SHOP NO	SHOP CITY	SUPV	

(c)

1)	MECH NO	MECH NAME	MECH AGE	SHOP NO
2)	SKLL NO	SKLL CAT		
3)	SHOP NO	SHOP CITY	SUPV	
4)	MECH NO	SKLL NO	PROF	

(d)

Figure 12.19. The Date-Wilson design technique: *(a)* establish base tables; *(b)* add attributes; *(c)* add foreign keys for one-to-many relationships; *(d)* add many-to-many relationships.

	Normalization Approach	Entity-Relationship Approach	Date-Wilson Approach
Relational	Normalization	Entity-Relationship diagram "dismantled" into a set of relations	Date-Wilson Technique
Pseudo-Relational	Normalization plus join tables or indexes	Entity-Relationship diagram "dismantled" into a set of relations plus join tables or indexes	Date-Wilson Technique plus join tables or indexes
Hierarchial	Normalization followed by hierarchical structuring	Entity-Relationship diagram converted to a hierarchical structure	Date-Wilson Technique followed by hierarchical structuring
Network	Normalization followed by network structuring	Entity-Relationship diagram converted to a network structure	Date-Wilson Technique followed by network structuring

Figure 12.20.   Database design summary chart.

based on dependencies among the fields. It decomposes the fields into subgroups based on those rules. Date-Wilson takes the opposite approach. It assumes an understanding of such concepts as foreign keys and many-to-many relationships and builds up or composes the tables from a null starting point in a progressive fashion.

Thus, the result of the Date-Wilson technique is a relational database design. Clearly then, the processes for the conversion of the Date-Wilson result into pseudo-relational, hierarchical, and network database designs are identical to those that we have already considered for the data normalization case.

Figure 12.20 is a summary chart of the four DBMS approaches and the three discussed database design techniques. It is interesting to note that in practice the data normalization and entity-relationship approaches to database design are sometimes used in tandem for the construction of a single database. For example, the designer might make initial assumptions about entities, attributes, and relationships in the style of the entity-relationship approach and then test those assumptions using data normalization.

Other Tools for Database Design

There are several kinds of software tools that can aid in the database design process.

Automated Database Design Aids

Within the last few years, several automated database design software products have been introduced. Typically, they require a list of the fields that will constitute the database and the relationships among those fields. In general, they are capable of performing logical database design, and in some cases, with some human intervention, physical database design for specific DBMSs. As part of their operation they can perform editing on the input data and in so doing find errors and inconsistencies.

Database design programs have met with mixed success in the field. The biggest complaint from their users is that specifying the fields and relationships in the depth and precision required (for any computer program) is too time-consuming. This, however, is an unfortunate attitude, since the set of fields and relationships *must* be specified precisely for database design, whether or not an automated tool is to be used. The result of doing otherwise is inevitably a poor database design.

Performance Prediction and Monitoring Aids

Once the logical and physical database designs are complete, there are various methodologies available to predict the eventual performance of the system. In order to be accurate enough to be of any real use, these methodologies must consider a substantial amount of information beyond the structure of the database. For example, they must also consider the relative frequency of occurrence of the different record types, the application program calling patterns, and the resource competition from other applications using the same or different databases. Some of the methodologies have been partially automated as simulation routines.

Conclusion

Once the database design process is completed, the focus of the application development process turns to the programmers. Presumably, program design was taking place simultaneously with database design. Thus the programmers can be presented at once with their coding assignments and with the necessary data structures to use.

There are some steps remaining in the sequence after coding. These include various levels of program testing, installation, and ongoing maintenance. All of the steps from programming through maintenance will greatly benefit from the careful and continuously flowing work that was done from the earliest stages of the application development process through database design.

References

Blaha, M. R., Premerlani, W. J., and Rumbaugh, J. E., "Relational Database Design Using an Object-Oriented Method," *Communications of the ACM* **31** (4), (April 1988): 414–427.

Chen, P. P., "Applications of the Entity-Relationship Model," *Proceedings of the NYU Symposium on Database Design* (May 18-19, 1978): 25–33.

Curtice, R. M., and Jones, P. E., *Logical Data Base Design*, 2nd ed., Van Nostrand Reinhold, New York; 1988.

Date, C. J., "A Practical Guide to Database Design," Technical Report TR03.220, IBM Santa Teresa Laboratory, San Jose, CA (December 1982).

Date, C. J., *An Introduction to Database Systems*, 4th ed., vol. I, Addison-Wesley, Reading, MA; 1986.

DeMarco, T., *Structured Analysis and System Specification*, Yourdon, New York; 1978.

Fidel, R., *Database Design for Information Retrieval*, Wiley, New York; 1987.

FitzGerald, J., and FitzGerald, A., *Fundamentals of Systems Analysis*, 3rd ed., Wiley, New York; 1987.

Fleming, C., and von Halle, B., *Handbook of Relational Database Design*, Addison-Wesley, Reading, MA; 1989.

Gane, G., and Sarson, T., *Structured Systems Analysis: Tools and Techniques*, Prentice-Hall, Englewood Cliffs, NJ; 1979.

Gillenson, M. L., "The Duality of Database Structures and Design Techniques," *Communications of the ACM* **30** (12), (December 1987): 1056–1065.

Gillenson, M. L., and Goldberg, R., *Strategic Planning, Systems Analysis, and Database Design*, Wiley, New York; 1984.

Hawryszkiewycz, I. T., *Database Analysis and Design*, Science Research Associates, Chicago; 1984.

Hubbard, G. U., *IMS (DL/I) Data Base Organization & Performance*, Van Nostrand Reinhold, New York; 1986.

Hursch, J. L., "Methods of Normalizing Databases," *Database Programming and Design* **1** (9), (September 1988): 52–58.

IBM Corporation, *Business Systems Planning—Information Systems Planning Guide*, 3rd ed., IBM Form No. GE20-0527-3 (1981).

IBM Corporation, *IBM DATABASE 2 Application Design and Tuning Guide*, IBM Form No. GG24-3004 (1986).

Inmon, W. H., *Effective Data Base Design*, Prentice-Hall, Englewood Cliffs, NJ; 1981.

Inmon, W. H., "Optimizing Performance with Denormalization," *Database Programming and Design* **1** (1), (January 1988): 34–39.

Ng, P. A., "Further Analysis of the Entity-Relationship Approach to Database Design," *IEEE Transactions on Software Engineering* **SE-7** (1), (January 1981): 85–99.

Perkinson, R. C., *Data Analysis: The Key to Data Base Design*, QED Information Sciences, Wellesley, MA; 1984.

Perron, R., *Design Guide for CODASYL Data Base Management Systems*, QED Information Sciences, Wellesley, MA; 1981.

Senn, J. A., *Analysis and Design of Information Systems*, 2nd ed., McGraw-Hill, New York; 1989.

Smith, H. C., "Database Design: Composing Fully Normalized Tables from a Rigorous Dependency Diagram," *Communications of the ACM* **28** (8), (August 1985): 826–839.

Teorey, T. J., and Fry, J. P., "The Logical Record Access Approach to Database Design," *Computing Surveys* **12** (2), (June 1980): 179–211.

Teorey, T. J., and Fry, J. P., *Design of Database Structures*, Prentice-Hall, Englewood Cliffs, NJ; 1982.

Teorey, T. J., Yang, D., and Fry, J. P., "A Logical Design Methodology for Relational Databases Using the Extended Entity-Relationship Model," *Computing Surveys* **18** (2), (June 1986): 197–222.

Vetter, M., and Maddison, R. N., *Database Design Methodology*, Prentice/Hall International, Englewood Cliffs, NJ; 1981.

Weinberg, V., *Structured Analysis*, Yourdon Press, New York; 1979.

Whitten, J. L., Bentley, L. D., and Ho, T. I. M., *Systems Analysis and Design Methods*, Times Mirror/Mosby, St. Louis, MO; 1986.

Wilson, M. L., "A Requirements and Design Aid for Relational Databases," Technical Report TR03.126, IBM Santa Teresa Laboratory, San Jose, CA (January 1981).

Questions and Exercises

12.1. What is database design?

12.2. Why should we be concerned about information systems strategic planning and systems analysis in conjunction with database design?

12.3. What is information systems strategic planning? What are its goals?

12.4. Explain how analyzing business processes and data classes can help to accomplish the goals of information systems strategic planning.

12.5. What is systems analysis? Where does it fit into the application development cycle?

12.6. Describe the structured systems analysis approach. Do you think that it would work well in a practical application situation?

12.7. How do you feel about the structured systems analysis concepts of keeping systems analysis diagrams free of physical computer component references and in a form that nontechnical users can understand?

12.8. Describe the flow of how data is considered in information systems strategic planning, in systems analysis, and in database design.

12.9. Discuss the issues that make a careful job of database design imperative.

12.10. In your own words, describe the data normalization process. What does it accomplish?

12.11. Discuss the data normalization process in terms of relational database. How does the end product of data normalization relate to a useable relational database design? What about the placement of join fields?

12.12. Describe the process for converting from normalized tables to hierarchical and network database designs.

12.13. What is the difference between logical and physical database design? Explain.

12.14. Describe the entity-relationship approach to database design.

12.15. Compare and contrast the data normalization–based approach to database design with the entity-relationship–based approach. What are the comparative advantages and disadvantages of the two?

12.16. Describe the Date-Wilson approach to database design.

12.17. Compare and contrast the data normalization–based approach to database design with the Date-Wilson–based approach. What are the comparative advantages and disadvantages of the two?

12.18. Wing-N-Prayer Airlines is developing a historical aircraft maintenance system to help it satisfy government safety regulations. In addition to producing information about individual airplanes, the system will also be expected to provide fast response to queries about individual mechanics and maintenance locations. Design a:

    a. Relational database

    b. Pseudo-relational database

    c. Hierarchical database

    d. Network database

for this application. The fields and some dependencies and restrictions follow. Note that some of the fields may indicate information that can be represented in ways other than as fields. Also state any additional assumptions that you make about the data in places where you feel the problem description is ambiguous.

Fields

    a. Aircraft serial number

    b. Aircraft type

    c. Aircraft passenger capacity

    d. Maintenance location

    e. Location manager

    f. Location building number

    g. Maintenance procedure

    h. Procedure length (time)

    i. Procedure frequency

    j. Date procedure was performed on a particular aircraft

    k. Date aircraft is next scheduled for procedure

    l. Location capable of performing a procedure

    m. Mechanic name

    n. Mechanic qualified to perform a procedure

    o. Mechanic education

    p. Tool (identification number) signed out to a mechanic

Dependencies and Restrictions

    a.   A given location may perform several procedures.

    b.   A given procedure may only be performed at one location (for all aircraft).

    c.   A location may have several buildings.

    d.   The database must maintain historical records on all maintenance procedure performances for the entire lives of all aircraft.

    e.   A mechanic may be qualified to perform several procedures, but may only perform those which are feasible at the location at which he or she currently works.

    f.   A mechanic may have several units of education and several tools signed out to him.

12.19.   The Federal Bureaucracy Administration (FBA) has decided to implement a new information system designed to maintain data about states, cities, and certain of their elected officials. Design a:

    a.   Relational database

    b.   Pseudo-relational database

    c.   Hierarchical database

    d.   Network database

for this application. The fields and some dependencies and restrictions follow. Note that some of the fields may indicate information that can be represented in ways other than as fields. Also state any additional assumptions that you make about the data in places where you feel the problem description is ambiguous.

Fields

    a.   City

    b.   City council member name

    c.   City council member occupation

    d.   City population

    e.   Mayor name

    f.   Mayor spouse

    g.   Mayor social security number

    h.   Senate committee

    i.   Senate committee location

    j.   Senate committee staff member

    k.   Senate committee year formed

    l.   Senator name

    m.   Senator social security number

    n.   Senator rank on committee

    o.   Senator spouse

    p.   State

    q.   State flower

    r.   State motto

    s.   State population

Dependencies and Restrictions

    a.   The senators are federal, rather than state senators.

    b.   Access to the data will generally be by state but may occasionally be by city or senator.

    c.   Senators generally serve on several committees at once.

    d.   Senate committee staff members are not senators and may only serve on one senate committee.

    e.   Each city has several city council members.

    f.   Each city council member holds one full-time job.

    g.   Mayor names are not unique.

    h.   City names are only unique within a state.

12.20.   The Football Players Association wants to design a database to support an information system that will maintain historical data about players and teams. Typical queries will involve getting all or some of the team-related information about a player, or all or some of the player-related information about a team. Also, there will be ownership-oriented queries. Design a:

    a.   Relational database

    b.   Pseudo-relational database

    c.   Hierarchical database

    d.   Network database

for this application. The fields and some dependencies and restrictions follow. Note that some of the fields may indicate information that can be represented in ways other than as fields. Also state any additional assumptions that you make about the data in places where you feel the problem description is ambiguous.

Fields

    a.   Team name

    b.   Player identification number

    c.   Player name

    d.   Team owner name

e. Player's current team
f. Player's past teams
g. Years player has been on a team
h. Average annual salary of a player on a team (one player on one team for all of the years he has played on that team)
i. Player position
j. Player home city
k. Player home state
l. Team city
m. Team state
n. Team mascot
o. Years an owner has owned a team
p. Head coach
q. Player's annual quality rating (over all teams played for in that year)
r. Dates of ownership

Dependencies and Restrictions

a. Data must be kept for the lifetime of each player.
b. A player may be temporarily unemployed.
c. Data must be kept on every previous team owner as well as on the current one.
d. A team may only have one owner at a time.

13

Data Dictionaries

Introduction

Like any other part of a business, a data processing installation consists of a number of generic components that have to be managed. It has an inventory: data. It has inputs: new data and requests about the data. It has products: reports, responses to requests about the data, and so on. It has equipment: the computers and all of the associated devices. It has a set of people who do the work. In the early days of data processing, and even today in small data processing installations, a bright data processing manager, with some rudimentary notes written here or there, could remember enough of the details about all of the components of the shop to manage them and the shop effectively. Actually, the fact of the matter is that the typical DP manager of the past never thought much about managing in the textbook sense. The DP manager tended to be so harried and pressured from all sides that "managing" became a matter of barely meeting deadline after deadline for specific jobs, rather than thinking of the broader implications.

Today, data processing departments are huge affairs, involving thousands of employees in the largest companies and hundreds in many others. Increasingly, DP managers have corporate vice president titles; many are generalists, not having come up through the ranks of data processing. They are being held accountable for running the data processing shop as a business within a business. The pressures have become enormous, as more and more of most companies' businesses have become dependent on data processing for their day-to-day functioning. At the same time, DP managers are responsible for the security of the data, controlling costs, alerting the rest of the company to the data that's available to them, and so on. Is there any help for the DP manager in running the data processing environment? The answer begins with a look at the kinds of help that the other functional heads of the corporation have available to them.

Remember that the purpose of data processing is to help all of the functional areas of a company perform more efficiently and effectively. The financial manager has a tremendous amount of accounting and modeling support from the firm's computers. The personnel manager has everything from home address to skills inventories at his or her fingertips for every employee. The manufacturing head has constantly updated raw materials inventories. The list goes on to include virtually every nook and cranny of the company.

But what about help for the data processing manager? Historically, DP managers were always so busy applying data processing to everyone else's needs that they neglected their own needs. One is reminded of the famous old parable of the shoemaker's children being the last ones to get shoes (see Figure 13.1.) It has only been recently that data processing has seriously considered applying its techniques to itself. From that effort has come a set of computer files that the data processing department uses to help manage its own affairs. This set of files is called a **data dictionary.**

Definition and Characteristics

Let's explore data dictionaries in two steps. In this section, we will take a look at the concept of data dictionaries at an overview level. In succeeding sections, we will go into more detail.

Figure 13.1. The shoemaker's children are the last to get shoes.

Figure 13.2 shows two rather common files found in the data processing installation of a typical manufacturing company. The personnel department is concerned with keeping track of the firm's employees, which we refer to as an entity set (each person is an entity). The kinds of facts that they have to store for each person include the person's employee number, last name, first name, and so on (each fact is an attribute of that entity). Similarly, one of the entity sets that the manufacturing department is concerned with is the set of items in its manufacturing inventory. For each item, it must store the part number, part name, and so on.

So both the personnel department and the manufacturing department have computer files (one of each department's files is shown in Figure 13.2) to help them manage their responsibilities. What equivalent support might the data processing department have for itself?

Figure 13.3 shows two files of what might be a 5- to- 10- (or more) file data dictionary: a set of files designed to help the data processing

EMPNO	EMPLAST	EMPFIRST	· · ·
06337	Jones	Fred	· · ·
09155	Smith	Susan	· · ·
16840	Adams	John	· · ·
· · ·			

Personnel File

PARTNO	PARTNM	· · ·
115248	Nut	· · ·
124770	Bolt	· · ·
173771	Screw	· · ·
· · ·		

Inventory File

Figure 13.2.   Two typical DP files.

FIELDNM	FIELDTYP	FIELDLEN	· · ·
EMPNO	Num	5	· · ·
EMPLAST	Alpha	20	· · ·
EMPFIRST	Alpha	10	· · ·
PARTNO	Num	6	· · ·
PARTNM	Alpha	20	· · ·
· · ·			

Fields File

FILENM	FILELEN	· · ·
Personnel	1000	· · ·
Inventory	15000	· · ·
·		

Files File

Figure 13.3.   Part of a data dictionary for the files in Figure 13.2.

department manage its own responsibilities. If personnel wants to keep track of people and manufacturing wants to keep track of its inventory items, among other things, what does data processing want to keep track of? Two of those "things"—entities that data processing must manage—are fields and files. Thus Figure 13.3 shows a Fields file and a Files file.

If personnel has decided that employee number, last name, first name, and so on, are attributes that it must store for each employee, and manufacturing has decided on part number and part name, and so on, what are the attributes for fields and files that data processing feels it must store in the data dictionary? Figure 13.3 shows that for fields some of the attributes are field name (FIELDNM), field type (FIELDTYP), and field length (FIELDLEN), and for files, file name (FILENM) and file length (FILELEN).

In the personnel file, each row represents one of the entities: an employee. In the inventory file each row represents a part. The equivalent in the data dictionary is that each row of the Fields file represents one of the fields in one of the application data files processed by the data processing department, and each row of the Files file represents one of the application files processed by the data processing department. Thus, in this example, we see that each row of the Fields file in Figure 13.3 represents one of the fields of one of the files in Figure 13.2. Also, each row of the Files file in Figure 13.3 represents one of the files in Figure 13.2.

What we have described thus far, the storage of data about data processing entities, is one of the two major dimensions in a data dictionary. The other major dimension is the storage of information about *relationships* among the entities. It's not enough to keep track of the items of importance in the data processing environment by themselves; it is equally important to maintain information on how they interrelate. The informal links between the two files in Figure 13.4 (which is Figure 13.3 with those links

FIELDNM	FIELDTYP	FIELDLEN	•••		FILENM	FILELEN	•••
EMPNO	Num	5	•••		Personnel	1000	•••
EMPLAST	Alpha	20	•••		Inventory	15000	•••
EMPFIRST	Alpha	10	•••		•		
PARTNO	Num	6	•••		•		
PARTNM	Alpha	20	•••		•		

Fields File   Files File

Figure 13.4. Part of a data dictionary showing relationships.

added) illustrate the relationships between the files and the fields shown. The facts that the fields EMPNO, EMPLAST, and EMPFIRST are in the file Personnel, and PARTNO and PARTNM are in Inventory, are clearly very important for a DP manager to know. For example, it may be that the same field is used in several files and there must be some coordination of that multiple usage.

Because the data dictionary contains descriptive information about personnel's files, manufacturing's files, and so on, we might refer to the data dictionary as storing "data about data," or "metadata."

Dictionary Contents

Let's take a more detailed look at the kinds of entities, attributes, and relationships that may be found in a data dictionary.

Entities

There are a number of data processing environment entities generally agreed upon for inclusion in a data dictionary. Depending on the installation's needs, a subset of them may suffice, or additional entities may be required.

The most obvious kind of entity to be considered in a data dictionary is the type that was used in the foregoing example: the directly data-related entity. As we have seen, fields and files are representative of this class. What about records as an entity? One could argue that a Records file should contain such information as record length and a set of pointers to the Fields file indicating which fields are in which records. Then the Files file would include such information as file length and a set of pointers to the Records file indicating which record types are in which file. But if there is only one record type in a file, which is the usual case (for linear files), then all of this information—record length, file length, pointers to fields in the records of the file—can be combined in the Files file. If a company uses a DBMS that uses hierarchical structures, network structures, file linking structures, or any other special structures, then it is appropriate to have entities for them set up in the data dictionary, too.

Another category of data processing environment entities is the set of software components that are involved in processing the previously named data entities. The most obvious such entity type is the program. Depending on the data processing systems in use, others include: transactions, operating systems, jobs, database management systems, and so on. A related type of entity is the set of control blocks needed by the DBMSs or other systems to describe and process the data. And if it is important to keep track of the software that processes the data, it is also important to know the hardware on which the data is processed. This might include the various computer systems that an organization has as well as the specific disk packs on which a file resides.

Another common data processing environment entity type is people. Clearly, from both a responsibility and a security standpoint, it will be necessary to maintain information about the people who are involved in data processing. Various output vehicles, such as reports, would also be dictionary entities.

In addition to these rather common data dictionary entity types, experimentation with and customization of data dictionaries have produced a wide variety of other dictionary entity types. These include entities involving data communications, information systems strategic planning (e.g., IBM's BSP methodology), and systems analysis.

Attributes

There are two classes of attributes for data dictionary entities: those of a general nature that are likely to be found with any of the entities and those specific to particular dictionary entities.

The most obvious of the general attributes is name. Clearly, any dictionary entity must have a name or some other identifier. Dictionaries often permit the specification of aliases of entity names. In addition, many dictionaries accept a free-form, textual description of the entity.

By far, though, the most prevalent dictionary attributes are those that are specific to particular entities. Some examples of this category include: the value range of a field, the length of a record, the home address of a person, the capacity of a unit of storage hardware, the language that a program is written in, and so forth.

Relationships

The relationship between virtually any pair of data dictionary entities can have value to some part of the data processing organization. Some data dictionaries specify a limited set of relationships among their entities that they are designed to handle. Others allow the relationship between every pair of entities to be used.

Some examples of common dictionary relationships, including the entities that they tie together, are:

- Record Construction: Which fields appear in which records
- Security: Which people have access to which files
- Impact of Change: Which programs might be affected by changes to which files
- Physical Residence: Which files are on which disk packs
- Program Data Requirements: Which programs use which files
- Responsibility: Which people are responsible for updating which files

System
Job
Program
Module
Transaction
PSB
Sys Def

User
Subjects
User
Relationships

Six DL/I HDAM Data Bases
Interrelated by Logical Relations

Figure 13.5. Entities and relationships in the IBM DB/DC Data Dictionary. (Reprinted with permission from *DB/DC Data Dictionary Guide*, IBM Corporation.)

As an example, Figure 13.5 shows the entities and relationships in the IBM DB/DC Data Dictionary. Four of the entity types have their own DL/I databases assigned to them: Database (DL/I hierarchies or non-DL/I data sets), Segment (including non-DL/I records), Element (field), and PCB (a DL/I control block). Another group shares a DL/I database. That group includes such entity types as Program, System, Job, Transaction, Module (part of a program), and PSB (another kind of DL/I control block). A sixth database is called the "extensibility" database. Using this database the user can define new entity types and their attributes and can create relationships between those newly defined entity types and any of the standard or other user-defined entity types. The connecting lines in Figure 13.5 illustrate the relationships.

Characteristics and Features

So far we've discussed the basic components of a data dictionary: data files that describe the data processing environment and the relationships among the data processing entities in those files. In this section we will look at some of the variations to be found among data dictionaries.

Some data dictionaries are what might be called "free standing," meaning that they are an independent set of linear files that can coexist with a variety of DBMSs and other systems. Other data dictionaries are designed to be applications of a particular DBMS, and their files conform to the file structure of that DBMS. Even in this latter case though, the dictionary is usually capable of storing data about data processing entities that are not involved with that DBMS. Whether free standing or not, the files of a data dictionary need the same protections that any other files need: security, integrity, and backup and recovery. If the files are based on a DBMS, then generally the DBMS file protection mechanisms will apply to it. If not (the free standing case), then the data dictionary system must provide its own.

A data dictionary, or more specifically the applications that use it, can be of either a batch or on-line nature. Obviously, certain applications requiring fast, direct response cannot be performed in a batch environment. Others, such as report generation applications, can. Taking this one step further, the data dictionary need not exist as a set of computer files at all. It could consist of a bunch of 3" × 5" cards in a filing cabinet, but in practice it is always implemented as a computer application. In this book we are assuming that data dictionaries involve computer files and applications, and generally have on-line access capabilities.

As we began saying earlier, some data dictionaries have a facility for adding additional entity types beyond the standard ones supplied. Such facilities vary in the number of entity types that can be added, in the attributes that can be associated with the entities (in some cases the attributes must be chosen from a supplied list; in others the user can describe and use any attributes), and in the degree to which relationships between new and old entities can be maintained.

Input Forms

There are four distinct ways of loading data into a dictionary: with batch forms, through individual on-line commands, on-line with full screen panels, and via extraction from existing software or commands. The following sections describe how they work.

Batch Forms

Many dictionaries have a facility that allows those performing dictionary input to fill out forms on paper describing the given dictionary entries. The data on these forms is then entered all at once in a batch. For example, there would be a form specifically for fields, which would include space for the field name, field type, field length, and so forth. This form could be filled out for any number of fields in the data processing environment whose descriptions are due to be entered into the dictionary. They then would all be entered in a batch mode, populating the Fields file in the dictionary. While doing anything in a batch mode may seem to be old-fashioned, this does have the advantages of not tying up the system at peak periods (assuming that the batch input is done during off-hours) and of allowing the work to be done by employees who would otherwise not have any interaction with the dictionary.

On-Line Commands

A second way of entering data is with single line commands. For example, the command:

A E EMPNO Type=N Bytes=6

when entered on a terminal in an interactive environment would mean add (A) a field (or element) (E) named EMPNO to the Fields file and set the type to numeric (N) and the length or bytes field to 6. Clearly, it would be rather cumbersome to enter large amounts of dictionary data using this method. But for small amounts of data or for making changes to existing data, this method is quite useful.

Full Screen Panels

The third dictionary input method involves preformatted screens displayed on video terminals. Figure 13.6 shows such a screen for entering data about fields into the Fields file. Notice that it includes space for a field's name, length, type, and so on. The dictionary description of a field can be entered fairly quickly by an experienced person tabbing through the

Figure 13.6 Preformatted screen for field input in the IBM DB/DC Data Dictionary. (Reprinted with permission from *DB/DC Data Dictionary Guide*, IBM Corporation.)

different fields on the preformatted screen. Some data dictionaries have a rather extensive collection of such screens. They may, in fact, be related so that one screen can lead to another and generate relationship connections between the dictionary entries in the process. For example, a preformatted screen used for entering information for a record into the dictionary would include space for the fields that are found in that record. Entering the field names in the record definition screen would create the relationship between the record and its fields, and with the proper commands would also allow the user to move from that screen to a field definition screen to enter more detailed information about the record's fields (as in Figure 13.6).

Extraction

The fourth means of data input is also the most exotic. Various dictionary packages include programs that read database control blocks, COBOL data division specifications, or the like, extract data from them that should belong in the dictionary, and enter the data in the dictionary. When properly used, such programs can obviously be a big savings in time and energy over the three other, more manual, modes of dictionary input. Remember, though, that for *new* application development efforts, such things as control blocks and program data specifications are created *after* the dictionary has been populated with basic data about the application.

Output Forms

Data dictionaries are capable of producing several kinds of output. Some of these outputs are in the form of reports for human consumption, others are in the form of software for the system to use.

Of the output forms for people to use directly, the most obvious is the simple printed listing. Such a listing might encompass all of the instances of a particular entity type (e.g., a list of all of the fields in the data processing environment, together with their attributes). It might include only a subset of them, with all or a subset of the attributes of each. Another kind of printed report is a cross reference listing. This would take the form of a list of all of the fields in a particular record, a list of all of the programmers who have access to a particular file, and so on. As an example of a dictionary report (from the IBM DB/DC Data Dictionary), Figure 13.7 shows a DL/I hierarchy, its segments, and the fields in each segment.

A second type of human consumption output is on-line query. An example of this is the use of the preformatted screens that we talked about for input for looking at the contents of the dictionary files. Instead of calling up an entity's description with a preformatted screen for the

```
REPORT DBS (D,P,DDSPDBS,0) NAME=HIER ;

* * * * * * * *          DB/DC DATA DICTIONARY REPORT          05/06/80   00:24:33
* * * * DBS => SEG => DTE REPORT * * * *                                  PAGE:0001

DBSNAME: DP DDSPDBS 0
      SEGMENTS: DA DBS 0                              LEVEL:1     PARENT:
              ELEMENTS: DA DBSNAME 0                  START: 1    /0       SEQ: U
                        DA DBSPFX1 0                  START: 1    /0       SEQ: G
                        DA DBSPFX2 0                  START: 2    /0       SEQ: G
                        DA DBSNMFL 0                  START: 3    /0       SEQ: G
                        DA DBSSFX 0                   START: 34   /0       SEQ: G

              DA DBSDTE 0                             LEVEL:2     PARENT:DA DBS        0
              ELEMENTS: DA DTENAME 0                  START: 1    /0       SEQ: U
                        DA DTEPFX1 0                  START: 1    /0       SEQ: G
                        DA DTEPFX2 0                  START: 2    /0       SEQ: G
                        DA DTENMFL 0                  START: 3    /0       SEQ: G
                        DA DTESFX 0                   START: 34   /0       SEQ: G

              DA DBSSEG 0                             LEVEL:2     PARENT:DA DBS        0
              ELEMENTS: DA SEGNAME 0                  START: 1    /0       SEQ: G
                        DA SEGPFX1 0                  START: 1    /0       SEQ: G
                        DA SEGPFX2 0                  START: 2    /0       SEQ: G
                        DA SEGNMFL 0                  START: 3    /0       SEQ: G
                        DA SEGSFX 0                   START: 34   /0       SEQ: G
                        DA PPNAME 0                   START: 35   /0       SEQ: G
                        DA PPPFX1 0                   START: 35   /0       SEQ: G
                        DA PPPFX2 0                   START: 36   /0       SEQ: G
                        DA PPNMFL 0                   START: 37   /0       SEQ: G
                        DA PPSFX 0                    START: 45   /0       SEQ: G
                        DA SEGLVL 0                   START: 46   /0       SEQ: G
                        DA SEGDSGNO 0                 START: 47   /0       SEQ: G
                        DA PAIREDLC 0                 START: 48   /0       SEQ: G
                        DA PCPNTRS 0                  START: 49   /0       SEQ: G
                        DA SEGTYPE 0                  START: 50   /0       SEQ: G

              DA SEGPATRB 0                           LEVEL:3     PARENT:DA DBSSEG     0
              ELEMENTS: DA FREQ 0                     START: 1    /C       SEQ: G
                        DA HPNTRS 0                   START: 5    /0       SEQ: G
                        DA TPNTRS 0                   START: 6    /0       SEQ: G
                        DA LTPNTRS 0                  START: 7    /0       SEQ: G
                        DA LPARNT 0                   START: 8    /0       SEQ: G
                        DA IRULE 0                    START: 9    /0       SEQ: G
                        DA DRULE 0                    START: 10   /0       SEQ: G
                        DA RRULE 0                    START: 11   /0       SEQ: G
                        DA WHRRULE 0                  START: 12   /0       SEQ: G
                        DA COMPRTN 0                  START: 13   /0       SEQ: G
                        DA CCRTNOPT 0                 START: 21   /0       SEQ: G
                        DA COMPINIT 0                 START: 22   /0       SEQ: G
                        DA CTR 0                      START: 23   /0       SEQ: G

              DA SEGPCHLD 0                           LEVEL:3     PARENT:DA DBSSEG     0
              ELEMENTS: DA PCSGNAME 0                 START: 1    /0       SEQ: G
```

Figure 13.7. A dictionary report describing a DL/I hierarchy by its segments and their fields (IBM DB/DC Data Dictionary). (Reprinted with permission from OS/VS/DB/DC *Data Dictionary Applications Guide* (SH20-9190-0) IBM Corporation.)

purpose of adding to it or changing it, we might want to simply look at it. A dictionary might also provide the capability for doing a keyword search. For example, if every field in the Fields file has a textual description stored with it, we might want to search for certain keywords in those descriptions to find out whether a particular field, whose name we obviously do not know, exists.

Probably the most common dictionary output used in the running of the system itself is the generation of control blocks required by the DBMS in use. Such control blocks are critical to the functioning of the system.

The slightest error in them will generally cause major operating problems. But assume that the information about files, records, fields, and so on, in the dictionary has been carefully entered and inspected, and that software exists that is capable of taking that information in the dictionary and creating DBMS control blocks from it. Then while there is still a margin for error in the instructions given to the control block generating software, the overall chance of error in control block generation will be reduced.

Another form of dictionary output is (like the control block situation) the inverse of one of the methods of dictionary input. Just as there are programs that can read the data description portions of a program and extract entries to be placed into the dictionary, there are also programs that can take entries from the dictionary and create program data description statements, such as those in a COBOL data division. Clearly, such programs must, as input, be provided with directions indicating which dictionary entries must be used and how they are to be juxtaposed.

Material in the data dictionary can also be funneled into other tools. Examples are database design aids, which require fields and the relationships between them as input, and report writers.

Implementation

Benefits

Data dictionaries can be of considerable use to a variety of people in the data processing environment. In this section we will look at the dictionary from the points of view of those people who use it.

The heaviest user of the dictionary clearly will be the data administration manager and staff. As we shall explore in more detail in a later chapter, data administration is charged with managing the data in at least the database environment and possibly in the entire data processing milieu. As we have seen, the data dictionary is the appropriate place to document the existence of files, fields, reports, and so on, and the relationships among them, and maintaining this information falls under the purview of data administration. In addition, data administration groups are usually charged with the job of generating control blocks for the DBMS. As we have already indicated, this is a task best done using the data dictionary. Data administration personnel are usually involved, at one of several levels, with database design. The database structures, fields, and so on, already stored in the dictionary from earlier applications might be needed or related to the data needed in the new design. Thus the dictionary can be a time-saver in that effort. Furthermore, as the new design is being developed, the dictionary is the appropriate place to store it away, both for documentation purposes and for such purposes as future control block generation.

There are a variety of other uses of the dictionary by data administration; most are based on relationship-type data. The following are merely three of many possible examples. If several programs share a file, and the owner of one of those programs proposes a change in that file, then data administration must touch base with the owners of all of the other programs to determine whether the change in the file will affect their programs (this is called "impact of change"). This can be accomplished using the relationship data between the file and program entities in the data dictionary. If confidential data has leaked out of a company, the investigation might begin by having data administration retrieve the relationship information between employees and files to see who (at least through normal channels) had access to the data. If a long-range planning effort is under way and a review is to be made of the data that is currently used in an application being restudied, then data administration can use the relationship between fields and database structures for this purpose.

Systems analysts and program designers can use the data dictionary in two major ways. One use is as a source of information on what fields, files, and so forth, already exist in the data processing environment that might be needed in a new application development effort underway. If data needed for a new system already exists, then the new application may be able to use it. If there are existing database structures that the application can add on to, to satisfy its requirements, then that might be a large cost savings. In those and related situations, the dictionary is the repository of information to be searched.

The other dictionary use for systems analysts and designers is as a documentation device for the new information that is generated as a result of their application development effort. In a sophisticated application development environment, the systems analysts begin the process by inserting nonphysical data about the fields (at least the field name) as they arise during their work. The systems designers can later add physical information about fields, as well as information about files, database structures, and so on. Thus the application developers have a natural vehicle for documentation, and the dictionary has a natural way of being populated with data concerning new applications.

Finally, there is the benefit of the data dictionary to higher-level data processing management, and for that matter to high-level corporate management in general. As data processing permeates increasing aspects and levels of organizations, it becomes increasingly important for management to understand the nature of the data in its systems. It is important from the viewpoint of understanding how the organization functions, as data is considered a resource that mirrors the workings of the organization. While the data administration personnel manage the data dictionary with that kind of data in it, it is management that ultimately benefits.

Costs

There are a number of costs associated with having a data dictionary. As with any other computer application, there are the costs of the dictionary programs themselves and the costs of executing and maintaining them. There are also the costs associated with teaching people how to enter data into the dictionary and with educating others on how they might benefit by using the dictionary.

The most controversial cost of the dictionary involves the initial and continuing efforts to populate it with data. When a data dictionary is introduced into a data processing environment, awaiting it are years and years of accumulated data processing entities ready for dictionary entry. Trying to enter all of that material into the dictionary overnight would be a bone-jarring task. The dictionary files often are gradually built up with appropriate pieces of data that are generated as a result of new application development efforts. We shall have more to say about this situation shortly, but for now suffice it to say that whether a large initial effort is made, a gradual dictionary build-up is undertaken, or both, there is a significant level of expense associated with the process.

Requirements for Success

The cost/benefit trade-off for data dictionaries is a tricky one, and there are a number of factors involved in having a successful dictionary installation.

It is clear that management must be supportive of the idea of installing a data dictionary. They must approve the initial outlay of money for the software, as well as the assignment of personnel to work with it. And they must be patient, allowing time to pass while the dictionary is being populated with data, until it can fully live up to expectations.

There are certain uses of the dictionary that do not require a tremendous amount of data in the dictionary files. An example of this is the database control block generation application. The only data that must be in the dictionary is the data that must go into these specific control blocks. In order to make the dictionary productive as soon as possible, it is often suggested that control block generation be one of the first applications of a new data dictionary for the foregoing reason.

The other side of the coin is that there are other uses of the dictionary that require a large, expensive effort in data entry into the dictionary before they can be implemented. For example, take the case of a systems analyst searching the dictionary to see if some data required in a new application under development already exists in the data processing environment. Unless all, or at least most, of the existing applications are reflected in the dictionary, the systems analyst is not going to have much confidence in a dictionary search that comes back with "not found." Maybe the data does exist but has not as yet been noted in the dictionary.

So the route to a successful data dictionary installation is a gradual one. First, management commitment to the idea of having a data dictionary must be obtained. Then, once the dictionary has been installed, data entry must be a well-planned and progressive undertaking. The route chosen often is to begin populating the dictionary with data derived from new data processing applications under development. Immediate use of such data, such as for control block generation, is one reason for doing this. But another reason is the convenience of the dictionary for documentation of the new application, something that would have to be done one way or another in any case. A third reason is the somewhat emotional point that a new application should be associated with the newest technologies. Finally, since this is the beginning of its "life," this application may be around for a long time and thus may make the longest use of the dictionary.

In addition, a schedule can be created for bringing the organization's existing applications into the world of the dictionary, over some reasonable period of time. Again, for this to work, management must believe in the long-term benefit of the dictionary and supply the resources necessary while being patient about the payback.

Other requirements for a successful dictionary installation also revolve around people. These individuals, whether data administration personnel, systems analysts, or programmers, must be educated in how to enter data into the dictionary and in how to use it. They must adhere to standards and to security arrangements in executing procedures involving the dictionary. And finally, it is preferable that management believe in the value of the dictionary, as even the strongest management orders to use it often have a way of slipping with time.

Active versus Passive Dictionaries

An increasingly important distinction in data dictionaries is the integrated or active data dictionary versus the nonintegrated or passive data dictionary. Actually there is no single, accepted definition for either of those terms, and there is a wide range of functions that have been connected with them.

Basically, a passive dictionary is one used just for documentation purposes. Data about the fields, files, people, and so on, in the data processing environment are entered into the dictionary and cross-referenced. Printed listings and terminal-based queries about the dictionary's contents are run as needed. The passive dictionary is simply a self-contained application and set of files used for documenting the data processing environment.

But what about the wide range of other potential involvements? Since most dictionaries today are closely associated, in structure, usage, or both, with a DBMS, let us consider the dictionary in this environment. One activity that we've already looked at that brings the dictionary closer to the functioning of the database environment is the generation of DBMS control blocks from data in the dictionary. One could add to that the programs that produce application program data definitions from data in the dictionary and the reverse, the programs that populate the dictionary with data derived from application program source code. All such off-line dictionary activities that either put more into it or derive system products from it form a step beyond a simple passive dictionary.

Another possibility, which makes the dictionary even a bit more active, is the *requirement* that functions like those described previously be performed. For example, a DBMS might force all application program database calls to pick up the physical details of the application data from the dictionary *at compile time*. Thus, given a field name by the application program, the dictionary might, at compile time, supply information about where and how the field is stored that would be compiled into the object code.

Another step upward in this line of reasoning would be for a database program to get information from, or be partially controlled by (depending on how you look at it), the data dictionary *during execution time*. The dictionary might pass information about the structure of the data at execution time that wasn't compiled into the application object program, or as another example, it might supply security information about which users or programs are entitled to have access to specific files.

Without specific human intervention, very active dictionaries might be capable of surveying database application programs being installed and executed to automatically extract information about them not already in the dictionary.

Originally, data dictionaries were considered to be functionally just one more application in the database environment. As we progress into the realm of increasingly active dictionaries, there are many who feel that in the future (and some vendors who claim that now) dictionaries will be at the heart of the DBMS environment. In some sense, the dictionary will be the central controller of the entire DBMS environment, managing the application files, security, backup and recovery operations, and even programming standards.

Relational DBMS Catalogs

Part of the concept of an SQL-based, relational database management system is the inclusion of a **catalog**. An SQL catalog is a highly active, but limited scope data dictionary that is very closely tied in to the operations of the relational DBMS. Significantly, the SQL catalog is itself composed of SQL tables and may be queried with the standard SQL commands.

While the SQL catalog varies in composition among different SQL implementations, it typically consists of 15-30 SQL tables, each of which describes a different set of system entities. Using IBM's DB2 system as an example, some of the typical catalog tables and some of their typical attributes include:

- SYSTABLES—A catalog table that contains one row for every table and one row for every view in the database environment. Attributes include the table or view name, creator, number of columns in the table, number of columns in the primary key, record length, number of rows, and others.
- SYSTABAUTH—A catalog table that indicates the operations that users are authorized to perform on tables and views. Attributes include the user ID and table name (obviously), plus the ID of the authorizer, the date and time the authorization was made, the type of operations authorized for that user on that table, and others.
- SYSCOLUMNS—A catalog table that contains one row for every column of every table and one row for every column of every view in the database environment. Attributes include the name of the column, the name of the table, the column type (integer, string, etc.), the column (attribute) length, the position of the column among the others in the table or view, and others.
- SYSINDEXES—A catalog table that contains one row for every index in the database environment. Attributes include the name of the index, the name of the table it indexes, whether the index is unique, whether the index is clustered, and others. Note that another catalog table, SYSKEYS, details the columns in the index.

Other tables include data about subdivisions of the database environment in which application tables can be contained ("data bases" and "table spaces" in DB2), additional user authorizations, precompiled modules of SQL statements, secondary storage devices, and more. The reason for the earlier remark that the SQL catalog is only a limited form of a data dictionary is that, although the catalog contains a wealth of information about the SQL environment, it does not include data about such other data processing environment entities as people (other than the IDs in the authorization tables), reports, non-SQL databases and files, and so on. In fact, some user organizations and some software vendors have extended their SQL catalogs with additional tables to make them look more like full-function data dictionaries.

Another interesting concept regarding the SQL catalog is the identity of its intended users. As we said earlier, data dictionaries were designed to be tools that data processing professionals could use to help in managing the data processing environment. But SQL catalogs, in addition to that use, are also helpful to end-users of the databases. Consider an end-user who has just been given authorization to view the data in one of the SQL tables. Clearly, that person is going to have to understand the structure, including the column names, of that table in order to issue SQL statements to it to view its data. What better way is there to get that information than by accessing the description of the table in the SQL catalog?

Finally, we note that the SQL catalog is a highly active and integrated form of a (limited) data dictionary. The SQL catalog is an integral part of the SQL database environment. The SQL optimizer uses data about application tables, indexes, and so forth, from the catalog to perform its function. The SQL system checks the authorization tables in the catalog before it allows users to retrieve data they request with a SELECT statement or to update, delete, or insert records in application tables. For the most part, the catalog tables themselves cannot be updated by users with the INSERT, DELETE, or UPDATE commands; changes in catalog table data can only be made by the system in the course of activities that would logically cause such changes to be made. For example, the issuing of a CREATE TABLE statement automatically inserts a new record, which describes that newly created table, into the SYSTABLES catalog table; the issuing of a GRANT authority command automatically inserts a new record into one of the catalog authorization tables. Recently, some relational DBMS products have begun to allow some user-updated catalog entries.

References

Allen, F. W., Loomis, M. E. S., and Mannino, M. V., "The Integrated Dictionary/Directory System," *Computing Surveys* **14**(2), (June 1982): 245–286.

Date, C. J., and White, C. J., *A Guide to DB2*, 2nd ed., Addison-Wesley, Reading, MA; 1988.

Dolk, D. R., and Kirsch, R. A. II, "A Relational Information Resource Dictionary System," *Communications of the ACM* **30**(1), (January 1987): 48–61.

Fidel, R., *Database Design for Information Retrieval*, Wiley, New York; 1987.

IBM Corporation, *IBM DATABASE 2 Reference*, IBM Form No. SC26-4078 (1986).

Leong-Hong, B. W., and Plagman, B. K., *Data Dictionary/Directory Systems*, Wiley, New York; 1982.

Narayan, R., *Data Dictionary*, Prentice-Hall, Englewood Cliffs, NJ; 1988.

Ross, R. G., *Data Dictionaries and Data Administration*, AMACOM, New York; 1981.

Van Duyn, J., *Developing a Data Dictionary System*, Prentice-Hall, Englewood Cliffs, NJ, 1982.

Questions and Exercises

13.1. In your own words, describe what a data dictionary is and why it is needed.

13.2. In the same style as the dictionary files in Figure 13.3, create a dictionary file for reports. What might the meanings of the relationships be between that Reports file and the files in Figure 13.3?

13.3. In the same style as the dictionary files in Figure 13.3, create a dictionary file for employees. What might the meanings of the relationships be between that Employees file and the files in Figure 13.3?

13.4. In the same style as the dictionary files in Figure 13.3, create a dictionary file for programs. What might the meanings of the relationships be between that Programs file and the files in Figure 13.3?

13.5. Describe possible data dictionary entities not mentioned in this chapter. What relationships might they have to the standard entities?

13.6. List a comprehensive set of attributes for the

   a. Fields file
   b. Files file
   c. Employees file
   d. Programs file

13.7. Choose five of the relationships shown in Figure 13.5 (identify them by the dictionary files they connect) and indicate a meaning for each.

13.8. What are the advantages and disadvantages of free-standing versus DBMS-specific data dictionaries?

13.9. Describe a significant advantage and a significant disadvantage of each of the four data dictionary input methods described in this chapter.

13.10. Design a full screen, preformatted panel for terminal input into a data dictionary for a

   a. Report
   b. File
   c. Program
   d. Employee

13.11. Design a data dictionary report format for a report describing the information in the

   a. Fields file
   b. Files file
   c. Employees file
   d. Programs file

13.12. Design a data dictionary report for cross-reference information between:

   a. The Fields file and the Files file.
   b. The Reports file and the Employees file.
   c. The Programs file and the Fields file.

13.13. Convince a data processing manager that he or she should install a data dictionary.

13.14. Describe the costs of installing and running a data dictionary.

13.15. In your own words, describe how you might gradually introduce a data dictionary into a data processing environment.

13.16. How would a data processing environment change with the use of a highly active data dictionary?

13.17. Would an active data dictionary change the way programmers, systems analysts, and operators do their jobs? Explain.

13.18. Defend or refute the following statement: "An active data dictionary is the central focus of the database environment."

14

Database Control Topics

Introduction

As we suggested in Chapter 4, there are certain concerns about data that must be addressed regardless of whether or not the data is being stored under the control of a database management system. These concerns include maintaining the security of the data, protecting the integrity of the data in concurrent update situations, being able to recover/restore the data to a correct state after a data error has occurred or the entire database has been destroyed, and being able to audit the data to see who has accessed or changed it.

Again, a database environment should provide solutions to all of these problems without programmers having to address them for each new application that comes along. Solutions to each can clearly be generalized for any data that fits within the framework of a given database environment. In this chapter, we shall take a brief look at each of these four database control topics.

Security

Security Breaches

Is it important to protect stored data from unauthorized access and unauthorized change? It certainly is and for several reasons. As more and more of our society's record keeping is computerized, an increasingly wider variety of kinds of data and a vastly increasing volume of data is being stored in computer files, including databases. Either the organizations holding the data, the people or organizations that the data describes, or both, have a vested interest in the security of the data. Governments must protect sensitive defense data from unauthorized intrusion. Companies must prevent their competitors from seeing their accounting data. Banks must be sure that the money they now hold in the form of computer data cannot be "stolen" (e.g., a field value representing the amount of money in an account cannot be tampered with). Individuals want personal information that insurance companies keep about them to remain confidential. And the list goes on and on.

Let's begin by considering the different kinds of security breaches possible in modern data processing facilities. Perhaps the most basic kind of breach is unauthorized data access, that is, someone seeing data they are not entitled to see. Another exposure is unauthorized data modification, that is, someone changing the value of stored data that they are not entitled to change. And a third problem, which is an extension of the first two, is unauthorized program modification in which someone changes a program so that it retrieves or modifies data in an illegal way.

The question then becomes one of thinking about the ways in which such deliberate compromises of the data can take place. Some possibilities are diagrammed in Figure 14.1. One method of breaking into a company's

Figure 14.1. Data security exposures.

database is to tap its communications lines as it transfers data between two of its computers or between a terminal and one of its computers. Another method, if the computer is accessible via ordinary telephone lines, is for the intruder to make him- or herself appear to the computer to be a legitimate, authorized user. This would mean, as we shall discuss more fully later, finding out the computer's telephone number, producing an identification tag that the computer recognizes, and supplying the correct password to go with it (shades of the movie *War Games!*). In a similar vein, the intruder might be able to surreptitiously enter the company's premises and use a terminal right on the site. Another "method" of gaining access to data is to steal the physical media on which it resides, including disk packs and printouts. Even bribes of authorized company employees have to be considered. The old adage that "a chain is only as strong as its weakest link" really does apply here.

To make matters more complicated, there is also the case of legitimate company employees who are authorized to access some of the company's data gaining access to other data that they are not authorized to see. And taking it even a step further than that, there may be a situation in which an employee attempts to modify data that he or she is authorized to look at, but not authorized to modify.

Security Measures

Which brings us to the essence of this subsection: What are the kinds of security measures that can be employed to protect stored data, especially (but not only) the data in databases? First, before a company considers the specific software and hardware devices that are usually associated with the idea of data security, there is the issue of the physical security of the company's premises. This aspect must not be underestimated. Anyone in the computer room or in areas in which there are terminals or other input/output devices must be a recognized company member or an approved visitor. This also applies to any areas that contain some of the company's data, from tape libraries to rooms with printouts. One would also hope that the company's employees are honest, but of course this is harder to control.

Then there is the issue of controlling access to the computer system. Here we assume that the potential intruder either has gained access to a terminal on the company's premises or has another (perhaps micro) computer with a modem and has learned the telephone number of the company's computer. Most systems today require that anyone attempting to use a computer produce an identification tag of several characters and enter a secret password that goes with it. Identification tags are often publicly known (at least within the company), but passwords must be kept as secret as possible, should be changed periodically, and should not be written down, to reduce the risk of someone else learning them. Passwords should not appear on the terminal screen when they are typed in, and they should be created by the user so that there is less chance of the user forgetting them.

Other forms of user identification have been suggested. One is to store personal information about the user (e.g., mother's maiden name) and have the system demand it when the user attempts to enter the system. Unfortunately, since that data doesn't get updated, there is a greater risk of its being compromised over time. Other possibilities for the future are selections from physical characteristics, such as the user's fingerprints, signature, or voice, as devices for recognizing them become sufficiently sophisticated.

Now let's assume that a particular person has been recognized by the system as a legitimate user. That person might in fact be a legitimate user or might not be but at any rate has convinced the system of it (perhaps by stealing someone else's identification tag and password). There are security features that can be used to protect data, given that someone has passed the first hurdle as an authorized user of the system. In terms of the database environment, perhaps the most basic is that all access to the data is controlled by and must pass through the DBMS. This leads to a number of useful features. One such feature involves data kept by the system that indicates which users (by identification tag) are permitted to retrieve and to update which data files, IMS segment types, CODASYL record types, and so on. Thus, if a particular person is a legitimate system user, but tries to access data that he or she is not entitled to see, the system will not permit that operation. For certain kinds of data the person might be permitted to see it but not to update it, and so that distinction must be made. There are many other variations on this theme that, as with the above security features, may or may not be built into specific DBMSs. For example, some systems will allow specific users to see some, but not all, of the fields in occurrences of specific record types. Some systems will restrict users from seeing data based not only on the record types involved, but also on the values in specific occurrences of those records. Another idea is to allow a user to see two different fields in the occurrences of a particular record type, but not at the same time. For example, a user might have permission to use a personnel file to get a list of the employees' names and to get a list of all of the salaries for statistical purposes, but not have permission to match specific people to specific salaries.

Another data protection feature, again pertaining to the situation in which a person has been recognized as a legitimate system user, is an additional use of passwords. We've been talking about the use of passwords to protect illegal entry to the system. But passwords can also be assigned to specific programs and to specific data files. The system would demand that the user produce the required password in order to execute a particular program or to access a particular file.

Unfortunately, none of the foregoing security techniques protects against data thefts in which the intruder does not attempt to extract the data through the computer and DBMS. Examples of this situation include wiretapping as the data is being sent over communications lines and theft of a disk pack. A solution to this problem is "data encryption." The term data encryption implies that the data, bit-by-bit or character-by-character, has been changed into a form that looks totally garbled. It must be reconverted—decrypted—back to its original form to be of use. The encryption/decryption process may take place only as the data is shipped along communications lines, or the data may actually be stored in an encrypted form on the disk.

The process of encrypting data can range from simple to highly complex. Obviously, the simpler the scheme, the easier it is for an intruder to figure it out and decrypt the data. Encryption generally involves an algorithm and a secret key. A very simple example of an alphabetic encryption scheme is as follows: Number the letters of the alphabet from A to Z plus "blank" as 1 to 27. For each letter in the data to be encrypted, add the secret key (some number in this case) and change that letter to the letter represented by the new number. Thus, if the key is 4, then an A (value 1) becomes an E (since $1 + 4 = 5$ and E is the fifth letter of the alphabet), a B becomes an F, and so on through the alphabet to the blank, which becomes a D (wrapping around from blank as the 27th "character" of the alphabet back to the beginning). The receiving program must be aware both of the algorithm and of the secret key so that it can work the algorithm in reverse and decrypt the data.

Generally, the more complex the encryption scheme, the more time it will take to encrypt and decrypt the data, which will slow down the overall operation of the database environment. Furthermore, if the data stored on the disk is encrypted, then every disk access, whether or not shipment on communications lines is involved, requires the time for decryption. Some encryption schemes, involving several levels of algorithmic transformations and very large keys (one common scheme has a 56-bit key) have been built into hardware for performance reasons.

SQL Security

The nature of the SQL database environment includes sophisticated security measures to protect its data with relative ease. The discussion of the SQL catalog in Chapter 13 pointed out that restricted access to the application data can be maintained in several catalog authorization tables, such as SYSTABAUTH. Users can be restricted to any subset of the retrieve (SELECT), update, insert, or delete operations on any subset of the available tables. The SQL command that allows these restrictions, or in the positive sense in which it is used, authorizations, to take place is the GRANT command. For example, to allow someone whose system ID is USER1234 to retrieve data from the Teams table, the owner of that table (in general, someone who has the authority to allow others access to the table) would issue:

```
GRANT SELECT ON TABLE TEAMS TO USER1234
```

To allow USER1234 to both retrieve data from the Teams table and to add new records to it (but still not to delete or update its records), the owner would issue:

```
GRANT SELECT, INSERT ON TABLE TEAMS TO USER1234
```

To allow USER1234 to have full access and modification privileges on the Teams table, the owner would issue:

```
GRANT ALL PRIVILEGES ON TABLE TEAMS TO USER1234
```

But what if you want someone to be able to access only certain rows (i.e., only certain records) and/or only certain columns of a table. That is when the SQL view capability comes in handy. The owner of a table can establish a view that includes only a subset of the rows and/or columns of a table and grant a user access only to that part of the table by granting access *only to the view*. A view can be defined as a restricted part of a table in very much the same manner that a simple SQL retrieval to retrieve only some of the data in a table can be set up. Using the baseball example in Figure 7.1, suppose you want to authorize USER1234 to see data in the Bats table, but only that data that pertains to bats manufactured by the Acme Company. The owner of the Bats table would issue:

```
CREATE VIEW BATXY58
    AS SELECT *
      FROM BATS
      WHERE MANUF = 'Acme'
```

and then issue:

```
GRANT SELECT ON TABLE BATXY58 TO USER1234
```

BATXY58 is, of course, an arbitrary name for the view.

Concurrency

The Concurrency Problem

Many of today's data processing application systems, and especially those that run within the database environment, assume that many people using those systems will require access to the same data files at the same time. Modern hardware and software systems are certainly capable of providing such shared data access. One very common example of this capability is in airline reservations, where several different reservations clerks may have simultaneous requests from different customers for seats on the same flight. Another example is in an industrial or retail inventory application in which several clerks seek the same item in inventory simultaneously.

When concurrent access involves only simple retrieval of data there is no problem. But when concurrent access requires data modification, the two or more users attempting to update the data simultaneously (or as simultaneously as a multiprogrammed system allows) have a rather nasty way of interfering with each other that doesn't happen if they are merely doing retrievals. This is certainly the case in the airline reservations and inventory examples, since selling seats on flights and using items in inventory require that the number of seats or inventory items left be revised downward.

Using the airline reservations application as an example, here is an illustration of what can happen. Suppose there are 25 seats left on Acme Airlines flight #345 on March 12. Two reservations clerks, Ms. Brown and Mr. Green, receive telephone calls at about the same time from two customers who are interested in this flight on that date. Brown's customer wants to book four seats on the flight, while Green's customer, with a larger family, wants to book six seats on it. Brown retrieves the record for the flight on that date from the database, notes that there are 25 seats available, and begins to discuss the price and other details with her customer. At about the same time, Green retrieves the same record (really another copy of it) for his customer. Both clerks make their respective sales and indicate them through their terminals to the database. Brown's transaction dictates that four should be deducted from the number of seats available on the flight and Green's indicates that six should be deducted.

The result in the database is shown in Figure 14.2. The record for flight #345 on March 12 now shows that there are 19 seats available. But shouldn't it be only 15, since a total of 10 seats were sold? Yes, but the point is that neither of the clerks knew that the other was in the process of selling seats on the flight at the same time that he or she was. Both Brown and Green started off with the premise that there were 25 seats left. When Brown deducted four seats, for a moment the record showed that there were 21 seats left. But then when Green deducted his six, he was deducting them from the original 25 seats that he saw when he originally retrieved the record from the database and not from the 21 seats that were left after Brown's sale.

By the way, you might question the probability of two clerks going after the same record simultaneously in a large airline reservations file. Have you ever tried to get a reservation on a flight from New York to Miami for Christmas week the week before? Similar circumstances occur in most applications of every type imaginable. You might also wonder if the same kind of error situation can take place in applications in which

Time		Ms. Brown	Mr. Green
	T1	Reads the record Finds 25 seats left	
	T2		Reads the record Finds 25 seats left
	T3	Deducts 4 seats and writes updated record indicating 21 seats left	
	T4		Deducts 6 seats and writes updated record indicating 19 seats left

But at this point the record
should show 15 seats left!

Figure 14.2. Integrity problem caused by concurrent update.

the retrieval/update operations execute in fractions of a second and not the minutes involved in Brown's and Green's telephone conversations with their customers. As should be fairly clear, the answer is very definitely yes, as a consequence of multiprogramming in today's commercial computer systems.

Locks and Deadlock

The usual solution to this problem is a technique known as "lockout." The DBMS is designed so that once one update operation has begun on a piece of data, any attempt to begin another update operation on that same piece of data will be blocked, or "locked out." One way or another, depending on the implementation, the bumped access request will be rescheduled. When the first query releases its lock on the data, the other one can lock it and use it for its own update operation. The level or "granularity" of lockout can vary. Lockout at a high level, for instance at the level of an entire file, unfortunately prevents much more than that one particular piece of data from being modified while the update operation is going on, but is a low-overhead solution. Lockout at a low level, the field level for instance, doesn't hold up the rest of the database, but is a comparatively high-overhead solution.

Unfortunately, as so often happens, the introduction of this beneficial device itself causes other problems that did not previously exist. Follow the next scenario:

Let's say we have a manufacturing inventory situation in which clerks must find out if a sufficient quantity of *each of two parts* is available to satisfy an order. A program has been written that is designed to accept information from a terminal on the two parts being sought, including the quantity of each required. It then searches the database for the records for those parts, retrieves the quantity of each currently on hand, and then, on approval from the clerk at the terminal, orders those parts to be shipped and reduces the quantity-on-hand field in the records accordingly. Suppose two clerks, Mr. White and Ms. Black, each request a quantity of nuts and bolts at about the same time. White happens to list the nuts before the bolts in his query, while Black happens to list the bolts before the nuts in hers. Both clerks begin their queries at about the same time. White's query grabs the nuts record and locks it, and at about the same time Black's query grabs the bolts record and locks it. White's query then tries to get the bolts record, but finds it locked by Black, and at about the same time, Black's query tries to get the nuts record, but finds it locked by White. Both queries then wait endlessly for each other to release what they each need to proceed. This is called "deadlock," or "the deadly embrace," and is shown in Figure 14.3. It actually bears a close relationship to the "gridlock" traffic problem that major cities worry about occurring during rush hour.

To solve the problem of deadlock, we can consider measures that would prevent it from happening outright or measures that would detect it when it happens and take appropriate corrective action. While prevention may sound more palatable than mere detection, it turns out that preventing deadlock is not always all that easy. Depending on the nature of the query, it may be that the program has to use information in one piece of data that it finds and locks to determine what other piece of data it must

		Mr. White	*Ms. Black*
Time			
	T1	Gets and locks the record for nuts	
	T2		Gets and locks the record for bolts
	T3	Tries to get (and lock) the record for bolts but finds it locked by Ms. Black	
	T4		Tries to get (and lock) the record for nuts but finds it locked by Mr. White
		DEADLOCK!	

Figure 14.3. Deadlock caused by the use of locks in concurrent update.

find and lock. If that second piece of data is already locked by someone else, then the query is stuck in the middle, holding one piece of data that it needs locked and finding the other unavailable. In addition, there are performance-related issues that make deadlock prevention less than desirable.

So the usual approach in this matter is to allow deadlock to occur, detect it when it happens, and then undo it. Deadlock can be detected either through a timeout (meaning that a query has been hung up for so long that the assumption is it must be deadlocked) or through a procedure that traces a chain of query wait situations to see if the chain begins and ends at the same query. For example, if Smith is waiting for something that Jones has locked, Jones is waiting for something that Williams has locked, and Williams is waiting for something that Smith has locked, then there is deadlock. The solution is to select one of the deadlocked queries and "roll it back" (see the following section on recovery), undoing any changes that it has made to the database up to this point of its execution, and releasing all of its locks so that the other queries can now use the data that it had locked. The bumped query can then be restarted.

Backup and Recovery

Introduction

No matter how sophisticated computers become, we have to assume that a variety of predicaments may, at one time or another, befall stored data. Trouble can come from something as simple as a user entering an incorrect data value into a field or as overwhelming as a fire or some other disaster destroying an entire computer center and everything in it. Thus the results can range in consequence from a single data value being rendered inaccurate to all of the installation's files or databases being destroyed, with many other possibilities in between. In the data processing business we have to assume that from time to time something will go wrong with our data, and we have to have the tools available to correct or reconstruct it. Clearly, in the database environment, those tools must be general enough to handle the different kinds of data and the volume of data stored in the database. The operations involved come under the heading of backup and recovery.

The basic ideas in backup and recovery are fairly straightforward in concept and have been around for a long time. This is not meant to imply, however, that there is no room for variation or that the implementation of the ideas cannot get complicated. For a database to be capable of recovering from a data error, a disk crash, or the like, two major actions must be taken, one on a regularly scheduled basis, and one on a constantly active basis. On a regularly scheduled basis the database files must be "backedup," that is, a copy of each file must be made. The copy (or a copy of the copy) should be kept in a different building or even in a different city, so that if a disaster strikes the computer center not all copies of the data will be lost. For example, disk-based files are copied onto other disk packs. From that moment onward, on a constant basis, every change to the database must be recorded on a special file called a "log" or "journal." The journal can be kept on either tape or disk, although the current trend is toward keeping it on disk. While the contents of a journal entry can vary, the basic notion is to record what piece of data was changed in a given transaction, what its value was before the change, and what its value is after the change. The question then is, "How can the database copy and the journal be used to solve the various kinds of recovery problems?"

Forward Recovery

First let's consider the case of a calamity that destroys a disk pack. The recovery procedure in this case is called "forward recovery" or "roll forward," illustrated in Figure 14.4. To re-create the disk that was lost, you begin by readying the most recent copy of the lost data and the journal of the changes to it. A program then starts reading journal entries, starting from the first one that was recorded after the copy of the database was made and continuing through to the last one that was recorded just before the disk was destroyed. For each of these journal entries, the program changes the data value concerned in the copy of the database to the "after" value shown in the journal entry. This means that whatever processing took place in the transaction that caused the journal entry to be made, the net result of the database after that transaction will be restored. Performing the operation for every transaction that caused a change in the database since the copy was taken (which is the same as saying for each entry in the journal), in the same order that these transactions were originally executed, will bring the database copy to the up-to-date level of the database that was destroyed.

There are a couple of variations on the forward recovery theme that are worth mentioning. One variation is based on the recognition that several changes may have been made to the same piece of data since the last database copy was made. If that's the case, then only the last one of those changes—which after all shows the value of this piece of data at the point that the disk was destroyed—needs to be used in updating the database copy in the roll-forward operation. If the database environment is a volatile one in which changes are made frequently and the same piece of data commonly is updated several times between database copy operations, then roll forward as we have described it may be needlessly inefficient. Instead, it may be worthwhile to sort through the journal prior to the roll-forward operation to find the last change made to each piece of data that was updated since the last database copy was made. Only those final

Figure 14.4. Roll-forward recovery.

changes need then be applied to the database copy in the roll-forward operation.

Another roll-forward variation is to record an indication of what the transaction itself looked like at the point of being executed, instead of recording before and after images of the data in the journal, along with other necessary supporting information. The roll-forward process then becomes one of re-executing all of the transactions in the order in which they were originally executed. This variation will take a lot longer as a recovery process.

Backward Recovery

Now let's consider a different situation. Suppose that in the midst of normal operation an error is discovered that involves a piece of recently updated data. The cause might be as simple as human error in keying in a value, or as complicated as a program ending abnormally and leaving some, but not all, of the changes to the database that it was supposed to make. Why not just correct the incorrect data and not make a big deal out of this? Because in the interim, other programs may have read the incorrect data and made use of it, thus compounding the error in other places in the database.

So the discovered error, and in fact, all other changes that were made to the database since the error was discovered, must be "backed-out." The process is called "backward recovery," or "roll backward," and is diagramed

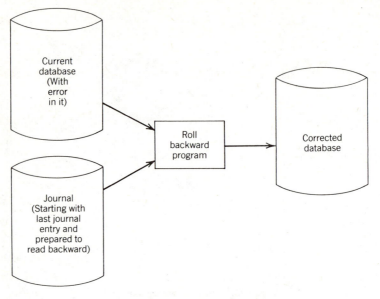

Figure 14.5.   Roll-backward recovery.

in Figure 14.5. Essentially, the idea is to start with the database in its current state (note: database copies have nothing to do with this), and the journal positioned at the *last* entry that was made in it. Then a program reads *backward* through the journal, resetting each updated data value in the database to its "before image" as recorded in the journal, until it reaches the point where the error was made. Thus the program "undoes" each transaction in the reverse order (last-in, first-out) from that in which it was made. If the error did affect other transactions, then those must be re-run, which may be a manual or automatic process, depending on a number of factors, including the nature of the information kept in the journal.

A couple of other notes about recovery: Some systems are capable of automatically initiating a roll-backward operation to undo the changes made to the database by a partially completed and then halted or failed transaction. This is called "dynamic backout." There are situations in which it is helpful to restore the database to a point at which there is confidence that all changes made to the database up to that point are accurate. Some systems are capable of writing a special record to the journal, known as a "checkpoint," which specifies that kind of stable state.

Auditability

An issue that has received relatively little attention in the past, but which is gaining in importance, is that of auditability of the database. The term "auditability" can have several connotations and we shall just touch on a couple of them here.

One sense of database auditing is surveying the database environment to make sure that the data is properly protected. This means that adequate security procedures, backup and recovery, and concurrency procedures are in place. Depending on the depth of the audit, it may also mean that the DBMS is being used properly and that its benefits are being exploited to an acceptable level.

Another sense of database auditing is being able to trace back to see who interacted with the database. This may be at the level of determining who made what changes to the database, or even at a level of simply finding out who retrieved what data from the database. The most obvious kind of vehicle for satisfying such a requirement is the journal. In fact, the same journal that is used for recovery operations could be used for auditing as well. If the goal in providing an "audit trail" is to be able to keep track of who made changes to the database, then the recovery journal would have to include who made the changes indicated in the journal entries. If the audit trail is to keep track of simple retrievals from the database, as well as updates to it, then the journal would have to include entries for simple reads in addition to its usual entries for updates. However, note that the latter requirement, in systems with high activity rates, would generate a huge journal, and would slow down the operation of the overall system as every database access would have to be recorded in the journal.

References

Bernstein, P. A., Hadzilacos, V., and Goodman, N., *Concurrency Control and Recovery in Database Systems*, Addison-Wesley, Reading, MA; 1987.

Date, C. J., *An Introduction to Database Systems*, vol. 2, Addison-Wesley, Reading, MA; 1983.

Denning, D. E., and Denning, P. J., "Data Security," *Computing Surveys* **11**(3), (September 1979): 227–250.

Everest, G. C., *Database Management*, McGraw-Hill, New York; 1986.

Fernandez, E. B., Summers, R. C., and Wood, C., *Database Security and Integrity*, Addison-Wesley, Reading, MA; 1981.

Gasser, M., *Building a Secure Computer System*, Van Nostrand Reinhold, New York; 1988.

IBM Corporation, *Audit and Control in the DATABASE 2 Environment*, IBM Form No. GE20-0783 (1987).

IBM Corporation, *IBM DATABASE 2 Reference*, IBM Form No. SC26- 4078 (1986).

Jaqua, D. J., "The Key to SQL Database Security," *Database Programming and Design* **1**(7), (July 1988): 26–34.

Knapp, E., "Deadlock Detection in Distributed Databases," *Computing Surveys* **19**(4), (December 1987): 303–328.

Kroenke, D. M., and Dolan, K. A., *Database Processing*, 3rd ed., Science Research Associates, Chicago, IL; 1988.

Leiss, E. L., *Principles of Data Security*, Plenum Press, New York; 1982.

Perry, W. E., *Ensuring Database Integrity*, Wiley, New York; 1983.

Pfleeger, P., *Security in Computing*, Prentice-Hall, Englewood Cliffs, NJ; 1989.

Verhofstad, J. S. M., "Recovery Techniques for Database Systems," *Computing Surveys* **10**(2), (June 1978): 167–195.

Wiederhold, G., *Database Design*, 2nd ed., McGraw-Hill, New York; 1983.

Questions and Exercises

14.1. In your own words, describe the different kinds of security threats to a company's data. Do you think the internal or the external (employees versus outsiders) threats are more serious? Why?

14.2. In your own words, describe the different kinds of security protection devices that can be employed to protect a company's data. Is any one of them more important than the others? Why?

14.3. Make a list of the different kinds of security threats and security protection devices and indicate which devices protect against which threats.

14.4. What are the security implications of having the computer generate random numbers as passwords (i.e., to have passwords that may be difficult for a person to remember)?

14.5. What are the security implications of using fingerprints, signature, or voice instead of passwords for the system recognition scheme? What if the recognition device isn't always perfect?

14.6. Devise a simple data encryption scheme. How long do you think it would take someone to break it?

14.7. Devise a sample situation that demonstrates the problem of concurrent update without locks.

14.8. Devise a sample situation that demonstrates the problem of deadlock.

14.9. Can you envision a situation in which someone doing a simple retrieval should be locked out until an update operation has completed?

14.10. If different queries that require multiple records from the same lock-protected file always request those records in ascending order by unique key value, can deadlock ever occur? Why or why not?

14.11. In your own words, describe the different kinds of destructive threats to a company's data.

14.12. Of the different kinds of destructive threats to a company's data, which ones require forward recovery and which ones backward recovery?

14.13. Consider the different items that can be written onto the journal for an update operation, including the before image of the data, the after image, and a description of the transaction itself. Which are needed for forward recovery and which for backward recovery? Explain.

14.14. What factors do you think govern the frequency with which database copies are made for potential recovery operations? What are the pros and cons of making copies more or less frequently?

14.15. Discuss the reasons for including auditing data in the journal. Are there disadvantages to doing so?

15

Data Administration

Introduction

Thus far in this book, we have been concerned primarily with the technical aspects of database and the database environment. But as with the components of any technology, they must be put to work by people, else they are no more than theory. Of course, there are many people in the database-oriented data processing milieu performing their database-related jobs. Programmers write programs for specific applications with DBMS calls embedded in them. Designers design databases for individual applications. End users seek information with query languages. Systems programmers build DBMS control blocks.

But all of these people performing their individual functions for individual applications would create a chaotic environment without some sort of coordination. Some of this chaos would surface as redundant data. Some of it would cause performance problems on a shared CPU. Some of it would show up as software maintenance headaches due to a lack of standards in database design and program construction. The problem is not a matter of inability to perform on the part of the individual data processing personnel, but rather a lack of overall direction and control. It's somewhat like a symphony orchestra without a conductor. The individual musicians may be quite talented, but without someone to blend their work together, the result will be less than pleasing, (see Figure 15.1).

In the late 1960s, as early DBMSs were starting to come into use, a few forward-looking companies began to recognize the need for an independent group whose job it would be to manage the database environment. As the years went on, some of those groups gained some responsibility

Figure 15.1.   Data administration coordinates like the conductor of an orchestra.

over data in non-DBMS files as well. In addition, some of them matured from a position of managing data only on an operational basis to additionally performing strategic planning and other, more broadly based duties.

In this chapter we will explore this subfield of the database discipline, which is now generally called **data administration**. We will look at the advantages of managing data with a data administration group, the responsibilities that such groups have or might have, the job categories involved, the placement of the group in the data processing organization, the impact of data administration on the data processing organization, and directions for the future.

The terminology that we will follow was developed by the GUIDE International Inc. user group organization (GUIDE, 1977). The term "data administration department" refers to a group that is responsible for managing a firm's data as a valuable corporate resource. It is responsible for "developing and administering the policies, procedures, practice and plans for the definition, organization, protection, and efficient utilization of data within a corporate enterprise." As Figure 15.2 shows, data administration is comprised of two parts, which, if the organization is large enough, may be arranged as two separate departments under the data administration umbrella. The two subfunctions are **data management** and **database administration**. The data management group is a planning and analysis function responsible for policy and standards setting, education, data resource control and accountability, and liaison support to systems analysts and programmers during application development. The database administration group is a more operationally oriented group responsible

Figure 15.2. Data administration and its subfunctions.

for the day-to-day monitoring of the database (and in some cases, of other data as well). The database administration group carries out the policies set by the data management group at the operational level. We will explore the full range of responsibilities in more depth later, but note that, even at this early point, there is no hard and fast rule on what set of responsibilities a data administration organization or its component parts must perform to be considered successful or full-fledged.

Advantages of the Data Administration Approach

In Chapter 4 we made a case for the advantages of the database approach to data processing. In this section we will demonstrate the advantages of the data administration approach to managing data both in the database and nondatabase portions of the data processing environment.

Data as a Shared Corporate Resource

As we said earlier, data should be considered a critical corporate resource, together with money, plant and equipment, personnel, and so forth. Some people have suggested that data is the most important corporate resource because, by its very nature, it describes all of the others. The very existence of an organized accessible database tends to increase the amount of a company's business procedures that use data processing, leading to a more efficient company in general, and the large-scale use of data and data processing can enhance a firm's competitive position by making it more responsive in the eyes of its customers and suppliers.

Data is also a shared resource. One of the basic tenets of the database approach is to reduce redundancy in the data in order to improve data integrity and reduce costs. One of the ways of reducing data redundancy is to have different users and applications that need the same data share it from one file, rather than each having their own copy in different physical files. In terms of data, another form of sharing is sharing the computer hardware that processes the data. A strain on those hardware resources caused by one application can adversely affect the performance of the other applications.

What all of this is leading to is simply this: Any shared corporate resource, including data, should be managed by an independent corporate group, which, in the case of data, we call the data administration department. It makes little sense to have an important resource either not managed at all, or managed part-time and half-heartedly by some group that has other responsibilities, too. It also makes little sense to have any one of the groups competing for the shared resource (e.g., a particular application development department) also managing it—the resource manager must obviously be impartial when a dispute arises.

Efficiency in Job Specialization

There are many functions involving the management of data, ranging from long-range planning and standards setting to database design and database performance monitoring. (We will develop a list of them shortly.) Some of those, such as database design, for example, *must* be performed by *someone* in the data processing organization, or no data processing will get done. But other functions, such as long-range planning, are somewhat optional, depending on the degree of sophistication of the data processing environment. But one thing about all of the functions is certain: They all require a high degree of employee specialization for optimum results.

The question then becomes one of who among the data processing personnel should be responsible for performing these tasks. There are two basic possibilities. One is for the tasks to be divided among the various data processing workers whose usual responsibilities resemble most closely those needed to manage data. The lead programmers would do the database design, the systems programmers would do the database performance monitoring, and so on. The other possibility is for an independent data administration department to take the responsibility for them.

The latter choice is by far the better one because of the complexity of the tasks and because of how important a competent execution of the tasks is to the efficient running of the data processing environment. Too many application developers, systems programmers, and other data processing workers already do too many other things; it isn't reasonable to expect that each of them can become as proficient at performing data-specific tasks as can people who become data administration specialists and do nothing but these tasks day in and day out. The argument is a very standard one for job specialization in general, and it is as important in this situation as in any other.

Data Detail Lifted from Programmers

Related to the preceding section, but important enough to be treated separately, is the question of the relationship between data administration personnel and programmers. With the advent of application generators, "fourth generation" languages, and other means of circumventing or speeding up the programming process, the exact nature of the programmers' job is currently a matter of some debate. There is also an aspect of this debate that relates to data.

One of the traditional programming tasks has been writing code to describe the data structure. Perhaps the best and most well-defined example of this is in the "Data Division" of COBOL programs. But who is best equipped to write COBOL Data Divisions or the equivalent in other languages, the application programmer or the data administrator? The argument here is that this is another data-intensive area in which the data administrator will become a specialist, allowing programmers to concentrate on the logic of the program, which should fundamentally be their area of greatest concern. Here again, the specialization factor also should produce fewer errors in the data description code.

Operational Management of Data

Earlier, we looked at data as a resource from a rather high level. Another aspect of looking at data as a resource is to view it from a lower operational level. A data administration department is necessary for the proper management and control of data on an operational level.

To begin with, there isn't even a close second choice after data administration as a place to put operational control of the data dictionary. Data administration is responsible for managing the company's data, and the data dictionary is the repository for information about what data exists, where it is, who has access to it, and so on. In addition, the independent data administration department is in the best position to see to it that the data dictionary continues to be an important and accurate source of information for all of the other data processing people who have to refer to it.

In the shared data environment there will always be some applications or users that depend on other applications or users to collect data and/or update the files on a regular or irregular basis. Clearly, it is prudent to have an independent data administration group keep track of who is responsible for updating which files and monitor whether they have kept to the expected schedule for the benefit of all of the others who use these files.

There are a number of other data-related tasks that should be managed by data administration specialists for the good of all who depend on the data. Data security, preventing the exposure of company data to the outside world, and data privacy, keeping sensitive data about customers, suppliers, and employees restricted, are two such issues. Also there is the question of managing (but not necessarily performing all of the details of) backup and recovery when the database is damaged. And there are the related jobs of data documentation and data publicity: keeping a record of the details of the data environment (e.g., through the data dictionary), and letting the rest of the firm know what data is available for use in the shared data environment.

Data Administration Responsibilities

As we said earlier, there is no right or wrong in terms of a required set of duties that legitimizes a data administration department. Similarly, there is some flexibility in dividing the duties between data management and database administration. The set of duties assigned to data administration and the breakdown between the data management and database administration subfunctions will vary with the maturity of the organization and with the technical and political atmosphere of the data processing organization and of the company as a whole.

In this section we will explore a wide range of data administration responsibilities, generally following the GUIDE International division between data management and database administration. Remember, data management is the planning and analysis side of data administration, while database administration is the operational side.

Data Management Responsibilities

Data Planning.   With data being treated as a critical shared resource, care must be taken in planning for its future.

The most important aspect of planning in this regard is the determination of what data will be needed for future application development and how that data should be integrated both with its own components and with existing data. There are a number of methodologies that have been developed to do such data planning, an example of which is IBM's BSP, which we discussed previously. Such methodologies take into account the business processes that the company performs as part of its normal operations and prioritizes them for future computerization. While they generally operate at a high "strategic" level, and may not get into the details of individual fields and database design, they do provide a broad roadmap from which to work.

Related to strategic data planning is the matter of what hardware and software will be needed to support the company's data processing in the future. Large data processing organizations usually have people who take this matter on as a full-time job, but clearly they should take input from the data management people regarding how much data there will be and what sort of processing will be done with it. The questions involved range from such relatively straightforward matters as how many disk packs will be needed to contain the data to broader issues of how much raw computing power will be needed to support the overall data processing environment.

A third form of data management planning is the issue of how the data dictionary should be put to use. This involves what data should be stored in the dictionary, what uses the dictionary should be put to, who should interact with the dictionary and how, and on what kind of schedule all of this should take place.

As a company builds more and more of its data processing around the database concept, it is still faced with a large number of existing applications that predated the introduction of database. So another aspect of data management planning involves the migration of these applications into the database environment: Which applications should be migrated, on what schedule, and how should the data needed by them be accommodated by the database?

Database Standards. In order to reduce errors, improve performance, enhance the ability of one data processing worker to understand the work done by another, and in general to provide a higher degree of coordination in the data processing environment, it is incumbent upon the data management function to set standards regarding data and its use. One example of standards is the control of the way that field names, file names, and other data-related names are formed. Normally, they must convey as much meaning in as few characters as possible and be approved by the data management people. Another example is insisting on consistency in the way the programs that access the database are written, especially in regard to the way that the database call instructions are written. Care here can help to prevent database call-related performance problems, as well as to ease maintenance by having standard, readily understood instructions.

Liaison to Systems Analysts and Programmers. As the liaison to application developers, the data management people (who are often called "data analysts" in this role) serve a key function. They are responsible for providing support to the systems analysts and programmers in all matters concerning the data needed by an application. During the systems analysis phase of application development that support may include help in determining what data is needed for the application and will also include help in finding out which of the data items needed for the application already exist in the active database. Another form of assistance to application developers is helping them to construct program data descriptions, such as COBOL Data Division specifications.

Another aspect of such liaison activity, which is really a topic in itself, is the question of database design. There is no doubt that the data analysts must be involved in database design at some level, but the decision of what that precise level of involvement should be depends on a number of factors. In a data processing environment in which the data administration organization is very strong and in which there is a significant amount of data sharing among different applications and different functional areas of the company, the data analysts may do all of the database design work themselves. Here again, they can stand as an impartial group creating the best design for the overall good of all of the sharing users. The other choice is for the application developers to do the database design with either the data analysts' active consultation or with their approval responsibility after the fact. In the active consultation role, the data analysts lend their expertise to the effort, as well as determine how the new data should mesh with data in the existing database, if there is to be such a merging. In the approval role, the application developers (usually the lead programmers for this activity) design the database. But since the data administration people are ultimately responsible for database performance, they must have approval capability, since a poor database design can not only adversely affect the performance of the applications using that database, but can also slow the performance of other applications, using other databases, which run on the same CPU.

Training. The data management people are responsible for training all those in the company, at a variety of levels, who have a reason to understand the database concept. Management personnel have to know why database is good for the company and for their individual functions specifically. Users must understand why their previously separate data files are now being shared with others, and why the data is still secure and private. Of course, application developers must be given substantial training in how to work in the database environment, including training in database concepts, database standards, how to write DBMS calls in their programs, possibly how to do database design, how to use the data dictionary to their advantage, and in general, what services they can expect to be provided by the data administration department. And of course, the data management function must provide education for the data administration department's own personnel.

Arbitration of Disputes and Usage Authorization. To introduce this heading, we should spend a moment on the question of data "ownership." Who "owns" a piece of data or a file? To be technical about it, since data is a resource of value to the company, the data "belongs" to the company's owners or stockholders. But in practical terms, data is often controlled by the user or primary user of it. Some day we may evolve to such an advanced level of data sharing that it will no longer be clear who the owner of some individual data is, and the responsibility will fall to data administration. But for now, data is usually identified with a particular user, and the data administration group acts as "custodian" of the data in the sense of providing security, backup, performance monitoring, and other such services.

If a new application requires the use of existing data, then it is the job of data management to act as an intermediary and approach the owner of the data with the request for data sharing. The owner can authorize this sharing, and then the data management people can instruct the database administration people to allow the new application access to the data. If there is a dispute over such data sharing, then the data management group acts as an arbitrator between the disagreeing parties. Incidentally, the data management group may also find itself acting as arbitrator between two database users who are sharing the same CPU and vying for better performance.

Documentation and Publicity. Using the data dictionary as its primary tool, the data management function is responsible for documenting the nature of the data-oriented environment. Such documentation includes what data exists; what files, programs, reports, and so forth, there are; what people have access to these items; and so on. Some of the information may be input by application development personnel and database administration personnel, but the data management group should be able to provide an overall picture of it.

As a related issue, the data management group should perform a publicity function, informing potential users of what data already exists in the database. Knowing what data exists might encourage people to automate more of their work and to integrate their work more directly with related business processes that are already automated.

Data Environment Management. Again using the data dictionary, the data management function must stand ready to respond to any question about how the data-oriented environment works. With the dictionary's interrelation capability, data management must always be ready to say who has access to which files, which files are used to generate which reports, which programs use which files (known as "change impact assessment" because a change in a file can affect a program that uses it), and the significance of all other meaningful combinations of data processing entities.

Database Administration Responsibilities

Usage and Security Monitoring. Database administration personnel are responsible for monitoring the database environment on an active, constant basis. In doing so they will appear to act as a cross between computer operators and systems programmers, and in fact, they are often referred to as "database systems programmers."

One of the tasks involved is to keep track of who is accessing the data in the database at any moment. Usually there are software utilities that enable such personnel to perform this function. Monitoring the users of the database environment is really done from several perspectives. One is the matter of security: making sure that only authorized personnel access the data. This includes the function of instructing the system to allow new users to access the database, as ordered by data management personnel in conjunction with the data owners. Another perspective is the need to maintain records on the amount of use the various users make of the database. This can have implications in future load balancing and performance optimizing work and may also be used in allocating system costs among the various users and applications. A related concern is database auditing. Even assuming that only authorized users have accessed the database, there are reasons involving accounting and error correction that require that a record be kept of who has accessed and who has modified which data items. Incidentally, if that function is to be performed, the tool that allows it to be accomplished is a log, similar to the one used for backup and recovery. Depending on the nature of the auditing, this log may have to record all simple data accesses, as well as all data modifications.

Performance Monitoring and Load Balancing. Another monitoring function performed by database administration is that of performance monitoring. Using utility programs, the database systems programmers can gauge the performance of the various executing database programs. This activity has a number of implications. For one thing, it is important to know how fast the various applications are executing, as an obvious data processing management function. This information is also pertinent to future hardware and software plans. Also, depending on the characteristics of the DBMS and the system it is running under, this information may be used to redistribute the database application load among different CPUs or among different memory regions within a system. Finally, performance information can be used to ferret out inefficient applications that may be candidates for redesign.

An additional note is that the database systems programmer must interface with the data processing organization's regular staff of systems programmers. The latter will usually still have certain DBMS-related responsibilities, such as installing new releases of the DBMS as they come out. The regular systems programmers may also have performance and troubleshooting responsibilities, which may overlap with those of the database systems programmers. The net of this is that it greatly facilitates matters if the two groups get along well with each other and can effectively work together as need be.

DBMS Troubleshooting. Inevitably, there will be a time when a DBMS application fails during execution. The reason can range from a bug in the application code to a hardware or system software failure. The question is, "Whom do the users call when it happens?" In a strongly controlled environment, the data administration personnel should be the troubleshooting interface. (Note that while some may believe that this heading belongs with the data management side of data administration, we place it here on the database administration side.) In practice, depending on the complexity and the nature of the problem, a variety of data administration people may become involved.

The key to the troubleshooting operation is making an assessment of what went wrong and coordinating the appropriate personnel needed to investigate and fix it. This may include systems programmers, operators, application programmers, and the data administration people themselves.

Data Dictionary Operations. The database administration group is responsible for the operations, as opposed to the planning aspects, of the data dictionary. This includes developing ways of interfacing with the dictionary data in terms of input and output techniques. It also means providing dictionary access to others (such as systems analysts), generating periodic dictionary reports as required by management, and providing management with answers to ad hoc questions about the data and the data processing environment.

Interface with Computer Operators. The independent computer operations function is still very much in evidence in the data administration environment. As always, computer operators start or restart the system as needed, mount tapes and disks, perform backup and recovery operations, and so forth. One of the jobs of database administration is to work with the operators, giving them instruction and training on how to do their jobs in the atmosphere created by the particular DBMS in place and by the needs of the application set. For example, they may need instruction on how to start jobs in the DBMS or how to execute a recovery operation after a system failure.

Data Administration Organizational Placement

Where does the data administration organization fit in to the data processing—or for that matter, the entire corporate—organization? We can begin to answer the question with a philosophical and somewhat futuristic thought: Are data and data processing two separate affairs or part of the same discipline? Traditionally, data has been part of data processing. But if we are now thinking of data as a critical corporate resource, isn't it an independent issue, with its processing a separate concern?

Before we get too carried away, let's take a look at the realities of data and data administration in today's corporations. In the vast majority of companies today, the data administration group is part of the data processing department. There are three basic reporting paths for data administration. One is for data administration to report directly to the chief data processing officer; this is diagramed in Figure 15.3. A second is for data administration to report to a manager of services or technical support

Figure 15.3. Data administration reports to chief DP officer.

who in turn reports either to the head of application development or to the chief data processing officer; this scheme is shown in Figure 15.4. The third choice is for data administration to report directly to the over-all head of application development, as shown in Figure 15.5. The data administration to services to chief data processing officer route is in prac-tice the most common of the three. One indisputable truth is that since the data administration function is in charge of a critical, shared resource, it must not be under the control of any of the corporate groups that are competing for the resource. Thus, placing data administration under one of several parallel applications development departments is unacceptable, because data administration must be impartial in allocating resources and

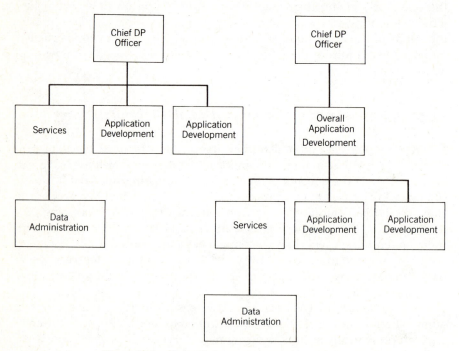

Figure 15.4. Data administration reports to Services.

Figure 15.5. Data administration reports to application development.

settling disputes among those competing for the data and for performance under the DBMS.

But there are significant variations to this theme, particularly among large firms and firms with very active data administration groups, and these variations will become more widespread as time goes on and both data administration and data processing activity increase. The most common such variation is for a company to have multiple data administration groups. This often happens when a large company has independent data processing organizations supporting either different divisions, or operations in different geographic locations, or both, and each one of these different data processing organizations develops its own data administration group. In that case, there may or may not also be a higher-level data administration function reporting in at the highest levels of the data processing organization, or even outside of the data processing organization entirely. This higher-level data processing group may vary from a corporate data standards setting and loose coordinating group to a powerful group that can dictate specific procedures and even common applications to the individual sites.

Data Administration Organizational Impact

The data administration approach to the management of data cannot be implemented in full overnight. It inherently involves changes in the job responsibilities of application developers and others and changes in data processing procedures in general. New data administration departments are likely to encounter resistance from managers who do not understand the concept, from application developers who are naturally suspicious of changes in their job responsibilities and in new ways of producing programs, and from users who are concerned about the concept of sharing their data with other users. Historically, we have seen that there is a learning curve associated with data administration for all concerned, and that successful data administration groups develop gradually in assuming more responsibilities.

How does the data processing environment differ after the successful introduction and development of data administration? With its stress on planning, data administration creates an awareness of the interrelationship of corporate data. It causes other data processing workers to study more carefully the business processes that they are trying to automate. Systems analysis is taken more seriously than before, and, it is hoped, management devotes more of the application development period to it.

As more of the data-intensive work is absorbed by data administration, applications programmers can concentrate on the logic aspects of their programming tasks. This, plus the improved database designs and more accurate program data specifications produced by the data administration specialists, leads to a more error-free application development process and a more solid final program. The quality and consistency of the data in the databases also improves as redundancy decreases and integrity improves.

In general, the increased emphasis on data as a resource puts the company's entire data processing operation in a new light in the eyes of corporate management. Management realizes that data is an asset that can be used to further the company's competitive position in its marketplaces. More emphasis is placed on data processing and a greater focus is placed on the data processing department's ability to automate more of the corporation's business processes.

Data Administration and New Computing Technologies

Recently there have been several new developments in data processing technology that are all somewhat related to each other and to the data administration concept. One development is the personal computer. Another is the so-called "fourth generation language." These provide a higher level of application development than that of standard languages such as COBOL or PASCAL, suitable for use by programming or nonprogramming oriented personnel. A third development is the concept known as the "information center," which provides programmers and nonprogrammers alike with access to computing through fourth generation languages, assistance with the use of personal computers, and other tools that avoid the normal data processing application development process.

The relationship of the information center and its tools to data administration is clear. Fourth generation languages, personal computers, and other "user-friendly" computer tools require the appropriate data to get any work done. A potential user of one of these tools who can approach the data administration department and get access to data that the user would otherwise have to laboriously collect has a tremendous head start in getting the job done. And that should come as no surprise at this point. Data is a resource that should be managed as such and that should be made available to those in the company who have a legitimate need for it. The information center, fourth generation languages, and personal computers provide the *means* for a wider variety of people in the corporation to use the data managed by the data administration function to further the company's goals.

Information Resource Management

Speculating about the future of data administration is an exercise that quickly turns into speculating about the future of data processing. Once again we have to ask, "Which came first, the 'data' or the 'processing'?" Historically, we have been concerned about the processing almost to the exclusion of the data. This ordering has slowly started to change with the advent of increasingly widespread use of DBMSs.

Already we can find chief data processing officers with titles like Vice President of Information Resources. The future may see this spirit trickle down from the highest level through the entire data processing organization, to the point that data is recognized as the critical concern and its processing is seen as more of a mechanical necessity than an end in itself.

As part of that transformation we will see more data and applications migrated to the database environment. This data and more of the non-database data will fall under the control or influence of the data administration organization. More kinds of data, such as pictorial data, will be held in the corporate databases. There will be increased growth towards data sharing, reduced redundancy, and a well-planned and integrated corporate database. We will approach and reach an environment that we can truly call *Information Resource Management*.

References

Chen, C. W., "The DBA's Changing Role," *Database Programming and Design* 1(10), (October 1988): 15–17.

Durell, W. R., *Data Administration*, McGraw-Hill, New York; 1985.

Everest, G. C., *Database Management*, McGraw-Hill, New York; 1986.

Gillenson, M. L., "The State of Practice of Data Administration—1981," *ACM Communications* 25(10), (October 1982): 699–706.

Gillenson, M. L., "Trends in Data Administration: 1981–1983," IBM Systems Research Institute Technical Report #TR73-027, New York (January, 1984).

Gillenson, M. L., and Goldberg, R., *Strategic Planning, Systems Analysis, and Database Design*, Wiley, New York; 1984.

GUIDE International Corp., "Establishing the Data Administration Function," Chicago (1977).

GUIDE International Corp., "Data Administration Methodology," Chicago (1978).

Martin, J., *Managing the Data-Base Environment*, Prentice-Hall, Englewood Cliffs, NJ; 1983.

McCririck, I. B., and Goldstein, R. C., "What Do Data Administrators Really Do?" *Datamation* **26**(8), (August 1980): 131–134.

Ross, R. G., *Data Dictionaries and Data Administration*, AMACOM, New York; 1981.

Tom, P. L., *Managing Information as a Corporate Resource*, Scott, Foresman, Glenview, IL; 1987.

Weldon, J. L., *Data Base Administration*, Plenum Press, New York; 1981.

Questions and Exercises

15.1. Choose one of the traditional corporate resources (e.g., money, plant and equipment, personnel, and so on) and outline the corporate organization in place to manage it.

15.2. Choose one of the traditional corporate resources (e.g., money, plant and equipment, personnel, and so on) and describe the effects on the corporation if there were no group responsible for managing it.

15.3. Describe the importance of sharing data from a management point of view.

15.4. How might data be shared between the

   a. Personnel and equipment management departments?

   b. Accounting and manufacturing departments?

   c. Research and manufacturing departments?

   d. Accounting and data processing departments?

15.5. Convince a company to create a data administration department.

15.6. Describe how the data administration function might change the jobs of others in the data processing department.

15.7. Outline the responsibilities of the *data management* portion of the data administration department. Which of these responsibilities do you think is the most important? Why?

15.8. How should the data planning function be coordinated with other corporate planning functions?

15.9. How would you respond to a programmer or systems analyst who considers the data management role as an intrusion into his or her profession?

15.10. Consider the distinction between data ownership and data custodianship. How comfortable would you feel as the data administration person responsible for arbitrating disputes concerning the sharing of data?

15.11. Outline the responsibilities of the *database administration* portion of the data administration department. Which of these responsibilities do you think is the most important? Why?

15.12. How would you respond to a programmer or systems analyst who considers the database administration role as an intrusion into his or her profession?

15.13. Describe the division of labor concerning the data dictionary between the data management and database administration personnel.

15.14. List a set of arguments for placing the data administration function:

    a. High in the data processing organization.

    b. Outside of the data processing organization.

    c. Partially inside of the data processing organization and partially outside of it.

15.15. Describe the impact of the introduction of the data administration group in the data processing organization.

15.16. Do you think data administration should be responsible for the data kept in a company's micro or personal computers? Why or why not?

15.17. Do you think that ultimately the rest of the data processing organization will report to the data administration organization? Why or why not?

16

Evolving Topics

Introduction

In this chapter we introduce four topics in database that are relatively new, considered relatively experimental, or both. A **database machine** is a hardware solution to improving performance in the database environment. **Distributed database** denotes the concept of a database split into parts, which are stored at different nodes on a distributed computing network. **Object-oriented database** involves an advanced way of considering data and the operations that can manipulate it. **Expert databases** and **knowledge bases** refer to the intersection of the field of database and the artificial intelligence subfield of expert systems.

Database Machines

The Database Machine Concept

Thus far in this book, our discussion of database has centered on software and data, as opposed to hardware. Except for the early description of disk devices, we've talked exclusively about database management systems, data dictionaries, data concepts, data structures, and so on. But there is a new branch of the field of database that is concerned with specialized hardware. This branch has come to be called database machines.

As we shall see in discussing the various approaches, work in database machines has proceeded in several different directions. The motivations have included:

- To free the host processor of its data access responsibility
- To improve performance in the database-oriented environment
- To permit access to data by multiple host processors
- To improve data security and integrity

Let's take a look at the approaches, discuss some of their advantages and disadvantages, and then conclude with the experience to date.

Database Machine Approaches

Backend Conventional Processor. Figure 16.1 shows a typical database environment, in which the host computer is responsible for running the DBMS. The responsibility for the host computer includes holding all or part of the DBMS in its main memory, processing requests for data stored in the database, and communicating these requests to the disk devices via their controllers. Some people have reasoned that if these functions were moved to a separate device, the host computer could spend more of its time performing other processing duties and the data requests could be satisfied more efficiently.

Figure 16.2 shows a database environment that employs a backend conventional processor as a database machine. A physically separate, small(er) conventional computer has been placed between the host computer and the disk storage medium. This database machine is simply a conventional computer configured to perform only one function: to run the DBMS. It takes requests for data from the host computer in the form of either calls from a program or ad hoc queries from a terminal, translates these requests into data access commands, retrieves the data from the disk storage medium, and returns the data to the host computer.

Associative Memory. A hardware solution has been proposed for the large number of compare operations that are an inherent aspect of relational DBMSs. The idea is to design special purpose data storage hardware that is capable of performing a given operation on different parts of a file in the database simultaneously. For example, the value of a given field in every record of a file may have to be compared against a specified value.

Operating system
Application programs

DBMS

Host computer/main memory

Database

Disk
storage

Figure 16.1. Typical database environment.

Figure 16.2. Database environment with a backend conventional processor.

This kind of operation is particularly common in the relational DBMS environment, so wouldn't it be desirable, from a performance point of view, to be able to test the field in several of these records in tandem and handle the results accordingly, rather than process them one at a time from the beginning to the end of the file?

Associative memory devices, also known as "content-addressable parallel processors," can be constructed in several ways. As an example, imagine a disk drive with a fixed read/write head *on every track of every cylinder.* Also imagine a microprocessor incorporated into every one of these read/write heads. When a data access request is made involving the kind of compare operation that we just described, each of those microprocessors can simultaneously be given directions to perform the operation. Conceivably, if the processing speed of those microprocessors is fast enough relative to the rotation speed of the disk, then every record in a file that's stored on the disk pack could be examined in a single complete rotation. Other variations on the theme might have a smaller number of microprocessors covering larger portions of the stored file. For example, there might be one microprocessor per cylinder, with all of the records on the cylinder being examined by the microprocessor in several revolutions of the disk pack.

Figure 16.3 shows two possible arrangements for the incorporation of an associative memory into the database environment. Figure 16.3*a* suggests that there is not a separate database processor as such, but simply that the secondary memory is of the associative type. Figure 16.3*b* indicates

Figure 16.3*a*. Database environment with an associative memory without a separate database processor.

Figure 16.3*b*. Database environment with an associative memory with a separate database processor.

that there is a separate database processor, which may or may not be part of the same physical unit as the associative memory (the reason for the dashed outline).

Other Database Machine Approaches. There is no clear agreement among those working in the field as to exactly what does and does not constitute a database machine. It's safe to say that everyone considers the two approaches discussed previously to fall within the database machine concept. Some think that these are the only two approaches; others would add to that group from among the following devices or arrangements.

First there is the "network node." The idea here is to have a database machine serve as a node in a distributed computing network. The database that is controlled by the database machine is made available to whichever processors in the network are authorized to use it.

Second is the "storage hierarchy." A series of data storage devices is arranged so that at one end of the series is a relatively small amount of very fast and very expensive storage, while at the other end is a relatively large amount of comparatively slow, but comparatively cheap storage. Most of the data in the database is stored at the slow, cheap end of the series, but the data that is active for a particular application percolates up to (is copied to) the faster end of the spectrum for rapid retrieval. Actually, one could argue that the usual main memory–disk secondary memory combination is a limited kind of storage hierarchy. A bit more apropos is the main memory–disk device–mass storage system sequence.

Finally, some practitioners consider a computer system such as the IBM System/38, which we discussed in Chapter 9, to be a database machine. The use of the term here refers not to the features that we've been discussing, but rather to the overall database-oriented environment that such computers are designed to support.

Database Machines Analysis

Advantages. A wide range of advantages have been suggested as justification for the use of database machines. Many of them are speculative or debatable. Some depend on the relative costs of rapidly changing hardware technologies, while others depend on the efficiency of the implementation of the particular database machine approach.

The most prominent reason for installing a database machine is to improve system performance. Unfortunately, the new level of communication between the database and the host computer that a database machine adds will very likely slow down the response time for any one particular database query. Any improvement in performance will come from the fact that operations involving more than one query can go on simultaneously, with the host computer and database machine operating independently. Of course, this brings up the point that the only way that a database machine makes sense in the first place is if the host computer is being used mostly in support of DBMSs and the queries being processed by them. Another point about performance improvement is that a sufficiently sophisticated associative processor database machine will, it is hoped, speed up the kinds of search operations that we described earlier; after all, that is what it is intended to do.

The fact that the database machine performs work that used to be done by the host computer frees the host in two ways. It frees the host from most or all of its database processing responsibilities, including processing queries and maintaining files, allowing it to devote that processing time to other uses. And it frees the primary memory space that contained DBMS modules during execution.

A database machine, and the data that it controls, can be shared by multiple host computers. Similarly, the database machine can be the data node on a distributed processing network. In fact, the host computers and their software need not be of any one particular configuration if the database machine has the capability of translating queries of different formats into a common form for processing.

The hardware in the database machine can be specialized, there being no need for items such as floating point processors, and can be of more advanced technology than that of the host, permitting an improvement in efficiency without the host having to be replaced. And conceivably, the acquisition of a new, larger host computer can be postponed because of newfound capacity in the existing one due to the off loading of some work to the database machine.

Additional arguments involve data security, integrity, and recovery. Since the data controlled by a database machine can only be accessed through a single interface, the security effort can be highly focused. There is no fear of someone skirting the DBMS to get to the data, as there is in the usual arrangement. Of course, there still must be a way of protecting against an unauthorized person's appearing to be authorized and coming into the database machine through the standard interface. Along the same lines, the integrity of the data can be better assured. As for recovery, a failure in the host computer is better insulated from the database, although failures in the database machine must still be contended with.

Disadvantages. The counterargument to the performance advantage has already been stated: the additional level of communication necessary for a single query. In addition, there are other issues concerning the fact that two different processors (the host and the database machine) exist in this arrangement. The two-processor approach can mean increased complexity and cost in development and maintenance, increased training and support, and a possible decrease in reliability because there are two machines that can fail. And if the two machines are manufactured by different companies, the coordination between the two could be a problem. Similarly, we talked about the advantages of multiple languages sending queries of different formats to the database machine, but that can be a significant problem to work out, too. In fact, even the single query format from a single host can require a significant effort in conversion to a form that the database machine understands.

Some other negative arguments include: Since hardware in general is getting progressively cheaper, the emphasis in the database machine approach on saving money through a better use of hardware may be fruitless. In fact, it may be simpler and cheaper to upgrade the main computer than to introduce a database machine. The two-processor, host computer–database machine approach is less flexible than a general multiprocessor approach because the specialization of the database machine restricts the capability to load-balance among the different processors. Finally, if several host computers are all sharing and accessing a database machine simultaneously, the flow of information into and out of the database machine could become a bottleneck that could slow the speed of all of these processors.

Conclusion. At the time of this writing there are several database machines on the market and others in various stages of experimentation, representing all of the major categories. There are those who think that they are worthwhile, those who are skeptical of their value, those who think that they work well only in certain application situations and not in others, and those who think that further breakthroughs in hardware speed and cost (particularly for the associative processor case) will be necessary before they can come into their own. Measured by amount of use, database machines are not a significant factor in commercial database practice today, but may become more so in the future.

Distributed Databases

The Distributed Database Concept

The usual centralized form of computer system design consists of a single processor together with its associated data storage devices. The system offers data processing capabilities to users who are located either at the same site or, through terminals, at geographically dispersed sites.

While the management of the system and its data can be controlled in a straightforward manner in this arrangement, there are also potential problems with it. For example, if the central site goes down, then everyone is blocked from using the computer until it comes back up again. Also, the communications costs from the terminals to the central site can be expensive. One solution to such problems—and an alternative design to the centralized processing concept—is distributed processing.

In a distributed processing or distributed computing system, computers located at different geographic sites can communicate with each other to facilitate a variety of processing modes. For example, an actual application task can be shipped to a free processor, instead of having to wait for a busy processor. But many of the aspects of distributed computing directly involve the ways in which the data is stored on the network and accessed by the application programs. As a result, an entire subfield of distributed processing—and of database—has come into being and has come to be known as distributed data or distributed database.

Since distributed database is a state-of-the-art topic, it is difficult to come up with a precise definition of it. Broadly stated, it is an arrangement by which data at different sites (or nodes) on a distributed computing system (or network) can be accessed by programs or users at other nodes on the network. And there is a wide variety of ways in which that dispersed data might be processed.

At one end of the spectrum is a distributed system that permits a program executed at one node to access data at another node. Such systems exist today as commercial realities. For example, DL/I databases at nodes in a distributed network can be accessed from other nodes through a feature called Multiple Systems Coupling (MSC) in IMS/DC environments, or through a feature called Intersystem Communication (ISC) in CICS environments. In the case of MSC, a program at one node orders the execution of a program at the node at which the required data resides and that second program performs the data access. The results are then shipped back to the original requesting node. In the case of ISC, a program at one node directly requests data from the DL/I database at another node on the network.

At the other end of the spectrum is a far more complex situation in which files required to satisfy a query that involves a relational join reside at different nodes on the network. In one way or another the data is brought together (or the query is split apart or both), the join is performed, and the result is sent back to the node that issued the query. Furthermore, the person issuing the query does not have to be aware that the data resides at different nodes or of how the join is accomplished. Work on such systems is at this point considered experimental.

Some people in the field have attempted to distinguish between the simpler and more complex cases just described by referring to the former as "distributed data" and the latter as "distributed database." While such a distinction may be useful, it is difficult to place each of the many variations into one bucket or the other, and so we shall not pursue this distinction any further here. What we will do is approach the subject of distributed database in the "traditional" fashion, by describing some of the major variations of the design options with which workers in the field have been experimenting. Specifically, we will look at some design choices for storing data on the network, some ways to handle the problem of updating data on the network if it is stored redundantly in more than one location, some choices for satisfying a query that requires data stored at two or more locations on the network, and some ideas concerning catalogs that give the systems information about which data is stored at which nodes.

The Placement of the Data

Most work on advanced concepts in distributed database has been done within the context of the relational approach to database management. So in the discussion of data placement in this section, and in the succeeding sections on this topic, this is the approach that we will assume is in use. Thus the question of data placement in the distributed network becomes one of deciding which relational files will be placed at which nodes of the network. As we look at the different data placement possibilities, keep in mind that a central issue involves whether or not files can be replicated at different nodes.

Perhaps the simplest way of distributing data on a network is to place specific files at specific nodes, with no data duplication. Figure 16.4 shows such an arrangement. The advantage here is that when some data must be updated, the update takes place at only one site, which eases data integrity

Figure 16.4. Distributed data with no duplication.

Figure 16.5.   Distributed data with all data duplicated at every node.

control. One disadvantage is that if a node goes down, the data at that node is inaccessible to everyone on the network. Also, depending on the nature of the data and the applications, there may be a great expenditure in cost and communication time if the various nodes often require data situated at other nodes. One could argue that this arrangement defeats much of the purpose of having a distributed system in the first place.

The arrangement in Figure 16.5 goes to the other extreme. All of the files are duplicated at every node. Accessing data is certainly fast and cheap, since every data retrieval operation can be done right at the node that requested it. But the amount of storage space taken up and the problems associated with having to perform data updates at every node on the network (since every node has a copy of every file) make this scheme unrealistic for virtually all application situations.

Figure 16.6 shows a more useful variation of the data duplication concept. All of the files are stored at one of the nodes (Los Angeles), while some of the files are also stored at *one* other node. The choice of where to store the files, other than at the node that contains all of them, is done on a "locality of reference" criterion. That is, they are stored at the sites that access them most frequently, which reduces the communications costs incurred by accessing data at nonlocal nodes of the network. But if the data required is not at the site requesting it, there is no doubt about which node to look to for the data. It will always be at the node that has a copy of all of the files. Since there is data duplication, even though it is limited, there is still the issue of updating duplicate data at more than one (in this case exactly two) nodes. Also, if the node that has all of the data goes down, then much of the work on the network might grind to a halt.

Figure 16.6. Distributed data with one node having a copy of all of the data.

For example, if Chicago needs data in file C, and Los Angeles is down, it is out of luck.

The most flexible of the arrangements is shown in Figure 16.7. Files can be duplicated at as many nodes as makes sense based on the application requirements. Thus a file that is used almost exclusively at one site might be stored only at that site. A file that is referenced frequently by programs or users at several sites, or for which there is a critical requirement that it

Figure 16.7. Distributed data with files duplicated at selected nodes.

be available at *some* site at *all* times (the problem being the possibility of sites going down) might be duplicated at several sites. The flexibility of this scheme makes it the most attractive of all of the possibilities for research. But while it has the advantages that data duplication in a distributed system brings, it also has the inherent problems. These problems, including updating duplicate data at separate sites, gathering data at separate sites needed in a single join operation, and finding data that is only stored at a few sites in a distributed network will be discussed in the succeeding sections.

As a final point in this section, note that we have been assuming that whether or not we duplicate the files at separate nodes on the network, each file or copy of a file remains whole. Another related issue is breaking files into pieces and storing different pieces at different nodes. Researchers have suggested dividing files horizontally, placing some records of a file at one node and other records at other nodes, and dividing them vertically, placing some fields of all (or some) of the records at one node and other fields of all (or some) of the records at other nodes. Clearly this is an even more complex proposition.

Integrity: Updating and Controlling Duplicate Data

In the last section, we made the point that having data duplicated at selected nodes of the distributed network is fundamental to the distributed database approach and we also noted that it introduces some significant problems. Let's take a closer look at them.

With files duplicated at several network sites, updating data becomes tricky. Look again at the distributed network in Figure 16.7. Let's say that a user at a particular site, for example Chicago, wants to update a particular piece of data in, for example, file A. First of all the system must find a copy of the file involved. If the file is stored at the user's site (as it is in this example), fine; otherwise, the system must find a copy of the file at another site. (In the more advanced distributed database thinking, the data locating operation is transparent to the user.) In either case, we might reasonably expect the system to update the data in that one copy of the file (file A at Chicago) and then update the same data in the other copies of that file around the network (at Denver and Los Angeles). But what if Denver or Los Angeles are down at the time, or what if the entire system goes down after some copies of the file have been updated, but before the rest are? The result will be an integrity problem, with different values for what should be the same data in different copies of the file at the different sites at which they are located.

A related problem can be described as follows. In Chapter 12 we discussed the concurrency problem involving two users attempting to update the same piece of data at the same time. As significant a problem as that is, its solution (in Chapter 12) was at least containable by the fact that for each susceptible piece of data, that piece of data only existed in one file in the central database. In the distributed database case, with duplicated files at different sites, we can still have the situation of two users trying to update the same piece of data at the same time. But now one user might be accessing a copy of the data at one site to update it, while the other user might be accessing a different copy of the data at another site to update it. Clearly this compounds the problem significantly. For example, what if the distributed database system is used for an airlines reservation application? Assume that there is one seat left on a particular flight on a particular date and that the information is correctly indicated in each copy of the appropriate file, say, file A at Chicago, Denver, and Los Angeles in Figure 16.7. It is entirely possible that sales agents in two different cities, say Chicago and Denver, may try to sell the seat to two different customers simultaneously. If the system processes the Chicago request against the Chicago copy of the file, and the Denver request against the Denver copy of the file, then each sales agent will sell the same seat before the system has had a chance to update all of the other copies of the file around the network. The copy of file A at Denver will be unaware that the copy of file A at Chicago has decremented its seat count from 1 to 0, and vice versa. By the time each site informs the other of the update, it's too late, and the seat has been sold twice.

Let's take a look at some of the proposed methods for overcoming these potential integrity problems. One method is based on an extension of the locking concept, which we discussed in Chapter 12. To refresh the point, the idea in locking is for one user to gain control over whatever data he or she is updating so that no one else can access or modify it (depending on the situation) until the update is complete. So in the distributed update case, the system would attempt to lock all of the copies of a file at all of the sites at which they are located before allowing the data to be updated in any one copy of that file.

One way of performing that multisite update is with a sequence of operations that has been called "global locking." The sites must not only be given orders on locking, they must acknowledge these orders as well. Note the following sequence (continuing with the use of Figure 16.7 as an example):

1. One node, say Chicago, issues a command to the other nodes on the network to lock a file, say file A. It also locks its own copy of file A.

2. Denver and Los Angeles, which also have copies of that file, lock their copies of file A (as soon as they become free of any other locks) and so inform Chicago.

3. Once Chicago is told that the copies of file A at Denver and Los Angeles are locked (and notes that its own copy is locked), it issues the order to perform the update to all of the copies of file A.

4. Chicago updates its copy of file A and so do Denver and Los Angeles, which inform Chicago that they have performed the update.

5. Chicago then releases the lock on its copy of file A and informs Denver and Los Angeles to do the same with the locks on their copies.

Unfortunately, in addition to having large communication costs associated with it, this procedure can result in a massive deadlock, with transactions at different sites contending for files that each other has locked. This has led to procedures for detecting such deadlocks, forcing one of the transactions to give up its locks to allow the other transaction to finish its work, and then restarting the one that was forced to retreat.

A variation on this theme involves declaring one node as the "dominant" node for each of the files. All updates for data in a particular file must be sent to the node at which the dominant copy of that file resides. With this kind of limitation, the node with the dominant copy can exercise a much stronger degree of control on updates to the particular file. Unfortunately, the dominant node might become a bottleneck for a volatile file. Also, if the dominant node goes down, all update activity on that file would have to stop, unless the system goes to another level of complexity with the ability to transfer "dominance" for a file from one node to another.

Yet another method for controlling updates in the distributed database environment involves not locks but **timestamps**. The idea is to record the time that every database transaction starts, as well as to record the time that every piece of data or record was last updated and last read. The integrity problem then can be controlled by forcing everything in the system to stay in sequence. For example, let's say that two transactions, X and Y, both attempt to update a record in file A in Chicago. The following time sequence and actions show how one of the several variations of the timestamping concept proceeds:

10:00 AM	Transaction X accesses the record to update it.
10:01	Transaction Y accesses the record to update it.
10:02	Transaction Y updates the record.
10:03	Transaction X attempts to update the record, but the timestamping protection prevents it. Transaction X is cancelled and restarted with a new timestamp. Why?

As part of its initial processing, transaction X read the old (10:00 AM) values in the record. But by the time it is ready to update the data at

10:03, these values have been rendered obsolete by transaction Y, which updated the record at 10:02.

Multisite Joins

In a truly distributed, relational database environment a transaction that involves a join may require files that are located at two or more different sites on the network. There are a variety of ways in which such a join can be performed, and the proper choice for a particular join can make a huge difference in the amount of communication time required on the network.

Perhaps the simplest choice is to ship all of the files to one site and perform the join there. This would probably take a fair amount of time, particularly for large files. Clearly, the choice of the target site is critical, as it would take a lot less time to ship a small file to a site where a large required file is already found, rather than vice versa.

The other major approach is to ship only parts of files to other nodes for further processing. If based on the query it can be determined that only certain records, and perhaps only certain fields in these records, are involved in the query, then that is the only data that needs to be shipped to the other node to complete the join. If three files are involved and two of them are at one site, then those two might be joined at their homesite and only the appropriate records of the result shipped for further processing.

Finally, a variation on this last approach would be to send the appropriate data from records in the file at one node to the other node one at a time, in a look-up kind of a mode, rather than to ship many records at once for a more formal join.

Directory Management

Earlier in this book we referred to control blocks as the vehicles for describing the data to the database system. Recall that there were control blocks, or more generally, system directories or catalogs to describe the physical data, the logical views of the data, security constraints, and so forth. Naturally, such information is also needed in the distributed database environment, with one addition: information on the location in the network of each of the data files. After all, up to this point in the discussion on distributed database we've been tacitly assuming that when a node needs data at another node to satisfy some kind of transaction, it "knows" where to find it. But that knowledge has to come from somewhere, and that somewhere is the directory.

Which brings up an interesting question: Where should the directory itself be stored? As with the matter of how to distribute the data files themselves, there are a number of possibilities, some relatively simple and others more complex, with many of the same kinds of advantages and disadvantages that we've already discussed. For example, the entire directory could be stored at only one site. This would make updating it easy, and each node would know exactly where to go to get directory information. But the amount of communications costs involved with all transactions going to that single node for directory information would clearly be prohibitive. If the directory node goes down, the entire system grinds to a halt. And even if the directory node stays up, it becomes a bottleneck, with transactions from all over the network needing to access it for directory information.

The other extreme is for the entire directory to be duplicated at every site. Actually, this is not as bad as trying to store the entire database at every node because there is much less data involved. Nevertheless, the amount of time and energy needed to update the directory at every site for every change to the directory can make this approach unappealing.

Another approach is to start with the premise that every node will have a directory that describes all of the data located at that node. But then what happens when a transaction at a particular node needs data at another node? Not only aren't the directory entries for the data at the transaction's node, there isn't even a guide to which node the needed directory entries are at (much less the data itself). Presumably the transaction will have to search every node for the needed directory information. However, we could go a step farther by additionally placing a copy of the entire directory at one of the sites. Every transaction would know where to go to get information about nonlocal data, but the arguments about the directory node being a bottleneck and the system stopping if the directory node goes down become factors again. And so the next logical extension would be to allow copies of the directories of each node to be placed at several arbitrary sites on the network. The advantages and disadvantages of this arrangement should be rather clear by now. One improvement for any of these local/nonlocal reference cases would be for a node to record the directory information that it just found in a nonlocal reference and hold the information temporarily. In many application situations it's likely that the node might need that same directory information again soon and finding it locally will speed things up.

As a final note, realize that the choice of these approaches to directory management should depend largely on the applications themselves and the data processing environment as a whole. Transactions that require mostly local data need the directory for the local data stored at the local site. If there is not much reference to nonlocal data, then storing many copies of each node's directory around the network is counterproductive. On the other hand, a high proportion of nonlocal data references would encourage duplication of the directory information, and a large amount of directory update activity would discourage duplication of the directory information. All of the factors must be carefully weighed.

Object-Oriented Databases

Very early in this book, we mentioned that there are several different data types in common use, not just in the realm of database, but in data processing in general. Among the more common types are numbers stored in the binary format, in the decimal format, and in the floating point format, as well as textual data stored in the character format. Many operations on data, particularly on numeric data, tend to be held in common among the different data types and are just assumed to exist. We take for granted, for example, that two numbers in any of the numeric formats can be added together, multiplied together, and so on. Data stored in traditional records and files, in relational tables, and in navigational database records all rely on the standard data types and the usual operations associated with them.

Recently, database researchers have begun exploring the possibility of greatly expanding the notion of what a data type is and of what kinds of operations can be performed on data stored in nontraditional data types. They have been developing the idea that programmers can create their own data types and define associated operations for data stored in those data types. They have also developed the idea that hierarchical classes and subclasses of objects can be defined so that properties of data classes can be "inherited" from classes above them in class hierarchies. These concepts characterize what has come to be known as object-oriented data storage and programming. Let's look at examples of these ideas.

A good example of a new data type (which already exists in some programming languages) is the Date type. Can dates be handled in traditional programming languages as simple character strings? Of course. But if Date is set up as a new data type, operations that pertain specifically to dates can be developed and used. The Date type might be defined as MM/DD/YYYY so that an instance of the date could be 03/24/1989. Note that MM (month) would be restricted to 1-12, DD (day) would be restricted to 1-28, 1-29, 1-30, or 1-31, depending on which month the date is in and whether or not it is a leap year. Operations could then be defined on this data type. For example, an operation called DATE_DIFFERENCE would take two date instances as arguments and return the number of days in between the two dates.

New data types can be built up from lower-level data types. For example, the Point type can be defined as consisting of an X, Y coordinate pair (X,Y). Then a Rectangle type can be defined by two of those Points, which define two diagonally opposite points of the rectangle. At the operational level, if the rectangle is instructed to alter its position, the lower-level points will move as well.

At another level in the object-oriented environment, an object can be thought of as an entity that can be described by attributes. In today's technology, an **object type** can be thought of as a record type with a specific object or entity being represented by a record occurrence. But in this environment, the idea of **inheritance** is also present. Thus, a Person type might include such attributes as First Name, Last Name, Age, and Telephone Number. A type of object subordinate to Person, also referred to a as a **subclass**, is Student. Another subclass is Plumber. Student has attributes Student Number, Class Rank, and Home Town. Plumber has attributes Years of Experience, Union Membership, and Plumber License Number. But both Student and Plumber inherit the attributes First Name, Last Name, Age, and Telephone Number from the higher-level class Person. Thus, an **inheritance hierarchy** can be created in which lower-level objects inherit properties from higher level objects.

Work has been done to merge some of the concepts of the object-oriented approach into existing database environments, most notably SQL. In fact, working with complex object types can circumvent some time-consuming SQL operations including the join. Work in this area is proceeding and will be interesting to watch in the coming years.

Expert Databases and Knowledge Bases

Artificial intelligence (AI) has been a research discipline in the field of computer science since the 1950s. During the 1980s, a branch of AI known as **expert systems** has become a commercial reality. An expert system is a complex computer program that combines expert knowledge about a problem area with an inferential capability to solve future problems in that environment. In many such systems, the expert knowledge is in the form of *rules* of an if–then nature. The inference capability in the software decides which rule to "fire" next, based on the results of the firing of earlier rules. Specialized AI programming languages, most notably LISP and PROLOG, have been used with success in writing expert systems. **Expert systems shells** have been developed, which contain a general-purpose **inference engine**. These shells can be used to create an expert system for any appropriate environment. The input to the shells includes data in the form of facts and rules about the environment.

The earliest, and still one of the best, example of a good expert system application is that of medical diagnosis. Facts for a diagnosis might include the patient's temperature, blood pressure, red blood cell count, and so on. An applicable rule might be, "If the temperature is over 100 degrees and the blood pressure is greater than 80/120 and the red blood cell count is normal, then the probability of pneumonia is 10 percent." Through the use of many facts, many rules, and complex inferential capabilities that can process a number of rules together in complex but highly beneficial ways, accurate diagnoses can be generated. With an expert systems shell, the same software can be used to perform a medical diagnosis or to troubleshoot a manufacturing problem, as long as an appropriate set of facts and rules is fed into it as input. Just as we have always referred to a collection of facts as a database, we can refer to a collection of rules and associated facts of the type described here as a **knowledge base**.

That the fields of database and expert systems would cross paths for their mutual benefit was inevitable. It is clear that a huge number of existing databases could be put to even better use than they already are by expert systems making sophisticated inferences from their contents. It is just as clear that expert system shells have a greater value if they have more data and situations on which to work. A combined system can be called an **expert database** system.

There are several ways to consider the interface between the concepts of database and expert systems. One is simply to work towards the efficient storage and retrieval of rules written in the form required by the expert system in a database of rules. Another is to find ways for an expert system to take advantage of all of the data stored in a traditional relational or navigational database. For example, an expert system, with its rules stored in its own "rule base," might access the data in a traditional database in much the same way that such data would be accessed in a call from a traditional programming language.

A very exciting research idea in this area involves combining expert system and object-oriented database concepts. In the previous paragraph, we began to explore how an expert system might access the data in a database. Again, at its simplest, an expert system could issue calls to a database just as an ordinary program can. But if the records in the database are organized as "objects" and the rules of the expert system are designed to process such objects, then the two can work together in a very direct, natural, and efficient manner. The potential for the future in this combined area is enormous.

References

Bray, O. H., *Distributed Database Management Systems*, D. C. Heath, Lexington, MA; 1982.

Bray, O. H. and Freeman, H. A., *Data Base Computers*, D. C. Heath, Lexington, MA; 1979.

Ceri, S., and Pelagatti, G., *Distributed Databases*, McGraw-Hill, New York; 1984.

Champine, G. A., "Six Approaches to Distributed Databases," *Datamation* 23(5),(May 1977).

Champine, G. A., "Four Approaches to a Data Base Computer," *Datamation* 24(13), (December 1978): 101–106.

Date, C. J., *An Introduction to Database Systems*, vol. 2, Addison-Wesley, Reading, MA; 1983.

Epstein, R., "Why Database Machines?" *Datamation* 29(7), (July 1983): 139–144.

Gardarin, G., and Valduriez, P., *Relational Databases and Knowledge Bases*, Addison-Wesley, Reading, MA; 1989.

Gray, J., "Transparency in Distributed Processing," *Database Programming and Design* 1(3), (March 1988): 46–52.

Harris, L. R., "The AI-Database Connection," *Database Programming and Design* **2**(2), (February 1989): 42–47.

Kerschberg, L., ed., *Expert Database Systems*, Benjamin/Cummings, Menlo Park, CA; 1986.

Larson, J. A., and Rahimi, S., *Tutorial: Distributed Database Management*, IEEE Computer Society Press, Silver Spring, MD; 1985.

Maryanski, F. J., "Backend Database Systems," ACM Computing Surveys **12**(1), (March 1980): 3–26.

Mohan, C., "Recent and Future Trends in Distributed Data Base Management," Research Report RJ 4240, IBM Research Lab, San Jose, CA (May 1984).

Ozkarahan, E., *Database Machines and Database Management*, Prentice-Hall, Englewood Cliffs, NJ; 1986.

Parsaye, K.; Chignell, M.; Khoshafian, S.; and Wong, H., *Intelligent Databases*, Wiley, New York; 1989.

Rauzino, V. C., "The Present and Possible Future Data Base Machines," *Computerworld* **17**(23), (June 6, 1983): 1–20.

Risch, T.; Reboh, R.; Hart, P.; and Duda, R., "A Functional Approach to Integrating Database and Expert Systems," *Communications of the ACM* **31**(12), (December 1988): 1424–1437.

Schur, S., "Intelligent Databases," *Database Programming and Design* **1**(6), (June 1988): 46–53.

Stein, J., and Maier, D., "Object-Oriented Data Management," *Database Programming and Design* **1**(4), (April 1988): 58–67.

Su, S. Y. W., *Database Computers*, McGraw-Hill, New York; 1988.

Questions and Exercises

16.1. What is a database machine? Discuss the motivations for the database machine concept. Do you think they are convincing?

16.2. What is a backend conventional processor? How might such a device aid the database environment.

16.3. What is associative memory? How might such a technology aid the database environment.

16.4. Describe the advantages and disadvantages of the database machine approach. Which do you think are the more compelling arguments? Why?

16.5. What is a distributed database? What is a distributed database management system?

16.6. Outline the major issues in distributed database.

16.7. Describe the different ways of distributing data on a network.

16.8. Outline the advantages and disadvantages of the different ways of distributing data on a network.

16.9. What is locality of reference? How important a role does it play in distributed database? Why?

16.10. How do you feel about storing files redundantly in a distributed network? What are the trade-offs involved?

16.11. What are the integrity problems associated with duplicate data on a distributed network?

16.12. Describe global locking for distributed database. What problem does it attempt to solve? How practical do you think it is to implement?

16.13. Describe timestamping for distributed database. What problem does it attempt to solve? How practical do you think it is to implement?

16.14. What are the advantages and disadvantages inherent in splitting files among different network nodes in terms of multisite joins? Is it worth the trouble? Why or why not?

16.15. Discuss the problem of directory management for distributed database. Do you think that as an issue, it is more critical, less critical, or about the same as the distribution of the data itself? Explain.

16.16. Outline the ways in which personal computers can be involved with database. What are the advantages and disadvantages of each?

17

The Future

The Growth of Database

So there you have them—all of the wide-ranging aspects of the burgeoning field of database. And database will not only continue to be an important aspect of data processing, it will in fact increase in importance as its benefits become more widely understood and as several factors that have limited its use evolve to more supportive levels of development.

As to the benefits of database, they are indisputable:

- The establishment of an atmosphere in which data is truly considered a corporate resource;
- The reduction of data redundancy for a manageable collection of data of high integrity and a well-integrated collection of data for the optimum benefit in combining different kinds of data to satisfy complex queries;
- The ability to easily handle multiple relationships between different entities in the real world environment;
- The establishment of the collection of data as a resource independent of the programs that use it (data independence);
- The freedom of having such chores as security, concurrency, backup and recovery, and auditability managed by a well-established and trusted set of procedures.

And then there are the factors that will improve to enhance these database benefits through more responsive implementations and more hospitable environments:

- Processor and data storage device speeds will increase, gradually reducing the performance limitations that have sometimes limited DBMS usage.

- Hardware costs will decrease, bringing the benefits of database to more and more potential users. (Of course, in a certain respect in the last few years, this has already happened with the advent of the microcomputer and of DBMSs designed for them.)

- Database management system software will continue to increase in sophistication.

- Corporate executives will increasingly become database advocates as they come to appreciate the ways that database can enhance their decision making capabilities.

- The costs of keeping redundant data and the consequences of data integrity problems will increase as more and more of the organization's data is kept in the automated data processing system.

- The costs of program maintenance will increase; this is a problem that can be reduced by the data independence and standardization afforded by the database environment.

- Standardized programs and packages, which can reduce applications development costs, will increase in popularity and will benefit from the same kind of standardized data processing environment that results from the use of DBMSs.

- Increasingly user-friendly interfaces to databases will be developed, permitting a wider range of technically unsophisticated users to take advantage of the data stored in them.

Several of these factors will give some of the more speculative technologies that we discussed in this book a chance to become commercial realities. Improved hardware and software techniques, particularly in the concurrency and recovery areas, along with new and cheaper communications channels, will aid the advancement of the distributed database concept. Further hardware miniaturization, together with decreasing costs and increasing speeds, may make the associative memory database machine an exciting reality.

Future Application Areas

We've talked about the factors to watch for in the increasing prominence of database in our mainstay, "bread and butter" data processing applications. But perhaps even more exciting will be the emergence of database as the foundation for the expansion of some existing application areas, and the development of an array of new and fascinating applications.

Computer graphics is a truly thrilling application area that has received a great deal of attention lately. The promise of computer animation, computer-aided design, and the pictorial display of business data is great and has only begun to be realized. One of the major challenges to database will be the development of the ability to store pictorial data. The data must be stored in such a way that it can manage complex pictorial images in meaningful ways, can be quickly displayed on graphics screens, and can accept rapid updates to reflect changes being made by users to the displayed pictures.

Database must be able to support the "factory of the future" concept, which entails the large-scale integration of computer control mechanisms into the manufacturing process, (see Figure 17.1). In this regard the database must be able to store graphic data that involves the design of the items to be manufactured, test data for testing the finished products, data to control robot manufacturing devices, data that tracks the status of the various manufacturing processes and tools, and traditional data processing data to manage the parts inventory in the manufacturing process, ordering details, shipping details, and so on. Furthermore, it must handle

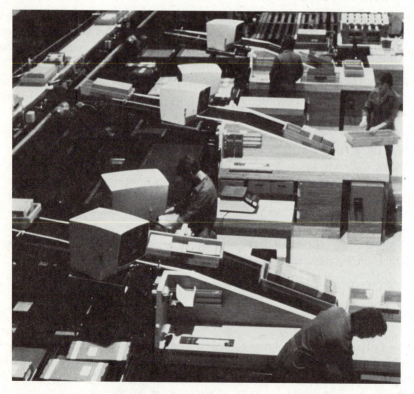

Figure 17.1. The factory of the future.

Figure 17.2. The office of the future.

all of this data in a highly integrated way, as it will be either shared, highly interrelated, or both.

Turning our attention from the blue-collar to the white-collar environment, the database must form the basis for the "office of the future." Here again, the database must be able to accommodate and integrate a range of data including text for word processing, pictures for business presentations, and the usual alphanumeric data for all of the expected record keeping functions found in everything from personnel to accounting chores in the typical office. Figure 17.2 shows such an office. The database will be interfaced to FAX machines and used in teleconferencing.

In the area of artificial intelligence and database, expert database systems hold the promise of bringing expertise to situations in which a human expert is too expensive or for some other reason can't be present. Physicians will be able to make diagnoses by accessing expert systems in mainframes in distant cities via telephone lines. Technicians will be able to determine which part of a complex piece of equipment is causing the whole unit to fail. Managers will be able to make better decisions using the data in their transaction processing systems.

Another AI application is natural language processing. Natural language processing involves the computer being able to interpret, convert, and use instructions and information given to it in human language form. The lexicon necessary for such a task, as well as elements of syntactic, semantic, and pragmatic interpretation rules, must be stored for highly efficient retrieval, and that is a form of a database problem.

Another area for database is the storage and retrieval of digitized images. Whether used in a simple storage and retrieval mode or operated on to discern features in them (a field known as "pattern recognition"), such images require a substantial amount of storage and present their own kind of database problem.

But beyond the specific areas that we've just mentioned, the extraordinary challenge lies in the sharing of the same data for different kinds of applications and in the integration of separately (and perhaps differently) stored data for yet other applications (as we alluded to in a couple of earlier comments). Imagine automated product design, linked to production in an automated factory, linked to office accounting operations, linked to an executive ad hoc query system. Further imagine these operations using a combination of traditional, textual, and pictorial data. And finally imagine all of these operations working smoothly from a single, integrated database. This is the challenge for the future.

We have come a long way in database in the last 20 years, but we have only begun to scratch the surface. Database will become the central focus of data processing as we come to recognize more and more that the term "data processing" means that we are concerned with a resource, *data*, that can serve us by the judicious processing of it. There is tremendous growth potential. The road ahead in database will be a very exciting one to travel.

References

Anderla, G., and Dunning, A., *Computer Strategies 1990-9*, Wiley, New York; 1987.

Dertouzos, M. L., and Moses, J., eds., *The Computer Age: A Twenty-Year View*, MIT Press, Cambridge, MA; 1979.

Hayes-Roth, F., Waterman, D. A., and Lenat, D. B., eds., *Building Expert Systems*, Addison-Wesley, Reading, MA; 1983.

Sowa, J. F., *Conceptual Structures*, Addison-Wesley, Reading, MA; 1984.

Wegner, P., ed., *Research Directions in Software Technology*, MIT Press, Cambridge, MA; 1979.

Questions and Exercises

17.1. Use your imagination and describe the different kinds of data that will be needed in the "office of the future" environment. How will this data be shared among the different applications to be found there?

17.2. Use your imagination and describe the different kinds of data that will be needed in the "factory of the future" environment. How will this data be shared among the different applications to be found there?

17.3. In your own words, describe the future technological and political developments in the computing field that will encourage the use of database.

17.4. Think of an application based on pictures and computer graphics and describe how the data used to describe these pictures can be shared with other nonpictorial applications.

17.5. Do you think that in the foreseeable future a company will be able to have a single corporate database that contains all of its data? Why or why not?

17.6. Do you think that the data administration manager of the future will report to the data processing manager, that the reverse will be true, or that the two will be equals? Defend your position.

Glossary

Access Method. The mechanism for retrieving data from a secondary storage device, based partially on the manner in which it is stored. (See *File Organization*.)

Association. The manner in which one entity relates to another. (See *Relationship*.)

Attribute. A descriptive feature of an entity.

Backup. The act or result (also called a "dump") of copying files or databases for potential use in recovering from a disastrous loss of the files or databases. (See *Recovery*.)

Backward Recovery. The process of working backwards through a log to reverse the operations performed on a file to the point at which an error was known to have occurred. (See *Backup, Recovery*.)

B-Tree. A class of hierarchical structures used to create efficient implementations of indexes in databases.

Candidate Key. A field or fields of a file which can be used as the primary key. (See *Key, Primary Key*.)

Catalog. A highly automated and integrated form of a data dictionary found in a relational database environment.

Checkpoint. Regarding database recovery, a time or juncture in the processing of a database when changes to the database are actually written to the disk and a record of that operation is recorded in the log.

CODASYL. Committee on Data Systems Languages, which devised the specifications for a widely used type of network-based database management system.

Collision. The attempt of a hashed file's hashing algorithm to place a record in a location already occupied by another record. (See *Synonym.*)

Concurrency. The state of two or more transactions operating on the same data simultaneously: often refers to the problems that occur when the transactions attempt to update a particular piece of data. (See *Deadlock, Lock.*)

Control Block. A set of specifications that the database designer writes to inform the DBMS of the structure and certain processing options of a database.

Cylinder. A unit of storage on a disk pack, consisting of the like-numbered tracks on each recording surface of the disk pack. (See *Track.*)

Data. Facts about an environment. (See *Information.*)

Data Administration. The deliberate management of an organization's data.

Data Communications. The mechanisms for transferring data between computers and between computers and terminals.

Data Definition Language. The form for describing to the system the physical arrangement of the stored data.

Data Dictionary. A database or set of files whose data describes the data processing environment.

Data Flow Diagram. A systems analysis documentation tool for describing the flow of data among business processes.

Data Independence. The degree to which a program's code depends on a specific stored data arrangement for its functioning.

Data Integration. The combining of data about related entities. (See *Join.*)

Data Integrity. The accuracy of stored data; often used in the context of a lack of data integrity in the situation in which a particular data value is held redundantly but the different copies are not all identical.

Data Management. The analysis and planning aspects of data administration. (See *Data Administration.*)

Data Manipulation Language. The set of commands used to access and modify the data in a database.

Data Normalization. A process for organizing fields into record types in such a way that data redundancy is eliminated, while semantic relationships between the record types are preserved.

Data Redundancy. The same fact about the environment stored more than once in one file or across several files.

Database. A collection of data, organized to reduce or eliminate redundancy and at the same time to promote data integration. (See *Data Integration, Data Redundancy, Database Management System.*)

Database Administration. The operational and systems programming aspects of data administration. (See *Data Administration.*)

Database Design. The organizing of fields into records and files (and then into hierarchies and networks, if applicable) to satisfy application access and performance requirements, while taking data redundancy and data integration factors into account.

Database Machine. A hardware processor designed to improve the performance of the database environment.

Database Management System. A software system (sometimes combined with specialized hardware) that manages one or more databases. (See *Database*.)

Database Performance. That aspect of the database environment concerned with the speed of data retrieval and associated operations.

Deadlock. The state in which two concurrently executing transactions each have locked data that the other needs for its continued processing. (See *Concurrency, Lock*.)

Direct Access. The retrieval of one (or, generally a small number) of records of a files based on the value of one or more of its fields.

Disk. A magnetic, secondary storage medium, characterized by one or more circular disks that spin on an associated drive.

Distributed Database. A database whose files, and often copies of those files, are resident in different nodes of a distributed processing network and are accessible to a greater or lesser degree of generality from other nodes in the network.

Division-Remainder Method. A common hashing algorithm used in hashed files.

Embedded Language. A database access design philosophy in which commands to retrieve or process data are placed at appropriate points within the logic of a higher-level or assembly language program. (For comparison, see *Query Language*.)

Entity. An object or event of which an organization has a need to keep track.

Entity-Relationship Diagram. A particular type of graphical representation used in systems analysis and design, and particularly in database design, capable of recording entities, their attributes, and the relationships among them.

Entity Set. A collection of a particular kind of entity. (See *Entity*.)

Expert Database. A database used by an expert system.

Field. An atomic unit of storage that represents an attribute of an entity. (See *Attribute*.)

File. A collection of like-structured records.

File Organization. The manner in which the records of a file are physically arranged on a secondary storage (disk) device. (See *Access Method*.)

Foreign Key. A field or fields of one file in a database that serves as the primary key of another file in the database. (See *Key*, *Primary Key*.)

Forward Recovery. The process of moving forward through backup and log files to recover from an accident in which a file was destroyed.

Hashed file. A storage arrangement in which a "hashing algorithm" performs a calculation on the value of a field in a record and stores that record in a location dictated by the outcome of that calculation.

Hierarchical Database. A database in which the record types and occurrences are arranged in a hierarchical fashion.

Information. Data processed to be of use for some purpose. (See *Data*.)

Index. An ordered file, consisting of data value – record pointer pairs, used as a mechanism to accomplish direct retrieval.

Indexed Sequential Access Method (ISAM). An access method characterized by a file organization in which a file is stored in physical sequence based on one (or more) of its field values and also has an index built over that same field.

Intersection Data. Attributes describing a relationship.

Join. The merging of related records from (usually) different files. (See *Data Integration*.)

Journal. A file, the records of which record the insert, delete, and update (and sometimes the retrieval) activity against a database.

Juncture Record. The type of record used to accomplish a many-to-many relationship and store intersection data in a CODASYL network database.

Key. A field or fields of a file whose values form a unique identifier for the records of the file.

Knowledge Base. A collection of rules and associated facts used by an expert system.

Link File. A file that indicates which records of different files are related in a pseudo-relational database.

Lock. A software device that prevents a record from being modified. (See *Concurrency*.)

Log. (See *Journal*.)

Logical Child Record. The type of record used to accomplish a many-to-many relationship and store intersection data (among other purposes) in an IMS database.

Logical Database Design. That part of database design concerned with organizing data into structures that will satisfy application retrieval requirements, but without respect to performance issues. (See *Database Design*.)

Logical View. The data as the programmer or end-user sees it.

Network Database. A database in which the record types and occurrences are arranged in a network fashion.

Object-Oriented Database. A database characterized by a variety of programmer-defined data types and operations designed to be applied to them.

Physical Database Design. That part of database design concerned with modifying a logical database design to accommodate for performance factors. (See *Database Design*.)

Physical View. The data as it is actually stored on the disk.

Primary Key. The one candidate key chosen to function as the main identifier for the records of the file. The requirement for having a primary key is often associated with the nature of a file organization and access method. (See *Key, Candidate Key*.)

Pseudo-Relational Database. A database in which the data is stored in linear files and related records of different files are linked by their physical addresses in additional link files.

Query. An operation that seeks to retrieve data from a database.

Query Language. A database access design philosophy in which commands to retrieve or process data can be issued to the database from a terminal on an ad hoc basis. (For comparison, see *Embedded Language*.)

Record. The representation of the data describing an entity.

Recovery. Rebuilding files or databases after a disastrous loss of data. (See *Backup*.)

Referential Integrity. The issue of whether a data value that serves as the foreign key of a record in one table has a matching primary key value in another table.

Relation. A collection of like-structured tuples (records) in a relational database. Sometimes referred to as a "table" or (less correctly) as a file.

Relational Database. A database environment characterized by data stored in (what appear to be) simple linear files and having an execution-time data integration or join capability.

Relationship. The manner in which two entities are associated with each other. (See *Association*.)

Schema. A physical database representation; the term is used particularly in CODASYL network databases.

Secondary Index. An index built on a file, additional to the file's primary access mechanism.

Segment. A record or record type in an IMS database.

Sequential Access. The retrieval of the records of a file in order based on the values in one or more of its fields.

Set. Two record types and the one-to-many relationship between them in a CODASYL network database.

Synonym. Either of two records that would be placed at the same storage location by a hased file's hashing algorithm. (See *Collision*.)

Table. Used synonymously with file or (more frequently) with relation in a relational database. (See *File, Relation*.)

Track. A circle (one of many concentric circles) on which data can be stored on the surface of a magnetic disk device; also, a longitudinal line used for the same purpose on a magnetic tape.

Transaction. In general, a processing activity in the database environment; sometimes, more specifically, a message sent from a terminal to the database management system to accomplish a unit of database work.

Tuple. The description of an entity in a relational database. (See *Record*.)

Index